Bed & Breakfast
American Style – 1987

Bed & Breakfast
American Style - 1987

Private Homes, Guest Houses,
Mansions, Farmhouses, Country and Village Inns,
Small Hotels, Seaside and Mountain Lodges

Northeast, West Coast, Northwest,
South, Southwest, Middle West, Rocky Mountains,
Middle Atlantic, Eastern Canada

By Norman T. Simpson
The Berkshire Traveller

PERENNIAL LIBRARY

HARPER & ROW, PUBLISHERS, New York
Cambridge, Philadelphia, San Francisco, Washington
London, Mexico City, São Paulo, Singapore, Sydney

TRAVEL BOOKS BY NORMAN T. SIMPSON

Country Inns and Back Roads, North America
Country Inns and Back Roads, Britain and Ireland
Country Inns and Back Roads, Europe
Bed and Breakfast, American Style

COVER: Briar Rose Bed & Breakfast, Boulder, Colorado
        by Barbara Bash

BOOK DESIGN AND DRAWINGS: Jan Lindstrom

BED & BREAKFAST, AMERICAN STYLE, 1987 Edition.
Copyright © 1986 by Harper & Row, Publishers, Inc.

Earlier editions of this book were originally published by the Berkshire Traveller
Press.

Library of Congress Cataloging in Publication Data

Simpson, Norman T.
  Bed & breakfast, American style—1987

  Includes index.
    1. Bed and breakfast accommodations—United States—
Directories. 2. Bed and breakfast accommodations—
Canada, Eastern—Directories. I. Title. II. Title: Bed and
breakfast American style—1987.
TX907.S55 1986   647.947303   86-45149
ISBN 0-06-096094-9 (pbk.)

86 87 88 89 90 10 9 8 7 6 5 4 3 2 1

In memory of Owen Johnson

CONTENTS

PREFACE

In a manner that is characteristic of our times, a bed-and-breakfast fever has literally swept through America. Only a few years ago, I explained in the first edition of this book that the term "bed and breakfast" or "B&B" had been associated almost entirely with the British. It evoked the image of the thrifty English housewife who tucked away a few extra shillings by renting out her two extra bedrooms and offering a bit of breakfast in the bargain.

No longer is the B&B a British institution. In typical fashion, Americans have turned B&Bs into an American phenomenon. B&Bs are popping up here, there, and everywhere, like daffodils in spring. They have become our new and thriving cottage industry.

A far cry from a distant cousin of the 1920s and '30s—the "tourist home" with its threadbare carpets, skimpy towels, and creaky beds—today's B&B is, at the least, comfortably and attractively furnished, and at the most, opulently outfitted, with all manner of blandishments, such as jacuzzis, hot tubs, breakfast in bed, shoeshine service, and the like, to tickle the fancies of its guests.

The American B&B "movement" is elastic, stretching to include everything from the small private home, like the British housewife's, with a couple of extra bedrooms tucked under the eaves, to imposing mansions with chandeliers and parquet floors, to rustic lodges on lakes or by the sea, to country inns and small hotels that offer a complimentary breakfast along with room service.

The main distinction between a B&B *home* and a B&B *inn* is not simply one of size; the atmosphere is obviously more intimate in a home where the hosts are living and where the guests usually share the living and dining rooms with the host family. The personal souvenirs, bibelots, photographs, bric-a-brac, and such, all reinforce the sense of being in someone's home. Sometimes "someone's" home even becomes a "friend's" home.

In a B&B inn, there are usually more bedrooms and at least one common room exclusively for the guests. The innkeepers often have private and separate living quarters.

Most of the time, in host homes, B&B means the bathrooms are shared, although there may be a bedroom or two with its own bath. However, just as country inns have become more responsive to the American public's preference for privacy, so have many host homes converted to private baths. There is a segment of inn-goers who have no problems with shared bathrooms—I, among them. Basically, B&B inns have more private bathrooms.

There is also a variety in the kinds of breakfasts offered and the manner in which they are served. In some instances, a lavish, full breakfast is served, but even the continental breakfasts could include homemade breads, pastries, and preserves. In small places guests might eat with the family in the kitchen or dining room; there are sometimes outside porches or terraces where breakfast can be enjoyed in the sunshine; or if you have a taste for luxury, there are a few places where you can be served breakfast in bed. Some places have dining rooms in which dinner is served regularly, and others will provide it on special request. There are a few exceptions where breakfast is not available, but which, for a variety of reasons, I felt should be included.

Swimming pools, tennis courts, or other recreational facilities are not common features among B&B homes, but can be found at some of the larger places and more often at inns. However, even a small B&B might be surrounded by grounds with nature and cross-country ski trails. Some places provide various kinds of indoor diversions beyond books and magazines, with television and video tape libraries, record collections, board games, jigsaw puzzles, chess, backgammon, and such. All of which can be a great boon when your vacation gets rained out. It should be noted that there is a growing trend toward restricting smoking to certain rooms, and sometimes it is entirely prohibited.

Inclusion in this book is not based on budget considerations, although most places have rates that compare favorably with nearby commercial facilities.

Rates for two people for one night are supplied in the Index and are intended as guidelines and not to be considered as firm quotations. They often include the low off-season rates as well as the high on-season rates, and in some cases, there is an added tax and service charge. The best policy, of course, it to call ahead and get all the details in advance of your visit. Also, because some places offer various kinds of plans, be sure to specify the B&B rate when you make your reservation.

I will be interested in receiving any comments, complaints, or criticisms you may have about the lodgings I have described herein, and, where necessary, will take up the matter with the proprietors.

IS OWNING A B&B FOR YOU?

The answer to that question has many "ifs." If you presently own your home free of mortgage entanglements and if you have a source of *other* income that would not be affected by the economic climate or the seasonal lag of travelers, then the answer *might* be yes.

Some B&B proprietors have painted rosy pictures of steady income and interesting, considerate guests beating a path to their doors. They have been fortunate enough to be located in an area where there is no dip in patronage during the off-season and to have had an 85% occupancy rate in a sufficient number of bedrooms to create a healthy profit.

I might add that in those popular (usually resort) areas described above, the market for buildings that might be used as B&Bs is so inflated I shudder to think of the people who have invested their life savings and mortgaged their future under circumstances that are very uncertain. Under-capitalization is a big problem.

Bear in mind that I am talking about individuals who will be buying property to convert into a B&B accommodation rather than those fortunate few who own easily adaptable property in an ideal tourist area where local codes are flexible.

Unless you are able to generate a sufficient amount of income from other sources allowing you to cover expenses during slack periods when there is insufficient cash flow from your bedroom rentals, you could have several months of discouragement and despair.

With those heavily cautionary remarks out of the way, I will simply suggest that there are a number of obvious questions you should ask yourself, such as what are your feelings about having people using your home and your belongings; do you enjoy having people in your home; are you comfortable and relaxed in your dealings with people; are you prepared to give up privacy; can you handle problems with equanimity? These are only a few of the points to be considered in deciding if owning a B&B is for you.

May I suggest an excellent book on this subject: *How to Open a Country Inn*, written by Karen Etsell and Elaine Brennan, former owners of the Bramble Inn on Cape Cod. Their book is available from your bookstore or directly from The Berkshire Traveller Press, Stockbridge, Massachusetts 01262 ($11.95 postpaid).

Note: This book is arranged alphabetically by state and then by name of inn. The Index lists towns alphabetically within each state and includes rates. To find a specific inn, please see Alphabetical List of Inns.

GUSTAVUS INN
Gustavus, Alaska

I have never visited the Gustavus Inn, and decided to include it when someone called it to my attention— much as I did with the California Guest House in Nelson, New Zealand. Eventually, I will visit each of them, but I hope that any readers who visit either of them will send me a postcard.

The Gustavus Inn is, according to its excellent brochure, located in southeastern Alaska, fifty air miles from Juneau at the gateway to Glacier Bay. A three-day stay is encouraged to allow the traveler to enjoy the fishing, bicycling, kayaking, and country life of the area— especially a visit by boat to the many tidewater glaciers in Glacier Bay National Park. There are several different package tours which include all meals and a day boat trip to the glaciers or an overnight boat trip aboard the *Glacier Bay Explorer*.

It's obvious that one just doesn't stop at the Gustavus Inn for bed-and-breakfast, but it is an original Alaskan homestead offering meals and it sounds like a definite open window to an Alaskan life-style.

The inn brochure mentions clean, but small, guest rooms accommodating singles, doubles, and twins. Singles may be asked to share. They have a limit of twenty houseguests to assure personal attention to each. All baths are "down the hall."

I've received a most enthusiastic report from a reader who writes of the "fresh, delicious country cuisine" cooked by innkeeper David Lesh and the "friendly, family-style atmosphere." "Altogether, a delightful experience" was the final word.

GUSTAVUS INN, Box 31-N, Gustavus, AK 99826; 907-697-2254. A country inn located on the edge of a great glacier area and Glacier Bay National Park in Alaska. Breakfast, lunch, and dinner served daily. Full American plan available, as well as special package rates. Open Apr. 1 to Nov. 1. Quite enjoyable for children. All descriptions of Alaskan adventure available, including many side trips. David and JoAnn Lesh, Innkeepers.

Directions: Alaska Airlines has daily connecting service to Gustavus from Juneau during the summer months. Charter service is available from Gustavus, Haines, Skagway, Juneau, and Sitka. Private boats find moorage in the Salmon River at Gustavus or Bartlett Cove. Especially essential to get full information directly by telephone or letter before planning further.

For rates, see Index.

GRAHAM'S BED & BREAKFAST INN
Sedona, Arizona

Bill and Marni Graham knew they wanted to build their own inn and were determined to find the ideal setting. After their retirement, they traveled from Port Townsend in Washington State throughout the Southwest, carefully examining each locale, until they discovered the Oak Creek area of Sedona. Both said, "This is it." This must be one of the most beautiful spots in the country. Not desert and yet not mountains, but located at an elevation of 4,300 feet, the inn is surrounded by starkly attractive peaks, viewed from the cathedral-like windows.

Bill and Marni turned to a local interior designer, who used the talents of the artists and artisans of the area to create a colorful, fresh, and interesting environment. Handmade woodwork, cabinetry, tiles, and custom-made marble tubs and washbowls are special features, while original paintings, prints, and metal and wood sculptures adorn the walls and entrance of the inn.

All of the guest rooms are attractively and individually furnished, with various-sized beds, comfortable chairs, and good lighting.

Marni and Bill prepare breakfasts that might include German pancakes or eggs rancheros, along with fresh fruit and home-baked breads, which they serve in the dining room in front of a cheery fire or on the patio beside the pool.

GRAHAM'S BED & BREAKFAST INN, 150 Canyon Circle Dr., Box 912, Village of Oak Creek, Sedona, AZ 86336; 602-284-1425. A 5-guestroom (private baths) newly built contemporary B&B home in spectacular "red rock country," 2 hrs. north of Phoenix. Complimentary full breakfast and afternoon refreshments. Open year-round. Air conditioning, ceiling fans, clock radios, some whirlpool baths. Swimming pool and spa on premises. An important area for Western and Indian art; excellent shops, galleries, and restaurants. Hiking, jeep rides into back country, Indian ruins and cliff dwellings, golf, fishing, picnicking, riding nearby. Grand Canyon 2½ hrs. away. No children under 12. Smoking restricted to outside areas. Bill and Marni Graham, Owner-Innkeepers.

Directions: From the north: at the intersection of Hwys. 89A and 179, the center of Sedona, proceed south on 179 for 6.4 mi. to Bell Rock Blvd. Turn right for 2 blocks, turn right again on Canyon Circle. From the south: 2 hrs. north of Phoenix on I-17 to Hwy. 179. Then 8.4 miles north to Bell Rock Blvd. Turn left and proceed as above.

For B&B rates, see Index.

THE LODGE ON THE DESERT
Tucson, Arizona

The Lodge on the Desert is a sophisticated resort that started in the fall of 1936 in the desert outside Tucson. Gradually, the city grew up around it, and today its six acres are separated from the Tucson residential area by a great hedge of oleander.

Guest rooms are one- and two-story adobe buildings built in the style used by the Pueblo Indians, and the furnishings are all in a distinctive Southwest style.

The center of activity is the pool area marked by three great palm trees. Here, guests may sit in the sun and enjoy the magnificent view of the mountains. The adjoining lounge area has a large library, where guests often gather in the evening to play cards and socialize.

Lunch and dinner are part of the amenities.

A very pleasant continental breakfast is included in the B&B rate and consists of fruit juices, a choice of breads or toast, and a beverage. Selections may also be made from the à la carte breakfast menu at an additional cost. Breakfast may be taken on the individual terraces connected with each of the rooms or suites.

The high season at the Lodge on the Desert is from November 1 to June 1, and it is often necessary to reserve even a one-night stay well in advance.

THE LODGE ON THE DESERT, 306 N. Alvernon Way, Tucson, AZ 85711; 602-325-3366. A 40-guestroom luxury inn within the city limits. Near several historic, cultural, and recreational attractions. American and European plans available in winter; European plan in summer. B&B rate available. Breakfast, lunch, and dinner served to travelers every day of the year. Swimming pool and lawn games on grounds. Tennis and golf nearby. Attended, leashed pets allowed. Schuyler and Helen Lininger, Innkeepers.

Directions: Take Speedway exit from I-10. Travel about 5 mi. east to Alvernon Way, turn right (south) onto Alvernon (¾ mi.). Lodge is on left side between 5th St. and Broadway.

For B&B rates, see Index.

AGATE COVE INN
Mendocino, California

We have visited many memorable inns, but Agate Cove is near the top for its spectacular and secluded view of the Pacific Ocean and the rugged coastline, all near the little northwestern California community of Mendocino.

With their B&B guests in mind, Joan and Tom Johnson added a breakfast room overlooking the ocean to their main house, which was built in 1860. Here, guests are treated to a sumptuous breakfast, including fresh fruit, juice, fresh baked breads, coffee, tea, and special omelets with a choice of fillings, as well as other good things cooked on an antique wood stove. With the surf crashing on the rocks below and exploding into colorful mists, it is a breakfast experience not to be forgotten.

Guests stay in modern bungalows amidst Pacific cypress and abundant apple trees, whose products may serve the breakfast table all year long. Each bungalow has a separate entry with parking nearby, and they all have either a king or queen four-poster bed, some with canopy tops.

Some of the rooms have wall wainscoting with patterned wallpaper above; others are fully paneled with wood from local pines. The clean and fresh breezes from the ocean invigorate and cause each building to sparkle as though it were just painted. All rooms have private baths, TV's, and coffee makers for the early risers. Last, but not least, every bungalow affords a view of the ocean.

This is an inn without a common guest area, but all the bungalows have outside decks with flower boxes and deck chairs, and you may either wave to your neighbor or stroll across the lawn for some pleasant conversation.

AGATE COVE INN, Box 1150, 11201 No. Lansing St., Mendocino, CA 95460; 707-937-0551. A 10-guestroom (individual and double bungalows with private baths) seaside B&B on the rugged Mendocino coast in northwestern California. Franklin fireplaces, heating, TV, coffee makers, king- or queen-sized beds, and ocean views. Complimentary big country breakfast. Open year-round. Fine galleries, antiques, artisans and craftsmen in shops, excellent restaurants in village and nearby. No children under 12. No pets. Smoking outside. Joan and Tom Johnson, Innkeepers.

Directions: From Hwy. 1, take Lansing St. exit westward toward ocean.

For B&B rates, see Index.

AMBER HOUSE
Sacramento, California

Sacramento, the capital city of one of America's largest states, has many fine inns. Among the best is the air-conditioned Amber House, completely restored by California craftsmen.

Only a few blocks east of the capitol, the house sits on a street lined with towering elm trees, distinguished by its clinker brick front, shiny redwood porch, tan awnings, and handsome brass nameplate.

The colorful stained glass creations sparkle in every room, and classical music lilts through the house. A working fireplace and a boxed beam ceiling dominate the impressive living room, where complimentary wine is served late afternoon.

There are four double-bedded rooms, two with private baths, all handsomely and individually furnished. The light and airy Sun Room is lined with windows on three sides and features an antique white iron bed. The Lindworth Room's private bath boasts a 70-year-old porcelain tub with brass and ivory fixtures.

A full and varied breakfast, consisting of seasonal fresh fruits, homemade pastry, quiche, or special cranberry kuchen, is served in the formal dining room, or guest's room, on stunning Limoges china, with sterling silver and crystal accessories.

Sightseeing in the city includes the completely restored state capitol, the Railroad Museum, and Old Town.

AMBER HOUSE, 1315 22nd St., Sacramento, CA 95816; 916-444-8085. A 4-guestroom (2 private baths) handsomely restored bed-and-breakfast inn 7 blocks from the state capitol. Open year-round. City sightseeing: Railroad Museum, Old Town. No children. No pets. No smoking. Off-street parking; also airline limousine terminal or local train station pick-up service available.

Directions: From the capitol, take East Capitol to 22nd St.; turn right for a half block.

For B&B rates, see Index.

AMERICAN RIVER INN
Georgetown, California

The American Hotel was built to serve the mine entrepreneurs who had swarmed into the peaceful village of Georgetown during the gold rush. Millions of dollars in gold had been mined here before a disastrous fire leveled the town. Rebuilt to serve itinerant visitors, as well as the traveling judge and court of the judicial district, the American Hotel persisted in state history.

The present young innkeepers have directed much love and substance into the exterior and interior of the building, which, with its wide porches running the full length of two sides, is a true legacy of a long-gone age.

The now like-new historic American River Inn can be one of the highlights of your gold country adventure. The exterior is done in pleasing cream, trimmed in light blue, and brick planters beautify the front sidewalk. To the right upon entering is the colorful dining room with fresh flowers and pretty quilted placemats on each table. Three sideboards from a 15th-century castle in Belgium, along with the handsome old chairs, create an interesting, eclectic look. Just beyond is a large guest lounge with a large display case in one corner, filled with beautiful antique glass objets d'art. These, along with antique furniture, quilts, and Tiffany lamps, are available for sale.

Each room boasts a valuable bedstead with beautiful quilted bedspreads, some so unique as to serve as wall hangings.

A full complimentary breakfast is served either in the dining room or on the patio. Wine and hors d'oeuvres are offered in the evening.

AMERICAN RIVER INN, Box 43, Main and Orleans, Georgetown, CA 95634; 916-333-4499. An 18-guestroom (private and semi-private baths) restored early Californian small hotel in a unique old mining town, with very wide streets and a saloon right out of "Gunsmoke." Separate Queen Anne house and 5 bedrooms. Complimentary breakfast. Open year-round. Swimming pool and spa in an acre of garden. Pheasant and dove aviary. Bicycles, wineries, hot-air ballooning, white-water rafting in American River nearby. Older children by prearrangement. No pets. Will and Maria Collin, Neal and Carol Lamorte, Innkeepers.

Directions: From Hwy. 80, take Hwy. 49 south and then Hwy. 193 to Georgetown. From Hwy. 50, take Hwy. 49 north and then Hwy. 193 to Georgetown.

For B&B rates, see Index.

THE BABBLING BROOK INN
Santa Cruz, California

The name of this inn is not irrelevant, since there is indeed a lovely babbling brook—actually Laurel Creek—that meanders through the terraced gardens surrounding the four separate buildings of the inn. From the private decks of most of the rooms can be seen little paths and footbridges, gazebo areas, rustic stone walls, a pond, and even a tiny waterfall—all part of the garden environment. Standing sentinel over all are huge redwood and laurel trees. The natural weathered shingles of the randomly arranged buildings blend beautifully into this charming landscape.

Gayle Brose, the enthusiastic owner and innkeeper, seems to have left nothing to chance in providing for the comfort and pleasure of her guests. The guest rooms boast private entries, king- or queen-sized beds, private baths, telephones, TV's tucked away in closets, and wood stoves, which are put to good use when the nearby Pacific Ocean chills the air.

In addition to the continental breakfast of fresh fruits and juices, homemade breads and muffins, fresh ground coffee and herb teas, guests are welcomed on arrival with a complimentary wine or sherry.

Ohlone Indians camped and prepared their food here centuries ago, and in 1796 mission fathers built a gristmill, whose four-foot walls are still a part of the inn. Early in this century a log cabin was also the site for a local thespian company and the first of the "Hopalong" Cassidy films done by William Boyd.

THE BABBLING BROOK INN, 1025 Laurel St., Santa Cruz, CA 95060; 408-427-2437. A 12-guestroom (private baths) relaxed and comfortable inn built around a winding stream located about midway between San Francisco and Monterey Bay. Breakfast included. Open daily. Nearby amusement center and many excellent restaurants featuring ocean catch. Picnic baskets and arrangements for hot air balloon rides, ocean excursions, or wine tastings. Children over 12 accepted. No pets. Smoking outside. Gayle Brose, Innkeeper.

Directions: Take Ocean St. turnoff from either Hwys. 1 or 17. Proceed to a right turn at Broadway, which becomes Laurel past the river. Continue to 1025.

For B&B rates, see Index.

THE BATH STREET INN
Santa Barbara, California

When this 1875 private home was redesigned and reconstructed in order to make it a bed-and-breakfast inn, a great deal of care was taken to preserve the Victorian atmosphere of the original building and at the same time to incorporate security and safety features that conformed to the strictest modern standards.

Each guest accommodation has its individual charm: a small front suite has a quaint flower-hung balcony; a luxurious rear bedroom has a delightful garden bath; the third-floor guest rooms adjoin a library and parlor aerie looking out to Santa Barbara's spectacular Santa Ynez Mountains.

In the morning a leisurely continental breakfast is served in the sunny dining room or in one of the garden patios.

The beach is a short drive or bike ride away, and bikes are provided upon request.

The Bath Street Inn is in a quiet residential area of Santa Barbara, and it is a very warm outreaching place with many, many books and magazines in evidence. The innkeepers, Susan Brown and Nancy Stover, obviously have a great deal of interest in the arts.

THE BATH STREET INN, 1720 Bath Street, Santa Barbara, Ca. 93101; 805-682-9680. A 7-bedroom (private baths) bed-and-breakfast inn in a very pleasant residential area of a beautiful southern California city. Open year-round. Ideally located for all of the historic, natural, and cultural points of interest in and near Santa Barbara. Not suitable for children. No pets. Susan Brown and Nancy Stover, Innkeepers.

Directions: From Rte. 101, take Mission St. off-ramp east 1 block to Castillo, turn right 3 blocks; left on Valerio 1 block; right on Bath (Bath is one-way). Inn is on the right, parking in the rear.

For B&B rates, see Index.

THE BAYBERRY INN
Santa Barbara, California

A gilded eagle and two American flags give a Colonial feeling to the imposing white entrance of the Bayberry Inn. Actually, it was built in 1886 as the summer residence for a French diplomat, and later served as a finishing school for young ladies. It is now painted a pleasing blue with a white trim.

Completely redecorated by two enterprising innkeepers, one an accomplished designer, the house is furnished in a post-Victorian style reminiscent of the period immediately following the first World War. Victorian furnishings are nicely blended with valuable art objects gathered from many countries. The guest lounge, with a fireplace, has a player piano and windows overlooking a large, well-manicured lawn, colorful garden, and large trees, bordered by a white, lattice fence.

The dining room is resplendent with silk wall coverings rimmed around the top by a wide strip of beveled mirrors that reflect the sparkling crystal chandelier over the table.

Just beyond this room is the sun porch with a player piano and a large bamboo bird cage holding unusual zebra finches. Outside is a patio with wicker furniture and tables, as well as a lawn croquet course and badminton court ready for use.

Some guest rooms have fireplaces and tiled baths and others possess canopied beds, thick carpeting, and warm comforters. All are in soft greens and yellows. Green plants and cut flowers are refreshing touches in guest areas and rooms.

An excellent complimentary breakfast is included. Hors d'oeuvres and wine are offered in early evening.

THE BAYBERRY INN, 111 W. Valerio St., Santa Barbara, CA 93101; 805-682-3199. An 8-guestroom (private baths) inn in the residential area of a seaside town, 5 min. from ocean beaches. A complimentary full breakfast included. Open year-round. Guidance to fine local restaurants. Hiking and riding available in nearby Los Padres National Forest. Historic courthouse, Santa Barbara Mission, fine art museum are only a short walk. No children. No pets. Smoking outside on deck only. Keith Pomeroy and Carlton Wagner, Innkeepers.

Directions: From Hwy. 101, take Mission St. off towards the mountains for 3 blocks to De La Vina, and then right on De La Vina 3 blocks. Turn left on Valerio.

For B&B rates, see Index.

BEAZLEY HOUSE
Napa, California

The key to a well-run bed-and-breakfast establishment is the personal touch. Carol and Jim Beazley, former residents of Nevada, exemplify this principle with warmth and enthusiastic hospitality at Beazley House.

Built in 1902 as the residence of a prominent Napa surgeon, and opened by the Beazleys in 1981 as the first bed-and-breakfast in Napa, Beazley House is situated on a quiet corner in a residential neighborhood. It was recently added to the list of historic houses.

The large, comfortable living room with its antiques is the setting for afternoon sherry and tea served from a teacart in front of the fireplace. The unusual "light" windows with eighteen tiny panes make it a sunny and inviting place for guests to visit or play games. The Beazleys' teenage daughter plays the cello for guests on Sundays in the adjacent Music Room. The formal dining room, its attractive redwood paneling stained to look like mahogany, is the scene for the continental breakfast, featuring fresh fruits, fruit juice, homemade muffins, jams, cheese, and coffee or tea.

A staircase with a window seat and half-round stained glass window leads to four attractive upstairs guest rooms. The Burgundy and Sherry suites are joined by a bath. The master bedroom, with a fireplace and beautiful brass and porcelain bed, shares its bath with the Wine and Roses Room, which overlooks the back gardens.

The Carriage House, completed in 1983, offers an additional five bedrooms, each with its own entrance; one with wheelchair access. Special features in these open-beam-ceiling rooms include fireplaces, double-paned windows, private cedar-lined bathrooms, some with double bathtubs complete with jacuzzis, and iron and brass queen- and king-sized beds with bright, handmade quilts.

BEAZLEY HOUSE, 1910 First St., Napa, CA 94559; 707-257-1649. An 8-guestroom bed-and-breakfast inn (many rooms with private bath), in the heart of the wine country. Open year round. Many recreational activities in the area. Children over twelve are welcome. No pets. No smoking. Carol and Jim Beazley, Innkeepers.

Directions: Take Rte. 29 into Napa; then the Calistoga fork to the Central Napa–First Street exit. Turn left on Second Street for 0.3 mi., and turn left on Warren and left onto First Street. The inn is at the corner of First and Warren. Ample parking.

For B&B rates, see Index.

THE BED AND BREAKFAST INN
San Francisco, California

San Francisco now has several interesting bed-and-breakfast establishments, but for many years there was only one: the Bed and Breakfast Inn, on Charlton Court, just off Union Street, in one of the more conservative and least tourist-oriented areas.

The guest rooms are named after various parts of London, and each room provides an entirely different experience. Many have completely different sets of sheets, pillow cases, and towels, and there are many varieties of beds, from those with carved Victorian headboards to traditional shiny brass headboards.

There are flowers everywhere, thermos jugs of ice water, many books, baskets of fruit, down pillows, and gorgeous coverlets and spreads.

The Bed and Breakfast Inn is within easy walking distance of Fisherman's Wharf and many of the San Francisco attractions, including connections with the cable cars.

Since some of the bedrooms have their own patios, breakfast can be enjoyed in a delicious privacy by guests in those rooms. The continental offerings include orange juice, hot croissants, and fresh ground coffee, and are frequently taken in the dining room because the atmosphere is so conducive to good conversation.

THE BED AND BREAKFAST INN, 4 Charlton Court, San Francisco, CA 94123; 415-921-9784. A 10-guestroom European-style pension in the Union Street district of San Francisco. Continental breakfast is the only meal offered. Open daily year-round. Convenient to all of the Bay Area recreational, cultural, and gustatory attractions. Not comfortable for small children. No pets. No credit cards. Robert and Marily Kavanaugh, Innkeepers.

Directions: Take the Van Ness Exit from Rte. 101 and proceed to Union Street. Charlton Court is a small courtyard street, halfway between Laguna and Buchanan, off Union.

For B&B rates, see Index.

BIG RIVER LODGE
(STANFORD INN BY THE SEA)
Mendocino, California

This section of the northern California coast is one of the most satisfying travel experiences in North America, and a particular treat is an evening walk in the sharp, clean air on the Mendocino headlands, while the dazzling sunset highlights the rugged coastline. Mendocino itself is now designated as a historic site and the restoration and architecture conform to the general feeling of the 1800s. Wandering through the town is like an expedition into the past.

It was a particular pleasure to visit Joan and Jeff Stanford at the Big River Lodge. I had met them a few years earlier when they were the innkeepers at a bed-and-breakfast inn in Carmel, but now they had relocated most happily in Mendocino and had an unusually attractive bed-and-breakfast hostelry that had begun life as a rather so-so motel.

The situation certainly provides a great advantage, because there is a beautiful view of the sea and some of the town of Mendocino. Each of the guest rooms opens into a deck that is lined with all varieties of flowers. All have chairs and a table so that guests can enjoy the splendid view, particularly of the sunsets.

The guest rooms have books, plants, secretaries, local art, and many interesting paintings. There are comforters and attractive tablecloths, four-poster beds, antiques, and antique reproductions.

Joan and Jeff will make dinner reservations, advise guests on galleries and sights to be seen. They have walked all of the walks, and they also provide bicycles at no additional charge.

BIG RIVER LODGE (STANFORD INN BY THE SEA), P.O. Box 487, Mendocino, CA 95460; 707-937-5615. A 23-guestroom (all private baths) elegantly rustic lodge, just a couple of minutes from the center of Mendocino with ocean and village views and woodburning fireplaces. Open every day in the year. Continental breakfast is the only meal served; however, ample advice is available about restaurants in the area. Centrally located to enjoy all of the historic, scenic, and artistic attractions of the Mendocino-Fort Bragg coast. Joan and Jeff Stanford, Proprietors.

Directions: From San Francisco, follow coastal Hwy. 1 north to Mendocino, or follow Rte. 101 to Cloverdale; 128 to coastal Hwy. 1 and then north. Two mi. north of Little River (just to the south of Big River) turn east on Comptche-Ukiah Rd. and look for the Big River Lodge sign.

For B&B rates, see Index.

THE BRIGGS HOUSE
Sacramento, California

Just a few blocks from the capitol of America's largest state is the "cube style" Colonial Revival Briggs House, built in 1901. Four years ago the house was purchased and completely remodeled before its opening as Sacramento's largest bed-and-breakfast inn.

One enters the inn from a wide four-columned porch, complete with swing and shaded by huge trees, so typical of this enterprising town and not unlike the Midwest. The library and parlor are on the right, comfortably furnished with antiques. A brick fireplace in the parlor could be blazing before the small breakfast tables used on inclement mornings.

One guest room with its own fireplace is on the main floor while four upstairs guest rooms are reached by a polished wooden staircase leading to a wide landing. Antique dolls, lace collections, and family memorabilia add atmosphere. Rooms have been individually decorated by the owners who are on hand to greet their guests on weekends. The original carriage house in the rear has been renovated to house two additional rooms, one above the other.

A large bricked patio with comfortable lawn furniture is shaded by tall trees and a latticed screen. Across the lawn is a huge wooden wine cask that has been made into a sauna.

A full breakfast, usually with a baked dish, is served in the parlor, in the shaded arbor, or in one's room.

Wine, fresh fruit, and toasted almonds are offered in the late afternoon. The innkeepers are glad to make dinner recommendations to a number of in-town restaurants, some within walking distance.

THE BRIGGS HOUSE, 2209 Capitol Ave., Sacramento, CA 95816; 916-441-3214. A 7-guestroom (private and shared baths) comfortable and homey B&B inn in the center of town in northern California. Complimentary breakfast and evening wine and refreshments. Open year-round. Bicycles, hot tub, sauna, redwood patio in shaded back yard, porch swing. Other diversions such as Greyhound city tour, Railroad Museum, Old Sacramento restoration, Sutter's Fort, Crocker Art Museum. Children by prearrangement. No pets. Sue Garmston, Innkeeper.

Directions: Seven blocks directly east of state capitol and its Capitol Park to 2209 Capitol Ave.

For B&B rates, see Index.

BRITT HOUSE
San Diego, California

The British Queen Victoria lent her name to a distinctive type of 19th-century architecture that flourished first in England, but it remained for American designers to bring it to full flower.

One of the more beautiful Victorian mansions is the Britt House, which has been lovingly restored and maintained by innkeepers Daun Martin and Robert Hostick.

An outstanding feature of the house is a lavish two-and-a-half-story stained-glass window, adjacent to the winding staircase leading to the second floor.

There are ten large guests rooms, each decorated differently with antiques, wallpapers reminiscent of the Victorian era, fresh flowers and plants, and original drawings by Robert Hostick.

The inn is fortunately within walking distance of Balboa Park and the famous San Diego Zoo.

The attractive guest rooms are most agreeable for enjoying an intimate breakfast. Daun is busy early in the morning, preparing individual baskets with freshly squeezed orange juice, two eggs, shirred or scrambled, freshly ground coffee, spiced or regular tea, homemade yeast breads with sweet butter and jam.

A formal afternoon tea is served, starting at four o'clock.

BRITT HOUSE, 406 Maple St., San Diego, CA 92103; 619-234-2926. A 10-guestrooom bed-and-breakfast inn (shared baths) just a short distance from Balboa Park with its world-famous zoo. Breakfast and afternoon tea included in room rate. (Special dinners can be arranged with advance notice). Open all year. Museum of Art, Man and Natural History, Reuben H. Fleet Space Theater, and the beaches, desert country, and Mexico (13 mi.) nearby. Jogging, biking, skating nearby. No pets. Not particularly suitable for young children. Daun Martin, Innkeeper.

Directions: Take Airport-Sassafrass turnoff coming south on Hwy. 5. Proceed on Kettner. Turn left on Laurel; left on Third; right on Nutmeg; right on Fourth St, and come down one block to the corner of Fourth and Maple.

For B&B rates, see Index.

BURGUNDY AND BORDEAUX HOUSE
Yountville, California

Here's an inn with a most rich and varied past. Burgundy House was built by Charles Rouvegneau around the 1870s and was used as both a brandy distillery and a boarding house. Rouvegneau constructed walls of enormous native fieldstone, over twenty inches thick. Heavy hand-hewn wooden beams and posts were used throughout the structure. Bob and Mary Keenan bought this old building in 1975, renovating and restoring it as an antique shop. Customers who came to browse and shop for antiques were so intrigued by the building that the Keenans decided they should take overnight guests. Soon thereafter, the shop became an inn with six guest rooms furnished with antiques and other pieces from around the world.

Nearby Bordeaux House, built recently, is a classically modern and more formal red brick building that is first glimpsed through a pair of rare old Italian pines. Its interior is elegant and understated with spacious rooms and contemporary furnishings. The guest rooms have pedestal beds, fireplaces, patios, air conditioning, and private baths.

Depending on the weather in the valley, breakfast is served in Burgundy House either before the blazing fire in a small, cozy room next to the front parlor or outside in the lovely garden. The menu consists of an assortment of pastries, juice, fruit, tea or coffee.

Burgundy and Bordeaux House, surrounded by vineyards, has extraordinary vistas in every direction one looks, of the mountains, the vines, and the valley. It's a peaceful and tranquil setting, and yet one is close to many restaurants and attractions in the valley.

BURGUNDY AND BORDEAUX HOUSE. 6711 Washington St., Yountville, CA 94599; 707-944-2855. A 12-guestroom inn with 6 rooms (some shared baths) in a restored 1870 stone building (Burgundy House) and 6 rooms (private baths) in an elegant modern brick building (Bordeaux House). Mobil 3-Star Award. Just off the main Napa Valley highway, about 1 hr. from San Francisco. Complimentary continental breakfast. Open all year except Christmas. Excellent restaurants nearby. No pets. Mary and Bob Keenan, Innkeepers.

Directions: Take Highway 101 north from San Francisco. Follow Napa green signs to Highway 29. Take turnoff to Yountville. Turn right on Madison St., and left onto Washington St.

For B&B rates, see Index.

CAMPBELL RANCH INN
Geyserville, California

While old Victorians are often the style among bed-and-breakfast inns, it is sometimes refreshing to enjoy the atmosphere of a warm and friendly home, viewing the verdant Sonoma valley with its thousands of acres of fruit trees and vineyards, as well as the distant mountains that separate it from the more publicized Napa Valley.

Such a place is the home of Mary Jane and Jerry Campbell, as pleasant and accommodating a couple as ever hosted a B&B. Not content with opening their extremely comfortable split-level ranch-style home with its spectacular view, its gardens, large swimming pool, and professional tennis court, they ply their guests with sumptuous breakfasts, poolside lemonade or iced tea, afternoon wine, bedtime snacks, fruit, and fresh flowers. Breakfast choices are made from a menu with over twelve items.

Perched on a hilltop, high above the Pedroncelli vineyard, one of California's premium winemakers, Campbell Ranch commands literally miles of scenery. One could sit all day and gaze at this view from the balcony off the two upstairs light and airy guest rooms. There is a third guest room on the main floor with a private bath. All of the rooms are fully carpeted and furnished in a contemporary style with king-sized beds. One room has a piano, and another has an extra bed, which could accommodate a family group.

The soaring beamed ceiling of the living room, the floor-to-ceiling used-brick wall with its "see-through" fireplace, and the open kitchen-breakfast-lounge area with view windows all around provide a most pleasant feeling of spaciousness.

CAMPBELL RANCH INN, 1475 Canyon Rd., Geyserville, CA 95441; 707-857-3476. A 3-guestroom (private and shared baths) split-level home on a hilltop with a magnificent view in the Sonoma County section of northern California. Complimentary full breakfast and refreshments. Open year-round; 2-day minimum stay on weekends. On-premises diversions include swimming, tennis, horseshoes, ping-pong, other indoor games, TV, VCR. Hiking nearby. Good restaurants within a few miles. Teenagers midweek only. No pets. No credit cards. No smoking. Mary Jane and Jerry Campbell, Innkeepers.

Directions: Take Geyersville off-ramp of Hwy. 101, and proceed immediately westward on Canyon Rd., 1.6 mi. Watch for Campbell Ranch sign on left.

For B&B rates, see Index.

CARTER HOUSE
Eureka, California

Eureka is an up-and-coming community. I've been visiting it off and on for about ten years, and it is definitely emerging as an area of considerable interest.

Symbolic, perhaps, of this emergence is the Carter House, a handsome redwood Victorian home that looks old but was actually completed in 1982. It is an architectural re-creation of the Murphy House, which was destroyed by the 1906 earthquake. The Victorian decor is further enhanced by marble and hardwood floors, oriental carpets, potted plants, and fresh-cut flowers.

In addition to a lobby, dining room, and sitting area, the first floor features a gallery where works of thirty different artists are displayed. There are seven guest rooms furnished in handsome Victorian antiques, and those on the third floor offer views of the Eureka marina and the extraordinary Carson mansion.

Breakfast includes a fresh tart or pastry, fruit compote, and homemade bran muffins; lox and bagels are offered when salmon is in season. Hors d'oeuvres are served in the early evening, and tea and cookies are served following the dinner hour.

The Carter House is just a few steps from Old Town Eureka, where there are many beautifully restored turn-of-the-century buildings. This downtown restoration ranks with some of the best I have ever seen, and is not as commercial as many.

So, Old Town Eureka and the Carter House are making Eureka a really compelling stop for the traveler on Route 101. If arriving by bus or train, arrangements can be made for a ride to the Carter House in a shiny black Bentley—the Carter House is definitely a class act.

CARTER HOUSE, Third & L Sts., Eureka, CA 95501; 707-445-1390. A 7-guestroom (private and shared baths) bed-and-breakfast recently re-created 1884 Victorian mansion in northern California. A full breakfast is served daily; dinner on weekends. Open all year. Conveniently located to visit many of the recreational, cultural, and natural attractions of Humboldt County. No pets. Mark and Christi Carter, Proprietors.

Directions: Eureka is approx. 200 mi. north of San Francisco on Rte. 101, the main north/south highway running the entire length of the West Coast.

For B&B rates, see Index.

DORYMAN'S INN
Newport Beach, California

A "flat-bottomed boat with high flaring sides, sharp bow, and deep V-shaped transom" describes a dory, according to Webster's latest, and since the early 1920s the building that is now Doryman's Inn provided overnight lodgings for fishermen who launched their boats each morning from the adjacent Newport Beach Pier. This building has now been designated as one of California's historic landmarks.

There is little to suggest those rough, early beginnings in the present sleek, urban facade of Doryman's Inn. At the sidewalk entrance, I walked under a lighted glass marquee through a pair of heavy swinging oak doors with shiny brass handles. After announcing myself over the telephone and being identified via a TV monitor, an elevator door opened and spirited me to the reception area on the second floor, where I was given a warm welcome by Ashley Lawrence, the manager.

No efforts have been spared in creating a lavishly decorated inn. The formerly long, dark corridors with heavy oak paneling have been transformed with handsome lighting, skylights, hanging ferns, and many paintings. The guest rooms behind the oak doors are distinctive and luxurious, with greenery and gas-burning fireplaces, ignited at the touch of a convenient wall switch.

The furnishings are Victorian, with thick carpets, Carrara marble bathrooms with sunken tubs and skylights, matching floral draperies and quilted bedspreads, gilt-edged mirrors, and etched French glass fixtures.

Six rooms have windows overlooking the beach, where the departure and return of the fishing boats can be seen; other rooms are off a sun-flooded and protected patio, where the complimentary continental breakfast may be served.

DORYMAN'S INN, 2102 W. Ocean Front, Newport Beach, CA 92663; 714-675-7300. A 10-guestroom (private baths) sophisticated inn on the ocean front at Newport Pier. Complimentary continental breakfast. Restaurant on premises. Open year-round. Swimming, boating, deep-sea fishing, windsurfing, restaurants, cabarets, boutiques nearby. Knott's Berry Farm and Disneyland within a 30-min. drive. No children under 16. No pets. Jeannie and Richard Lawrence, Hosts.

Directions: From Hwy. 405, take the San Diego Freeway, turning off at Newport Blvd. off-ramp, Hwy. 55, to Newport Beach. Continue on Newport Blvd. to 32nd St., turning left to Balboa Blvd., then right at sign to Newport Pier.

For B&B rates, see Index.

EAGLE HOUSE
Eureka, California

Eagle House is one of the oldest and yet newest of California inns. Overlooking an important bay of the Pacific Ocean and in the northwest corner of the state, the building was constructed in 1888 as an excellent example of high Victorian Stick architecture. Initially, it served as the Buon Gusto Hotel, with a popular pub for local and visiting deep-sea fisherman. Now, it is completely renovated and has been an important step in the revival and establishment of the Eureka Old Town neighborhood.

A performing arts theater occupies the ground floor, and the Eagle Crest, one of Eureka's finest restaurants, is located on the second floor.

The third and fourth floors of Eagle House are devoted entirely to the inn, with a keyed elevator for guest use. Done in Victorian style with furnishings and antiques purchased in and brought from England, the third floor accommodates the lounge and some of the twenty-four newly furnished guest rooms and suites, completed in half-wood paneling with old wallpaper patterns above. Each room offers private facilities. Large, comfortable beds are covered with warm, European-style "puffs," as the ocean air and not unusual rainfall demand warmth even in summer months.

The fourth floor contains additional guest rooms and a breakfast room, whose tables are set with china and fresh flowers for a generous continental breakfast in the morning. Windows are on all four sides, with views of the city, Humboldt Bay, and the lumber mills that have made Eureka so famous.

Exploring the many new and old shops of Old Town, all within sight of Eagle House, is a novel experience.

EAGLE HOUSE, 2nd and "C" Sts., Eureka, CA 95501; 707-442-2334; in Calif.: 800-522-8686. A 24-guestroom (private baths) preserved and restored former 1888 hotel, now a B&B inn in a historic harbor town in northern California. Guestrooms on 3rd and 4th floors with electronically coded elevator. Facilities for disabled; jacuzzi. Complimentary continental breakfast and refreshments. Open all year. Explore Old Town, watch fishermen with catch, shopping, many good restaurants. No pets. Jerry Loring, General Manager.

Directions: From Hwy. 101, turn towards the bay on "C" St. and continue to 2nd St.

For B&B rates, see Index.

FOOTHILL HOUSE
Calistoga, California

From the early summer days of newly budded vines until the final grape press in the fall, the Napa Valley with its many wineries has a constant stream of visitors. Most of this activity can be avoided by continuing north on busy Highway 29 for some twenty miles to Calistoga where tourists infrequently venture.

Nestled in the foothills just north of Calistoga is the Foothill House, acclaimed by one knowledgable guest as "probably the best place to stay anywhere in the world."

In a lovely country setting surrounded by trees and mountains, innkeepers Michael and Susan Clow offer their guests a very special brand of hospitality with three guest suites.

Colorful, handmade quilts were the beginning, and each room was then decorated to blend in with their colors. Aided by indirect and concealed lighting, a guest steps into a literal fairyland. There are four-poster queen-sized beds, separate outside entrances, small refrigerators, and wood-burning fireplaces. In the private baths, towels are thick and rich, and replaced as they are soiled.

Upon your return in the evening from any one of the fine nearby restaurants, your bed will be turned down, soft lights will glow, and a miniature cookie jar filled with homemade cookies and a decanter of sherry will be on your bedside table. Possibly, also, a personal note from your innkeeper wishing you pleasant dreams.

A full continental breakfast is served in the morning in the Sunroom or on the patio, shaded by a huge tree whose base is a flower bed and a fountain. If you prefer privacy, a breakfast basket will be brought to your room.

The house has many 100-year-old trees, as well as private patios, and provides a great view of Mt. Helena on the eastern side of the valley.

FOOTHILL HOUSE, 3037 Foothill Blvd., Calistoga, CA 94515; 707-942-6933. A 3-suite (private baths) remodeled country farmhouse nestled in the foothills on the northern edge of Napa Valley. Breakfast and afternoon refreshments included. Open year-round. Famous Calistoga healing waters and mud baths, winery visits, ballooning, Sharpsteen Museum, and Robert Louis Stevenson State Park nearby. Hiking, biking, swimming, antiquing. Children over 12. No pets. No smoking. Michael and Susan Clow, Innkeepers.

Directions: Hwy. 29 north to Calistoga. Take Hwy. 128 for 1½ mi. to Foothill House. Follow to 3037.

For B&B rates, see Index.

THE FOXES
Sutter Creek, California

The little town of Sutter Creek is a historical gem, eagerly visited by Californians as an authentic reminder of the gold country and the Forty-Niners. Architecture is affectionately termed "mother lode" style and is reminiscent of old Western movie sets with second stories and porches overhanging store fronts, and rough sidewalks, where careful steps are advised.

In the center of town is the Foxes, lovingly watched over by its owners, Min and Pete Fox. The 1857 home reflects the New England origins of the builders. A second floor was added by raising the ground floor when the house suffered a fire many years ago. Three new guest rooms have been added to the rear, with car parking underneath.

Min operated an antique shop before opening the inn, so the furniture in each guest room is most admirable. A beamed cathedral-type ceiling with chandeliers and a huge armoire grace the front Anniversary Suite, the Honeymoon Suite has a living area with a cozy fireplace, and the Victorian Suite is equally impressive, with a nine-foot-tall Victorian headboard and matching dresser.

Each guest room boasts a queen-sized bed and its own breakfast table, set with linen tablecloths, lovely china, and gleaming silver, where a full breakfast is served each morning. A restaurant-type kitchen offers the Foxes an opportunity to show off their culinary skills. Late-afternoon refreshment revives their guests while the innkeepers make suggestions as to the various local restaurants where dinner may be taken.

There is much of historical interest to be investigated in and around Sutter Creek, along with the many antique and crafts shops, art galleries, wineries, and old gold mines. Outdoor activities are possible on the nearby lakes and in El Dorado National Forest. Or sitting in the garden gazebo, admiring all the flowers, might be just what the doctor ordered.

THE FOXES, Box 159, 77 Main St., Sutter Creek, CA 95685; 209-267-5882. A 6-guestroom (private baths) mid-19th-century B&B in the center of a historic gold rush town. Complimentary full breakfast and afternoon refreshment. Open year-round. Minimum of 2 nights on holiday weekends. TV on request. City walking tour, antiquing, wineries, exploring gold mines, along with recreational outdoor activities, all within easy walks or drives. No children. No pets. No smoking. Pete and Min Fox, Innkeepers.

Directions: On State Hwy. 49, follow Main St. into town.

For B&B rates, see Index.

GATE HOUSE INN
Jackson, California

Not only miners rushed to the mother lode country of California's Sierras when gold was first discovered, but also merchants and traders to meet the needs of those miners. One such family was the Chichizolas, who established a general store in Jackson, offering supplies, clothing, food, hardware, and whatever else was needed. The success of this family's efforts was later evidenced by the construction in the early 1890s of the largest and most pretentious Victorian home in the area.

In 1981, Ursel and Frank Walker bought the home (only its third owners) to offer a bed-and-breakfast inn with the same service and attention to the guests that has typified their years as owners of the Palace Restaurant in nearby Sutter Creek, acknowledged to be the finest in the gold country.

All rooms in the inn are beautifully decorated and furnished, some with original Early American wallpaper in floral designs still in perfect condition. Light fixtures are Italian imports, installed when the house was constructed, as is the marble in the living room fireplace. Marble-topped chiffoniers and sinks are prominent in the bedrooms.

A unique and separate accommodation is in the "Summerhouse," originally the caretaker's quarters and later the summerhouse for the private residence.

A full breakfast with coddled eggs, fresh fruit and juices, accompanied by an assortment of pastries and muffins, is served in the morning on Ursel's bone china and antique crested bronzeware.

GATE HOUSE INN, 1330 Jackson Gate Rd., Jackson, CA 95642; 209-223-3500. A 5-guestroom turn-of-the- century bed-and-breakfast inn, including a separate cottage (all private baths) 45 mi. southeast of Sacramento and 2 mi. from Amador County Airport. A full breakfast is the only meal served, but four restaurants are within walking distance. Open all year. More than 20 excellent Amador County wineries are nearby, featuring fine chardonnay, zinfandel, and Johannisberg Riesling. Also old and historic mining towns, museums, antique stores, gold-panning, golf, skiing, and water sports nearby. Regretfully, no children. No pets. No smoking. No credit cards. Ursel and Frank Walker, Innkeepers.

Directions: From either north or south on Hwy. 49, turn off on Jackson Gate Rd. just north of its intersection with Hwy. 88 from Stockton to the west.

For B&B rates, see Index.

THE GINGERBREAD MANSION
Ferndale, California

When an entire village is given Historical Landmark status by a state government as a result of its well-preserved and colorfully painted Victorian shops, homes, and farmhouses, a visit there is very much in order. Then, when the most photographed building in that village is a bed-and-breakfast inn, you know it must be something special.

Yet "special" is a minimal word to describe the Gingerbread Mansion, with its widow's walk, weathervanes, turrets, gables, and intricately carved finials and spoolwork. It is all made even more pleasing to the eye by the exterior tones of soft peach and gold, the well-groomed hedges and topiaries, and a formal English-style garden with brick walkways and a magnificent holly tree.

Built in 1899 by a local physician in an unusual combination of Queen Anne and Eastlake architectural styles, the mansion has had a varied past as a private home, a hospital, a rest home, and an apartment building, until it was purchased by its present two young innkeepers Wendy Hatfield and her husband, Ken Torbert.

Now beautifully restored with period pieces and replicas of Victorian wallpaper, the mansion has five guest rooms with private baths and three very comfortable second-floor bedrooms that share two large baths. One of these is as spectacular as the mansion itself, with a claw-footed tub on a raised platform, surrounded on three sides by a white, spindle-posted railing.

Two inviting parlors with fireplaces and a separate adjoining well-stocked library are on the main floor, as is the breakfast room, where Wendy has a full continental offering each morning with freshly squeezed orange juice, a seasonal fruit plate, a cheese tray, and an assortment of home-baked breads with locally made jams.

THE GINGERBREAD MANSION, 400 Berding St., Ferndale, CA 95536; 707-786-4000. An 8-guestroom spectacular Victorian mansion in a historic landmark village, 20 mi. south of Eureka in northern California. Continental breakfast included in room rate. Open all year. Village sightseeing, including antique shops and crafts, all within walking distance. Bicycles available. Children over 10 by prior arrangement. No pets. No smoking. Wendy Hatfield and Ken Torbert, Innkeepers.

Directions: Turn off U.S. 101 at the Ferndale exit, 20 mi. south of Eureka. Ferndale is 5 mi. west. At the mint green Bank of America building, turn left for one block.

For B&B rates, see Index.

THE GLENBOROUGH INN
Santa Barbara, California

Jo Ann Bell and Pat Hardy, proprietors of this bed-and-breakfast inn in the residential section of Santa Barbara, feel so enthusiastic about their occupation that they, along with four other innkeepers, have formed the Innkeepers Guild of Santa Barbara. If you think you want to be an innkeeper I'd suggest that you write to them for further information about frequent seminars. In-depth workshops have been offered in March and October for five years, resulting in a dozen new inns throughout the country.

Guests at the Glenborough Inn are invited to a late afternoon-early evening get-together with hot mulled cider or wine and hors d'oeuvres on the parlor sideboard or a cool glass of Pat's wine punch or iced tea on the shady lawn.

All of the rooms enjoy the softness and warmth of plants and fresh flowers. Rooms have delightful old quilts, many turn-of-the-century wall hangings and samplers, and here and there a Norman Rockwell reproduction.

One of the features at the Glenborough is the outdoor, fully enclosed hot tub with large, fluffy bath towels for spa users. This is available for private use by reservation.

A full gourmet breakfast in bed, or sometimes enjoyed outside on the lovely grounds, is served on fine china or handmade pottery and silver with linen napkins. Incidentally, smoking is not allowed in the main house.

THE GLENBOROUGH INN, 1327 Bath St., Santa Barbara, CA 93101; 805-966-0589. A 4-guestroom (shared baths) 1906 home and a 4-guestroom 1880s cottage (private baths) including 2 fireplace suites. Private hot tub use included with room rate. Open all year. Within walking distance of the many historic, natural, and cultural advantages of Santa Barbara. Children under 12 and pets discouraged; smoking and non-smoking rooms. Jo Ann Bell and Pat Hardy, Innkeepers.

Directions: From Rte. 101 take off-ramp at Carrillo. Go east to Bath St. and turn left; go 3½ blocks to inn.

For B&B rates, see Index.

GLENDEVEN
Little River, California

This section of northern California on Highway 1 is rapidly becoming a weekend and midweek vacation area for residents of the Bay area. The drive up the coast with its tremendous cliffs and headlands is most spectacular. Little River is just a mile and a half south of the historic coastal town of Mendocino, with its interesting shops, galleries and restaurants.

Innkeepers Jan and Janet de Vries explained that the original farmhouse, barn, and watertower were built by a man from the state of Maine, one Isaiah Stevens, in 1867. I must say that he picked a very gracious location and today this Victorian house is a cheerful bed-and-breakfast inn.

The center of activity is the living room with a fireplace, a baby grand piano, and windows along the south side affording an extraordinary view of the well-tended garden and the bay. It is obvious that both Jan and Janet de Vries are involved in contemporary arts and crafts as evidenced by the ceramics, the paintings, and the numerous gallery notices.

The guest rooms have quite unusual furnishings with a generous number of French antiques as well as contemporary decorations. The Eastlin Suite has its own fireplace; all guest rooms have views of the bay or the gardens. A recent addition, called Stevenscroft, has four spacious rooms with views, fireplaces, and private baths.

The continental breakfast is generous, including fresh fruit or baked apple, muffins, morning cakes, coffee, tea, and baskets of brown hard-boiled eggs.

GLENDEVEN, 8221 No. Highway One, Little River, CA 95456; 707-937-0083. A 10-guestroom bed-and-breakfast inn (8 with private baths). Open year-round. Most convenient for enjoyable excursions to the northern California coastal towns and many nearby parks and beaches. Breakfast is the only meal served. No pets. Credit cards by special arrangement. Jan and Janet de Vries, Proprietors.

Directions: Either follow coastal Hwy. 1 all the way from San Francisco, skirting the shores of the Pacific, or follow Rte. 101 to Cloverdale; Rte. 128 to Hwy. 1, and then proceed north to Little River.

For B&B rates, see Index.

THE GOSBY HOUSE INN
Pacific Grove, California

Pacific Grove is a delightful oceanside resort and residential area situated on the famous Monterey Peninsula where the waters of the Pacific Ocean and Monterey Bay converge. Four miles of freely accessible sandy beaches and a rocky, coved shoreline afford unsurpassed enjoyment to young and old alike—for the sunbather, swimmer, skin diver, beachcomber, fisherman, or artist. It is a paradise of coastal wonders and marine life, with seals, seabirds, sea otters, emigrating whales, and coastal flora. The beautiful Monarch butterflies spend their winters here.

It is also the location of a bed-and-breakfast establishment that should delight the eclectic imagination of any Victorian enthusiast— The Gosby House Inn.

The exterior has all of the turn-of-the-century delights: a cupola with a conical roof, several different gabled sections, stained-glass windows, and many different types of siding.

The interior, including the many bedrooms, has quite a few original Victorian pieces along with some excellent reproductions. There are several old framed newspapers adorning the walls and decorative Victorian prints in the bedrooms. Ten bedrooms have their own fireplaces.

The reception area has a display case with some lovely dolls dressed in period costumes of various kinds. The building is in the National Historic Register.

THE GOSBY HOUSE INN, 643 Lighthouse Ave., Pacific Grove, CA 93950; 408-375-1287. A 22-guestroom (mostly private baths) bed-and-breakfast inn within a short distance of the Pacific Ocean in a relatively quiet residential section. Open year-round. Convenient for visits to Cannery Row in Monterey, Old Fisherman's Wharf, Monterey Bay Aquarium, Carmel, 17-mile Drive, Pebble Beach. Smoking is not permitted in the main house.

Directions: From Hwy. 1, take the Pebble Beach—Pacific Grove exit (Rte. 68 west) 5 mi. to Pacific Grove and follow Forest Ave. 3 mi. to Lighthouse Ave. Turn left 3 blocks.

For B&B rates, see Index.

GRAPE LEAF INN
Healdsburg, California

Healdsburg, Geyserville, and Cloverdale are just a few moments apart on Route 101, which leads to upper northern California.

In Healdsburg, the Grape Leaf Inn, at one time a private home, is located on a rather quiet residential street. Proprietor Terry Sweet has furnished this restored eighty-two-year-old home to reflect the turn of the century.

The first thing that impressed me upon walking into the entry hall was the parlor and dining-living room with its very comfortable couch, love seat, fireplace, swag lamp, and lots of flowers.

The seven comfortably furnished bedrooms, all with private baths (including whirlpool tub/showers for two), are named after the wines of the Alexander Valley. The new rooms upstairs have skylight roof windows and air conditioning. Within a twenty-minute drive of the inn there are fifty-three wineries that are still family-owned. During the wintertime especially, you can go right into the winery and talk to the winemaker. There is also a canoe company nearby where rental canoes are available for day trips on the Russian River, which runs through Healdsburg.

Full breakfast served by Kathy Cookson, resident innkeeper, includes freshly ground coffee that is roasted nearby, fresh orange juice, fresh fruit, eggs prepared in a variety of ways, and home-baked muffins or coffee cake. In addition, in the afternoon, Kathy pours a red or white local premium-quality wine to be enjoyed with Sonoma County cheeses.

GRAPE LEAF INN, 539 Johnson St., Healdsburg, CA 95448; 707-443-8140. A 7-guestroom bed-and-breakfast home in the northern Sonoma wine country. Open year-round. Breakfast is the only meal served. Conveniently located to visit all of the cultural and historic attractions and wineries. Night tennis, bicycles, canoe trips and other recreation nearby. Terry Sweet, Proprietor; Kathy Cookson, Innkeeper.

Directions: From San Francisco, follow Rte. 101 north, exiting at Healdsburg Ave. (the second exit from Healdsburg) and continue in the same direction for 4 traffic lights. Turn right at Grant St., go 2 blocks to Johnson St. and turn right. Grape Leaf is on the right with a small, unobtrusive sign.

For B&B rates, see Index.

THE GREEN GABLES INN
Pacific Grove, California

If you're ever planning to be in Pacific Grove, by all means telephone in advance in the hope that there will be accommodations available at the Green Gables.

Located right on the water on Ocean View Boulevard, this many-gabled Victorian beauty, with its white fence and well-kept garden, can only be described as "delicious."

Large bay window alcoves, antique furnishings, and a unique fireplace framed by stained glass panels make the living room a gracious gathering place for guests.

The six guest rooms in the main house are exceptionally comfortable and have leaded casement windows with a view of the Pacific Ocean as it crashes on the great rocks. There are four additional guest rooms in the carriage house.

A generous breakfast is served in a lovely little dining room with its own view of the ocean, too. There is a substantial main course, which could be quiche, a frittata, Belgian waffles, or crêpes, combined with fresh fruits, homemade breads, juices, and coffee or tea.

A complimentary social hour is held in the afternoon, when hors d'oeuvres, wine, sherry, and hot cider are offered.

THE GREEN GABLES INN, 104 Fifth St. (corner of Ocean View Blvd.), Pacific Grove, CA 93950; 408-375-2095. A 10-guestroom B&B home by the bay. Open all year. Breakfast included. Conveniently located for all the Monterey Peninsula recreational, cultural, and historic attractions, including the famous golf courses and Cannery Row. Not suitable for children. No pets. No credit cards. No smoking. Roger and Sally Post, Owners; Linda Kravel, Innkeeper.

Directions: Exit Hwy. 1 on Rte. 68 west; continue to Pacific Grove (5 mi.) and then follow Forest Ave. to Ocean Blvd. and then turn right on 5th St.

For B&B rates, see Index.

THE GREY WHALE INN
Fort Bragg, California

Fort Bragg is located on Route 1 on the romantic north coast, where forest meets the sea, just nine miles north of Mendocino village. Guests at the Grey Whale can enjoy beachcombing amid the twisted driftwood, whale-watching as the giant grey whales migrate between December and March within sight of shore, attend a salmon barbecue in July, along with such other diversions as the Foot-lighters' Gaslight Gaieties summer theater and Gloriana light opera.

A walk on the secluded, unspoiled miles of beaches has something very special for everyone. There's something special, too, about the Grey Whale which, for many years, was the Redwood Coast Hospital. The rooms and corridors are spacious, and in one of the oceanview suites, an old gimbaled surgery lamp is a reminder of the building's past. There is a guest room with a fireplace.

The large suites with kitchens are ideal for an extended bed-and-breakfast experience. One spacious first-floor room has superior facilities for the guest in a wheelchair.

Breakfast at the inn is served buffet style in a cozy breakfast room from 7:30 to 11:00 A.M., and includes fruit juice, prizewinning homemade breads and coffee cakes, fresh fruit, yogurt or cheese, and hot beverages.

THE GREY WHALE INN, 615 No. Main St., Fort Bragg, CA 95437; 707-964-0640. A 13-guestroom inn located on Hwy. 1 at the north end of Fort Bragg. Complimentary breakfast included in room rates. (Only meal served.) Open every day in the year. Wheelchair access. Many natural, historic, and recreational attractions within a short distance. Available by Greyhound Bus and Skunk Train. Beachcombing, scuba diving, fishing, and hiking nearby. John and Colette Bailey, Innkeepers.

Directions: From the south, follow Hwy. 101 to Cloverdale, take Rte. 128 west to Hwy.1, and follow north to Fort Bragg. Alternate route: Exit Hwy. 101 at Willits, then west on Rte. 20 to Fort Bragg. Driving time from San Francisco, 3½ hrs. Another alternate: Hwy. 1 along the coast. Driving time from San Francisco: 5 hrs.

For B&B rates, see Index.

THE HANFORD HOUSE
Sutter Creek, California

This modern inn is an unexpected find in a very historic California town in the gold country. The original site supported an old Spanish bungalow, to which extensive additions were made in recent years. The result is reminiscent of an old San Francisco brick warehouse. The inn is decorated with lovely antiques that create a warm and comfortable atmosphere. Floors have been completely covered with slate gray carpeting so unobtrusive yet complementary that every flower arrangement and piece of furniture is highlighted.

Guests are greeted in an attractive lounge with a cathedral-type ceiling, which opens into a dining area immediately beyond. One receives an instant impression of orderliness without a feeling of formality.

There are four guest rooms in the main house and five in a wing. Headboards for the beds are often old Spanish doors, or even barn doors turned sideways, making great conversation pieces. An old prayer bench may serve as a plant stand, while full, tilting mirrors, armoires, and wicker furniture are found elsewhere.

An expanded continental breakfast is served in the dining room. In late afternoon, a complimentary bottle of local wine or soft drinks may be enjoyed on the large deck overlooking the countryside or on the shaded patio. Many good restaurants are nearby. The small converted home next door, the Pelargonium, seems particularly good.

THE HANFORD HOUSE, Box 847, 3 Hanford St., Sutter Creek, CA 95685; 209-267-0747. A 9-guestroom (private baths) contemporary inn in a historic gold rush town in northern California. Complimentary breakfast and afternoon wine. Open year-round. Handicapped accessible. Panning for gold, wineries, antique and specialty shops, city walking tour among western movie-type buildings. All kinds of recreational activities. Children over 12. No pets. Smoking and non-smoking rooms. Jim and Lucille Jacobus, Innkeepers.

Directions: At the corner of Hanford and Main St., the latter being Hwy. 49 in town.

For B&B rates, see Index.

THE HAPPY LANDING
Carmel-by-the-Sea, California

Just a half block from Ocean Avenue, the principal shopping street of Carmel, stands the Happy Landing, a collection of English-type pink cottages built around a courtyard with a delightful lily pond and a gazebo, where weddings and receptions are often held.

Built in 1925 as a family retreat, this early Comstock-designed group of buildings has evolved into one of Carmel's entrancing accommodations. They are in keeping with the Carmel tradition of individual and family comfort.

There are seven of these little cottages set amongst the rose trellises, and almost all of them have cathedral ceilings and individual fireplaces. Some are furnished in wicker and others have antiques and brass. The pink theme is continued throughout, even to the pink towels. When you open your curtains in the morning, it is the signal that you are ready to have breakfast brought to your room by Aiko, the Japanese maid. It consists of various breakfast breads, fresh fruit, juice, and coffee or tea. Many guests sit out in the garden enjoying the Carmel sunshine and the ubiquitous birds.

Although the Happy Landing is not on Carmel Bay, it is possible to get a glimpse of the bay through the trees. Views of both the ocean and the garden can be enjoyed from the large reception room with its stone fireplace, where tea is served in the afternoon.

THE HAPPY LANDING, Box 2619, Monte Verde between 5th and 6th Streets, Carmel, CA 93921; 408-624-7917. A 7-guestroom (private baths) bed-and-breakfast inn; including 2 suites with king-sized beds. Open every day of the year. In a very quiet section of Carmel, a short distance from the beach and a pleasant walking distance to shops and restaurants. Conveniently located for drives through Pebble Beach and Big Sur. No pets. Bob Alberson and Dick Stewart, Innkeepers.

Directions: Take the Ocean Ave. exit from Hwy. 1 and continue to Monte Verde. Turn right for 1½ blocks. The Happy Landing Inn is next to the Christian Science Church.

For B&B rates, see Index.

THE HEIRLOOM
Ione, California

Slightly west of the famous California towns of Jackson and Sutter Creek lies the country village of Ione. Well off the main road, in a beautiful garden setting, is the town's historical center—a brick antebellum mansion with classic columns and wisteria-entwined porticos. Built in 1863 by a Virginian, the windows are deep-set in Southern style, a fan transom covers the front entrance, and the living room is all in off-white paneling. A Colonial staircase and mantel complete the background for the antique furnishings in this charming home.

The four seasons provide themes for the decor of the guest rooms, and innkeepers Patricia Cross and Melisande Hubbs have used jonquil yellow in the Springtime room, seafoam and dusty rose for Summer, maple-leaf colors for Autumn, and Winter is evoked with burgundy and blue. Three of the rooms have balconies and there are double and king- and queen-sized beds. A handcrafted adobe (rammed earth) cottage, with woodburning stoves and skylights, contains the Early American Room and the Early California Room.

Usually attired in long skirts, Patricia and Melisande serve their guests a full breakfast. A typical meal will offer fresh orange juice, home-baked breads or popovers, an entrée of crêpes, soufflés, quiche, or eggs Benedict, and the very best of coffees. Breakfast may be enjoyed in bed or on the balcony, in the garden, or in the fireside dining room.

On arrival in late afternoon, guests are served sherry, white wine, or tea. Guests will find fresh flowers, fruit, and candy in their rooms.

THE HEIRLOOM, 214 Shakeley Lane, P.O. Box 322, Ione, CA 95640; 209-274-4468. A 6-guestroom (3 private baths) historic bed-and-breakfast inn (circa 1863) in the heart of the gold rush country in the foothills of the Sierra Nevadas, west of Jackson and Sutter Creek. Open year-round. Bicycles available for exploring country roads. Historic sites, antiquing, wineries nearby. No children under 12. No pets. No credit cards. Patricia Cross and Melisande Hubbs, Innkeepers.

Directions: From Hwy. 88 or 16 take Hwy. 124 to Ione. Watch for the Heirloom sign on left. A short lane leads to the inn.

For B&B rates, see Index.

HERITAGE PARK BED & BREAKFAST INN
San Diego, California

Some of the finest examples of San Diego's Victorian past are to be found in Heritage Park, a historical preserve maintained by the county. In a rather unique arrangement, the county leases the buildings to private concerns, which are responsible for the renovation and maintenance of the interiors.

Lori Chandler and her family have created a delightful bed-and-breakfast inn with authentic Victorian antiques in one of the classic homes in the park. Built in 1889 by H. Timberlake Christian, one of the signers of the original city charter, the graceful Queen Anne house is characterized by a variety of chimneys, shingles, a corner turret, and an encircling veranda.

"Most of the money for remodeling really went into the milling," Lori told me, "for you don't just phone a lumberyard and order Victorian." Many of the original walls have been restored, and rich wood paneling, newly milled and finished, has been placed in the parlor and chambers to duplicate the original woodwork. The distinctive guest rooms have authentic period antiques, documented Victorian wall-coverings, handsome quilts, and oriental rugs.

Lori spares no effort in making her guests feel comfortable and at home, including making picnic lunches and candlelight dinners. Breakfast, delivered to the room on an antique tray and fitted with a sugar bowl and creamer to match the room, is sumptuous, with all sorts of homemade offerings, including Lori's award-winning "strawberry jam loaf." On sunny days, you could enjoy a fresh-air breakfast in the garden or on the veranda.

HERITAGE PARK BED & BREAKFAST INN, 2470 Heritage Park Row, San Diego, CA 92110; 619-295-7088. A 9-guestroom (private and shared baths) gracious Victorian B&B in Heritage Park, a historic preservation, adjacent to San Diego's Old Town. Complimentary full breakfast and evening social hour. Picnic lunch and dinner available on request. Open year-round. Nightly film classics; purchasable antiques and collectibles on premises. Balboa Park and Zoo, walking tours, bicycle taxi tours, San Diego Bay boat tours, shops, galleries, restaurants nearby. Facilities for disabled. No children under 14. No pets. No smoking. Lori Chandler, Innkeeper.

Directions: From downtown San Diego, take I-5 to Old Town Ave. exit and turn right on Old Town Ave. Turn left on San Diego Ave. and then right on Harney St. to Heritage Park.

For B&B rates, see Index.

HERMITAGE HOUSE
San Francisco, California

Extensive scrubbing, oiling, painting, paperhanging, and up-dating plumbing and wiring have brought this 1903 home of Judge Charles Slack back up to snuff. When Hermitage House, a four-story Greek Revival mansion, was purchased by the Binkleys in 1978, it had been used as a drug rehabilitation center and was much in need of restoration and care. Innkeeper Marian Binkley was skillful in her renovation, as she kept much of the mansion's original character and beauty intact, and then transformed the building into a cozy and convenient inn.

Hermitage House has six bedrooms with baths, four of which have working fireplaces. Not only are the rooms beautifully papered with floral patterns and attractive turn-of-the-century furniture, but the beds are four-postered or brass. Each room has a special name, such as Game Room, Guinevere, or Green Gables; but one of the most interesting bedrooms is Judge Slack's study on the top floor of the house. It is noteworthy for its high, beamed ceiling, walls lined with bookshelves, a massive stone fireplace, and a dormered window, providing a special vista of the Twin Peaks district of San Francisco.

The cheery breakfast room, off the main entrance, is where the morning fare is served buffet style. Each morning there is a buffet filled with freshly squeezed orange juice, a variety of cold cereals, an assortment of rolls and croissants, fruits, tea, coffee, and chocolate. I was given a tour of the kitchen, where Marian Binkley pointed with pride to the original 1900 Wedgewood stove. Marian boasts, "It's in grand condition and I only had to get two new gadgets for it—a self-lighter and a thermostat!"

HERMITAGE HOUSE, 2224 Sacramento St., San Francisco, CA 94115; 415-921-5515. A 6-guestroom bed-and-breakfast inn lo-cated in the city's Pacific Heights district, with limited off-street parking facilities for guests. Continental breakfast only. Open all year. Convenient local public transportation (the bus stops at the corner) to many districts in the city. Walking distance to Union Street and Fillmore. Children discouraged. No pets. Ted and Marian Binkley, Innkeepers.

Directions: Take Van Ness exit from Rte. 101 to Sacramento St. Inn is between Laguna and Buchanan Streets.

For B&B rates, see Index.

HILL HOUSE INN
Mendocino, California

Query knowledgeable Californians as to the beauties of their state's 800-mile Pacific Ocean frontage, and you will hear unanimous praise for the coasts of Big Sur and Mendocino County. While Big Sur provides a picturesque drive, it is generally without public accommodations, but Mendocino offers both spectacular scenery and the best of creature comforts—and high on the list is the Hill House Inn.

One's first view of the inn, across the quarter-mile of open, green-belt land separating it from Highway 1, is a bit startling, for the three low-profile buildings provide an outward appearance not unlike what one would expect in New England or on the East Coast. The pleasing olive-painted siding, trimmed in white and topped by dark gray roofs, appears most inviting, and this feeling is immediately confirmed when you step into the central reception building with its comfortable couches, flowers and greenery, large fireplace, and neatly patterned wallpaper.

As they are shown to their rooms, guests invariably stop to admire the colorful flower beds and the luxuriant plantings in the atrium areas within each of the two guest buildings.

The decor of the bedrooms is a proper mix of modern and Victorian furnishings and offers either two double beds or a single king-sized bed; some rooms have fireplaces. Marble-topped end tables with excellent reading lights flank the beds, while a color TV is discreetly concealed in a cabinet. There are comfortable chairs and a writing table placed in front of view windows overlooking either the ocean or the gardens.

A continental breakfast of juice, hot breads or muffins, and freshly brewed coffee is served in a spacious dining room overlooking a panoramic view of the Mendocino coast.

HILL HOUSE INN, P.O. Box 625, Mendocino, CA 95460; 707-937-0554. A 44-guestroom (private baths) New England-style inn with restaurant in historic Mendocino county, overlooking the Pacific Ocean. Continental breakfast included. Open all year. Shops, galleries, restaurants, and Mendocino Headlands State Park nearby. Children welcome. No pets. Monte and Barbara Reed, Owners.

Directions: From either north or south on Hwy. 1, take Little Lake exit toward the ocean, one block to Lansing, then right to the top of the hill.

For B&B rates, see Index.

HOPE-MERRILL HOUSE
Geyserville, California

The Hope-Merrill House is one of the most impressive renovations and restorations I have seen. Earlier "modernizations" had installed new windows and lowered ceilings that covered up the original Gothic arches over the bay windows throughout the house—all of which had to be torn out and the moldings retrimmed. Turn-of-the-century wainscoting is a highlight of the interior—it is known as Lincrusta-Walton and is the same wainscoting that has been restored in the state capitol. Even the original silk-screened wallpapers are custom-designed.

This loving effort extends to the very elegant guest rooms that are decorated with Victorian carved headboards, a wicker chaise lounge, a free-standing mirror, a marble-top dresser, and nice old sepia and tinted prints. One room has wallpaper designed from a set of random mathematical tables that simulate the positions of stars as you would see them in the sky. The bathrooms are equally elegant with lots of pictures on the walls.

Favorite spots for relaxation and conversation are the swimming pool, latticed gazebo, and large grape arbor.

Bob and Rosalie Hope also own the Hope-Bosworth House, located immediately across Geyserville Avenue, so if one house is filled, there is a good chance you can be accommodated in the other one. The Hope-Bosworth House has five guest rooms and a very pleasant atmosphere.

Rosalie and Bob offer a unique wine country tour, called "Stage-a-Picnic" in a horse-drawn stage or a "depot wagon," that includes a scrumptious picnic lunch.

HOPE-MERRILL HOUSE, 21253 Geyserville Ave. (P.O. Box 42), Geyserville, CA 95441; 707-857-3356. A 5-guestroom (some private baths) restored Victorian home. Reservations can also be made for the Hope-Bosworth House, across the street, with 5 guestrooms and a very pleasant atmosphere. Swimming pool on grounds. Conveniently located to enjoy all of the wine country scenic and historical attractions. No pets. Not suitable for children. Bob and Rosalie Hope, Proprietors.

Directions: From San Francisco, take Rte. 101 north 80 mi. to the Geyserville exit, drive east 1 block to Old Redwood Hwy., turn left on Geyserville Ave. (Old Redwood Hwy.), and go 1 mi. north. The two houses are across the road from each other.

For B&B rates, see Index.

THE HOUSE OF SEVEN GABLES
Pacific Grove, California

It is difficult to imagine a more dramatic marine outlook than that afforded to the guests of the House of Seven Gables. Above the shoreline of Monterey Bay, it has an unobstructed view from large picture windows of the bay's half-moon-shaped beach, stretching far, far into the distance. Lucie Chase, a well-to-do civic leader, built this showplace Victorian home in 1886, parking her electric car in front to further display her affluence.

Seven Gables has been the Flatleys' home for many years. Their children, who now operate the house as an inn, have modernized only the baths. The large comfortable rooms are furnished with English and French antiques—carved armoires with bevelled pier mirrors, inlaid-wood pieces, chandeliers, and oriental rugs. Most rooms are further enhanced by the filtered light of antique Tiffany-quality stained glass windows.

Mornings, seated in loge-view seats, praising Nora Flatley's sumptuous breakfast of fresh orange juice, a huge family-style bowl of mixed fresh fruits, crisp croissants, and a hot apple cobbler, guests are treated to a show few people ever see.

Between early December and late February, migratory gray whales cavort below the windows, sending up spouts of vapor, then revealing broad backs before sounding into the deep waters of the bay with a final wave of huge tails. These mammoth creatures use this protected water as a haven to break their long journey between the Sea of Cortez and the Arctic Ocean. Even if your visit is at a different time of the year, you will always enjoy a performance by the frisky California sea otters and the proliferating marine bird life. One can take a pleasant stroll along the ocean path to the world-famous aquarium or Cannery Row.

THE HOUSE OF SEVEN GABLES, 555 Ocean View Blvd., Pacific Grove, CA 93950; 408-372-4341. A 14-guestroom Victorian bed-and-breakfast inn on the ocean front of the Monterey Peninsula. All rooms with private baths and ocean views. Breakfast included in room rate. Open all year. Convenient to Monterey golf courses, Cannery Row, Carmel, Big Sur, Butterfly Trees, 17-Mile Drive. Adults only. No pets. No smoking. No credit cards. The Flatley Family, Owners and Innkeepers.

Directions: From Hwy. 1, take the Pebble Beach-Pacific Grove exit (Rte. 68 west). Continue 5 mi. to Pacific Grove and follow Forest Ave. to its end at Ocean View Blvd. Turn right 2 blocks to Fountain.

For B&B rates, see Index.

THE INN AT UNION SQUARE
San Francisco, California

There are probably few inns in America that deliberately strive to be inconspicuous in their outward appearance. Yet, at a very select location in San Francisco, directly across from the Post Street entrance of the Westin St. Francis Hotel on Union Square, amidst fine shops, international airline ticket offices, and some fifty steps from the cable cars, is the Inn at Union Square.

Only a neat awning and brass plate identify the inn, formerly a sixty-room hotel that Norm and Nan Rosenblatt (she, an interior decorator by profession) completely remodeled into a very comfortable thirty-room inn, all with Georgian furniture, colorful fabrics, private facilities, direct dial telephones, and TV's concealed within stylish armoires.

For guest convenience, each of the five floors has its own common room with fireplaces, icemakers, and refrigerators. It is here or in the guest's room that a continental breakfast of fresh fruits and juices, scones, croissants, and hot drinks is served in the morning, with the latest news and financial papers.

As security is paramount in any centrally located, metropolitan inn, 24-hour desk and concierge service is provided. Access to upper floors is by a keyed elevator.

Most of the well-furnished guest rooms are above adjacent buildings and face east, so natural lighting, while brightest in the morning hours, continues throughout the day. The overlook is made even more pleasing by the colorful flower garden on the neighboring roof. Turndown bed service is provided in the evenings and shoes will be given a gratis shine if placed in the hallway upon retiring.

The inn staff assures constant attention to guests. Earliest possible reservations are necessary.

THE INN AT UNION SQUARE, 440 Post St., San Francisco, CA 94102; 415-397-3510. A 30-guestroom bed-and-breakfast inn in the very heart of San Francisco's fine shops, hotels, and theaters. All rooms with private baths, concealed TV's, and direct dial telephones. Breakfast only meal served. Open year-round. Cable cars a few steps away. Valet parking if desired. Minimal accommodations for children; inquire in advance. No pets. Advance reservations a must. Norm and Nan Rosenblatt, Innkeepers.

Directions: At the Union Square corner of Post and Powell, across from Post St. entrance to St. Francis Hotel.

For B&B rates, see Index.

THE J. PATRICK HOUSE
Cambria, California

Visitors to California should plan to see Hearst Castle, fabled one-time home of the newspaper tycoon, William Randolph Hearst, who built this museumlike showplace in San Simeon, high in the Big Sur coastal mountains, overlooking the Pacific Ocean. Now state owned, the castle and grounds are open to the public, and tours provide a glimpse of the opulence created when early Hollywood was in its heyday.

Nearby in the town of Cambria is a delightful spick-and-span inn, the J. Patrick House. Molly Lynch, the innkeeper, is a true Irish colleen and has named each of her guest rooms for the counties of Ireland. The warmth and charm of her inn are enhanced by the woodsy setting, with its filtered sunlight and carpets of pine needles.

Molly's modern two-story log cabin–type home has cozy areas for guests' reception, lounge, and breakfast room on the ground floor, while the second story contains her private quarters.

Housed in a building at the rear, separated from the main house by vine-covered arbor and a guest parking area, the guest rooms are reached across a pleasant lawn landscaped with many flowers and vines.

Whether you stay in the Dublin, Kilkenny, Donegal, Tipperary, or another room, you will be treated to a rocking chair, hooked rugs, pleasing decorations, a wood-burning fireplace, and an excellent bath.

A hearty continental breakfast is served in the bright, cheery breakfast room overlooking the garden, and afternoon refreshments await by the fire in the living room. One cannot be a stranger here for long.

THE J. PATRICK HOUSE, 2990 Burton Dr., Cambria, CA 93428; 805-927-3812. A 7-guestroom (private baths) rustic inn just off scenic Hwy. 1 in a peaceful community on the central California coast. Complimentary continental breakfast and afternoon refreshments. Open year-round. A telephone is accessible, but no TV. Hearst Castle, Morro Bay, Big Sur, San Luis Obispo, beaches, wineries, shops, and restaurants all within an easy drive. Adults only. No pets. No smoking. Molly Lynch, Innkeeper.

Directions: From the north on Hwy. 101, turn west on Hwy. 46. At Hwy. 1, turn north to blinking light at Burton Dr., then turn right. From the south, take Hwy. 1 north at San Luis Obispo, and turn right at blinking light at Burton Dr.

For B&B rates, see Index.

THE JABBERWOCK
Monterey, California

The whimsy of Lewis Carroll and his Jabberwock poem from *Alice in Wonderland* is matched by the imagination of Barbara and Jim Allen, proprietors of the Jabberwock. They have turned a towered and turreted former convent, built in 1911, into a seven-bedroom bed-and-breakfast inn. Unique touches abound, starting in the foyer with the gumball machine and shoe-shiner set among antiques and oriental rugs, along with a needlepoint wallhanging of the Jabberwock poem.

Opened in March of 1982, Jabberwock is one of the very few bed and breakfasts in Monterey. Its unique setting overlooking Monterey Bay offers guests a magnificent view. Situated on a quiet corner, the large lot includes a lush garden with a waterfall and ponds.

The homey living room with its wallpaper, antiques, and dark green rug is the place where homemade cookies and milk are set out for guests after dinner. A glassed-in sunporch with comfortable rattan chairs for reading and tables for puzzles and games offers a wonderful view of Monterey Bay. Fresh flower arrangements adorn all the rooms.

The dining room, with its fireplace and charming wallpaper, has a mirror on the table to help guests read the breakfast menu, printed backwards. Breakfast is Barbara's specialty and she uses made-up names, such as "Razzleberry Flabjous" or "Snarkleberry Flumptious." Breakfast can also be served in the guest's room.

A lovely stained-glass window on the landing helps lead the guests to the bedrooms on the second and third floor, each decorated with flowered wallpapers, antique furniture, goosedown quilts, and lace-trimmed sheets. Some rooms have fireplaces and telescopes or binoculars.

THE JABBERWOCK, 598 Laine St., Monterey, CA 93940; 408-372-4777. A 7-guestroom bed-and-breakfast inn (3 rooms with private bath, 4 share baths) overlooking Monterey Bay. Open year-round. Minimum 2 nights on weekends, 3 nights at special times, i.e. Monterey Jazz Festival, Crosby Tournament. Mature teenagers accepted. No credit cards. No pets. Jim and Barbara Allen, Innkeepers.

Directions: From San Francisco, take Del Monte Ave. off Hwy. 1 into Monterey, following signs to Cannery Row through the tunnel to Lighthouse Ave. Turn left on Hoffman and left on Laine. Pick-up service at Monterey Airport.

For B&B rates, see Index.

JOSHUA GRINDLE INN
Mendocino, California

A New Englander searching for a place to remind him of his home should pay a visit to Mendocino. Not only is the spectacular coastal scenery reminiscent of New England, but many of the wooden Victorian homes resemble those built in the Northeast.

In the 1870s, Joshua Grindle, a native of Maine, came to Mendocino to try his hand in the lumber business. He built a beautiful Italianate house for his bride in 1879, and went to work at a nearby mill.

Californians Gwen and Bill Jacobson, although not New Englanders, were also taken by the beauty of Mendocino and were delighted to be able to buy the Grindle house in 1977, which they then turned into a gracious bed-and-breakfast inn.

The Joshua Grindle Inn's five guest rooms in the main house all have private baths and are exquisitely decorated with early American furnishings, handmade quilts from New England, etchings, and oil paintings. In a cottage adjacent to the inn are two other bedrooms complete with Franklin fireplace. A recently completed watertower houses two more guest rooms, each with fireplace.

The main visiting room off the entrance is beautifully wallpapered, has a baby grand piano and a fireplace decorated with tiles made in England. Here on a chest there is always sherry and a bowl of fresh fruit provided by the Jacobsons. Hospitality abounds in the dining room, where guests may relax at a long pine table while Gwen serves up a delicious, full continental breakfast, complete with fresh fruit, homemade breads, eggs, coffee, and tea.

As the inn is only a few short blocks from the main street, it is best to set aside time to walk, browse, and explore the many little alleys, paths, shops, art galleries, and historic buildings that make up Mendocino.

JOSHUA GRINDLE INN, Box 647, 44800 Little Lake, Mendocino, CA 95460; 707-937-4143. A 9-guestroom (private baths) attractive Victorian inn on California's northern coast. Continental breakfast included in room rate. Open all year. Many cultural, recreational, and historic attractions nearby. No telephone, no television. Children discouraged. No pets. No credit cards. Gwen and Bill Jacobson, Innkeepers.

Directions: Starting from San Francisco, travel on Hwy. 101 north to Cloverdale, then Rte. 128 and take Hwy. 1 north to Mendocino. Alternate route is to take scenic Hwy. 1 north to Mendocino.

For B&B rates, see Index.

LA MAIDA HOUSE
North Hollywood, California

This large, historic Hollywood mansion, built in 1926 on the corner of two quiet residential streets, is just what a movie-buff would expect. Now overseen by a sparkling young proprietor and her mother, the manicured lawns and flower gardens, the myriad stained-glass windows, hallways, and ceilings, the guest rooms with comfort almost to an excess, reflect an inn that everyone should make an effort to visit.

Fleeing Rhodesia, now Zimbabwe, the owners have literally "bootstrapped" themselves from nothing to positions of envy. Megan Timothy, with a delightful accent that may have opened many otherwise closed doors, is a self-taught chef and handywoman, whose talents, recipes, and flower photography have appeared in *Better Homes and Gardens*, *Bon Appetit*, and national "how-to" magazines.

Purchased in a complete state of disrepair, the inn's oak floors, handsome mahogany, and even the Carrara marble fireplace have been meticulously restored to their original splendor. Be certain to call it "La-my-da" House, both the house and the street having been named as a tribute to the original builder and owner.

As might be expected, breakfasts are exceptional, prepared to guests' preferences, with freshly blended fruit and vegetable juices, freshly baked breads, and freshly ground coffee.

La Maida is an "experience," particularly if you will draw out the innkeeper, who is a very modest, though multitalented person, along with her mother, who tends and arranges flowers and plants like a professional horticulturist.

Celebrities have been known to slip in for a quiet and anonymous stay at this very special place.

LA MAIDA HOUSE, 11159 La Maida St., North Hollywood, CA 91601; 818-769-3857. A 10-guestroom (private baths) Italianate villa on a quiet street in North Hollywood. Included are bungalows across the street. Complimentary breakfast, afternoon wine. Dinner available with advance arrangements. Open year-round. Near Burbank Airport, NBC Television and Universal Studios tours, Hollywood, Los Angeles, and Pasadena attractions: Hollywood Bowl, Norton Simon Museum, Rose Bowl. Children over 16. No pets. No smoking. No credit cards. Megan Timothy, Innkeeper.

Directions: From Hollywood Freeway, exit at Magnolia, turn east at first light, turn right on Tujunga Blvd., proceed to next light, left on Camarillo St., 3 blks. to Bellflower. Turn left 1 block to La Maida.

For B&B rates, see Index.

LA RÉSIDENCE COUNTRY INN
Napa, California

In a two-acre country setting with large, old magnolias and California live oaks, a few miles north of Napa, sits La Résidence, a three-story Gothic Revival-style house with a Southern flavor. Built in 1870 by Harry C. Parker, a New Orleans river pilot, who came to California during the 1849 gold rush, this beautiful house with its wide, columned porch has been turned into a very special bed-and-breakfast inn by its proprietor, Barbara Littenberg.

With her background as both fashion designer and archaeologist, and influenced by English country inns, Barbara has decorated La Résidence in the style of a 19th-century country house, with fresh flowers in each room, antique armoires, sofas and queen-size replicas of brass and cast-iron beds covered with quilted eyelet or floral spreads and ruffled pillows. Each bedroom has its own sitting area.

Several of the seven bedrooms have marble or brick fireplaces and all have large windows. Four rooms have private baths. Two large second-floor rooms have french doors leading to the balcony at the front of the house. The smaller but cozy and charming third-floor rooms have wallpapered eaves. There is central air conditioning throughout.

An additional building completed in 1984, the Barn, has eight rooms with private baths and fireplaces. Furnished in English pine furniture with English chintzes and French fabrics, each room has a sitting area. The country French dining room is the setting for the complimentary continental breakfasts of fresh orange juice, fresh fruit, croissants, tea or coffee, as well as for dinners. The kitchen in the main house is available to guests for preparing snacks.

LA RÉSIDENCE, 4066 St. Helena Highway North (Hwy. 29), Napa, CA 94558; 707-253-0337. A 7-guestroom (4 private baths) Gothic Revival country house just north of Napa in the wine country. Also 8 guestrooms (private baths) in the Barn. Wheelchair access to some rooms. Continental breakfast included in rate. Open all year. Minimum stay of 2 nights on weekends. Convenient to wineries and all the other attractions of the Napa Valley. No telephones or television. No children. No pets. Barbara Littenberg, Innkeeper.

Directions: Take Highway 29 beyond Napa, past Salvador Rd., turn right at Bon Appetit Restaurant, where a sign will take you to the inn, which faces the highway.

For B&B rates, see Index.

MOUNTAIN HOME INN
Mill Valley, California

A visitor to San Francisco can see towering Mount Tamalpais, across the Golden Gate Bridge, from almost any vantage point. For many years, a radar station on its peak has surveyed incoming Pacific Ocean air and sea traffic, while its lower slopes shelter one of the city's great tourist attractions, the huge redwoods of the Muir Woods.

The only way to climb Mt. Tam, as it is locally known, was by cow trail until 1886, when a scenic railroad was constructed, and a beer garden near the top immediately became a favorite luncheon destination for San Franciscans.

With the advent of the auto and the decline of the Mt. Tam Railway, Ed and Susan Cunningham, the present owners and innkeepers, purchased the property to build a new three-tiered inn with skylights, hardwood floors, and redwood columns in keeping with the natural, rugged setting.

Lunching on the large veranda is an event in itself, looking out over the sleepy town of Mill Valley and beyond to San Francisco Bay below.

All of the comfortable guest rooms have views of San Francisco Bay, the Tiburon Peninsula, and the East Bay hills; some have private balconies or fireplaces.

A continental breakfast may be enjoyed on an outside deck or in the overnight guests' private dining room. Evening meals are served in an upper-level dining room.

MOUNTAIN HOME INN, 810 Panoramic Highway, Mill Valley, CA 94941; 415-381-9000. A 10-guestroom (private baths) rustically luxurious new inn at the 1,000-foot level of Mt. Tamalpais, 15 min. from the Golden Gate Bridge, overlooking San Francisco Bay. Complimentary continental breakfast. Picnic lunches available. Dinner served to the public daily. Open year-round. Hiking, nature walks into Muir Woods National Monument with huge redwoods; 250 mi. of trails in Mt. Tamalpais State Park; spectacular drives; beachcombing on Muir Beach, Stinson Beach, or at Pt. Reyes; horse stables nearby. No pets. Ed and Susan Cunningham, Owners; Cathy Larson, Innkeeper.

Directions: From downtown San Francisco, take Hwy. 101 across Golden Gate Bridge. Turn right at Hwy. 1 off-ramp at Mill Valley. Turn left at light, which is Hwy. 1. After 2½ mi., turn right on Panoramic Hwy. and continue 3½ mi. to inn.

For B&B rates, see Index.

OLD MONTEREY INN
Monterey, California

Built in 1929, this three-story, half-timbered English Tudor-style home was converted into an inn eight years ago and continues to be one of the very best. The proprietors, Gene and Ann Swett, have lived here for more than a decade.

Located in the heart of the city of Monterey, in a quiet residential neighborhood, the acre-plus grounds are studded with old oak, pine, and redwood trees, thick ivy, and even a running stream. Secluded outdoor sitting areas invite guests to relax and enjoy the gardens filled with fuchsias, begonias, rhododendrons, and a formal rose garden.

In the inn itself, a blend of beautiful antiques and contemporary furnishings reflects an air of casual elegance. Most guest rooms have wood-burning fireplaces, skylights, and stained glass windows. Each room has a view of the peaceful gardens. There are canopied beds (either queen or king), European goose-down comforters and pillows, and visually beautiful color schemes. Outside one guest room is a flower-filled Mexican fountain; in another is an antique chaise lounge, and a couple have rocking chairs. A generous continental breakfast may be enjoyed in bed or downstairs in front of a fire, where early evening wine and cheese is also served.

OLD MONTEREY INN, 500 Martin St., Monterey, CA 93940; 408-375-8284. A 10-guestroom (private baths) English country house B&B on a hillside in a residential section of Monterey. Continental breakfast and refreshments included. Open year-round. Minimum stay of 2 nights on weekends. Many golf courses, including the challenging Crosby fairways, 17-mile Drive, seal and whale watching, beaches, Cannery Row with aquarium, Carmel and Monterey shopping nearby. Excellent restaurants. Mature teenagers accepted. No pets. No credit cards. No smoking in rooms. Ann and Gene Swett, Innkeepers.

Directions: From Hwy. 1, take Munras Ave. exit heading toward the ocean. Turn left on Soledad Dr., then right on Pacific St. Martin St. is 6/10 mi. on your left.

For B&B rates, see Index.

THE PELICAN INN
Muir Beach, California

The thin line on your map (probably red in color) that runs adjacent to the Pacific Ocean along most of the length of California is the famous Coastal Route 1. After you cross the Golden Gate Bridge in San Francisco, follow Route 101 north to the Mill Valley exit, turn left at the traffic lights, and there is Route 1 waiting for you to enjoy its curves and undulations all the way to Rockport, where it goes inland and becomes part of Route 101 again at Leggett. This scenic route offers spectacular views of the Pacific at almost every turn of the road. There are several B&Bs located on this road and among them I have chosen three.

The first is actually about twenty minutes from the Golden Gate Bridge and is as romantic a country inn as can be imagined this side of England's west country.

The innkeeper, Charles Felix, is, as he proudly announces, "the son of a publican," and with his distinctive white hair and moustache, there's no mistaking him as he moves among the patrons in the low-ceilinged dining room with its heavy exposed posts and beams, beautiful old tables, hutches, and sideboards. These have been sent over from England and many of them are almost two hundred years old. At one end of the dining room there is a great brick Inglenook fireplace, complete with a chamber for smoking hams.

The six Tudor-style guest rooms have exposed beams, white plaster walls, Hogarth prints, and English countryside scenes, as well as half-tester beds, and a profusion of fresh flowers.

The breakfast is full and hearty in the true English style, complete with "bangers" (sausages), bacon and eggs, broiled tomatoes, and other things dear to the heart of a Briton. The coffee pot is always available and an English tea is served throughout the day.

THE PELICAN INN, Muir Beach, CA 94965; 415-383-6000. A 6-guestroom English inn on the northern California coast, 8 mi. from the Golden Gate Bridge. Price of lodging includes breakfast. Lunch and dinner served Tues. thru Sun. Swimming, backroading, walking, and all San Francisco attractions nearby. Charles and Brenda Felix, Innkeepers.

Directions: From Golden Gate Bridge follow Rte. 101 north to the Stinson Beach–Hwy. 1 North exit, turn left at traffic lights and follow Hwy. 1 about 5 or 6 mi. to inn.

For B&B rates, see Index.

PETITE AUBERGE
San Francisco, California

The attractions of San Francisco, combined with the comforts of a centrally located inn, just three blocks from Union Square, and appropriately named Petite Auberge, add up to an assured formula for enjoyment in everyone's "favorite city."

Sally and Roger Post, owners of three other successful inns on the Monterey Peninsula, purchased an old five-story hotel, gutted its insides, and then fashioned a twenty-six-room, truly French-style country inn. From the moment I walked into the attractive entrance area with its antique carousel horse and multicolored helium balloons tied to the neck, a Post-owned-inn trademark, I knew a unique lodging experience was at hand. The host and hostesses, outfitted in chic Pierre Deux dresses, carried out the French theme to perfection.

Before being shown to my room, I visited the lower guest lounge, with its comfortable seating arrangement around the fireplace, and the adjacent breakfast room, with tables for two and four, opening onto a small, flowered courtyard. A sumptuous breakfast buffet is offered each morning with fresh fruits, cereals, egg dishes, and fresh breads and pastries from the inn's own kitchen. An icemaker and refrigerator, the latter containing gratis soft drinks, are always available for guests to use.

The bedrooms are reached by an old-fashioned cage elevator, its brass bars shined to perfection and affording a view of each floor as you ascend. My room was comfortably furnished with an inviting, quilted bed coverlet, windows draped and louvered, a gas fireplace, and the TV cleverly concealed within an armoire. A small sign informed me my shoes would be carefully shined were I to set them in the hallway before retiring. After dinner at a small nearby restaurant, I found my bed neatly turned down with a fresh flower and Swiss chocolates on the pillow. Needless to say, you are well cared for at the Petite Auberge.

PETITE AUBERGE, 863 Bush St., San Francisco, CA 94108; 415-928-6000. An exceptional French-style 26-guestroom bed-and-breakfast inn (all private baths) just 3 blocks from San Francisco's most fashionable department stores, shops, theaters, and hotels. Cable cars 1½ blocks away. TV and telephones in all rooms; 18 with fireplaces. No pets. Earliest possible advance reservations necessary. Suzie Baum, Manager and Innkeeper.

Directions: Between Taylor and Mason on Bush Street.

For B&B rates, see Index.

PUDDING CREEK INN
Fort Bragg, California

Rumor has it that there might be jewels buried on the grounds around Pudding Creek Inn! Could be, as the inn—actually two homes connected by an enclosed garden court—was built in 1884 by a Russian count, who is said to have fled his homeland with riches that were not his own! Marilyn and Gene Gundersen bought the property in 1979, and soon after they set about restoring and redecorating it. In 1980, they opened the home as a bed-and-breakfast inn.

Pudding Creek Inn has ten guest rooms, all with private baths, and two have original working fireplaces. The rooms, cozy and comfortable, are attractively decorated in a country style and many are paneled in redwood, the native wood lumbered in this area.

On the main floor is a country store and an old-fashioned kitchen, complete with the original cast-iron stove and hand water pump. A continental breakfast, consisting of fresh fruit, juice, Marilyn's delicious homemade coffee cakes and breads, and coffee and teas, is served in this kitchen or in the enclosed court. The enclosed garden area, separating one house from the other, has a little fountain and an abundance of fuchsias, ferns, impatiens, and begonias. In the early evening it's an ideal place to relax and meet the other inn guests and enjoy a quiet social hour.

Pudding Creek is in a convenient location on Main Street in the north part of Fort Bragg. The ocean, the famous Skunk Train Depot, shops, and restaurants are within easy walking distance of the inn. And the city has much to brag about when it comes to nearby scenic excursions and recreational activities. There is boating, diving, tennis, whale-watching, and fishing. And don't forget, when you feel lucky and adventurous, you could strike it rich by uncovering the count's hidden treasure!

PUDDING CREEK INN, 700 North Main St., Fort Bragg, CA 95437; 707-964-9529. A 10-guestroom (private baths) inn on Ft. Bragg's main street. Continental breakfast included. Open all year. Restaurants nearby. Skunk Railroad, and all the diversions offered by a seaside town nearby. No telephones, no televisions. Children over 10 welcome. No pets. Marilyn and Gene Gundersen, Innkeepers.

Directions: Driving from the south, take Hwy. 101 to Cloverdale, then Rte. 128 west to Hwy. 1, and continue north to Fort Bragg. Inn is located at the north end of the city.

For B&B rates, see Index.

RIVER ROCK INN
Placerville, California

Seldom will a country inn be associated with the thrills of white water rafting, but at River Rock a guest may choose either to participate directly or just enjoy the sight of hundreds of rafters floating past the inn with helmets and inflatable rubber boats, ready for a long and rough downstream journey.

This is the South Fork of the American River, world-famous for rushing rapids and the currently successful efforts of the Sierra Club to prevent any alteration of the environment. A favorite raft-launching point from April to September for some fifty different river companies is the beach below Chili Bar, a quarter-mile upstream. All rafts pass in front of the inn's long deck, where the first rapids are encountered, while the less adventuresome inn guests just watch and enjoy their late-morning coffee. During the remaining six months of the year, when waters do not have the force of the snow melt, the American River is equally enjoyable to the observer.

The inn is a contemporary home with a large lounge and a fireplace in one wall that is faced entirely with smooth river rocks. Three comfortable guest rooms have large sliding glass doors opening onto the observation deck. The ever-present sounds of the river create a melodious background. The fourth guest room is opposite the river side but is equally enjoyable.

Innkeeper Dorothy Irvin enjoys cooking and she makes breakfasts of fresh fruits, homemade jams, and various cooked dishes that seldom will be experienced elsewhere. Breakfast is served on the carpeted and enclosed sunporch where you can enjoy the wild scenery of this deep and heavily wooded valley.

RIVER ROCK INN, 1756 Georgetown Rd., Placerville, CA 95667; 916-622-7640. A 4-guestroom (private and shared baths) comfortable and somewhat rustic B&B located on the American River within a valley of California's mother lode gold country, 2½ mi. from Placerville and transcontinental Highway 50. Breakfast included in room rate. Open year-round. Air conditioning, TV, telephone. Observe river life or relax on spacious sun deck; hot tub. River rafting, fishing, gold panning, hiking, exploring nearby. Wineries, summer playhouse, Apple Festival in Oct. Children accepted. No pets. No credit cards. Dorothy Irvin, Innkeeper.

Directions: From Hwy. 50 in Placerville, take Hwy. 49 north. Soon turn right on Hwy. 193 to bottom of valley. Cross American River bridge at Chili Bar and immediately turn left, remaining on blacktop which ends at inn.

For B&B rates, see Index.

ROCK HAUS
Del Mar, California

Ideally situated in the heart of the village of Del Mar, a few furlongs from the Del Mar Race Track and minutes from La Jolla, Rancho Santa Fe, and the Torrey Pines Golf Course, the Rock Haus, an early California, bungalow-style house, has served variously as a private home, a place of worship, a gambling parlor, a hotel, and now as an excellent bed-and-breakfast inn.

Most of the six upstairs guest rooms enjoy a pleasant view of the water. One room, the Whale Watch Room, has a raised bed so guests can watch for those strange, wonderful creatures and also enjoy a beautiful sunset.

The decorations and furnishings reflect Carol and Tom Hauser's preoccupation with the beautiful, tasteful things of life. Furthermore, many of the unique paintings were done by Carol's mother.

The living room at Rock Haus has a low, peaked ceiling, cream walls, and brown beams. Through the living room is the veranda, closed in with glass, also overlooking the Pacific. Breakfasts are served on the veranda and include fresh fruit, juice, muffins, breads, and coffee or tea.

Del Mar is located on Amtrak, and the inn provides courtesy pick-up at the station.

ROCK HAUS, 410 15th St., Del Mar, CA 92014; 619-481-3764. A 10-guestroom (4 with private baths; 6 share 3 baths) bed-and-breakfast inn just 2 blocks from the ocean in one of southern California's attractive towns. The Huntsman's Room has a private fireplace. Breakfast, included in the room rate, is the only meal served. Open year-round; 2-night minimum stay required on weekends. Conveniently located to enjoy all of the many historic, natural, and cultural attractions of southern California. No children. No pets. No smoking. Carol and Tom Hauser, Innkeepers.

Directions: Once in Del Mar inquire for 15th Street.

For B&B rates, see Index.

SAN ANTONIO HOUSE
Carmel-by-the-Sea, California

Carmel has been described as one of the jewels of the California coastline. Nature has provided the setting—the surging Pacific Ocean, a crescent-shaped sweep of sandy beach, a dramatic shoreline embroidered with the delightful and colorful flora that abounds in the region.

Fortunately, the planners of Carmel have also intelligently augmented this heaven-bestowed natural beauty with protective laws that should preserve Carmel's beauty indefinitely.

Couple all of the above with the attractive shops, stores, galleries, and restaurants, and it will become evident why Carmel is such a popular destination for holiday-seekers.

Located just one block from the beach, the San Antonio House, a circa 1900 three-story brown shingle, quite reminiscent of New England, can provide a bed-and-breakfast experience that is entirely in keeping with the Carmel ambience.

Set in a gentle grove of Monterey pines, with a handsome, large holly tree, colorful gardens, and stone terraces, this little cottage has four spacious suites, all of which have their own woodburning fireplaces and refrigerators. Guests will also find a decanter of sherry, a coffee pot and fresh ground coffee and tea. Each of these rooms has been most tastefully furnished with antiques by Karen Levett, who, with her husband, Dennis, has carefully supervised the rejuvenation of this quiet, conservative, small guest house.

Continental breakfast is served in your suite and this is one of the few places where the word "continental" is truly defined, since the breakfast features two kinds of cheeses, juices, warm, freshly made breads and muffins, hard-boiled eggs, and fresh fruit.

If you are planning a visit to Carmel, the San Antonio House would be a wonderful place to stay.

SAN ANTONIO HOUSE, San Antonio Ave., Carmel-by-the-Sea, CA 93921; 408-624-4334. A graceful bed-and-breakfast inn with four guest suites. Continental breakfast served to houseguests only. Open all year. Conveniently located for the beach, the shops and galleries of Carmel, and all of the recreational offerings of the area. Karen and Dennis Levett, Jewell Brown, Innkeepers.

Directions: Turn into Ocean Ave. from Rte. 1, and proceed toward the ocean, turning left on San Antonio. There is a discreet sign in front of the inn.

For B&B rates, see Index.

THE SANDPIPER INN AT-THE-BEACH
Carmel-by-the-Sea, California

Carmel-by-the-Sea! Even the name has a melodious, inviting sound and I can assure many of our readers who have never visited Carmel that it is an experience to be treasured. South of San Francisco and north of Big Sur on U.S. 1, the California coastal highway, Carmel's gentle weather, beautiful homes and *chic* shops make it a very popular vacation area and I would suggest that reservations be made well in advance for even a short stay.

The Sandpiper Inn, fifty yards from Carmel Beach, is in many respects similar to a British country house. In fact, both Irene and Graeme Mackenzie are Scottish. There are country house touches, including great pots of flowers and overflowing window boxes and eye-catching quilts and pleasant draperies and colorful pictures.

Accommodations are in fifteen handsomely furnished rooms and cottages all with comfortable beds and private bathrooms. Some have views of Carmel Beach and others have woodburning fireplaces.

Guests congregate in front of the beautiful stone fireplace in the living room which has a distinctive cathedral ceiling. Many of them have come to Carmel to test the challenge of the area's famous golf courses.

Breakfast may be served in a number of different places. For example, it may be enjoyed by the fire in the living room/library or it can be taken on a tray to the bedroom or the patio. Breakfast leads off with sugar-free chilled orange juice, two hot fresh-baked danish pastries, and a wide assortment of breakfast beverages.

THE SANDPIPER INN at-the-Beach, 2408 Bayview Ave. at Martin St., Carmel-by-the-Sea, Ca. 93923; 408-624-6433. A 15-room bed-and-breakfast inn near the Pacific Ocean. Open all year. Breakfast only meal offered. Carmel and Stuarts Cove beaches, Old Carmel Mission, Point Lobos State Reserve, 17-Mi. Drive, and Big Sur State Park nearby. Ten-speed bicycles available; jogging and walking on beach. Arrangements to play at nearby private golf and tennis clubs with pools and hot tub. Children over 12 welcome. Please no pets. Graeme and Irene Mackenzie, Innkeepers.

Directions: From the north, on Hwy. 1 turn right at Ocean Ave. through Carmel Village and turn left on Scenic Dr. (next to ocean), proceed to end of beach to Martin St. and turn left.

For B&B rates, see Index.

THE SEAL BEACH INN & GARDENS
Seal Beach, California

The Seal Beach Inn & Gardens is a classic, Old World, French Mediterranean-style inn located in a lovely little seaside village. Each one of the twenty-three rooms of the inn is unique, with a character of its own, filled with antiques and objets d'art. Among its more distinctive features are the lush gardens replete with antique statuary.

A lavish complimentary continental breakfast, consisting of freshly baked croissants, muffins, granola, cereal, homemade preserves, fresh fruits, cheeses, soft- or hard-boiled eggs, and strudels, along with fresh-squeezed orange juice and imported blends of coffee, is served each morning in the tea room or by the pool. Picnic lunches may be arranged by advance reservation.

Location is a bonus, for the inn is just 300 yards from the beach and, via the freeway, only a short distance from all major southern California attractions, such as Disneyland, Knotts Berry Farm, Marineland, and Universal Studios, as well as a nearby romantic gondola ride.

THE SEAL BEACH INN & GARDENS, 212 5th St., Seal Beach, CA 90740; 213-493-2416. A 23-guestroom classic country inn located in a quiet seaside village, 300 yards from beach. Breakfast included; picnic lunches available by advance reservation. Open all year. Swimming pool. Near Disneyland, Knotts Berry Farm, the Queen Mary, Catalina Island (20 mi. offshore) with California mountains and lakes 2 hours away. Long Beach Playhouse, Music Center, tennis, biking, skating, golf, parks nearby. No pets. Marjorie and Jack Bettenhausen, Innkeepers.

Directions: From Los Angeles Airport take Freeway 405 south to Seal Beach Blvd. exit. Turn left toward the beach, right on the Pacific Coast Highway; left on 5th St. in Seal Beach, which is the first stoplight after Main St. Inn on corner of 5th and Central Ave.

For B&B rates, see Index.

THE SPRECKELS MANSION
San Francisco, California

Amongst the prestigious families of San Francisco's late 19th century, none had greater prominence than that of sugar baron Claus Spreckels. In 1898 he built a stately mansion of the Colonial Revival style on the northern slope of the city's Twin Peaks, directly across from the green, expansive lawns of Buena Vista Park. For more than eighty years it has been maintained as a single family home with a succession of artistic people in residence, including Jack London. Even in a city with more than a thousand Victorian buildings, San Franciscans have always looked upon the home with reverence and awe. When advertised for sale in 1979, two talented young men, Jeffrey Ross and Jonathan Shannon, were first in line for its acquisition and have since turned it into a spectacular inn.

As I ascended the front steps to the columned portal area, I experienced a sense of anticipation that was further heightened by the Corinthian columns, Meissen chandeliers, and leaded, stained glass windows in both the hall and parlor.

The bedrooms all have queen-sized beds and most have working fireplaces, for there are seven fireplaces in all, including one in front of the free-standing tub of the Sugar Baron Suite bathroom.

A handsome Edwardian building next door, built in 1897 as a wedding present for one of the Spreckels children, has also been acquired and is now part of the inn.

Each morning, trays and breakfast baskets of fresh juice, croissants, and coffee are brought to the bedrooms. A social hour is hosted each evening in the library.

THE SPRECKELS MANSION, 737 Buena Vista West, San Francisco, CA 94117; 415-861-3008. A 10-guestroom (8 with private baths) imposing and elegant Victorian mansion and an adjacent, equally grand Edwardian mansion on quiet, residential Buena Vista Hill, above San Francisco. Breakfast, included in room tariff, is the only meal served, but recommendations to the many fine restaurants are available. Open year-round. Within 15 min. of the city: Union Square, the Waterfront. Golden Gate Park with its museums and gardens nearby. No children. No pets. No cigars. Direct-dial telephones in all rooms. Jeffrey Ross and Jonathan Shannon, Proprietors.

Directions: Proceed south on Masonic; then a left turn to Fredrick; then a left turn to Buena Vista West, to Spreckels Mansion, adjacent to Buena Vista Park, 737 Buena Vista West.

For B&B rates, see Index.

SUTTER CREEK INN
Sutter Creek, California

Located in California's gold rush country on Route 49, the Sutter Creek Inn was the first B&B inn that I visted in California, and that was back in 1967.

Since that time, innkeeper Jane Way, who is also a graphologist, has become one of the outstanding keepers of such accommodations on the West Coast, and is well known for having a very comfortable and unusual inn.

The building is a replica of a New Hampshire house and was built in this gold rush town during the second half of the 19th century. A beautiful, colorful living room is filled with books and music. Many of the guest rooms have fireplaces, some have canopied beds, some are tailored and simple, and all have private baths.

It is surrounded by green lawns, a grape arbor, and impressive gardens.

Guests are called to breakfast at 9 A.M. when a melodious bell peals forth. Everyone troops into the big kitchen and dining room to sit around the harvest table. Breakfasts are different each morning, and I've enjoyed such appetizing dishes as scrambled eggs, french toast, pancakes, and the like. Conversation is apt to be animated since everyone easily gets acquainted and is eager to share his or her gold country adventure.

SUTTER CREEK INN, 75 Main St., Box 385, Sutter Creek, CA 95685; 209-267-5606. A 19-guestroom New England village inn with a 4-star Mobil rating on the main street of a historic mother lode town, 35 mi. from Sacramento. Lodgings include breakfast. Open all year. Water skiing, riding, fishing, and boating nearby. No children under 15. No pets. Mrs. Jane Way, Innkeeper.

Directions: From Sacramento, travel on the Freeway (50) toward Placerville, exiting at Power Inn Rd. Turn right and drive one block, noting signs for Rte. 16 and Jackson. Turn left on Folsom Rd., approx. ¼ mi., follow Rte. 16 signs to right for Jackson. Rte. 16 joins Rte. 49. Or take Hwy. 88 out of Stockton to Hwy. 49. Turn left— Sutter Creek is 3 min. away.

For B&B rates, see Index.

TOLL HOUSE INN
Boonville, California

The hilly, partially wooded pastureland between the northern California towns of Boonville and Ukiah for more than a century was the domain of pioneer sheep ranchers. One of the largest was the 2,400-acre spread of the Miller family, who, in 1912, built a head-quarters home six miles from Boonville and an access road. The Millers exacted a charge for the use of this road by muleskinners hauling redwood logs to inland mills, so the home became known as the Toll House.

In 1981, Beverly Nesbitt purchased the building as a home and an inn, transforming it into a gracious and restful place, which quite appropriately can be described as the "quintessence of quiescence." The comfortable lounge, the bright and cheery breakfast room, and guest rooms are all tastefully decorated in floral prints.

Large redwood patios seem to beckon from every window, and an inviting hammock and secluded hot tub, the latter surrounded by trees, lawn, and colorful flower beds, compete for guest attention.

A recent pet project was converting the bicycle shed in the garden into a cozy little guest room, called fittingly enough, the "Bicycle Room."

The professional kitchen in the house would be envied by many restaurants, as one of its former owners, an amateur chef, left nothing to be desired. This is Beverly's pride and joy, and she turns out what seems to be a never-ending stream of breakfast delicacies each morning, with fresh breads, waffles, pancakes, omelettes, and fresh fruits and juices of the season.

THE TOLL HOUSE INN, P.O. Box 268, Hwy. 253, Boonville, CA 95415; 707-895-3630. A 4-guestroom (2 with private bath and fireplace) former ranch house in the secluded Bell Valley and the Mendocino wine country. Full breakfast included. Open all year. Dinner available by prior arrangement. Hot tub, sundeck, garden, birdwatching on grounds. Wineries, Mendocino, the Skunk Railway, and Fort Bragg nearby. No children under 10. No pets. No credit cards. Smoking discouraged. Beverly Nesbitt, Innkeeper.

Directions: From the north on U.S. 101, exit Rte. 253 south of Ukiah. Watch for inn on your right about 6 mi. north of Boonville. From the south on U.S. 101 exit Rte. 128 on the northern outskirts of Cloverdale. Upon reaching Boonville, turn right on Rte. 253 and the inn will be on your left after 6 mi.

For B&B rates, see Index.

THE UNION HOTEL
Benicia, California

About halfway between San Francisco and the wine country, the small and largely undiscovered town of Benicia perches at the edge of the Carquinez Straits, where oceangoing freighters pass on their way to the inland California ports of Sacramento and Stockton. Sailing vessels and windsurfers dot the water and one of the largest "mothball" fleets from World War II huddles in a protected cove.

In the center of this haven for persons who enjoy browsing is the Union Hotel, which housed legislators in 1852, when the Benicia City Hall served as the temporary California state capitol. Gutted to its shell in 1982, the hotel has been completely renovated by its present owners.

As one enters the inn, the lounge and parlor is to the left with an exquisite hand-carved bar that once graced the Old Senate Hotel in Princeton, New Jersey. Here are low marble-topped tables, armchairs, love seats, and floor-to-ceiling windows of stained and beveled glass, all reminiscent of the 1880s. The dining room to the right of the entrance is nicely hosted and attended, offering an unusual menu that has drawn praise from such knowlegeable sources as James Beard, *Bon Appetit, Gourmet,* and *Travel & Leisure.*

The upper guest rooms are reached by an elevator operated only by a guest's room key. All guest rooms have queen- and king-sized beds, with each room having a completely different decor, along with the latest in accessories, including jacuzzis in the private baths.

This is a "can't miss" inn where only a single night is better than not having visited at all.

THE UNION HOTEL, 401 First St., Benicia, CA 94510; 707-746-0100. A 12-guestroom (all private baths) hotel in a quiet harbor town on northern California's Carquinez Straits, halfway between San Francisco and the wine country. Continental breakfast with homemade breads and muffins included in room rate. Excellent dining room. Open year-round. Antiquing, fishing, state parks, historic sites, crafts studios, bird watching. Children by prearrangement. No pets. Handicapped accessible. Therese Varney, Innkeeper.

Directions: From either Hwys. 80 or 680, take Hwy. 780. Exit at Central Benicia 2nd St. off-ramp. Proceed under freeway to stoplight at Military Ave. Turn right to First St. Turn left to corner of "D" Street.

For B&B rates, see Index.

UNION STREET INN
San Francisco, California

San Francisco is truly one of the great places in the world to visit, or even to live in. It's a good, clean city, easy to get around in, has some great restaurants and is filled with lighthearted people.

While there are some spiffy hotels, to me the way to visit San Francisco is to stay in an elegant B&B and that exactly describes the Union Street Inn and its proprietor, Helen Stewart.

Helen is a former San Francisco schoolteacher who restored this handsome turn-of-the-century Edwardian building, using tones and textures that not only are of the period, but also increase the feeling of hospitality.

The guest rooms have intriguing names such as Wildrose, Holly, English Garden, and Golden Gate. Some have private bathrooms and others have shared bathrooms. The Carriage House in the garden has a jacuzzi, bay window, and lovely garden view with a little white picket fence.

During most of the months of the year it's possible to enjoy breakfast on the wooden deck that overlooks the garden. Helen Stewart calls it continental, but it seems pretty hearty to me. There's freshly squeezed orange juice, freshly ground coffee, fresh-baked croissants, and an assortment of homemade jams and jellies, including kiwi, pomegranate, wild grape, and assorted plums.

The inn is located in the city's most pleasant shopping and entertainment areas, and it's an easy walk to Fisherman's Wharf, Ghirardelli Square, Pier 39, and other downtown San Francisco attractions.

UNION STREET INN, 2229 Union St., San Francisco, CA 94123; 415-346-0424. A 5-guestroom (private and shared baths) bed-and-breakfast inn; also Carriage House. Convenient to all of the San Francisco attractions including the cable car line. Breakfast only meal served. Open every day except Christmas and New Year's. Well-behaved young children are welcome; no accommodations for infants. No pets. Helen Stewart, Innkeeper.

Directions: Take the Van Ness exit from Rte. 101 to Union St.; turn left. The inn is between Fillmore and Steiner on the left side of the street.

For B&B rates, see Index.

VAGABOND'S HOUSE
Carmel-by-the-Sea, California

For most of our Eastern readers, Carmel, California, represents a kind of Arthurian grail, an objective to be achieved, a place to be visited sometime "when we can get away."

Let me assure you that the whole of Monterey Peninsula, which includes Pacific Grove, Monterey, Pebble Beach, Del Monte, Carmel, and Carmel Valley, is just about as beautiful and enjoyable as you can imagine. The sea, beaches, golf courses, mountains, trees, and the flowers, as well as the beautiful homes, make it an Elysian experience. However, there are times when it can be quite crowded.

The Vagabond's House, at the corner of Fourth and Dolores Streets in Carmel, provides an almost magic withdrawal. It has a three-sided courtyard with many beautiful trees, flowers, and shrubs, and guest rooms are in twelve completely different cottage rooms or suites, many of which have their own woodburning fireplaces. These are pleasingly furnished with Early American maple furniture, quilted bedspreads, and antique clocks. Most rooms are supplied with coffee pots and fresh ground coffee for brewing.

The innkeepers have outdone themselves with a full continental breakfast, featuring juices, muffins, breads, danish, hard-boiled eggs, and hot beverages—all of which are served on a silver tray and can be enjoyed in the guest rooms or shared with other guests in the courtyard.

Carmel is justly famous for its shops and galleries. A walk along Ocean Avenue provides some great browsing on the way to the spectacular beachscape.

A word of caution: advance reservations are almost always necessary at the Vagabond's House.

VAGABOND'S HOUSE, Fourth & Dolores Sts., P.O. Box 2747, Carmel-by-the-Sea, CA 93921; 408-624-7738 or 408-624-7403. A 12-guestroom village inn serving a full European breakfast for houseguests only. No other meals served. Open every day of the year. Bike renting, golf, natural beauty, and enchanting shops nearby. Not ideal for children. Dennis and Karen Levett, Owners.

Directions: Turn off Hwy. 1 onto Ocean Ave., turn right from Ocean Ave. onto Dolores, continue 2½ blocks. Parking provided for guests.

For B&B rates, see Index.

VENICE BEACH HOUSE
Venice, California

Venice, named for its well-known European counterpart, upon the completion in 1900 of many dredged canals, and the building of grand piers, boardwalks, and bathhouses, achieved a proper likeness to the old Italian city. It became a romantic seaside escape for southern Californians.

Citizens of Los Angeles doubted the continued success of the project, and, unfortunately, they were correct, for Venice soon reverted to what it is now, a beach community. But Warren Wilson, then owner and editor of the Los Angeles Daily Journal, decided Venice would be an ideal place to live, and built a home there that was later to become the Venice Beach House.

This is now a pleasing, old, bungalow-style, shingled house set back behind a well-weathered picket fence enclosing an extensive yard with flower gardens. One enters the house through a portion of a trellised veranda, where on sunny mornings a continental breakfast may be served, into a large, sun-filled living room with a fireplace for those cool ocean evenings, a large Persian rug, and comfortable furniture.

THE VENICE BEACH HOUSE, 15 Thirtieth Ave., Venice, CA 90291; 213-823-1966. An 8-guestroom (private and shared baths) gray shingled 2-story bungalow a short distance from the Pacific Ocean, and 10 min. from Los Angeles Int. Airport. Continental breakfast included in room rate. Open year-round. Fine beach for swimming and walking, bicycling, ocean pier fishing, excellent and varied restaurants nearby. Good shopping in Marina del Rey with fine private boat moorage. Children over 10 welcome. No pets. Smoking outside only. Penny Randall, Innkeeper.

Directions: Take Washington St. in Venice towards the ocean to Pacific Ave. Turn right and then left onto 29th Pl. (30th Ave. is a walkway). Venice Beach House is at the end of the street on the left side.

For B&B rates, see Index.

VILLA ROSA
Santa Barbara, California

This delightful inn was formerly a small apartment-hotel. The present owners, a young architect and a young builder, each with a talented wife, removed complete sections of the ground floor during the inn's renovation to provide both a large, comfortable lounge with a working fireplace and a separate breakfast room.

French doors of the lounge open directly onto a secluded, solar-heated pool protected by tall hedges, a jacuzzi, and a fountain terrace where the continental breakfast may be enjoyed. Colonial Spanish furniture with a contemporary flair, used throughout the inn, offers complete comfort and is complemented by pots and baskets of tropical plants.

Guest rooms offer lounge areas and the fabrics and carpeting are soft-textured in warm, soothing tones. The queen- and king-sized beds and furniture are very comfortable and room accessories are of the finest. Such amenities as turn-down service, pool robes and towels are some of the niceties offered.

The prestigious French reviewers, Gault and Millau, say, "without a doubt our favorite little inn in Santa Barbara." Guests, however, are always aware of the inn's setting with the nearby Pacific Ocean, adjoining red tile roofs, colorful bougainvillea, and squat banana palms to be seen everywhere.

VILLA ROSA, 15 Chapala St., Santa Barbara, CA 93101; 805-966-0851. An 18-guestroom (private baths) two story, Spanish-style inn a very short walk from a wide, sandy beach. Continental breakfast and other refreshments included. Minimum 2-night stay on weekends. Pool, jacuzzi, TV on request, room telephones. Bicycling, picnics, shopping, arts and crafts shows on weekends, excellent restaurants, Stearn's Wharf with attractions and day-long fishermen nearby. Children over 14. No pets. Beverly Kirkhart, Proprietor.

Directions: From Hwy. 101, turn towards the Pacific Ocean at the Chapala Ave. stop light and continue to 15 Chapala.

For B&B rates, see Index.

VINTNERS INN
Santa Rosa, California

From a distance the red-tiled roofs of Vintners Inn, clustered in the midst of a fifty-acre expanse of vineyards, give the impression of a small French village. Closer inspection reveals four modern stucco buildings grouped around a small plaza with a fountain and colorful flower-bordered tile walkways.

Innkeepers John and Francisca Duffy, also the owners of the surrounding vineyard, have spent much time and effort in creating a European ambience in their inn. In the course of their travels in Europe and especially in Provence in the south of France, they garnered both ideas and furnishings for the inn. A French craftsman in Orleans, whose main trade was in small French villages, made the copper light fixtures. Many furnishings were purchased in Belgium; however, the massive bedsteads were faithfully reproduced here from drawings of old French farm beds. Even the outside electric light poles were discovered in an old Belgian foundry.

In the main reception building there is a lounge area, a library, and a breakfast room, where a continental breakfast is served in front of a cozy fireplace.

The large guest rooms in three two-story buildings are attractively and comfortably furnished, with elegant private baths, balconies or patios; some have wood-burning fireplaces. There are also color TV's, AM-FM radios, and telephones in each guest room.

Although the Duffys live in a separate farmhouse nearby, they are always on hand to see to the needs of their guests, and there is also a concierge who has all kinds of information on local wineries and other attractions.

VINTNERS INN, 4350 Barnes Rd., Santa Rosa, CA 95401; 707-575-7350. A 45-guestroom new inn complex in 4 buildings, nestled in the center of a vineyard in the heart of the Sonoma Valley in northern California. Complimentary continental breakfast. Open year-round. Disabled-equipped rooms. Winery tours, golf, Luther Burbank Gardens & Center for the Arts. Children welcome. Pets by arrangement. Some guest rooms restricted for smoking. John and Francisca Duffy, Innkeepers.

Directions: From Hwy. 101 about 3 mi. north of Santa Rosa, take River Rd. turnoff west. First left turn is Barnes Rd.

For B&B rates, see Index.

WHALE WATCH INN BY THE SEA
Gualala, California

Whale Watch is a contemporary and newly constructed inn, perched on sheer rock cliffs above the Pacific Ocean on one of the most beautiful sections of northern California's rugged coastline.

If you are fortunate enough to be at one of the inn's many vantage points during winter or early spring, you will observe the two-way migrations of the great gray whales, first southward from their homes in Arctic waters to the birthing deeps of the Gulf of California, and then northward again with their newly born calves. Thus the name, Whale Watch.

A perpendicular staircase, securely fastened to the rock cliff wall, leads to the sheltered rocks and beach below.

Four of the inn's five buildings offer sixteen rooms, each room is individually decorated in a contemporary style with its own fireplace, private deck, and ocean view. There are various amenities, such as fully equipped kitchens, coffee makers, bathtubs with whirlpools, skylights for those on the second floor, and larger units accommodating three or four people.

An octagonally shaped building flanked by two guest rooms, has a circular free-standing fireplace, a wide redwood deck, and many windows overlooking the coastline, extending into the far distance. Guests gather here for wine and hors d'oeuvres in the early evening, and they may choose to enjoy their breakfast baskets here by a blazing fire on cool, foggy mornings.

Otherwise, the extended continental breakfast, which features fresh fruit, juices, breads or scones, as well as cheeses or yogurts, is brought to your room, where, on beautiful mornings, you can have breakfast on your private deck while you admire a breathtaking ocean view.

WHALE WATCH INN BY THE SEA, 35100 Hwy. 1, Gualala, CA 95445; 707-884-3667. An 18-guestroom (private baths) contemporary, redwood, small inn on rock cliffs over the Pacific Ocean, about 3 hrs. north of San Francisco, in northern California. Extended continental breakfast included. Open all year. Whale watching in winter or early spring. Beach and driftwood exploring. Good restaurants nearby. No children. No pets. No smoking in rooms. Beth Bergen, Innkeeper.

Directions: On the ocean side of Hwy. 1, just above Anchor Bay, 5 mi. north of Gualala. Or Hwy. 101 to Hwy. 116 to Hwy. 1.

For B&B rates, see Index.

THE WINE COUNTRY INN
St. Helena, California

The sunny Napa Valley of California is one of the happy experiences for San Franciscans and others who wish to make a quick escape from city cares.

In 1975 when Ned and Marge Smith built the Wine Country Inn, which is fashioned after the inns of New England, it was the first such accommodation in the valley. Each of its rooms is oriented to rural views and many overlook the nearby vineyards. Combining the old and the new, all rooms are individually decorated with country antique furnishings and lovely fresh colors reflecting the seasonal moods of the valley.

Jim Smith, now the innkeeper, reports that over the last several years the Napa Valley has become one of the nation's centers for fine dining. Seventeen restaurants within a ten-mile radius of the inn offer outstanding cuisine of various countries and styles.

On beautiful mornings, of which there are many in the Napa Valley, guests may enjoy their continental breakfast on the patio, sitting around the harvest tables in the common room, or they can take a tray to their bedrooms. Although the hot sticky buns are my choice, there are many other types of breakfast treats, including nut bread, pumpkin bread, raisin-bran muffins, and a selection of fine fruits in season. Breakfast is always a good time to get to know other guests.

The inn's pool and spa is a perfect place to unwind after a grueling day of wine-tasting or hot-air ballooning.

THE WINE COUNTRY INN, 1152 Lodi Lane, St. Helena, CA 94574; 707-963-7077. A 25-guestroom country inn in the Napa Valley, about 70 mi. from San Francisco. Continental breakfast served to houseguests; no other meals served. Open daily except Dec. 19-25. This inn is within driving distance of a great many wineries and also the Robert Louis Stevenson Museum. Pool and spa on premises. Golf and tennis nearby. Not suitable for children. No pets. Jim Smith, Innkeeper.

Directions: From San Francisco take the Oakland Bay Bridge to Hwy. 80. Travel north to the Napa cutoff. Stay on Hwy. 29 through the town of St. Helena, for 1¾ mi. north to Lodi Lane, then turn east ¼ mi. to inn.

For B&B rates, see Index.

BRIAR ROSE BED & BREAKFAST
Boulder, Colorado

The enthusiasm for bed-and-breakfast accommodations has reached through all parts of North America, including Colorado. However, the Briar Rose can puff with pride over being the first bed-and-breakfast inn in the most interesting city of Boulder.

The Briar Rose is a lovely little Queen Anne cottage with brickwork on the bottom and fancy shingles up above, with some very attractively ornamented windows. The entryway has a cozy fireplace on the left and a bright sitting room on the right, with carefully chosen Victorian and Regency furniture that blends well with the architecture of the building.

With the recent addition of a small building off the garden, the Briar Rose has eleven bedrooms, six of which have private baths. There are many special touches such as beautiful down comforters on all the beds, baskets of fruit, and many flowers. Several of the rooms have their own private patios.

Breakfast on the sunporch at Briar Rose includes warm, fresh croissants, pastries, European-style yogurt, fresh orange juice, and market-blend coffee. Dinner is available on request, consisting of a single-entrée meal that also includes a salad and simple sweet for dessert. It is not a public restaurant, but arrangements can be made to accommodate the guests.

Visitors to Boulder have unusual opportunities, not only to enjoy its proximity to the great mountains nearby, but also to participate in the very active arts programs for which the community is justly well known. There are regular concert series and chamber music concerts, including occasional informal offerings on Sunday afternoons at the Briar Rose!

BRIAR ROSE BED & BREAKFAST, 2151 Arapahoe Ave., Boulder, Colo. 80302; 303-442-3007. An 11-bedroom inn located in a quiet section of a pleasant, conservative Colorado city, approx. 1 hr. from Denver. Some bedrooms with shared baths. Open all year. Breakfast included in lodging rate. Evening meal available upon request. Afternoon tea served. Convenient for all of the many recreational, cultural, and historic attractions nearby. Limousine service available to and from Denver airport. Emily Hunter, Innkeeper.

Directions: From Denver follow I-25 north and Rte. 36 to Boulder. Turn left on Arapahoe Ave. Briar Rose is on the right on the corner of 22nd St.

For B&B rates, see Index.

THE DOVE INN
Golden, Colorado

Golden, Colorado, nestled against the foothills of the Rockies, is a lovely small town with an abundance of quiet, tree-lined streets. It's also less than twenty minutes from downtown Denver, and for travelers in this region seeking relaxed and reasonably priced bed-and-breakfast accommodations within easy reach of big-city attractions, the Dove Inn in Golden offers the perfect opportunity.

Built in 1889, this Victorian-style inn has four guest rooms, two of which have private baths. The rooms are tastefully done in casual, country-inn decor, reflecting innkeeper Jean Sims's former career as a decorator. My favorite room, furnished with an antique writing desk and chair, had a light and airy bay window looking out on a giant blue spruce in the front yard.

The landscaping is exquisite. Besides the blue spruce, which must have been there since the inn was built, there are beds of poppies and bushes thick with yellow roses. A large bed of Shasta daisies was just coming up when I was there in early spring, and grapevines were growing like ivy along some of the walls.

Breakfasts are hearty and delicious. Jean makes homemade cinnamon rolls and blueberry muffins. There is always an egg dish, bacon or sausage, fruit or fruit compote, cereals, coffee, tea, and juice. Guests may have breakfast whenever they choose during the morning and may enjoy it on the wooden front-porch deck with its comfortable white lawn furniture and gliding love seat.

Golden was the territorial capital of Colorado, and there are many beautiful old homes along the streets near the Dove. Conveniently close to Denver, yet located in the peaceful, small-town atmosphere of Golden, the Dove offers guests the best of both worlds.

THE DOVE INN, 711 14th St., Golden, CO 80401; 303-278-2209. A 4-guestroom (2 private baths) Victorian inn located in this small town approx. 12 mi. west of downtown Denver. Breakfast included in lodging rates. No other meal available but many restaurants within walking distance. Air conditioning and TV in rooms; phone service available. Open all year. Convenient to both Denver and the mountains. No unmarried couples. Small, obedient pets with advance arrangement. Smoking in restricted area only. Jean and Ken Sims, Innkeepers.

Directions: From Denver, follow I-70 west approx. 9 or 10 mi. to Hwy. 58 (Golden, Central City) Exit 265. From Hwy. 58, take Washington Ave. exit south for 7 blocks to 14th St. Take a left on 14th St. and the Dove is on the right.

For B&B rates, see Index.

ELIZABETH STREET GUEST HOUSE
Fort Collins, Colorado

Honestly, I was back in my Aunt Estelle's house in Elmira, New York, fifty years ago. I could almost hear her playing the piano as I walked in the front door of the Elizabeth Street Guest House. Sheryl Clark referred to the building's architectural style as American Foursquare, including an unadorned, boxlike shape and a low hip roof. It was built in 1905 and still retains some of the original features such as leaded glass in the dining room windows and handsome hardwood floors.

The living room has quite a few rocking chairs, an old wooden chest, shelves with knickknacks, and other things associated with the first three decades of the 20th century. A small collection of Santa Claus dolls, made by Mrs. Clark and her mother, are displayed in a former clock case. Another interesting feature that took me back to an even earlier time in my own life was the high piano window. These were placed to accommodate the then popular upright pianos. There is a TV set, but it is hidden behind a screen when not in use.

The three guest rooms are named after places where the Clarks resided before moving to Fort Collins. There is an Alaska room, a Barbados room, and a Kansas room, all furnished in late-Victorian furniture with very appropriate quilts and wall-hangings. Mrs. Clark prefers that guests not smoke in the guest rooms; however, smoking is allowed in the living room.

Breakfast, served in the guest rooms if preferred or in the dining room, features breads and muffins and also baked egg dishes.

The Elizabeth Street Guest House is an intimate experience. Guests who had been there for a week told me it was a very happy experience.

ELIZABETH STREET GUEST HOUSE, 202 E. Elizabeth St., Fort Collins, CO 80524; 303-493-2337. A 3-guestroom (sharing one bath) guest house in a quiet residential section of a Colorado college town. Each guestroom has its own sink. Breakfast, the only meal served, is included in the room rate. Open all year. Conveniently located to enjoy all of the scenic, recreational, and cultural attractions in the area. No pets. Sheryl Clark, Manager.

Directions: Driving north from Denver on I-25, take the Fort Collins Exit (Colo. 14), drive west toward the mountains, and south on Remington. The inn is at the corner of Elizabeth and Remington Sts.

For B&B rates, see Index.

THE HEARTHSTONE INN
Colorado Springs, Colorado

The Hearthstone Inn is a magnificent Queen Anne mansion near Pike's Peak in the Colorado Rockies. It is rapidly becoming one of the showplaces of the community. An elaborate building when it was a private home in the 1880s, it has been lovingly restored by Ruth Williams and Dorothy Williams.

The exterior is trimmed in lavender, plum, peach, and bittersweet, all authentic Victorian colors. Dorothy and Ruth bought the dilapidated building in 1977, and as a result of a complete, authentic renovation it has been included on the National Register of Historic Places.

All of the guest rooms, halls, and landings have their own special decor, and each antique piece has been chosen with great care. Some rooms have working fireplaces; others have private balconies; and all but two guest rooms have a full private bath.

A completely different breakfast is served each morning in the sunny dining room, and special treats such as old-fashioned gingerbread, fresh peaches, and eggs Florentine are a few of the morning offerings.

The Hearthstone is an excellent center for enjoying all of the wonderful advantages of the Pikes Peak area.

THE HEARTHSTONE INN, 506 N. Cascade Ave., Colorado Springs, CO 80903; 303-473-4413. A 25-guestroom (mostly private baths) bed-and-breakfast inn within sights of Pikes Peak, located in the residential section of Colorado Springs. A full breakfast is included in the price of the room. Open every day all year. Convenient to spectacular Colorado mountain scenery as well as the Air Force Academy, Garden of the Gods, Cave of the Winds, the McAllister House Museum, Fine Arts Center, and Broadmoor Resort. Golf, tennis, swimming, hiking, backroading, and Pikes Peak ski area nearby. No pets. Dorothy Williams and Ruth Williams, Innkeepers.

Directions: From I-25 (the major north-south hwy.) use Exit 143 (Uintah St.) and travel east (opposite direction from mountains) to third stoplight (Cascade Ave.). Turn right for 7 blocks. The inn will be on the right at the corner of St. Vrain and Cascade.

For B&B rates, see Index.

HELMSHIRE INN
Fort Collins, Colorado

Fort Collins, Colorado, is 4,984 feet above sea level, and to an Easterner, this boggles the mind because that is almost as high as the highest mountain in New England. To the west of the city itself, the site of one of the campuses of Colorado State University, are what Coloradians refer to as the foothills. At the time of my visit in late April there had been an unexpected snowfall, and the mountains gleamed white above the green fields and the farmlands.

Although the Helmshire Inn is newly built, it has some of the warmth and charm of a historic landmark. The suites are all individually decorated and appointed with English and American antiques. Each room is furnished with handsome linens and quilts and features a small snack bar with a refrigerator and a microwave oven. When one adds color television, telephone, and air conditioning, it looks like the best of all possible worlds.

Harry and Evie McCabe are the proud innkeepers and owners, and in speaking of the breakfast, Harry says, "We serve a buffet-style breakfast every morning from seven to nine, which includes juice, fresh fruit, a hot dish such as french toast or quiche or waffles, homemade rolls or coffee cake, and coffee. This is served in our regular dining room."

Evie and Harry showed me most of the very bright, airy, and cheerful guest rooms, many with queen-sized beds. The fixtures and the furniture are all Victorian or late-Victorian reproductions for the most part. An elevator is a welcome convenience.

The inn is adjacent to the Colorado State University campus, only minutes from historic "Old Town," and Fort Collins, I'm told, abounds in fine restaurants. There are sample menus at the inn.

If it is possible for the guest to stay for more than one night, there are tennis courts, a jogging track nearby, and the inn has a well-equipped exercise room and game room.

HELMSHIRE INN, 1204 So. College Ave., Fort Collins, CO 80524; 303-493-4683. A 27-guestroom, newly built bed-and-breakfast hotel in a college town near the foothills and mountains of eastern Colorado. Breakfast is included in the room rate. Open year-round. Many diversions available on grounds and nearby. No pets. Harry and Evie McCabe, Innkeepers.

Directions: Fort Collins is 1 hr. from Denver, 40 min. from Cheyenne, Wyoming, and 30 mi. from Estes Park. South College Ave. is a part of U.S. 287.

For B&B rates, see Index.

MARDEI'S MOUNTAIN RETREAT
Frisco, Colorado

MarDei's is a cozy, European-style bed and breakfast surrounded by large Douglas firs at the the end of a quiet, residential street.

Martha Elliott is the innkeeper here and one-half of the inn's name; the other half being her friend and partner, Deidre Wolach. When I was there, Martha was on vacation after a busy winter season, but her temporary innkeepers, Tino and Ann Pestalozzi, provided friendly and gracious hospitality. Tino serves a rich buffet breakfast of pancakes, french toast, eggs, bacon or sausage, bagels or english muffins, cereals, fruit, coffee, tea, juice, and milk. Guests take their breakfast family-style at the large dining room table. They may use the kitchen throughout the day for making tea or coffee and heating snacks.

The living room is filled with soft, cozy chairs and sofas; there's a game table surrounded by plush leather chairs, a television with a VCR, and a fireplace.

All of the guest rooms, as well as the living and dining rooms downstairs, are warm and inviting, important features in this high mountain climate. The choice of guest rooms ranges from a master bedroom with a king-sized bed and a fireplace to a "dorm" with four single beds.

Frisco, about an hour west of Denver on I-70, is a small mountain town surrounded by four ski areas and Lake Dillon, a year-round recreation facility with twenty-five miles of shoreline. The air is pure and sweet, and it would be hard to find an area offering a wider variety of outdoor activities. Within walking distance of MarDei's is downtown Frisco and a number of restaurants and shops.

MARDEI'S MOUNTAIN RETREAT, P.O. Box 1767, 221 So. Fourth Ave., Frisco, CO 80443; 303-668-5337. A 5-guestroom (private and shared baths) European-style bed and breakfast in a small mountain town, about 60 mi. west of Denver. Breakfast is included in room rate. Restaurants nearby. Open every day. Convenient to skiing, boating, fishing, hiking, biking, and many other outdoor activities. Reservations advised during winter. No pets. No credit cards. Martha Elliott, Innkeeper.

Directions: From Denver, take I-70 west approx. 60 mi. to Exit 201 (Frisco, Main St.). Go west on Main St. not quite 1 mi. to Fourth Ave. and take a left on Fourth. Go 2 blocks and MarDei's is on the right.

For B&B rates, see Index.

OUTLOOK LODGE
Green Mountain Falls, Colorado

Outlook Lodge is a country Victorian inn, literally on the lower slopes of Pike's Peak. It is only fifteen miles from Colorado Springs, but worlds apart in a great many other ways. The village is at an altitude of almost eight thousand feet, and the inn is next to the historic "Church in the Wildwood."

Impy Ahern, the innkeeper, shows a genuine interest in each of her guests and has an amplitude of friendliness and enthusiasm.

There are bowls of fruit in the twelve guest rooms, hanging plants, bookcases, and dresser scarves that enhance the Victorian atmosphere.

A typical breakfast consists of a choice of two kinds of fruit juices (one always being freshly squeezed orange juice), fresh fruits, such as strawberries, kiwi, melon, and so forth, homemade breads and other hot offerings, such as scones, cinnamon rolls and muffins.

Outlook Lodge is convenient to wonderful sightseeing opportunities during all seasons of the year. These include Pike's Peak, the Cog Railway that runs to the top, the old gold-mining town of Cripple Creek, and the Air Force Academy. Back roads have magnificent pine-scented views of the impressive mountain scenery.

OUTLOOK LODGE, P.O. Box 5, 6975 Howard, Green Mountain Falls, CO 80819; 303-684-2303. A 12-guestroom rustic lodge on the slopes of Pike's Peak, 15 mi. from Colorado Springs. European plan. All lodgings include continental breakfast. No other meals served. Open from Memorial Day weekend through Labor Day. Immediately adjacent to all the copious mountain recreational activities as well as the U.S. Air Force Academy, Colorado Springs Fine Arts Center, Cripple Creek Gold Camp. Tennis, swimming, horseback riding, lake fishing, backroading, all nearby. Impy Ahern, Innkeeper.

Directions: Green Mountain Falls is 15 mi. west of Colorado Springs on U.S. 24. Outlook Lodge is located next to the historic Church in the Wildwood.

For B&B rates, see Index.

PARRISH'S COUNTRY SQUIRE
Berthoud, Colorado

The owners of this Colorado bed-and-breakfast ranch, Jess and Donna Parrish, have some interesting and unusual backgrounds. Donna was at one time a rodeo queen; in fact, she was Miss Rodeo Colorado. On the other hand, Jess was a real calf roper. They first met at a rodeo and later fell in love and were married.

Now they have a 1,400-acre ranch where they raise commercial Herefords. The rustic ranch house has a marvelous view of the valley with the Little Thompson River flowing through and the mountains beyond. It's a most serene place.

This is an authentic Colorado experience. Guests are welcome to watch the hands branding or working cattle, and as Donna points out, "We have a couple of little ponds nearby that we swim in. We frequently go down there to have a good time and cook hot dogs."

The rustic log ranch house was built by the Parrish family themselves, and the rusticity is found throughout, with guest rooms furnished in Colorado ranch style. One guest room on the top floor would be very appropriate for young people. There are modern bathrooms and a very contemporary kitchen. The ranch atmosphere is carried out to the triangle on the porch, used to call guests to meals.

Guests enjoy breakfast and other meals in the Great Room, with its massive stone fireplace, which serves as both a dining and sitting area.

Breakfast is included in the room rate, and it's a real ranch repast, with bacon, eggs, hash browns, pancakes, homemade biscuits and gravy, or whatever you want.

PARRISH'S COUNTRY SQUIRE, 2515 Parrish Rd., Berthoud, CO 80513; 303-772-7678 or 678-8834. A 4-guestroom (private and shared baths) working cattle ranch B&B in the foothills of Rocky Mountain Nat'l. Park in northern Colorado. Complimentary ranch breakfast; the evening meal is available at an additional charge with advance reservation. Open from midspring to midfall. Swimming, horseback riding, and hiking on grounds. Carter Lake nearby has sailing, boating, and fishing. Suitable for younger children. Jess and Donna Parish, Proprietors.

Directions: From Denver, take I-25 north to the Lyons and Estes Park turnoff and go west on Hwy. 66. Turn north on Rte. 287 to County Rd. 4, also marked 41600W. Turn west for 5 mi. and look for the ranch sign as the road enters the foothills.

For B&B rates, see Index.

TARADO MANSION
Arriba, Colorado

The Tarado Mansion has got to be one of the most delightfully surprising bed and breakfasts in the country. Located on the high plains of eastern Colorado, where long, low horizons offer little in the way of variety, this white, plantation-style mansion sits about one-quarter-mile south of I-70 in the small town of Arriba, clearly visible from the highway and looking for all the world like a long-lost relative from the land of magnolias and spanish moss.

The owners have been in the antique business for over twenty-five years and have furnished their bed and breakfast entirely in antiques. Rugs, china, crystal, pianos; a 600-year-old tapestry here, a 400-year-old vase there—it's like walking into an unusually relaxed museum. There's a music room with a 32-rank pipe organ, a Reproducto player organ, and a piano. There are three large and elegant guest rooms, all with private bath.

At breakfast the house specialty is Aebelskivers, a Danish dish similar to pancakes, served with eggs, bacon (sometimes ham), breakfast puffs (muffins), fruit in season, fresh-squeezed orange juice, coffee, and tea. English muffins, toast, and yogurt are also available, and jams and jellies are homemade. The light and spacious breakfast room is graced with flowering bougainvillea.

With so much treasure on the premises you might expect the atmosphere at Tarado to be somewhat reserved and tense, but such is not the case.

"We're not a museum," innkeeper and part-owner Jim Petersen says, "people should feel comfortable here, they don't have to tiptoe around. We've spent all our lives finding and saving these pieces, and they're to be enjoyed."

Jim, founder of the Eastern Colorado Preservation Society, is an exceedingly gracious host and excellent source of information about the area.

THE TARADO MANSION, Rte. 1, Box 53, Arriba, CO 80804; 303-768-3468. A 3-guestroom (private baths) elegant Southern Colonial mansion on the high plains of eastern Colorado, about 110 mi. east of Denver. Complimentary full breakfast; dinner available with advance notice. Open all year. The area is rich in historical lore. Pets are not encouraged. Restricted smoking. Jim Petersen, Innkeeper.

Directions: From Denver, go east on I-70 about 110 mi. to Exit 383 in Arriba. Continue south approx. ¼ mi., and Tarado is on the right. It's visible from the highway.

For B&B rates, see Index.

BEE AND THISTLE INN
Old Lyme, Connecticut

The quiet and peaceful atmosphere of historic Old Lyme encourages guests of the Bee and Thistle to remain for more than one night. That's why it is most appropriate that dinner is served every evening except Tuesday.

Situated in the historic district of the village, the old inn, built in 1756, has yellow clapboards, a garrison roof, and is set well back from the street. It has many fireplaces, antiques, and comfortable bedrooms. It recalls early-American gracious living.

A carved staircase leads to the second-floor bedrooms, all but two of which have private baths, and some have canopy or four-poster beds.

Breakfast (à la carte) is on the porches, or before the fire in the little dining room, and includes freshly squeezed orange juice, a variety of fruits, homemade bigger-than-life muffins, and delicious omelettes. Lunch is also offered with soups, chowders, and other seasonal dishes.

Dinners include hearty New England fare prepared to order and served in a romantic candlelit setting.

The Lieutenant River flows through the back of the property. Bicycles are available and there are several good jogging routes to follow, as well.

BEE AND THISTLE INN, 100 Lyme St. (Rte. 1), Old Lyme, Ct. 06371; 203-434-1667. A 10-bedroom (2 rooms with shared bath) inn located in an as-yet-unspoiled Connecticut village, near the border of Rhode Island. À la carte breakfast served daily. Lunch and dinner daily, except Tuesday. Sunday brunch. Open year-round. Conveniently located to visit Gillette Castle, Goodspeed Opera House, and Essex Steam train and train rides. Mystic Seaport, Essex Village, Ivoryton Summer Theater nearby. No pets. Bob and Penny Nelson, Innkeepers.

Directions: Coming north on I-95 take a left at the bottom of Exit 70. At the first light take a right. At the second light, take a left and then follow Rte. 1 (Lyme Street) to inn.

For Lodging rates, see Index.

BISHOPSGATE
East Haddam, Connecticut

Guests might fancy they hear the strains of delightful music, so close is Bishopsgate to the Goodspeed Opera House. And there's more than simply physical proximity (down the hill and around the corner) that forms a bond with the Goodspeed; hostess Julie Bishop has had a long and intimate association with it, as evidenced by her gallery of photographs of stage celebrities who have appeared there.

In her cozy 1818 Colonial house, tucked into a niche in the bustling village of East Haddam, Julie offers the most special of bed-and-breakfast experiences with her own buoyant and infectious brand of hospitality. The recently renovated and redecorated rooms are beautifully furnished with family heirlooms and antiques and oriental rugs adorning the wide pine floorboards.

Four sparkling bedrooms boast working fireplaces; one has a lovely Jenny Lind spool bed with a fishnet canopy; and there is a smashing suite with a cathedral beamed ceiling, an outside sun deck, and a luxurious dressing room and bath with a stall shower and a sauna.

The kitchen-dining room with its Colonial dutch oven and fireplace with a crane is the scene of the breakfast gathering at a long harvest table, where guests might enjoy such delightful offerings as homebaked apple crisp or freshly baked scones with jams and jellies.

East Haddam offers a number of diversions with fine shops and restaurants, tennis, golf, and river cruises—not to mention the musicals at the Goodspeed Opera House from April to the end of November. And, of course, there are the historic and fascinating communities of Essex, Old Lyme, Mystic, and Old Stonington, all within an easy drive.

BISHOPSGATE, Goodspeed Landing, East Haddam, CT 06423; 203-873-1677. A 6-guestroom (2 with shared baths) Colonial home within walking distance of the famed Goodspeed Opera House. Open year-round. Continental breakfast included with room charge. Convenient to all the historic, cultural, and recreational attractions that abound in the area. Not suitable for children under 6. No pets. No credit cards. Julie Bishop, Hostess.

Directions: From NYC or Boston, take I-95 to Exit 69 and Rte. 9. Continue on Rte. 9 to Exit 7 and East Haddam. From the Goodspeed Opera House take Rte. 82 one block to Bishopsgate driveway on your left. Drive in to the rear entrance.

For B&B rates, see Index.

THE CANDLELIGHT
Kent, Connecticut

Route 7 is one of the most scenic and enjoyable ways to go from New York City or Connecticut north to the Berkshires and beyond. I would suggest using Route 22, branching off to the east at Wingdale, and picking up Route 7 at Gaylordsville.

The Candlelight is a very pleasant stop for guest room accommodations in the most attractive town of Kent, Connecticut, which, among other things, is the home ground of the artist and author Eric Sloane. In fact, he designed the folder that gives the town history and supplies some valuable facts about the region.

Kent is also the location of the Kent School and the South Kent School. As a result there are some weekends when there are never any rooms available at the Candlelight; these include Memorial Day weekend, June 7, October 11, and October 26 (or the nearest weekends to those dates).

Because there is a constant flow of prospective students to these schools, the Candlelight is also busy at other times throughout the year, and it is well to reserve ahead. Mr. and Mrs. Edwards told me they have visitors from all over the world who are anxious to place their sons or daughters at these schools.

The four guest rooms at the Candlelight share one and a half baths. They are very pleasantly furnished and it is, indeed, like being in someone's private home.

Breakfasts are not served at the Candlelight, but I had a very acceptable breakfast in the little local restaurant, just about five minutes away on foot. An excellent lunch and dinner are served at the Fife and Drum restaurant on the main street of this picturesque Connecticut village.

The road alongside the Housatonic River makes this an exceptionally enjoyable drive. It's worth an overnight stop at the Candlelight just to make the remainder of the journey by daylight.

THE CANDLELIGHT, Kent, CT 06757; 203-927-3407. A 4-guest-room (1½ shared baths) home on Rte. 7 in the picturesque Housatonic Valley. Call ahead for reservations in order to avoid disappointments. No pets. No credit cards. Albert and Helen Edwards, Proprietors.

Directions: Kent is about 2½ hrs. from NYC on Rte. 7. It sits on the east side of the main street, back of a rather broad lawn, and it is almost across the street from a white Carpenter Gothic church.

For Lodging rates, see Index.

THE FELSHAW TAVERN
Putnam, Connecticut

The day I visited the Felshaw Tavern the elegant honeymoon room was ready for a couple arriving later for their wedding night.

"We've had a lot of guests on their honeymoons since we opened in 1982," said Terry Kinsman. She and her husband, Herb, moved from California to northeastern Connecticut in 1980 and began restoring this two-story center chimney Colonial house, built as a tavern by John Felshaw around 1742. During the 19th century the tavern became first a post office and then a private home.

There is a working fireplace in each of the two luxuriously large guest rooms, furnished with antiques and a four-poster queen-sized bed. The honeymoon room also has two inviting sitting areas, including one by the fireplace for snowy winter evenings. In an oak-paneled library on the second floor, guests can read or watch television.

Herb, who has been interested in cabinetry and residential architecture all his life, did the restorative work on the house himself and made many of the reproductions of antique furniture that grace the rooms. Among the antiques the Kinsmans have acquired over the years is a beautiful oak grandfather clock made in Scotland in 1789, with instructions inside the case on how to set the clock by starlight.

The Kinsmans serve a full breakfast either in a formal dining room or in a breakfast room that looks out on a red barn and the edge of thick woods that extend for five miles to the Rhode Island border.

The house is only one and a half miles from I-395, but its setting is very rural in an attractive section of Putnam Heights, known for its old white clapboard houses, lush green lawns, and stone walls.

THE FELSHAW TAVERN, Five Mile River Rd., Putnam, CT 06260; 203-928-3467. A 2-guestroom (private baths) restored pre-Revolutionary tavern, now a pleasant B&B in northeastern Conn., about 20 mi. from Mass. Tpke. Complimentary full breakfast. Open year-round. Less than an hour from Old Sturbridge Village in Mass. Herb and Terry Kinsman, Proprietors.

Directions: From Mass. Tpke., take Exit 10 and go south on I-395. Take Exit 96, go east for 1 1/2 mi. to blinking red light (Rte. 21). Cross Rte. 21 to Felshaw Tavern, the first house on the left. From the south, take Rte. 95 to I-395 and proceed as above.

For B&B rates, see Index.

FLANDERS ARMS
Kent, Connecticut

I would be hard put to find a more idyllic setting for a bed and breakfast than the grounds of Flanders Arms on Route 7 in rural northwestern Connecticut. A beautiful Federal Colonial, the earliest part of which is circa 1750, it is set among lawns and gardens, and shaded by huge old maple trees, one of which, Marc De Vos tells me, is at least 200 years old.

Marc is a distinguished-looking, cosmopolitan former advertising agency executive who lived abroad for many years. He and his wife, Marilyn, after some of their children had left the nest, decided the best thing to do with their many-roomed house was to turn it into a B&B.

This section of Kent has been called Flanders ever since anybody can remember, and nobody knows how it got the name, but it is on the National Registry of Historic Places, as are several houses in the area, including Flanders Arms, also known as the John Lewis House.

The house has a well-documented history, and there is a little framed chronology, starting in 1738, that hangs on the wall of the entry. The sign for Flanders Arms is a copy of the one used in the 1920s when it was a full-fledged inn.

The four guest rooms are pleasingly furnished with double and twin beds, quilted comforters, and hanging plants. The living room and dining room are most attractive with many antique pieces that Marc and Marilyn have collected in their travels.

A continental breakfast is served in the cozy, many-windowed dining room at a marble-topped table from Spain under an interesting candelabra from Paris.

FLANDERS ARMS, Route 7, Kent, CT 06757; 203-927-3040 or 4224. A 4-guestroom (private and shared baths) circa 1750 beautiful home in rural northwestern Conn., near Kent School. Complimentary continental breakfast. Open year-round. Do not drop in; reservations must be made in advance. Good restaurants nearby. Near the Housatonic River with kayaking, canoeing, fishing; hiking at Kent Falls State Park where there is a natural pool for swimming, a stream, waterfall, and picnicking area. No facilities for children under 6. No pets. Marilyn and Marc DeVos, Hosts.

Directions: From the south, I-84 intersects with Rte. 7 at Danbury, Conn. Continue north on Rte. 7 through the village of Kent. Flanders is 1.7 miles north of the center of Kent.

For B&B rates, see Index.

GRISWOLD INN
Essex, Connecticut

On I-95 at New Haven, on what we refer to as the "New England Corridor," the traveler is faced with the choice of either following I-91 north to Sturbridge and on to Maine on I-495, or following I-95 to the eastern end of Connecticut and across Rhode Island and north to Boston and beyond. One of the reasons to take the latter course would be to stop at Essex, Connecticut, to enjoy the Griswold Inn.

The main building of the inn was the first three-story structure in Connecticut, and, with the exception of the removal of the second-floor gallery, the building has remained structurally unchanged for two centuries.

During the War of 1812, the inn was occupied by British mariners who burned the entire Essex fleet.

Today, Essex is mainly a residential, yachting, and holiday area and is particularly well known for its unusual number of very pleasant shops and boutiques.

In summer, sailors from the world over make Essex a port of call.

Guests are comfortably ensconced in antique-furnished country inn lodging rooms. Breakfasts are informal and guests can wander down to the library-dining room and help themselves to orange juice, coffee, and toasted english muffins.

The dinner menu is basically American with a wide selection of fish, beef, and lamb dishes. Every Sunday a Hunt Breakfast is served featuring great tables of fried chicken, herring, lamb, kidneys, eggs, creamed chipped beef, and the inn's own brand of 1776® sausage.

GRISWOLD INN, Main St., Essex, Conn. 06426; 203-767-0991. A 22-room inn in a waterside town, steps away from the Connecticut River, and located near the Eugene O'Neill Theatre, Goodspeed Opera House, Ivoryton Playhouse, Gillette Castle, Mystic Village, Valley Railroad and Hammonasset State Beach. All rooms with private baths. European plan. Complimentary continental breakfast served daily to inn guests. Lunch and dinner served daily to travelers. Hunt breakfast served Sundays. Closed Christmas Eve and Christmas Day. Day sailing on inn's 44-foot ketch by appointment. Bicycles, tennis, and boating nearby. Victoria and William G. Winterer, Innkeepers.

Directions: From I-95 take Exit 69 and travel north on Rte. 9 to Exit 3, Essex. Turn right at stoplight and follow West Ave. to center of town. Turn right onto Main St. and proceed down to water and inn.

For B&B rates, see Index.

HEDGEROW HOUSE
Thompson, Connecticut

If you are visiting Thompson Hill at noon or 6 P.M., you will hear the carillon at the white-steepled Thompson Congregational Church pealing out over the common and the stately houses nearby. Thompson Hill, one of ten villages that make up the town of Thompson, is only about a mile from I-395, but it has one of the most attractive village commons in New England.

In Colonial days this common was at the juncture of the major roads between Hartford and Boston and between Springfield and Providence. Today, Thompson Hill is off the beaten path. The nearest attraction for tourists is Old Sturbridge Village in Massachusetts, about a thirty-minute drive away.

Within an easy stroll of the common is the Hedgerow House, an Italianate villa built in 1875 with a sweeping front porch and an outdoor salt-water pool. Innkeepers Harriett and Norman Macht, after a long search, bought and opened it as a bed and breakfast house in 1984.

Guests enjoy afternoon tea in a leather-walled library and a full breakfast in an elegant dining room copied from a Bavarian Castle with a hooded fireplace, rosewood paneling, and painted canvas murals. Breakfast usually features a hot dish, which may be an omelet, a quiche, or a ham-and-cheese soufflé, along with home-made biscuits, breads, and muffins.

The three guest rooms on the second floor look out over the gardens and pastures, belonging to a neighboring farm. They are all attractively furnished with Persian rugs, original art works, and down quilts.

An excellent restaurant in an 18th-century inn is a few doors away.

HEDGEROW HOUSE, 1020 Quaddick Rd., Thompson, CT 06277; 203-923-9073. A 3-guestroom Italianate villa, circa 1875, a few doors away from a historic and beautiful village green in north-eastern Connecticut. Complimentary full breakfast and afternoon tea. Open all year. Swimming pool, antique shop on grounds. Old Sturbridge Village within 30-min. drive. No pets. No credit cards. No smoking. Harriett and Norman Macht, Innkeepers.

Directions: From Mass. Tpke. take Exit 10, then south on I-290, which becomes I-395. Take Exit 99, turn left and go ⁸⁄₁₀ mi.

For B&B rates, see Index.

THE HOMESTEAD INN
Greenwich, Connecticut

Forty-five minutes from Manhattan on the much-traveled NYC-New Haven-Boston corridor, the Homestead Inn sits in a quiet residential area surrounded by old trees and lovely homes. A sophisticated inn with antique-filled rooms and old chestnut beams, it was originally a 1799 farmhouse that had been Victorianized and made into an inn a hundred years ago. Neglected and tired in 1979, it was purchased by its present owners and completely renovated by the eminent New York City designer, John Saladino. Now it has lovely bedrooms, each with its own bath, cozy public rooms, and a famous French restaurant that serves dinner seven nights a week and luncheon Monday through Friday. Continental breakfast—croissants, preserves, orange juice, and coffee—is served on the sunny enclosed porch, and is included in the price of the rooms. A heartier breakfast is also available.

Patronized by a variety of travelers—executives visiting the many corporate headquarters in the area, inn-lovers on their way through New England, European tourists, and escapees from the hectic pace of New York City—the Homestead extends a warm welcome to those who seek a sophisticated country charm at the very gateway to New England.

THE HOMESTEAD INN, 420 Field Point Rd., Greenwich, CT 06830; 203-869-7500. A 24-guestroom elegant inn located in the residential area of a suburb, 45 min. from New York City in one direction and New Haven in the other. Continental breakfast included in room rate. Luncheon served Mon. thru Fri. Dinner served daily, save for a few holidays. Located a short distance from Connecticut countryside, shore scenes, and many corporate headquarters. Easily accessible by train or car from NYC. No pets. Lessie B. Davison, Nancy K. Smith, Innkeepers.

Directions: Rte. I-95 to Exit 3 to Greenwich. Off ramp, turn west toward the railroad bridge and take a left (just before the bridge) onto Horseneck Lane. Drive to the end and turn left onto Field Point Rd. The inn is ¼ mi. on your right.

For B&B rates, see Index.

MANOR HOUSE
Norfolk, Connecticut

Probably most remarkable among many unusual features in this baronial-looking mansion is the amazing fireplace with a huge raised stonework hearth and a curious roughened plaster wall in which a Roman frieze is embedded. Diane Tremblay, who with her husband, Hank, is the innkeeper, told me that sometimes guests can get into rather lively conversations about the origins of that frieze.

It's hard to know just where to start in describing this 1898 house—its builder, Charles Spofford, clearly had eclectic and aesthetic tastes, as can be seen in the many Tiffany and leaded-glass windows, intricate moldings, rich, hand-carved woods, ornate fixtures, and Moorish arches. Although the surroundings are imposing and elegantly Victorian, there is a casual air of easygoing informality in this spacious house.

There's a wide variety in the eight guest rooms—from a palatial master bedroom with a huge working fireplace and one with a private elevator and balcony to the two smaller, cozier rooms on the third floor. All are furnished with interesting antique pieces and down comforters.

Breakfast might be blueberry pancakes, poached eggs with lemon-chive sauce, scrambled eggs and bacon, orange-spice waffles, or french toast. The honey comes from their own bees, and the maple syrup is local. Breakfast can be served almost anywhere—in bed, in the formal dining room, in the small breakfast nook, on the sun porch, in the living room in front of the fire—take your choice.

MANOR HOUSE, P.O. Box 701, Maple Ave., Norfolk, CT 06058; 203-542-5690. An 8-guestroom (private and shared baths) Victorian baronial manor in the picturesque village of Norfolk in northwestern Conn. Complimentary full breakfast. Open year-round. Summer weekends and holidays, 2-night minimum stay. Chamber music concerts presented in the living room twice a year. Summer concerts at Yale Summer School and Music Mountain nearby. Tennis, golf, lake swimming, canoeing, horseback riding, biking, carriage and sleigh rides, skiing, antiques, shopping, nearby. Children over 12 welcome. Kennel facilities nearby. Smoking in restricted areas. Diane and Henry Tremblay, Innkeepers.

Directions: From NYC: Take I-84 to exit for Rte. 8 north (Waterbury, Conn.). At Winsted, turn right to Rte. 44 west. In Norfolk, look for Maple Ave. on right opposite village green. From north: Take Rte. 7 to Canaan, Conn., then Rte. 44 east to Norfolk. Rte. 44 takes a sharp left turn in front of village green; look for Maple Ave. on left.

For B&B rates, see Index.

THE MAPLES INN
New Canaan, Connecticut

I am continually impressed by the number of families who seem to be relocating, sometimes from one coast of North America to the other. That's why I was particularly glad to learn about the Maples in New Canaan, one of the attractive suburbs of New York City.

Actually, I believe the Maples, in a quiet residential area, has three types of patrons: business people paying calls to the Fortune 500 businesses located in the area, families who need a comfortable base from which to search for new homes in the area, and city dwellers who find the atmosphere conducive to a pleasant weekend away from the hustle and bustle.

A large, rambling, homelike building with a broad porch, the Maples has guest rooms and individual apartments to fulfill the differing needs of its guests. The rooms are all attractively furnished, some with fireplaces or porches, and all with color TV and telephones. The corporate relocation apartments range from two to six rooms, complete with kitchen facilities and a full complement of housekeeping services.

A buffet-style continental breakfast of juice, hot danish, cereal, and coffee is served early for New York commuters, and comes complete with the *New York Times.*

No other meals are served at the inn, but there is a restaurant right next door, and Cynthia Haas has a collection of menus from good local restaurants in Fairfield County.

By the way, the Maples is within a very pleasant walk of the New Canaan railroad station, where there are many trains every day to and from New York City.

THE MAPLES INN, 179 Oenoke Ridge, New Canaan, CT 06840; 203-966-2927. A suburban inn with many apartments, suites, and rooms (private and shared baths) in one of New York City's attractive suburbs. Color TV. Open year- round. Continental breakfast included in room rate. Many good restaurants nearby. New Canaan Nature Center with 40 acres of trails, antiques, art galleries, and other recreational attractions nearby. No pets. Cynthia Haas, Innkeeper.

Directions: From NYC via I-95, use Exit 11, turn left under the overpass, and go four lights. Turn left on Rte. 124. You are in Darien, Conn. Stay on Rte. 124 through the town of New Canaan and look for the Maples on the right-hand side. From the Merritt Pkwy., use Exit 37 and turn north on Rte. 124.

For B&B rates, see Index.

OLD RIVERTON INN
Riverton, Connecticut

Riverton is a small, late 18th- and early 19th-century village typical of the many that thrived in northwest Connecticut 150 or more years ago. Today, besides the Old Union Church which is now the museum, visitors to Riverton can enjoy several excellent antique shops, craft galleries, the Hitchcock factory store, the Seth Thomas factory outlet, and especially the Old Riverton Inn, which has been providing for the "hungry, thirsty, and sleepy" since 1796.

The inn was restored in 1937, much as it might have been at its original opening. However, the popularity of this village inn neccessitated the addition of a wing and some remodeling. The combination of the old floors and fireplaces and the old hemlock beams with modern decor has created a very pleasant atmosphere.

The many visitors to the Hitchcock Chair Factory, which is just a short stroll across the river, find it most convenient to plan either luncheon or dinner at this inn. Overnight visitors have the added advantage of a full complimentary breakfast of bacon, eggs, toast, juice, and coffee.

It is well to note that the Old Riverton Inn dining rooms are closed on Mondays, but open all the remaining days of the week. Overnight accommodations are available every evening.

Traditional furniture for every room may be found in the Hitchcock Chair Factory store in Lambert Hitchcock's original factory.

The area abounds in wonderful scenic drives, including trips to the Saville Dam, the Granville State Forest, and the village of Winchester.

OLD RIVERTON INN, Route 20, Riverton, CT 06065; 203-379-8678. A restored 18th-century inn about 3½ mi. northeast of Winsted, Ct., in a most pleasant northwest Connecticut village. Complimentary breakfast offered to overnight guests. Lunch and dinner served every day except Mon. Open year-round, except first 2 wks. in Jan. A few steps from the Hitchcock Chair Factory Store and several other small shops. Excellent for browsing. Xc skiing, white-water canoeing, downhill skiing, golfing, tennis, backpacking, hunting, nearby. Mark and Pauline Telford, Innkeepers.

Directions: Riverton is located 3½ mi. northeast of Winsted on Rte. 20. Winsted is on Rte. 44, the main road from Salisbury to Hartford.

For B&B rates, see Index.

SAMUEL WATSON HOUSE
Thompson, Connecticut

Children are as welcome here today as they have been since 1767, when Samuel Watson built this home for his wife and eight children. The three-story, white clapboard house on the Thompson Common remained in the Watson family until 1814, when it was bought by George Larned, whose daughter, Ellen Larned, was born here in 1825. Miss Larned was the author of several volumes of Windham County history.

"This house has always been full of people, and to me, it gives back a glow when the rooms are full of people now," says Jo Godfrey, who with her husband, Bob, opened their home as a bed and breakfast house in 1984 once their children were grown.

The Godfreys are avid bird watchers, bird carvers, and bird painters. In one guest room Jo has stenciled a border of birds common to the area: blue jays, cardinals, purple finches, and chickadees.

Guests may relax in the sitting room or play a game at a pool table. "It's strictly informal—the way you'd want to be treated in your own home," Jo says. The full breakfast includes fresh fruit, sweet rolls or popovers, and sometimes blueberry pancakes or waffles. Jo serves breakfast either in a formal dining room or in a breakfast niche with bird feeders at the window.

Only a short walk away is the Vernon Stiles Inn, which serves lunch and dinner but does not accommodate overnight guests. The inn was the refuge in 1814 for Thomas Dorr, the instigator of Dorr's Rebellion in Rhode Island, who crossed the border into Connecticut and evaded government agents by using a complex series of stairways in the inn.

SAMUEL WATSON HOUSE, Rte. 193, Box 86, Thompson, CT 06277; 203-923-2491. A 4-guestroom (shared baths) 18th-century Colonial home on the green of a quiet, pre-Revolutionary village in northeastern Conn. Complimentary full breakfast. Open year-round. Sea Wings Gallery and Workshop on premises. Beautiful old homes, crafts and antique shops nearby. Old Sturbridge Village, Mystic Seaport, state parks, golf courses, Thompson Speedway within an easy drive. Children welcome. No pets. No credit cards. Jo and Bob Godfrey, Hosts.

Directions: From Mass. Tpke., take Exit 10, then south on I-290, which becomes I-395. Take Exit 99, turn left and continue to Rte. 193 and the village green.

For B&B rates, see Index.

SHORE INNE
Groton Long Point, Connecticut

Even if Mystic, Connecticut, with its restored seaport, marine life aquarium, museum, submarine memorial, and many interesting shops, were not nearby, the Shore Inne is a delightful place to stay overnight or for as long as two weeks.

This white clapboard building overlooks the water, and there's even a beautiful copper beech tree shading some wooden benches, tables, and chairs, where you can eat lunch and enjoy the ocean view.

Innkeeper Helen Ellison says, "My location is unique and superb and the beaches here are as beautiful as you'll find in Connecticut. It's not the Caribbean, but the water is pure, the beach is lovely, there are eight tennis courts nearby, and we're just three-and-a-half miles from Mystic Seaport.

"We're solidly booked in advance during July and August, but June, September, and October are more quiet and we can probably accommodate a certain number of people who want to stay for just one night. Of course, they frequently stay longer when they realize how unusual we are."

Helen has had so many requests for her buttermilk bran muffins served piping hot every morning that she's happy to supply every guest with a copy of the recipe. It's quite simple—I've made them myself.

SHORE INNE, 54 East Shore Rd., Groton Long Point, Ct. 06340; 203-536-1180. A 7-bedroom waterside guest house in a very quiet residential area (3 rooms with private baths). Open every day from April 1 to Nov. 1. Continental breakfast is the only meal served. Mystic Seaport, Mystic Marine Life Aquarium, Fort Griswold, Coast Guard Academy, swimming, fishing, sunning, biking, tennis nearby. No pets. Helen Ellison, Proprietor.

Directions: Going east on I-95 take Exit 88 and turn right on Rte. 117 to Rte. 1, then left. Turn right on Rte. 215 (do not go toward Noank). Take first left after the Fisherman Restaurant to East Shore Rd. Park in rear off Middlefield St.

For B&B rates, see Index.

WEST LANE INN
Ridgefield, Connecticut

Nestled among the gently rolling wooded hills that are graced with small lakes and streams, Ridgefield is located on the outermost reaches of New York City suburbia. There are many fascinating antique shops, historic sites, the Aldrich Museum of Contemporary Art, the Hammond Museum, and a host of interesting countryside shops.

The West Lane Inn with its broad lawn and flowering shrubs is set among majestic old maples. The lobby has rich oak paneling and deep pile carpeting. A fire is often crackling on the hearth. The original building was constructed as the home of one of the wealthy landowners of the early 1800s.

Each of the somewhat oversized guest rooms has either one king-sized or two queen-sized beds. All have a full private bath and some are equipped with working fireplaces.

Breakfast may be taken in the breakfast room, the guest rooms, or on the very pleasant porch. A continental breakfast is included in the room charge. Hearty "breakers of the fast" may enjoy melon, yogurt, berries, poached eggs, cereals, english muffins, bagels and cream cheese, and other offerings at an additional charge.

The West Lane is a very convenient overnight stop for travelers in and out of upper New England and New York City.

WEST LANE INN, 22 West Lane, Ridgefield, CT 06877; 203-438-7323. A 20-guestroom inn in a quiet residential village in southwestern Connecticut. Approx. 1 hr. from N.Y.C. Open every day in the year. Light snacks available until 11:30 P.M. Convenient to many museums and antique shops. Golf, tennis, swimming, and xc skiing and other outdoor recreations available nearby. No pets. Maureen Mayer, Innkeeper.

Directions: From New York: follow West Side Hwy. (Saw Mill River Pkwy.) to Exit 6, turn right on Rte. 35, 12 mi. to Ridgefield. Inn is on left. From Hartford: Exit 3 on I-84 to Rte. 7 south and follow Rte. 35 to Ridgefield.

For B&B rates, see Index.

YESTERDAY'S YANKEE
Salisbury, Connecticut

The only original Cape Cod cottage in the village of Salisbury seems tiny in its setting among towering maples that have probably stood here since the first section of the house was built in 1744.

Dick Alexander, who with his wife, Doris, runs Yesterday's Yankee, told me how the Tories who built this house cannily kept their two-foot-wide floorboards on the second floor, where the king's collector wouldn't spot them. (Any planks over nineteen inches wide were supposed to be sent to the king). Much of the house retains its original Colonial feeling in the low ceilings, whitewashed walls, and the nine-over-six windows.

I challenge anyone to tell which are the original antiques and which are Dick's reproductions in the cozy little parlor, where another fireplace sports a cheery fire on brisk mornings.

Three simple, Colonial-style bedrooms with towel racks, braided rugs, and comforters share a completely modern bathroom.

The tick-tock of the old Regulator wall clock accompanies breakfast at the oval table in the keeping room. On sunny mornings the redwood deck with its white garden furniture beckons. While enjoying Doris's fresh fruit with Grand Marnier, shirred eggs, or frittata with Brie or fresh asparagus, french toast, homemade breads, coffee or tea, guests can guess the names of some of the herbs in the pretty little garden flanking the deck . . . parsley, orange geranium, lemon geranium, lavender, fennel, English thyme, golden thyme, rosemary, mint, nasturtiums. . . .

YESTERDAY'S YANKEE, Route 44 East, Salisbury, CT 06068; 203-435-9539. A 3-guestroom (shared bath) restored Colonial home in a lovely village in the northwestern corner of Conn. Complimentary full breakfast. Open year-round. Summer weekends and holidays, 2-night minimum. Appalachian Trail, Sharon Playhouse, Music Mountain, Lime Rock sports car racetrack, "Noble Horizons" retirement community, Hotchkiss, Salisbury, Berkshire, and several other private schools in the area. Canoeing on Housatonic River, biking, hiking, lake swimming, antiquing nearby. Kennel facilities nearby. Smoking allowed downstairs. Doris and Dick Alexander, Hosts.

Directions: From NYC: Hutchinson River Pkwy. to Rte. 684, then Rte. 22 to Millerton. Take Rte. 44 east to Salisbury, 2 mi. from state line. Or take Taconic Pkwy. to Rte. 44 east. From Boston: Mass. Tpke. to Exit 2 (Lee) and Rte. 7 south to Canaan. Turn west on Rte. 44 approx. 3 mi. Look for small sign on right.

For B&B rates, see Index.

THE DAVID FINNEY INN
New Castle, Delaware

First settled by the Dutch in the 1600s and a major seaport in Colonial times, New Castle, Delaware, is beyond a doubt one of the best-preserved historic areas in this country. Off the beaten track, it is just south of the Delaware Memorial Bridge.

The village where William Penn first set foot in America is a rare living restoration rather than a group of replicas. Home to three signers of the Declaration of Independence, it is nationally known for "A Day in Old New Castle," held in May, when Colonial churches, public buildings, and numerous privately owned Colonial homes are open to the public.

The David Finney Inn, whose earliest beginnings date back to 1683, is named for the 18th-century attorney who made the building his home for over thirty-five years, and is located at an ideal point overlooking the truly remarkable village green and the Immanuel Church.

With thirteen double rooms and four two-room suites, the inn is furnished with authentic antique pieces. Original paintings by noted artists are featured, as well as ship models of exquisite detail, in keeping with New Castle's history as a major Colonial seaport. The inn serves three meals a day, including a complimentary continental breakfast for inn guests.

The combination of visiting New Castle, with its notable array of homes, churches, and public buildings spanning over a hundred and fifty years of American architecture and history, and enjoying the hospitality of the David Finney Inn is a most rewarding experience.

THE DAVID FINNEY INN, P.O. Box 207, 216 Delaware St., New Castle, DE 19720; 302-322-6367. A 17-guestroom (private baths) meticulously restored 18th-century inn in a historic riverfront village, 35 mi. south of Philadelphia. Continental breakfast included in tariff. Breakfast, lunch, and dinner served every day of the year. Many historic, recreational, and cultural attractions in New Castle or nearby. Convenient off-street parking available. No entertainment facilities for children under 10. No pets. Tom and Louise Hagy, Owners; Judy Piser, Manager.

Directions: Coming south on the New Jersey Tpke., take the first exit after crossing the Delaware River Bridge and turn south on Rte. 9, which goes directly into New Castle. The inn is located in the historic section of Old New Castle.

For B&B rates, see Index.

SEA-VISTA VILLA
Bethany Beach, Delaware

Many readers in Washington, D.C., Baltimore, and Philadephia need no introduction to the Delaware shore. They are aware of the fact that the beaches are extremely attractive and popular. That was why I felt particularly fortunate in discovering the Sea-Vista Villa, the personal residence of Dale Duvall, on the shore of a small lake just about five blocks from the beach at Bethany Beach.

The residence is a townhouse in the country with all modern conveniences. The guest bedroom for use by B&B travelers is bright and airy, and includes a full breakfast served by the host.

The tennis courts and swimming pool are available to guests in season, as is a canoe on the salt pond.

Advance reservations are definitely required and Mr. Duvall will provide the most explicit directions at that time. There are also some delightful housekeeping villas available by the week from Memorial Day to Thanksgiving.

SEA-VISTA VILLA, Box 62, Bethany Beach, DE 19930; 202-223-0322, 305-539-3354. A 1-guestroom private townhouse made available for B&B guests. The host serves a full breakfast. Within convenient distance of the beach and also other outdoor sports. Tennis courts, swimming pool. Open from May to Thanksgiving. No credit cards. No pets. Children welcome at housekeeping villas. Dale M. Duvall, Host.

Directions: Obtain explicit directions from Mr. Duvall.

For B&B rates, see Index.

CHALET SUZANNE
Lake Wales, Florida

The title of this book says "American Style," but here at Chalet Suzanne, I think it might be better to refer to "World Style," because there are several different types of accommodations to be found, including Bavarian, Swiss, Oriental, French, English, Turkish, and Chinese.

All of this didn't happen by accident. Back in the 1930s, Bertha Hinshaw was a world traveler and thought it would be fun to bring whole sections of rooms and small houses back to central Florida to add to her growing collection of lodging and restaurant facilities.

Today, Chalet Suzanne is known the world over, not only for its funky architecture, but also for its restaurant, one of the ten top-rated in the country, where its equally famous chicken Suzanne may be found on both the lunch and dinner menus. There is also the Chalet Suzanne Soup Factory, where the most delicious soups and sauces are concocted and canned. And there is an airstrip.

The breakfasts, which are available at various à la carte prices, include fruit, any style of eggs, bacon, ham or sausage, and the specialty—tiny Swedish pancakes served with lingonberries imported from Sweden. Breakfasts are served in the dining room, on the patio, at poolside, or in the individual guest rooms.

Expect to be surprised at Chalet Suzanne, but never bored.

CHALET SUZANNE, P.O. Box AC, Lake Wales, FL 33859; 813-676-6011. A 30-guestroom phantasmagoric country inn and gourmet restaurant, 4 mi. north of Lake Wales, between Cypress Gardens and the Bok Tower Gardens near Disney World. European plan. Open daily for lodgings year-round. Dining room open from 8 A.M. to 9:30 P.M. daily. Closed Mon., May thru Nov. Pool on grounds. Golf, tennis, riding nearby. Not inexpensive. The Hinshaw Family, Innkeepers.

Directions: From Interstate 4 turn south on U.S. 27 toward Lake Wales. From Sunshine State Pkwy. exit at Yeehaw Junction and head west on Rte. 60 to U.S. 27 (60 mi.). Proceed north on U.S. 27 at Lake Wales. Inn is 4 mi. north of Lake Wales on Country Road 17A.

For Lodging rates, see Index.

HOTEL PLACE ST. MICHEL
Coral Gables, Florida

Tucked away in the midst of Coral Gables' many stylish boutiques and modern, glass, corporate office buildings is a delightful and unexpected European-style inn. The Hotel Place St. Michel is an anachronism in this setting, but a relaxing oasis and fortunate serendipity for those who first discover it.

Built in 1926, this intimate thirty-room, three-story hotel was once known as the Sevilla and hosted many discriminating travelers of that period. Complete restoration as the Hotel Place St. Michel by owners Stuart Bornstein and Alan Potamkin has retained the architectural integrity of this landmark. The gleaming hand-tiled floors, soaring arches, and vaulted ceilings are evidence of their success.

All of the guest rooms have an individual character, and each contains authentic antiques carefully culled from shops in Scotland, England, and France. Highly polished armoires, writing desks, and nightstands eclectically harmonize with color television sets tastefully mounted atop treadle sewing machine bases. White lace curtains frame the windows and paddle fans whirr from the high ceilings. Freshly cut flowers scent the rooms and antique gold-and-white telephones sit on the night tables.

A continental breakfast of freshly baked croissants with an assortment of marmalades and jams, fruit juices, and hot coffee are included with the room rate and may be enjoyed in the lobby-level dining room or the more informal cafe-style lounge. If you wish to take breakfast in your room, room service will oblige.

HOTEL PLACE ST. MICHEL, 162 Alcazar, Coral Gables, FL 33l34; 305-444-1666. A charming 28-room restored 1926, European-style hotel in the heart of Coral Gables, 7 min. from Miami International Airport and 10 min. from downtown Miami. All rooms with private baths and air conditioning. Continental breakfast included in room tariff. Open year-round. Dining room open daily for breakfast, luncheon, and dinner. Sunday brunch. Within 3 blocks of shopping mecca of Miracle Mile, and easy walking distance to theaters, galleries, and boutiques. Children welcome. No pets. Stuart Bornstein and Alan Potamkin, Owners and Proprietors.

Directions: Follow I-95 south into U.S. 1 (Dixie Hwy.). Continue south to Ponce de Leon Blvd. Right turn onto Ponce, continuing to 2135 Ponce. Right turn onto Alcazar.

For B&B rates, see Index.

THE 1735 HOUSE
Amelia Island, Florida

This is the ideal answer for a stop on the way north or south through Florida. Amelia Island is at the northernmost point of the scenic ocean drive of Route A1A. It's just a fifteen-mile detour from I-95.

Unquestionably, the outstanding feature of The 1735 House is its situation directly on the seashore. It's about fifteen steps across the sand to the ocean.

There are six bedrooms and, in some cases, bunk beds for families traveling with children. A complimentary breakfast basket with fresh fruit, juice, fresh-baked goods, and beverage, as well as the morning paper, is furnished each morning.

The innkeepers are David and Susan Caples whom I first met a number of years ago when I spoke at the Cornell Hotel School where they were enrolled in the graduate program.

In addition to being a good overnight stop, The 1735 House is an ideal place to stay for travelers continuing on to Cumberland Island. The unusual recreational opportunities on Amelia Island make it an excellent place to stay for three or four nights as well.

THE 1735 HOUSE, 584 So. Fletcher (Rte. A1A), Amelia Island, Fla. 32034; 904-261-5878. A 6-bedroom country inn located directly on the beach near Fernandina, Florida. Open year-round. Breakfast only meal served. Convenient to golf, tennis, swimming, fishing, sailing, boating, and the historic seaport of Fernandina Beach. Free pick-up service is provided at the Jacksonville or Fernandina Beach Airports or the Marine Welcome Station. David and Susan Caples, Innkeepers.

Directions: Amelia Island is located near the Florida/Georgia border. It is 15 mi. east of the Yulee exit on I-95 and 35 miles north of Jacksonville.

For B&B rates, see Index.

BALLASTONE INN
Savannah, Georgia

Ballast stones were used to weight down the empty holds of cargo ships coming to Savannah for loads of cotton in the days of sail. The same ballast stones were used to pave the streets as well as shore up the foundations of Savannah houses. The Ballastone Inn, built as a private residence for the Anderson family in 1835, was redesigned in 1890 by the same architect who was responsible for the old Cotton Exchange.

The word "Ballastone" was chosen for its special significance, as the literal welcome mat of Savannah, when the Anderson house became an inn in 1980. All the innovations of full hospitality have been brought into play: overnight shoe polishing; fresh fruit in the rooms; terry cloth robes in the baths; flowers and newspapers on the tray of continental breakfast; lemonade and afternoon tea in the courtyard.

There are nineteen rooms, each different, in the Ballastone. In fact, you may want to discuss your preference at the time you make your reservation. On the other hand, any surprise is sure to be a pleasant one.

"What I like about staying here is the feeling of being part of Old Savannah," a guest told me. "Anything else is just a room with a bath."

THE BALLASTONE INN, 14 E. Oglethorpe Ave., Savannah, GA 31401; 912-236-1484. A 19-guestroom (private baths) bed-and-breakfast inn in the Historic District next door to the birthplace of Juliette Gordon Low, founder of the Girl Scouts. Complimentary continental breakfast. Open year-round. Close to restaurants and shops. Limited off-street parking. No pets. Paula Palmer, Manger.

Directions: Take I-16 into Historic District; north on Montgomery to Oglethorpe. Turn right to inn on the northeast corner of Oglethorpe and Bull Sts.

For B&B rates, see Index.

FOLEY HOUSE INN
Savannah, Georgia

Two 1896 townhouses were combined to form Foley House, the pretty bed-and-breakfast inn at the corner of Chippewa Square. Now a new annex has been added bringing the number of rooms to twenty. In a city of courtyards, Foley House has two, one with a spa. Guests may choose a courtyard setting for their continental breakfast or take it from a silver tray in the bedroom while reading the morning newspaper.

The comforts of home are important to inn manager Muril Broy, an old friend from the Wayside Inn in Middletown, Virginia. She supervises every aspect of Foley House, making sure the housekeeping is immaculate, the service prompt, and the welcome warm and typically Southern.

The rooms at Foley House are all different—though each has its own charm—and share such important traveler comforts as good reading lights. Many have jacuzzis and fireplaces with gas-jet controls. Outside, the sidewalk is paved with oyster shells, and in the park across the street is a fine Daniel Chester French statue of General Oglethorpe, who laid out the city in 1733.

Savannah has the largest National Register Historic District in the United States. Foley House is nicely placed in the middle of it.

FOLEY HOUSE INN, 14 West Hull St., Savannah, GA 31401; 912-232-6622; outside Georgia: 800-647-3708; inside Georgia: 800-822-4658. A 20-guestroom (private baths) bed-and-breakfast inn created in 2 townhouses in the Historic District. Complimentary continental breakfast. Open year-round. All restaurant and shopping facilities nearby. No pets. Muril Broy, Manager.

Directions: Entering the Historic District on I-16E at Montgomery, go 1 block to Liberty St., turn right and continue to Bull St. Turn left to Chippewa Square (2 blocks), circling the square to Hull St. Foley House will be on your right, on the northwest corner of the square.

For B&B rates, see Index.

THE GASTONIAN
Savannah, Georgia

"Restoration" is not exactly applicable to the pair of 1868 town-houses near Forsyth Park that opened late in 1985 as the Gastonian. The original owners were prosperous, but the new inn has quarters that are clearly opulent, prime contenders in the no-expenses-spared category of lodgings. The scope of Savannah history in the 18th and 19th centuries has been accounted for, along with some flights of fancy that are clearly of other times and places.

There is, for example, an enormous Roman bath in the Caracalla Suite; a honeymoon suite in the Carriage House, done in Chinese red and with a canopied Chinese wedding bed. In another room you can sleep under a tent of shirred peach satin.

Most of the rooms, however, are just beautifully furnished period rooms with fine antiques and interesting innovations like interior stained glass windows between some bedrooms and baths. Wallpapers and fabrics are especially well chosen. All of the guest rooms have working fireplaces and many have whirlpool baths.

The Gastonian breakfast is complete and to your order when taken in the parlor; continental when served in the room or courtyard. Tea is served in the afternoon.

Had the present Gastonian been operating during the occupation of Savannah, I doubt if General Sherman would have left.

THE GASTONIAN, 220 E. Gaston St., Savannah, GA 31401; 912-232-2869. A 13-guestroom (private baths) (including 3 suites) elegant bed-and-breakfast inn in the National Historic Landmark area of Savannah. Complimentary full breakfast and tea. Open year-round. Off-street parking. Limousine service to airport and restaurants. No pets. Non-smokers preferred. Hugh and Roberta Lineberger, Innkeepers.

Directions: From the I-16 entrance to the Historic District, take the W. Broad St. exit, crossing Broad St. onto Gaston. Inn is on the corner of Gaston and Lincoln, on your left, 2 blocks beyond Forsyth Park.

For B&B rates, see Index.

LIBERTY INN
Savannah, Georgia

Few of the historic houses in Savannah are really well set up for the traveling family, but Liberty Inn is the exception. Not only are there original beams and walls and antique and period furniture in the five guest suites, but each has a private entrance to the garden courtyard, a completely equipped kitchenette, and private parking.

Frank and Jane Harris restored the once derelict Liberty-Dent House while raising five children in its spacious quarters. However, the Harrises originally saw the place when, on their first date, they had dinner in the cafe then operating on the first floor. Although there is no longer a cafe downstairs, they now own three well-known Savannah restaurants in addition to the inn.

Liberty Inn was built in 1834 by Colonel William Thorne Williams, six-time mayor of Savannah and a prominent bookseller and publisher of the early 1800s. Midcentury it became a center of social life, when it belonged first to Solomon and Miriam Cohen, then to the Cohen's youngest daughter, Miriam Cohen Dent.

Today it is once again a showpiece, its public rooms full of comfortable chairs, books, and all the accouterments of fine 19th-century living. Also the location is perfect: easy walking to the riverfront with its shops and restaurants, the Civic Center, the Visitors' Center, and all the sights of the old town.

LIBERTY INN, 128 W. Liberty St., Savannah, GA 31401; 912-233-1007. A 5-suite bed-and-breakfast inn, with private baths and fully equipped kitchenettes, in the heart of historic Savannah. Continental breakfast "fixings" in your room. Open year-round. Private off-street parking. Air conditioned, color cable television, laundry center in each suite, spa in courtyard. All restaurant, shopping, and sightseeing nearby. No pets. Janie and Frank Harris, Innkeepers.

Directions: Hwy. 16 is the major route into Savannah. Follow it until it becomes Montgomery St. Turn right on Liberty St. and go 2 blocks. Liberty Inn is on the northeast corner of Barnard and Liberty Sts.

For B&B rates, see Index.

ALDRICH GUEST HOUSE
Galena, Illinois

Historic Galena, with its rolling hills, Victorian architecture, and streetside shops, is today a mecca for both history buffs and tourists. Over twenty bed-and-breakfast spots mark this county. One of the nicest is one of the newest: the Aldrich Guest House, tucked at the end of a quiet lane.

The house itself dates back to 1845, when Cyrus Aldrich, veteran Whig and Illinois state representative, built a one-room brick cottage. Other owners, all Galena politicians, added grander wings in later years.

The home has been beautifully restored in period decor with traditional Victorian hues of mauve and green, airy white woodwork, plenty of antiques, quilts, and crocheted coverlets. Even the bathrooms have clawfoot tubs with showers and high-tank pull-chain commodes (the behind-the-scenes plumbing is purely 20th century). Judy Green, the proprietor, also provides such amenities, usually found only in more costly lodgings, as bed turndowns, chocolate mints on the pillow, and a wake-up knock in the morning.

Judy serves a wonderfully fragrant full breakfast—you might sample coffee cake, french toast with sliced fruit, eggs, or quiche, complete with silver service in the gracious dining room. Guests are welcome to use the large front parlor and screened-in porch at all times.

ALDRICH GUEST HOUSE, 900 Third St., Galena, IL 61036; 815-777-3323. A 4-guestroom (private and shared baths) elegantly restored brick home circa 1845, a stone's throw from the heart of downtown Galena and the Galena River. Lodgings include full breakfast and complimentary beverage during check-in period. Open year-round. Antiquing, shopping for gifts or crafts, all kinds of historic tours and special events are available in this area. Children over 6 welcome. No pets. Smoking in parlor only. Judy Green, Proprietor.

Directions: Take U.S. 20 into Galena. Turn north onto Third St. Aldrich Guest House is last home on right side of lane.

For B&B rates, see Index.

OLD ILLIOPOLIS HOTEL
Illiopolis, Illinois

I'll never forget my visit to the Old Illiopolis Hotel. I'll tell you why as soon as I share the important details of this truly unique establishment, which was built at the same time that the Great Western Railroad came through Illiopolis, and was used as a stopover for the railroad crew and passengers.

The owners of this unusual Midwestern landmark are James Browne and Kathleen Jensen-Browne. Mrs. Jensen-Browne is a special education teacher at the school and her husband is an assistant professor of management at nearby Millikin University.

The old-fashioned parlor on the first floor sets the tone with a loveseat, a working player piano and lots of piano rolls, and groups of great photographs of the family. The kitchen has a high, beamed ceiling, and a big, round table. There is all manner of interesting paraphernalia on the walls, including an old cornet, a few photographs, and a mounted butterfly collection.

Abovestairs there are five smallish, very comfortable bedrooms, sharing two bathrooms. Each room is individually decorated and offers a real touch of yesteryear. I couldn't help but feel that the house has grown along with the times. There are pictures of various national and international notables covering the past 100 years.

Breakfast is taken in the wonderful kitchen, where everybody sits around the table and enjoys rolls, fruit juice, milk, hard-boiled eggs, whole-wheat toast, and there is more than enough to eat. Breakfast can be served in the bedrooms, also.

It may be of interest to add that I met several engaging members of the community and, in addition to being presented with a key to the town by Mayor Ed Bliler, I was interviewed by two radio stations and my visit was covered by three newspapers and a TV crew. Don't tell me that small towns are sleepy and out of date.

OLD ILLIOPOLIS HOTEL, 608 Mary St., Box 66, Illiopolis, Ill. 62539; 217-486-6451. A 5-bedroom bed-and-breakfast hotel (sharing two bathrooms). Open all year except Christmas. Telephone in evening after 4 P.M. No smoking in any of the bedrooms. No credit cards. James Browne and Kathleen Jensen-Browne, Proprietors.

Directions: Turn off I-72 and proceed into the town, turning right on Matilda Street. Turn left on 5th St. and right on Mary St. The hotel is right across the street from the public library.

For B&B rates, see Index.

CREEKWOOD INN
Michigan City, Indiana

'Round the bend on a backwoods road and there it is: the Creek-wood Inn, nestled on a 33-acre wooded estate near the Lake Michigan shore.

Built in the 1930s as a physician's residence, the original brick house with its steeply pitched roof and low-hanging eaves was expanded in 1983 by owner and innkeeper Mary Lou Linnen. She envisioned a gracious retreat for urban-weary Chicagoans and other travelers. By all appearances, she has created just that.

A tiny bell jingles a welcome to guests as they open the front door. Guest rooms, each with private bath, desk, reading lamp, and windows overlooking the well-kept grounds, have names such as "Primrose" and "Wildflower" etched on oval brass plaques. They are also equipped with TV, telephones, and refrigerators.

Hot chocolate may be served before bedtime; in the morning, guests may take their complimentary breakfast of homemade breads and fresh fruit to the white wicker chairs on the sunporch or the bay window in the parlor. Its dark wainscoting, pegged hardwood floors, and handhewn beams make it the cosiest of places.

Stay around the inn itself and you can play lawn croquet, volleyball, basketball, ride bicycles, or wander along several nature trails down to the creek for which the inn is named. Explore the Michigan City area and you'll find activities popular in any lakeside city: charter boat fishing, swimming, beaching, golf, tennis, riding. The magnificent Indiana Dunes National Lakeshore, with its wind-and-water-sculpted beachfront and Visitors Center, maintained by the National Park Service, is just a short drive away.

CREEKWOOD INN, Route 20-35 at I-94, Michigan City, IN 46360; 219-872-8357. A 12-guestroom (plus executive suite) (private baths) elegant country inn on a wooded estate near Lake Michigan. Continental breakfast included with lodging; afternoon tea with sweets upon request. Catered dinner served on Sat. eve. Closed Mar. 3 to 14. Croquet, volleyball, basketball, bicycles, nature trails on grounds. Nearby is the Indiana Dunes Natl. Lakeshore. Charter boat fishing and other lakeside sports are available. Mary Lou Linnen and Margaret H. Wall, Innkeepers.

Directions: Take I-94 to Exit 40B. Exit onto Rte. 20-35 and look for the first road to the left (you'll see the Creekwood Inn sign). Follow that road and the first drive on the left is the inn's entrance.

For B&B rates, see Index.

HOLLINGSWORTH HOUSE INN
Indianapolis, Indiana

The inn's front door, flanked by white pillars, overlooks suburban Indianapolis. But gaze out the back and you'll see another world—that of a rural Indiana farmer, tilling his broad meadows by a rippling creek half-hidden with forest.

Five generations of Hollingsworths, an old Indiana farm family, grew up here. Family history has it that the original land grant was given in the 1820s by John Quincy Adams. A one-room cabin was built some years later. Since then the house has been expanded to its present form: a gracious two-story mansion with floor-to-ceiling windows and plenty of modern comforts.

The old stone fireplace is still the same, though. It marks what is now the breakfast room, where guests may eat overlooking those broad meadows. Innkeepers Susan Muller and Ann Irvine serve the breakfast with accouterments those early Hollingsworths never knew: Limoges china, Lunt sterling, linen napkins, and fresh flowers. Larger groups or families may take their breakfast in the formal dining room. At night, its antique chandelier may be lit with real candles.

In restoring this farmstead, Susan and Ann scoured area antique shops for period furniture and linens. The inn shows such attention to detail with satiny down comforters, silver soap dishes, everywhere a touch of old-fashioned lace. Even the staircase is hand-stenciled in a graceful pattern.

HOLLINGSWORTH HOUSE INN, 6054 Hollingsworth Rd., Indianapolis, IN 46254; 317-299-6700. A 5-guestroom (private baths) elegant 1854 farm mansion, listed in National Register of Historic Places. Lodgings include full breakfast. Open year-round. Downtown Indianapolis is nearby, with such attractions as the Children's Museum and the Indianapolis Motor Speedway. Children over 12 welcome. No pets. No cigars. Susan Muller and Ann Irvine, Innkeepers.

Directions: Take the Lafayette Rd. exit from I-65. Turn north onto Lafayette Rd. and go to 56th St. Turn right on 56th and go to Georgetown Rd. Turn left and go to 62nd St.; turn left on 62nd, and a short block later turn left again on Hollingsworth Rd. You'll shortly see the inn on your right.

For B&B rates, see Index.

INDIANA STATE PARK INNS

In my experience, some of the best places to stay in the Indiana countryside are the inns in the state parks, which are maintained by the state.

There are six of these inns and each of them has something special to recommend it. For example, the Potawatomi Inn in Angola has an indoor swimming pool, sauna, and jacuzzi, with riding stables, hiking, boating, and other outdoor sports. In winter there is even a refrigerated toboggan run and cross-country skiing.

At Turkey Run Inn there are four tennis courts for guests and you can hike to the beautiful covered bridge area.

Spring Mill State Park also has an early pioneer village and gristmill, and it is near the Virgil Grissom Memorial.

The Canyon Inn, located in the McCormick's Creek State Park, has horseback rides, hiking trails, and forest paths, as well as a pool.

In Brown County, the Abe Martin Lodge, along with individual cabins, is located in 15,000 acres of bluegreen, heavily pine forested, rolling hills, and flowering dogwood and redbud trees.

The Clifty Inn is in Clifty Falls State Park in beautiful Madison, and from the verandas is a view of the Ohio River. It is reminiscent of the days of Mark Twain.

All of these inns are open year-round and offer very acceptable accommodations. Many of them have swimming pools as well. Accommodations and food are under the European plan and breakfast is not included with the cost of the room.

Turkey Run Inn, Turkey Run State Park — 317-597-2211
P.O. Box 444, Marshall, In. 47859

Canyon Inn, McCormick's Creek State Park — 812-829-4881
P.O. Box 71, Spencer, In. 47460

Spring Mill Inn, Spring Mill State Park — 812-849-4081
Box 68, Mitchell, In. 47446

Potawatomi Inn, Pokagon State Park — 219-833-1077
R.R. 2, Box 37, Angola, In. 46703

Abe Martin Lodge, Brown County State Park — 812-988-4418
P.O. Box 25, Nashville, In. 47448

Clifty Inn, Clifty Falls State Park — 812-265-4135
P.O. Box 387, Madison, In. 47250

For Lodging rates, see individual listings in Index.

OPEN HEARTH BED AND BREAKFAST
Bristol, Indiana

Open Hearth is an unusually attractive bed-and-breakfast inn. It is actually a guest house at Echo Valley Farm, just below the Michigan border in northern Indiana.

There are three bedrooms, a cozy living room with a fireplace and walls decorated with prints by Indiana artists, and a kitchen. There are paths to follow, birds to watch, farm animals to enjoy.

There is a beautiful, large pond with a gazebo on one corner, where it is great fun to sit and watch the fish and ducks.

This is a wonderful place to bring children. Michele and Dick Goebel have children of their own and the place has all kinds of farm and domestic animals, including—according to a late bulletin— nine baby lambs.

Michele is the daughter of Arletta Lovejoy of the nearby Patchwork Quilt Country Inn, and she can make arrangements for her guests to dine there every evening except Sunday and Monday. Also, Michele and Arletta give guided tours through the Amish heritage country.

Incidentally, Michele is a marvelously innovative cook and gives cooking classes in the Open Hearth kitchen.

Breakfasts include some of Michele's own recipes, including pecan sticky buns, apple-raisin coffee cake made with oatmeal, zucchini and oatmeal muffins, as well as homemade jams and jellies.

OPEN HEARTH BED AND BREAKFAST, 56782 State Rd. 15, Echo Valley Farm, Bristol, In. 46507; 219-848-5256. A 3-bedroom (shared bathroom) bed-and-breakfast home located in the beautiful rolling farmland of northern Indiana. Accommodations are in a separate small house adjacent to the main house. Accommodations available Mon. through Sat. nights. Most conveniently located for many of the area's points of interest including quilt shops, cheesemaking, buggy shops, summer theaters, winter skiing, snowmobiling, and country fairs. Near Shipshewana Auction and many other antique shops in Indiana's Amish country. Children welcome. No pets. No alcoholic beverages; no smoking in guestrooms. Dick and Michele Goebel, Proprietors.

Directions: Just ⅛ mi. north of the intersection of U.S. 20 and Indiana Rte. 15.

For B&B rates, see Index.

PATCHWORK QUILT BED AND BREAKFAST
Middlebury, Indiana

Patchwork Quilt, which has long been in *Country Inns and Back Roads* as a prime example of the best in American farm cookery, has now added overnight accommodations and bids fair to set new standards for such establishments.

There are three guest rooms. One called "The Treetop" features a canopied bed, a hand-painted armoire, and a turquoise velvet chair. It is paneled in white and turquoise and has a beautiful print above the Franklin fireplace. Another room, known as "The Meadow," is paneled in wattled walnut hardwood. The Early American cannonball bed has a mini-canopy made from an apricot quilted counterpane. A leather-top lady's pigeon-holed desk and wall unit displays Pigeon Forge pottery. The third has two double poster beds.

Breakfast on the farm is served in a very pleasant little room with windows looking out over the fields and orchards. It is a most generous continental-style breakfast, featuring freshly baked breakfast cake or roll every day and generous helpings of fruit and orange juice.

The Patchwork Quilt Country Inn dining room has gained national fame for its prizewinning recipes for both chicken and strawberries. It is open by reservation every evening except Sunday and Monday.

PATCHWORK QUILT BED AND BREAKFAST, 11748 C.R. 2, Middlebury, IN 46540; 219-825-2417. A 3-guestroom bed-and-breakfast inn (shared baths) located near the Michigan border of Indiana in an interesting Amish community. Rooms available every night in week. Dinner at Patchwork Quilt by reservation nightly except Sun. and Mon. Conveniently located for the Shipshewana auction and flea market. Not convenient for children. No pets. No alcoholic beverages; no smoking in guest rooms. No credit cards. Milton and Arletta Lovejoy, Innkeepers.

Directions: From east or west, exit Indiana Toll Rd. at Middlebury (Exit 107) and go north ¼ mi. to County Rd. 2 and proceed west 1 mi. to inn. From Middlebury, follow Indiana Rte. 13 for 8 mi. north to County Rd. 2 and west 1 mi.

For B&B rates, see Index.

THE ROCKPORT INN
Rockport, Indiana

Rockport is a small community on the Ohio River, ten miles north of Owensboro, Kentucky, and thirty miles east of Evansville, Indiana.

The area in and around Rockport is rich in Lincoln lore, since Honest Abe grew up near here. In fact, he left from Rockport on his famous trip to New Orleans.

The Rockport Inn, a full-service inn, was built as a private residence about 1855. It was expanded into a rooming house about 1870 and then into a small hotel about 1920. The building has been thoroughly renovated, with as much of the original design and spirit being retained as has been feasible and possible. It is one of the oldest structures in the area.

There are six guest rooms of varying sizes. Each has a private bath and air conditioning, which can be quite welcome in this part of the world. There are four dining rooms of different sizes, and the furnishings, both upstairs and down, are turn-of-the-century.

At the time of my visit, lunch was served Tuesday through Saturday, and dinner was served Wednesday through Saturday. There is also a Saturday brunch.

The Rockport Inn is probably the most unique lodging experience of its kind in southern Indiana.

THE ROCKPORT INN, Third at Walnut St., Rockport, IN 47635; 812-649-2664. A 6-guestroom village inn in a small Ohio River town in southern Indiana. Continental breakfast included in room rate. Lunch served Tues. thru Sat. Dinner served Wed. thru Sat. Early dinner served on Sun. Open year-round. Excellent backroading along the river, especially to the east. Emil and Carolyn Faith Ahnell, Innkeepers.

Directions: Rockport is on Rte. 66 between Evansville and Cannelton in southern Indiana. It is just north of Owensboro, Kentucky. The inn is in the business section of town.

For B&B rates, see Index.

DIE HEIMAT
Amana Colonies, Iowa

To the traveler weary of crossing the Midwest plains, Die Heimat (pronounced "dee hy-mat" and meaning "the home place") is a welcome sight.

Painted blue-gray with white trim, this sturdy nineteen-room inn stands on a quiet lane in Homestead, one of the seven Amana Colonies here. Inside, zither music drifts through the hallway. Lamplight spills across the soft blue walls. A German house blessing graces every room.

"People come here to relax," says innkeeper Sheila Janda, who with her husband, Don, turned the one-time village kitchen into a bed-and-breakfast haven in 1982. "They walk. They bike. They look at the stars."

Travelers also wander about the flat, open farm fields of the Amanas, settled years ago by German immigrants who sought refuge here for a religious and communal way of life. Today, the Amana Colonies, aided by the sterling reputation of Amana craftsmen, are a bustling tourist spot. They hum with commercial interests competing with more traditional concerns. The Jandas know the Colonies well and can point out copycats from authentic craftsmen.

Breakfast is served on a wooden teacart, covered with a red-and-white checkered tablecloth. It includes stout rolls made at one of the local Amana bakeries: pecan, cinnamon with raisin, and the special Oma (means "grandmother" in German) with a fruit-and-frosting top. Guests may chat or wander about the living room, eyeing some of the unusual antique furnishings and art that hint at the village's old ways.

Guest rooms, furnished in the Amana pieces, are up to date with private baths, air conditioning, and television.

DIE HEIMAT, Main St., Amana Colonies, Homestead, IA 52236; 319-622-3937. A 19-guestroom (private baths) former communal kitchen of the Amanas; now a fully restored country inn. Lodgings include a continental breakfast. Open year-round. Reservations recommended. Nearby are the 7 historic villages of the Amana Colonies. Hayrides and sleigh rides arranged upon request. Museums, wineries, bakeries, woolen mills, furniture shops, arts/crafts/gift/antique stores nearby. No pets. Don and Sheila Janda, Innkeepers.

Directions: Take Exit 225 off I-80. Head 5 mi. north. You'll see the sign at the junction of Hwys. 6 and 151. Turn left past Bill Zuber's Restaurant. The inn will be on your right.

For B&B rates, see Index.

THE REDSTONE INN
Dubuque, Iowa

Everybody who's ever read Huckleberry Finn dreams of floating down the Mississippi River.

In Dubuque, Iowa, a classic, hardworking river city, you'll get your chance on one of the great paddle-wheel excursion boats that dock here. You'll tour the river-boat museum, walk the decks of the William M. Black side-wheeler to the beat of old-time steamboat music. Maybe you'll ride the cable car up the steep side of the river bluffs. And when you're done with your day, you may stroll back to lodgings at the new Redstone Inn.

A fashionably restored brick Victorian mansion with peaked turrets and red sandstone trim, it was built as a private residence in 1894. Guests may sleep in any of its fifteen rooms, each with private bath, coordinated wallpapers and quilts, and antique furnishings.

An à la carte continental breakfast, served downstairs in the dining room, is a pleasant affair with white tablecloths and beribboned vases, warm muffins and fresh fruit. Tea, with sweets such as strawberry pie and lady finger cake, is served in the afternoon. And reading material is always available in the parlor, decked out with lacy curtains and ancestral portraits.

You'll find plenty to do and see in Dubuque for a day or so, whether you shop for the country crafts of Dubuque homemakers or sample Midwestern produce at farmers' markets. Don't miss a glimpse of the working grain terminals at the city's edge. Tugboats and barges, heaped with corn and coal, show the traveler what the Mississippi's all about today.

THE REDSTONE INN, 504 Bluff St., Dubuque, IA 52001; 319-582-1894. A 15-guestroom (private baths) brick Victorian mansion built in 1894 in the heart of Dubuque. Continental breakfast and afternoon tea not included in most room rates. Open year-round. Easy walk to Mississippi River boat cruises, museum, farmer's market, antique and specialty shops, cable car railway up the side of river bluffs with view of three states. Gail Naughton, Innkeeper and General Manager.

Directions: Enter Dubuque by any of the highways that serve the city, such as Rtes. 20, 151, or 52. Head for the center of town and proceed to the corner of Bluff and Fifth Sts. (like most Midwestern towns, the streets are consecutively numbered).

For Lodging rates, see Index.

STOUT HOUSE
Dubuque, Iowa

If you've ever wanted to feel like an old-time millionaire, the Stout House gives you the chance.

Built by 1890s lumber baron Frank D. Stout, this three-story sandstone mansion shimmers with wealth. Stained and leaded glass. Marble fireplaces, with inlaid mosaic hearths. Silver-trimmed sinks. Fragrant cedar closets. And everywhere, the gleam of polished woods—rosewood, sycamore, maple, oak—intricately carved and quartersawn to reveal the delicate graining.

The house was maintained over the years by the Catholic Archdiocese of Dubuque, which purchased it as a home for its archbishop in 1911. Then, in 1985, the privately held Dubuque Historic Improvement Co. bought it for use as a tour home and bed-and-breakfast inn. Tours, offered to the public for two dollars on Fridays and weekends from noon to 3 P.M. during tourist season, are free to guests.

The Stout House's five guest rooms are furnished in brass beds and antiques, with windows that open wide to admit the Mississippi River breeze. Guests may relax in the evening with a complimentary beverage in the second-floor lounge, with television and phone, or downstairs in the library or parlor. There you can ask Jim Borden or Barbara Kopperud, the husband-and-wife innkeeping team, to play the Steinway grand player piano. The instrument comes complete with such tunes as "Showboat Medley" and "Rhapsody in Blue."

The morning meal, including cinnamon rolls and croissants, is served in the dining room. There, the sounds of the wakening river city mingle with the quarter-hour chime of the grandfather clock. Breakfast, generally about 8:30 A.M., will be served earlier upon special request.

STOUT HOUSE, 1105 Locust St., Dubuque, IA 52001. Reservations, cancellations, and information handled through the Redstone Inn, 504 Bluff St., Dubuque, IA 52001; 319-582-1894. A 5-guestroom (private and shared baths) historic three-story sandstone mansion in downtown Dubuque. Complimentary continental breakfast and beverage. Open year-round. Formal tours of the mansion free to houseguests. Children under 12 in same room with parents, no extra charge. No pets. Jim Borden and Barbara Kopperud, Innkeepers.

Directions: Enter Dubuque by any of the highways that serve the city, such as Rtes. 20, 151, or 52. Head for the center of town and proceed to the corner of Locust and 11th Sts.

For B&B rates, see Index.

THE BEAUMONT INN
Harrodsburg, Kentucky

The Bluegrass Parkway, I-64, and I-75 all converge in the vicinity of Lexington, Kentucky, a place well known for its predilection for fast and beautiful horses.

Fortunately, Routes 127 and 68 provide an enjoyable and quick journey to Harrodsburg, where there are two very pleasant and unusual inns that offer bed and breakfast. One of these is the Beaumont Inn.

It is hard to imagine an atmosphere more steeped in Kentucky history and tradition than this lovely old red brick inn with its majestic white pillars and climbing ivy.

The front hall is adorned with many pictures of Robert E. Lee, and the sitting rooms have stunning rose decorations around each wall and are graced by elegant fireplaces.

The guest rooms are large, commodious, and air conditioned and are furnished with the same attention to detail.

In Kentucky, the Beaumont Inn is famous for its menu, and I hope that everyone traveling with this book will plan on arriving in time for dinner.

The full breakfast, which is included in the B&B rate, features all kinds of juices and fruits in season, cereal, any style of eggs, sausage or bacon, grits, hot biscuits, strawberry preserves, and probably the most famous of all: lacy-edged cornmeal batter cakes served with an old-fashioned brown-sugar syrup.

THE BEAUMONT INN, Harrodsburg, KY 40330; 606-734-3381. A 29-guestroom destination-resort inn in the heart of Kentucky's historic bluegrass country. European plan. B&B rates also available. Lunch and dinner served to travelers; all three meals to house-guests. Open every day from mid-March to mid-Dec. Tennis, swimming pool, shuffleboard on grounds. Golf courses and a wide range of recreational and historic attractions nearby. No pets. The Dedman Family, Innkeepers.

Directions: From Louisville: Exit 48 from east I-64. Go south on Ky. 151, to U.S. 127 south to Harrodsburg. From Lexington: U.S. 60 west, then west on Bluegrass Parkway to U.S. 127. From Nashville: Exit I-65 to Bluegrass Parkway near Elizabethtown, Ky., then east to U.S. 127. From Knoxville: Exit north I-75 at Mt. Vernon, Ky., then north on U.S. 127 to Beaumont Inn entrance, on east side of highway as you enter Harrodsburg.

For B&B rates, see Index.

BLUE HARBOR HOUSE BED & BREAKFAST
Camden, Maine

The town of Camden, first visited in 1605 by an Englishman, Captain George Weymouth, and permanently settled in 1768, is one of the busiest places on the northern coast of Maine. Even during the dead of winter (when, incidentally, the Blue Harbor House Bed & Breakfast is also open) there is a bustle of activity in the center of town and along the town dock, from which the famous Windjammer cruises depart. June is probably the best month to visit—the weather is usually fair, and the town isn't terribly crowded.

Blue Harbor House Bed & Breakfast is at the south end of the village of Camden, just a few minutes' walk from many fine restaurants and shops. Each of the seven guest bedrooms is individually decorated with Maine country furniture, handmade, hand-tied bed quilts, and ruffled country curtains. All of the rooms will accommodate at least two guests, and some larger rooms, up to four. Five of the guest rooms have shared baths, and two have a private bath. Private suites and housekeeping apartments are available.

Thomas and Lorraine Tedeschi do not offer televisions or radios in the guest rooms; however, soft music plays in the sitting rooms, where there are all sorts of comfortable furniture and lots of books and magazines.

Lorraine prepares egg dishes, warm muffins, fruit juices, homemade breakfast breads, and freshly brewed coffee and tea, all served on the sun porch at no additional charge.

For any length of stay, the Blue Harbor House Bed & Breakfast has a most friendly atmosphere.

BLUE HARBOR HOUSE BED & BREAKFAST, 67 Elm St. (U.S. Rte. 1), Camden, ME 04843; 207-236-3196. A 7-guestroom bed-and-breakfast inn (private and shared baths) in a busy harbor village. Breakfast is included in the room rate. Open all year. Conveniently situated to enjoy the dozens of recreational, cultural, and historical attractions of the area. Just a few moments from Rockland and other ferry terminals. Well-behaved children over 8 welcome. No pets. No credit cards. Nonsmokers, please. Thomas and Lorraine Tedeschi, Innkeepers.

Directions: Blue Harbor House Bed & Breakfast is at the south end of Camden Village on Rte. 1.

For B&B rates, see Index.

BLUE HILL INN
Blue Hill, Maine

Blue Hill is on the east Penobscot peninsula, which extends into Penobscot Bay, south of U.S. 1 between Bucksport and Ellsworth. The village of Blue Hill nestles underneath a mountain at the head of Blue Hill Bay. There are beautiful homes, historic landmarks, handcraft and pottery shops, and the Kneisel School of Music.

The Blue Hill Inn, built in 1832 right in the center of the village, is as neat and tidy a New England inn as can be found anywhere. The country-inn guest rooms are roomy and have attractive, appropriate furniture and private baths. The many chairs and sofas in the living room invite getting acquainted with the other guests.

The inn is open all year and serves both breakfast and dinner, the latter including succulent chowders, homemade bread or popovers, and a different entrée each evening, such as roast beef, roast lamb, or roast pork. A full country-style breakfast can be had for three dollars and a continental breakfast is also available.

The inn is the focal point for day trips to the picturesque harbor towns on the peninsula, as well as Mt. Desert Island and the Acadia National Park. Reservations for the summer season and weekends almost any time of the year must be made well in advance.

BLUE HILL INN, Blue Hill, ME 04614; 207-374-2844. An 11-guestroom traditional village inn in the center of picturesque Blue Hill on the Maine coast. Open year-round. Breakfast and dinner available. Historic landmarks, Kneisel School of Music concerts, the famous Rowantrees and Rackliffe Pottery Studios in Blue Hill. Tennis, golf, and beach facilities are available nearby. Exploring and xc skiing in Acadia Nat'l Park nearby; day trips to Deer Isle, Northeast Harbor, and Seal Harbor. No pets. Rita and Ted Boytos, Innkeepers.

Directions: From U.S. 1 take Rte. 15 to Blue Hill, to Rte. 177 in village.

For Lodging rates, see Index.

THE BRANNON-BUNKER INN
Damariscotta, Maine

The U.S. 1 Coastal Route traveler, hunched foward over the steering wheel, intent on reaching Bar Harbor, Calais, New Brunswick, or Nova Scotia, would do well to take one of the several local byways that lead down to the end of the peninsulas along the rocky coast of Maine. For instance, Route 129 is such a road, and it passes the Brannon-Bunker Inn with its spacious front lawn, trees planted along the highway, and the pleasant look of an old Maine homestead.

The entrance leads into a low-ceilinged breakfast room furnished with many of the accouterments of bygone days. Beyond the breakfast room is a large room with a whitewashed fireplace, an old school clock, a corner cupboard, and a chess set. I realized that I was walking around in a barn that had been converted into an inn. In one corner of the room is the guest kitchen with a refrigerator that guests can share for lunch and dinner.

Bedrooms have a real New England country look—ruffled curtains at the windows and an assortment of twin and double beds. There are lots of books everywhere.

One of the things that guests enjoy is watching the seals at play in the river. It's a good place for sunning and lazing away the day in a lawn chair, if you like.

A light breakfast that includes warm homemade muffins is served.

The inn is just a short distance away from a golf course.

THE BRANNON-BUNKER INN, Rte. 129, Damariscotta, ME 04543; 207-563-5941. An 8-guestroom village inn on the Damariscotta River; 5 rooms share 2 baths and 3 rooms have private baths. Open year-round. Continental breakfast included with lodgings. Breakfast only meal served. Many good restaurants in the area. All water sports, excursion boats, sightseeing, tennis, golf, sandy beach, lighthouse, historic fort nearby. Only minutes away from Boothbay Harbor, Wiscasset, and Camden-Rockland activities. Jeanne and Joe Hovance, Innkeepers.

Directions: From U.S. 1 turn south on Rte. 129 at Damariscotta. The inn is on Rte. 129, 5 min. away from U.S. 1.

For B&B rates, see Index.

BREEZEMERE FARM
Brooksville, Maine

The East Penobscot Bay region of Maine, south of Mt. Desert Island and north of Penobscot Bay, is one of the most unspoiled places where trees, birds, flowers, and marine life abound. There are beautiful homes, historic landmarks, crafts shops, golf, tennis, swimming, horseback riding, antiquing, and sailing.

Right in the spirit of this as-yet-to-be-discovered area is Breezemere Farm, an inn on sixty acres at the head of Orcutt Harbor.

The day begins with a big country breakfast, including Breezemere granola and other treats such as blueberry pancakes with genuine maple syrup.

The atmosphere at Breezemere is friendly, informal, and unhurried. Some guests prefer to spend most of their time on the farm, setting off by foot to explore the coast or crossing field and wood to discover a hidden cove. Trails take you to open blueberry fields or deep through the woods. A favorite hike is up the rock ledges to the observation tower, which commands a magnificent 360° view. (If you'd like a hiking companion, Packy, a friendly beagle, is at your service.)

Even if only staying for one night, be sure to get there in time for dinner—and remember, don't tell a soul about East Penobscot Bay; we'll keep it our own little secret.

BREEZEMERE FARM, Box 290, Brooksville, ME 04617; 207-326-8628. A 7-guestroom circa 1850 saltwater farmhouse plus 6 cottages. Sixty acres of farm and blueberry fields and forest at the head of Orcutt Harbor. Shared baths in the inn. Large farm breakfast included with the lodgings. Dinner by reservation. Open from Memorial Day to Oct. 15. In Aug., 3-day minimum stay. Bicycles, rowboats, Day Sailer, Hobiecat, woodland and coastline exploring, clamming and musseling, shuffleboard, and indoor recreation on grounds. Charter boat tours, golf, tennis, crafts and antique shops nearby. Pets allowed in cottages only. Joan and Jim Lippke, Innkeepers.

Directions: From Bucksport via Rtes. 1 or 3, take Rte. 175 to No. Brooksville. Turn right onto 176W. The first right after Cape Rosier Rd. is Breezemere Farm.

For B&B rates, see Index.

THE CAPTAIN LORD MANSION
Kennebunkport, Maine

Kennebunkport is a picturesque seacoast village that contains an unusual number of stately homes built in the late 18th and early 19th centuries. Its quiet tree-shaded streets and the nearby river, where there are many ocean-going fishing boats, provide visitors with an honest "New England" experience.

The Captain Lord Mansion, which is listed on the National Register, was built during the War of 1812 by ships' artisans who were idled by the British blockade. With its three stories topped by a cupola, it is the most impressive structure in Kennebunkport today. There are at least twenty-four rooms in the mansion, and sixteen have been set aside as guest rooms. All of them have their own private baths. Eleven have working fireplaces.

All of the guest rooms are named for ships built by the original owner. They are individually decorated with fine antiques. Some rooms overlook the river and the Arundle Yacht Club, and others have a view of the extensive gardens and historic homes in the quiet residential neighborhood.

At breakfast everyone gathers around the great table in the kitchen for some of Bev's homemade muffins, hot breads, and boiled eggs. This is where plans are hatched (no pun intended) for the day's activities, as well as selecting a restaurant for the evening meal.

As one might imagine, advance reservations are almost always necessary at the Captain Lord Mansion.

THE CAPTAIN LORD MANSION, Box 800, Kennebunkport, ME 04046; 207-967-3141. A 16-guestroom inn located in a mansion in a seacoast village. Near the Rachel Carson Wildlife Refuge, the Seashore Trolley Museum, The Brick Store Museum, and lobster boat tours. Lodgings include breakfast. No other meals served. Open year-round. Bicycles, hiking, xc skiing, deep sea fishing, golf, and tennis nearby. No children under 12. No pets. Bev Davis and Rick Litchfield, Innkeepers.

Directions: Take Exit 3 (Kennebunk) from the Maine Turnpike. Take left on Rte. 35 and follow signs through Kennebunk to Kennebunkport. Take left at traffic light at Sunoco Station. Go over drawbridge and take first right onto Ocean Ave., then take fifth left off Ocean Ave. The mansion is on the second block on the left. Park behind building and take brick walk to office.

For B&B rates, see Index.

THE CARRIAGE HOUSE INN
Searsport, Maine

U.S. 1 is one of the principal routes to northern Maine, and it continues on into New Brunswick, Prince Edward Island, and Nova Scotia. There are some very attractive Maine towns en route, including Bath, Wiscasset, and Camden.

North of Camden, to the east, between the stands of trees and an occasional motel, is beautiful Penobscot Bay. In Searsport, which would be an ideal stop for the weary traveler, there are two bed-and-breakfast places directly across U.S. 1 from each other. I'm certain if you called Nancy or Susan at the Carriage House and they were full, they would recommend the Homeport, and vice versa with Mrs. Johnson.

I think each inn is equally comfortable, hospitable, and friendly, although they differ in some interesting ways.

The Carriage House shares the spotlight with the main house, and this truly impressive building is now a gift shop. During past years, the property was owned by the late Waldo Peirce, a renowned Maine painter, and was used as his summer home and studio.

Built during the mid-19th century, this mansion has high ceilings and large, cheerful guest rooms with appropriate furnishings.

The kitchen-brunch room is one of the most interesting rooms in the house. Its tongue-and-groove walls and ceiling create a very cozy feeling. In addition to the continental breakfast, coffee and tea are available for guests at any time.

THE CARRIAGE HOUSE INN, Rte. 1, Searsport, ME 04974; 207-548-2289. A 6-guestroom guest house in an impressive Victorian mansion. Lodgings include continental breakfast; coffee or tea available at all times. All of the Penobscot Bay recreation and natural attractions are easily accessible. Open all year. Nancy and Susan Noqueira, Proprietors.

Directions: The Carriage House Inn is on U.S. 1 in Searsport.

For B&B rates, see Index.

CHARMWOODS
On Long Lake, Naples, Maine

Route 302 connects with I-89 at Barre, Vermont, and swings across New Hampshire, providing a spectacular journey through Crawford Notch into North Conway. It then cuts into the lake country of Maine through Fryeburg. It is a favorite road for Canadians.

A very pleasant overnight stop on this road would be Charmwoods, a unique type of guest house set in an area of great natural beauty on Long Lake in Naples, Maine.

Once a private lakefront estate, Charmwoods radiates all the flavor and ambience of the Maine woods, but is a mere two-and-a-half hours' drive from downtown Boston.

The focus of activity at Charmwoods is frequently in the commodious and gracious living room with its massive fieldstone fireplace and panoramic view of lake and mountains. In fact, every handsomely appointed guest room suite enjoys a view of the lake.

A "glorified" continental breakfast, included in the B&B rate, is served either in the dining room or on the terrace overlooking the lake. It is one of the most congenial hours of the day, as I discovered when I realized that two hours had gone by!

CHARMWOODS, Naples, ME 04055; 207-693-6798 (winter: 617-469-9673). A 4-guestroom and cottage (private baths) lakefront estate on the west shore of Long Lake, approx. ½ hr. from Maine Tpke. Open June to Oct. Breakfast is the only meal served (to houseguests only). Tennis, swimming, boating, canoeing, shuffleboard, and horseshoes on grounds; horseback riding, golf, nearby. Summer playhouse just down the road. Not suitable for children under 12. No pets. No credit cards. Marilyn and Bill Lewis, Innkeepers.

Directions: From Boston: follow Rte. 1 north to I- 95 to Exit 8 (Portland-Westbrook). Turn right and follow Riverside St. 1 mi. to Rte. 302. Turn left (west) to Naples. Charmwoods is just beyond the village on the right with an unobtrusive sign. From North Conway, N.H.: follow Rte. 302 through Bridgton. Charmwoods sign and driveway off Rte. 302 just west of Naples village.

For B&B rates, see Index.

CLEFTSTONE MANOR
Bar Harbor, Maine

I had three letters of recommendation before I visited this inn, and I must say that every one of them was absolutely correct.

Each of the eighteen guest rooms is individually furnished with tasteful antiques chosen by the owners, Don and Phyllis Jackson. There are three large rooms for guests to enjoy—a living room and a large dining room, both with fireplaces, and a very light and airy sunroom. All of the guest rooms are exceptionally attractive and comfortable with handmade crafts in each, and every bed is supplied with a down comforter for those cool Maine nights.

A continental breakfast is included in the room rates, and Phyllis bakes homemade blueberry, bran and cinnamon muffins, as well as raisin bread to go with the fruit, orange juice, and coffee. Four o'clock is teatime and guests are invited to sample herbal teas and homemade Scottish shortbread. Everyone gathers in the sunroom and shares their activities of the day. At 8:00 P.M., there is additional refreshment offered, including several types of cheeses and crackers.

Cleftstone Manor is an excellent place to stay for several days to enjoy all of the many attractive features of the Mount Desert area, and it is just 500 yards from the Bluenose Ferry to Nova Scotia. If it served the evening meal I would certainly include it in *Country Inns and Back Roads, North America*.

CLEFTSTONE MANOR, Eden St., Bar Harbor, ME 04609; 207-288-4951. An 18-guestroom (13 with private bath) elegant country inn within walking distance of the Bluenose Ferry to Nova Scotia. Open May 15 through mid-Oct. Continental breakfast, afternoon tea, and evening refreshments included in room rate. Ideal for honeymooners and longer stays to enjoy many of the natural, historical, and cultural attractions of Mt. Desert Island. Hot-air balloon flights are also available through the inn. The Jackson Family, Innkeepers.

Directions: Follow Rte. 3 to Bar Harbor. The inn is on the right-hand side, plainly marked.

For B&B rates, see Index.

THE COUNTRY CLUB INN
Rangeley, Maine

Rangeley, Maine, is one of those places in the world that has a special kind of charisma. There are few locations that offer such beauty and grandeur in all seasons. The combination of wide skies, vast stretches of mountain woodland, and the placid aspect of Rangeley Lake were drawing people to this part of western Maine long before the roads were as passable and numerous as they are today.

The Country Club Inn sits at a high point overlooking all of the marvelous panorama of lake, sky, and mountains. The cathedral-ceilinged living room has heavy beams, wood paneling, many, many different types of sofas, rocking chairs, and armchairs. I saw several jigsaw puzzles in various states of completion, a huge shelf of books, and a great moose head over one of the two fireplaces.

An 18-hole par-70 golf course is just a few steps from the front door and there is excellent fishing for square-tailed trout and land-locked salmon in all of the Rangeley Lakes. And, of course, magnificent cross country skiing on the grounds, downhill skiing on nearby Saddleback Mountain, and over 100 miles of snowmobile trails.

The dining room has a spectacular view of the lake and mountains, and the full hearty breakfasts fortify the vacationer for a lovely day in the outdoors. At breakfast there are hot muffins made from blueberries grown on the nearby hillside, as well as a choice of pancakes, corned beef hash, eggs any style, and homefries.

THE COUNTRY CLUB INN, P.O. Box 680 BB, Rangeley, ME 04970; 207-864-3831. A 25-guestroom resort inn on Rangeley Lake in Maine's beautiful western mountain lakes country, 45 mi. from Farmington. European, modified American plans. B&B rates available. Open late May to mid-Oct.; and mid-Dec. to mid-Mar. Breakfast and dinner served to travelers. Near many cultural, historic, and recreational attractions. Swimming pool and lake swimming, horseshoes, bocci, and 18-hole golf course on grounds. Fishing, saddle horses, water skiing, canoeing, tennis nearby. Xc skiing on grounds; downhill skiing and snowmobile trails on nearby Saddleback Mt. Bob and Sue Crory, Innkeepers.

Directions: From Maine Tpke.: take Auburn Exit 12 and follow Rte. 4 to Rangeley. From Vt. and N.H.: take I-91 to St. Johnsbury; east on Rte. 2 to Gorham, and Rte. 16 north to Rangeley.

For B&B rates, see Index.

DOCKSIDE GUEST QUARTERS
York, Maine

There's something very romantic about awakening in the morning to the sound of sea gulls and the chug-chug of fishing boats putting out to sea. That's what the guests at the Dockside Guest Quarters enjoy, because it is located right on the harbor of York, Maine, and the action begins at dawn when the lobster and fishing boats head out to sea, guided by hundreds of shore birds.

This section of southern Maine is a very happy combination of seaside life and a generous dollop of history.

The Dockside Guest Quarters includes the original New England homestead of the 1880s, called the Maine House, as well as several other cottage buildings of a contemporary design, each with its own porch and water view.

One of the uncrowded times to visit is in late May and early June, when it's fun to wander along York beach, enjoy golf and tennis, or perhaps rent a sailboat for scooting around the harbor.

The Dockside Dining Room, an excellent restaurant on the grounds of the inn, is an excellent place to dine after a long day of travel.

On nice mornings, guests may bring their à la carte continental breakfast, consisting of fruit juices, fresh doughnuts and coffee cake, as well as bread and preserves, to the sunny porch on the ocean side of the Maine House. It's a good time to get acquainted.

DOCKSIDE GUEST QUARTERS, Harris Island Rd., York, ME 03909; 207-363-2868. A 20-guestroom waterside country inn 10 mi. from Portsmouth, N.H. Some studio suites in newer multi-unit cottages. York village is a National Historic District. American plan available. Continental breakfast not included in room rate. Dockside Dining Room serves lunch and dinner to travelers daily except Mon. Open from Memorial Day weekend in May thru Columbus Day in Oct. Lawn games, shuffleboard and badminton, fishing, sailing, and boating from the premises. Golf, tennis, and swimming nearby; safe and picturesque paths and roadways for walks, bicycling, and jogging. Credit cards are not accepted for any amounts over seventy-five dollars. Personal checks accepted for payment of food and lodgings incurred by registered guests. David and Harriette Lusty, Innkeepers.

Directions: From U.S. 1 or I-95, take exit at York to Rte. 1A. Follow 1A through center of Old York Village, take Rte. 103 (a side street off Rte. 1A leading to the harbor), and watch for signs to the inn.

For B&B rates, see Index.

ELFINHILL
Newcastle, Maine

The twin villages of Newcastle and Damariscotta face each other across the Damariscotta River, about six and one-half miles north of Wiscasset. Elfinhill is the first of two bed-and-breakfast inns on the River Road about a half-mile from Route 1. My notes about the Captain's House, immediately next door, are also in these pages.

Elfinhill is unique, if for no other reason than because Ms. Emma Stephenson is originally from Kent, England, and as she says, "We are a true British-American-style B&B."

Of course, I was intrigued by the name "elfinhill," and with a twinkle in her eye she pointed out the biggest elf I'd ever seen, seated in the garden in the rear of the inn. He's five feet eight inches tall with a jolly smile, red cheeks, yellow hat, blue pants, red jacket, and a big yellow tie. Emma explained that he was obtained when the Danbury Fair in Connecticut closed a few years ago.

There are three bedrooms here with shared bathrooms. At breakfast time, Emma says, she specializes in coffee cakes. There are blackberries from the garden and fresh fruit in season, along with eggs, pancakes, homemade preserves and jellies and, of course, a wide choice of coffee and English teas. Incidentally, she also does a brisk business in specialty baking, and she serves afternoon tea.

Elfinhill enjoys a very pleasant view of the Damariscotta River, and I must point out that it was through her generosity that I learned about the Mill Pond Inn, also located in Damariscotta.

ELFINHILL, 20 River Rd., Newcastle, ME 04553; 207-563-1886. A 3-guestroom (shared baths) bed-and-breakfast accommodation with a real British air about 6 mi. north of Wiscasset. Open all year. Breakfast is included in the room rate. Conveniently located to enjoy the many natural and recreational attractions on the Pemaquid and Boothbay peninsulas. Second floor area is non-smoking. No pets. No credit cards. Personal checks accepted. Emma Stephenson and Donald Smith, Innkeepers.

Directions: About 6½ mi. past Wiscasset, on Rte. 1, turn right, following signs for Newcastle. Take River Rd. and watch for Elfinhill on the left, 6/10 of a mi. from Rte. 1.

For B&B rates, see Index.

ENGLISH MEADOWS INN
Kennebunkport, Maine

English Meadows Inn is a 19th-century Victorian farmhouse that has been operating as an inn for over eighty years. From Route 35 it's easy to identify the inn by the lilac-tree-lined drive and a weathervane in the shape of a whale.

From the front yard it's possible to look across the trees and fields to the tower of the church in Dock Square in Kennebunkport where there is a collection of shops, restaurants, churches, and galleries, as well as deep-sea fishing boats.

When I first visited this inn I was greeted enthusiastically by two friendly dogs, Ramona and Buttons, who seemed to lead me naturally to the sideporch where I could look through the large windows into a spotlessly clean kitchen. And it was here, the next morning, I enjoyed one of Claudia Kelly's wonderful full New England breakfasts.

Claudia is the daughter of Gene and Helene Kelly who came to Kennebunkport a few years ago and turned this Victorian gem into a trim bed-and-breakfast inn.

There are fourteen lodging rooms furnished with brass and iron beds, hooked rugs, early quilts, and wonderful prints.

The Kelly family's interest in antiques is reflected in their own Whaler Antiques Shop which has country furniture and accessories, and wicker folk art.

ENGLISH MEADOWS INN, R.F.D. 1, Rte. 35, Kennebunkport, ME 04046; 207-967-5766. A 14-guestroom bed-and-breakfast inn (2 have private baths, 12 share 6 baths), just a short distance from the center of Kennebunkport. A full breakfast is the only meal offered. Open from April to the end of Oct., and winter weekends. A beautiful beach that is spectacular in all weather nearby, as well as some splendid shopping, antiquing, and backroading. No credit cards. The Kelly Family, Innkeepers.

Directions: Use Exit 3 from Maine Turnpike. (If coming north, slow down and be sure you take the correct turn.) Follow Rtes. 35 and 9A to Kennebunkport. The inn is on the right-hand side 5 mi. from Exit 3 toll booth.

For B&B rates, see Index.

GOOSE COVE LODGE
Deer Isle, Maine

Although Goose Cove Lodge is a modified American plan inn, George and Elli Pavloff have set aside a few weeks at the beginning and end of the season to offer the readers of this book a delightful bed-and-breakfast experience. See the dates in the italicized paragraph below.

Goose Cove Lodge, like most of the other bed-and-breakfast inns included in this book, represents an unusual, and distinctive accommodation. Located on a gorgeous bay and secluded cove, the bedrooms are in individual cabins and cottages tucked into a wooded hillside. They all have private bathrooms and fireplaces that are particularly welcome during the late spring and mid-fall.

A combination of the really spectacular beauty of the place, as well as its privacy, combine to make Goose Cove Lodge something quite special. Innkeeper Elli Pavloff says, "It is one of the very special places with a magic all its own—there aren't many places that are still unspoiled."

I had better emphasize that Sunset, Maine, is not really on the road to anywhere except the fishing village of Stonington, a few miles away. The reader will see from the directions that one wouldn't just happen to be "driving by," but would be making a special effort to drive down the Penobscot Bay Peninsula, across the bridge, and into Deer Isle.

Please note that bed-and-breakfast rates and accommodations are available only at certain times during the year.

GOOSE COVE LODGE, Sunset, Deer Isle, Me. 04683; 207-348-2508. A 22-room (60 people) resort-inn on beautiful Penobscot Bay approx. 1 hr. from Rte. 1 at Bucksport. Open May 1 to mid-Oct. B&B rate available May 1 to mid-June; mid-Sept. to mid-Oct. Modified American plan mid-June to mid-Sept. Meals served to houseguests only. Swimming, boating, canoeing, hiking, and birdwatching all available at the inn. Other outdoor sports, including backroading, golf, tennis, etc., nearby. Especially adaptable for children of all ages. Elli and George Pavloff, Innkeepers.

Directions: From Bucksport, drive 4 mi. north on Rte. 1 and turn right at Rte. 15 down the Blue Hill Peninsula to Deer Isle Village. Turn right in village at sign to Sunset, Maine. Proceed 3 mi., turn right at Goose Cove Lodge sign. Follow dirt road 1½ mi. to inn.

For B&B rates, see Index.

GRANE'S FAIRHAVEN INN
Bath, Maine

Bath is one of those interesting communities on U.S. 1 (the coastal route) leading to Camden, Mt. Desert, and points north into Canada.

Somewhat separated from the rather interesting downtown section of Bath on the Kennebec River where the world's largest naval crane can be seen for miles around, is Grane's Fairhaven Inn, overlooking this selfsame river.

It has beautiful plantings on green lawns, cross-country ski trails leading into the woods, and a very quiet and pleasant aspect.

The building dates to about 1790 and was lived in by members of the same family for 125 years. The present owners, Jane Wyllie and Gretchen Williams, have done much to preserve the original warmth and Maine-coast ambience.

There are several places to curl up quietly with a book or listen to music in the sitting rooms, and the bedrooms are all furnished with appropriate country-inn furniture.

An à la carte breakfast is available each morning—plenty of fresh fruits, hot and cold cereal, homemade jam or marmalade, piping-hot biscuits, muffins, or bread, bacon and eggs, and various types of soufflés and omelets on occasion.

GRANE'S FAIRHAVEN INN, No. Bath Rd., Bath, Me. 04530; 207-443-4391. A 9-bedroom old country home with shared baths on 27 acres of woods and fields on the Kennebec River. Open year-round. Full country breakfast available. Hiking, nature walks, cross-country skiing, snowshoeing on grounds. Swimming, golfing, picnicking, tennis, boating, fishing nearby. Performing Arts Center offers Fri. & Sat. concerts (classical, jazz, bluegrass). Jane Wyllie and Gretchen Williams, Innkeepers.

Directions: From U.S. 1 south in Bath follow signs for Congress Ave., turning right off U.S. 1 and right again on Congress Ave. At 4-street intersection, take Oak Grove (first street on left). Follow Oak Grove 1½ miles and turn right immediately beyond large barn. Look for inn sign ½ mile on left.

For B&B rates, see Index.

136

GREY ROCK INN
Northeast Harbor, Maine

Grey Rock Inn on Mt. Desert Island on the upper coast of Maine was built as a private estate in the early 1900s. The inn has an alpine setting of evergreens and berry bushes and has quite a few woodland walks on the property.

The guest rooms are quite large, many with handsome brass beds, which are turned down for guests each night. Each room faces the harbor and has its own bath. They are cool and shady in the summertime and most pleasantly decorated.

My first visit to Grey Rock came in 1974 when I discovered that Janet Millett is British, having been brought up in England. This means that very frequently she invites her guests to join her in the living room for a cup of tea in the late afternoon. The scene is most reminiscent of an English country house hotel. Guests are frequently en route to New Brunswick by land or Nova Scotia by ferry. Many stay longer to enjoy the wonderful attractions at Acadia National Park.

Some of the real treats at the continental breakfast are the various kinds of muffins, baked fresh every morning. These include blueberry, ginger pecan, date, raisin, and honey muffins, as well as prune danish, cranberry bread, cheeses, and croissants. English touches are provided with the marmalade, preserves and tea. In summer, it's fun to breakfast on the porch.

GREY ROCK INN, Harborside Rd., Northeast Harbor, ME 04662; 207-276-9360. A 9-guestroom village inn in the town of Northeast Harbor, adjacent to Acadia National Park and all of the attractions of this unusual region. European plan. Continental breakfast served to houseguests only. No other meals served. Small cottage available for minimum 4-night stay. Season from early spring to Nov. 1. Children 14 yrs. and older preferred. No pets. No credit cards. Janet Millett, Innkeeper.

Directions: Located on the right-hand side of Rte. 198 approaching the town of Northeast Harbor. Note sign for inn. Do not try to make a right-hand turn at this point, but proceed about one block, turn around and approach the inn on the left up the steep hill.

For B&B rates, see Index.

HARTWELL HOUSE
Ogunquit, Maine

Ogunquit is a seaside village where the flavor of old Maine remains zesty and alive. Among other reasons that tourists flock to it every year are the beautiful beach and the Marginal Way that meanders at cliff's edge past innumerable picture-postcard Maine seascapes and fabulous rock formations.

In addition to the lure of the forest and the sea, there is summer theater, art galleries, boutiques, and many restaurants.

Hartwell House is on the road from the center of Ogunquit to Perkins Cove. It is a two-story, pleasantly designed building, fronted with many Moorish arches. There are most pleasant gardens in the front and a considerable lawn in the rear.

There are nine guest rooms, including two efficiency apartments; all have private baths and all are furnished entirely in Early American and English antiques, featuring four-poster beds and handsome bedspreads.

It's within walking distance of the beach and also on a minibus route that serves the town.

A European-style continental breakfast is served with juice, fresh fruits, homemade muffins, croissants, breads, pastries, herbal teas and coffee—and at the innkeeper's whim, a baked surprise.

HARTWELL HOUSE, P.O. Box 393, 116 Shore Rd., Ogunquit, ME 03907; 207-646-7210. A 9-guestroom inn (private baths) providing a very compatible atmosphere for a limited number of guests (2 rooms may be rented as complete apartments). Open year-round. The ocean, Perkins Cove, the Marginal Way, Ogunquit Playhouse all within walking distance. Fishing, golf, swimming, bicycles, sailing, and tennis nearby. Not suitable for children under 14. No pets. Trisha and Jim Hartwell, Innkeepers.

Directions: Follow I-95 north through New Hampshire to Maine; take last exit before Maine toll booth; north on Rte. 1, 7 mi. to center of Ogunquit. Turn right on Shore Rd. approx. ¾ mi. Hartwell on right.

For B&B rates, see Index.

HILLTOP HOUSE
Boothbay Harbor, Maine

The traveler on U.S. 1, the coastal route through Maine, is in for a treat if he turns off on Route 27 and drives the twelve miles down the peninsula into Boothbay Harbor. There's much to see and enjoy and it is well worth an overnight stay and even more. I would advise stopping at the first information booth and getting a booklet and a map or two to help in getting oriented.

Hilltop House, as well as its neighboring guest house, Topside, is right down on the harbor at the top of McKown Hill. It is a real "down home" type of place with comfortable rooms, and the operating family has been here for forty years. It's a big old house with an inviting front porch and a tree with a swing on it, and some satisfying views of Boothbay Harbor.

A continental breakfast of hot muffins and coffee is included in the room rate.

I visited Boothbay Harbor shortly after Labor Day and although there were still quite a few people there, I can imagine that during July and August the one-way streets would be jammed. I can't see why anyone who can come to Maine in September and October would possibly want to go to this section of the Maine coast in July or August.

HILLTOP HOUSE, McKown Hill, Boothbay Harbor, Me. 04538; 207-633-2941. A 6-bedroom farmhouse lodging with shared baths (1 rm. with private bath) on a hill overlooking Boothbay Harbor; also a family unit with complete kitchen and bath. Open year-round. Continental breakfast included. All summertime activities within a 3-minute walk—sightseeing, fishing, excursion boats, antiquing nearby. Swimming beaches within easy driving distance. No credit cards. Mrs. Cora Mahr, Manager.

Directions: From Rte. 1 north of Bath, follow Rte. 27 to Boothbay Harbor and continue on through, watching for a sign for McKown Hill on the left.

For B&B rates, see Index.

THE HOMEPORT INN
Searsport, Maine

Searsport on Penobscot Bay is one of the antiquing centers of Maine. According to a little folder on the town there must be at least twenty antique shops plus a few galleries.

During the last century Searsport was well known as a lumbering port. Maine lumber was carried to many parts of the world.

The original owner of the Homeport Inn was a sea captain, who provided this house with a widow's walk that, I understand, can be used today as a guest room in an emergency.

The house itself befits such a sophisticated individual and a hundred or so years later, the furnishings, I'm sure, would be most pleasing to him, including the impressive flocked wallpaper, marble fireplace, and crystal chandelier.

Abovestairs, the guest rooms are almost opulently furnished. Some beds have a canopy and there are attractive lace curtains and appropriate wall hangings. Six of the rooms have private baths.

Breakfast is served in a long, narrow room, which at one time was a porch looking out over the fields to Penobscot Bay. In clement weather, breakfast can be enjoyed on the patio, with a view of the English garden, the fountain, and the bay. A full breakfast, along with homemade muffins, juices, and coffee, is offered.

The Homeport is right across U.S. 1 from the Carriage House, and I'm sure that both are equally comfortable. If you call one and it is full, I'm sure they'll recommend the other.

THE HOMEPORT INN, Searsport, ME 04974; 207-548-2259. A 10-guestroom elegantly furnished New England sea captain's mansion. Convenient to recreational, cultural, and natural attractions in the Penobscot Bay area. Breakfast only meal served. Open year-round. Edith and Dr. George Johnson, Innkeepers.

Directions: Mrs. Johnson suggests, as an alternate to Rte. 1, following I-95 to Augusta and then taking Rte. 3 to Belfast, just below Searsport.

For B&B rates, see Index.

HOMEWOOD INN ON CASCO BAY
Yarmouth, Maine

I think the best time to visit Maine is in September and October. The sun is still high, the water is still warm, and the principal roads are relatively free of the heavy traffic found in July and August.

That's why I was delighted to find my good friends, Fred and Colleen Webster, at the Homewood Inn offering bed-and-breakfast accommodations in June, September, and October.

Guest rooms are in a group of waterside cottages overlooking scenic Casco Bay. In the early fall on chilly evenings they are very cozy with the crackling fires in the fireplaces.

There is much to do in the area, including shopping at Portland's Old Port Exchange, L.L. Bean, and the outlet shops in Freeport and visiting the many state parks and museums up and down the Maine coast.

Recreation on the grounds includes a swimming pool, shuffleboard, croquet, saltwater swimming, tennis, and bike rentals. The inn also boasts the Maine Craft Shop, which features authentic "down east" crafts.

Late spring and early fall B&B guests can take advantage of the full breakfast as a part of their room rate. It is a welcome start for another day on the Maine coast.

HOMEWOOD INN, P.O. Box 196B, Drinkwater Point, Yarmouth, ME 04096; 207-846-3351. A 46-guestroom waterside inn on Casco Bay, north of Portland. European plan. B&B only available in June, Sept., and Oct. Breakfast and dinner served to travelers daily, except Mon. when steak or lobster cookout at night available (by advance reservation). Open early June to mid-Oct. Bicycles (incl. tandems), pool, tennis, croquet court, hiking, saltwater swimming on grounds. Golf, riding, fishing, state parks, theater nearby. Fred and Colleen Webster, Ted and Doris Gillette, Innkeepers.

Directions: From the south, take Exit 9 from Maine Tpke. (I-95) to Rte. 1-N, or Exit 17 from I-295 to Rte. 1-N, and follow signs to inn. From north (Brunswick area), from I-95, take "Yarmouth, Rte. 1" exit and follow signs to the inn.

For B&B rates, see Index.

KENNISTON HILL INN
Boothbay, Maine

It was the gracious, rather stately, white clapboard exterior of this inn on a little knoll in a wonderful grove of trees on Route 27, between Boothbay and Boothbay Harbor, that originally attracted me. I'm delighted to say that both the interior and the atmosphere generated by Paul and Ellen Morrisette confirmed my initial impression.

Eight large, tastefully decorated rooms (four with fireplaces) have homelike accommodations created by handmade quilts, delicately colored wallpaper, and something I always like to find at an inn—fresh flowers.

The entrance leads into a very impressive living room boasting a gorgeous fireplace with a big mantel and lots of interesting, fancy decorations. The small library with another fireplace is a sort of quiet little place for reading and games.

By virtue of Paul's experience as owner of the well-known Country Kitchen Restaurant in Brattleboro, Vermont, for many, many years, bed-and-breakfast guests are treated to what he assures me is "not a continental breakfast."

"Today we had a blend of orange juice, bananas, and lemon juice for a drink, followed by zucchini and walnut pancakes with spiced apples and raisins, and bacon and coffee."

One might say that Kenniston Hill Inn is the right combination of Maine and Vermont.

KENNISTON HILL INN, Rte. 27, Boothbay, ME 04537; 207-633-2159. An 8-guestroom 200-year-old Colonial bed-and-breakfast inn (mostly private baths) 1 mi. from Boothbay Harbor. A full breakfast is included in the room rate. Open April thru Dec. Shopping, boat trips, fishing, golf, bicycling, restaurants, and theater nearby. No pets. Paul and Ellen Morrisette, Innkeepers.

Directions: The Kenniston Inn is located in Boothbay on Rte. 27. Turn off Rte. 1 just after Wiscasset, inn is on the left, 1 mi. from Boothbay Harbor.

For B&B rates, see Index.

MILL POND INN
Newcastle, Maine

Here's an inn that has its own resident American eagle, as well as loons, herons, otters, and all varieties of ducks. These furry and feathered friends can be seen from the deck, the Keeping Room, and many of the bedrooms overlooking the mill pond.

Three or four things remain in my mind after a June visit. I was impressed by the fresh flowers in all the rooms, as well as the rocking chairs and colorful afghans. I was also delighted to find oversized cotton bath towels.

There are beautifully furnished bedrooms and a handsome Keeping Room, used as the breakfast room, with walls of extra-wide wood paneling. A red brick fireplace now has a very efficient-looking Franklin stove that burns on chilly mornings.

Innkeeper Gloria Krellman fled the world of academe and found this really exceptional location overlooking the mill pond, just across the village street from the south end of Lake Damariscotta. It's actually in Newcastle, Maine, but the little community is called Damariscotta Mills. It's a gray-shingled house with white trim.

Gloria assures me that a full breakfast is served from 7:30 to 9:00 A.M. From 9:00 to 9:30, it's possible to get coffee and rolls. I noticed that she was grinding her own coffee beans.

As lovely as the mill pond is and as attractive as the setting may be, I think the Mill Pond Inn would be a hit in any location.

MILL POND INN, RFD 1, Box 245, Newcastle, ME 04553; 207-563-8014. A 7-guestroom (5 with private baths) bed-and-breakfast inn a short distance from Rte. 1 in the Damariscotta/Newcastle area. Breakfast is included in the room rate. Open all year. Conveniently located to enjoy the unusual ambience of the mid-Maine coast historic, recreational, and cultural attractions. No credit cards. No pets. No smoking. Gloria Krellman, Innkeeper.

Directions: Coming north on Rte. 1, exit at Damariscotta/Newcastle. Follow signs to Rte. 215 north for 2 mi.

For B&B rates, see Index.

THE MOORELOWE
York Harbor, Maine

For the traveler going north on I-95 and the Maine Turnpike, York Harbor is the first exit after crossing the Piscataqua River Bridge between Portsmouth, New Hampshire, and southern Maine. This bridge, incidentally, is a very graceful span and is a welcome replacement for the drawbridge that was used for many years and quite frequently held up traffic.

York is a quiet, peaceful village, and a very appropriate introduction for first-time travelers to Maine. The Historic District has a group of fine old buildings and historical sites, including the Old Gaol Museum, Jefferds Tavern, the Elizabeth Perkins House, and other splendid pre-Revolutionary dwellings.

The Moorelowe is a yellow building on the right-hand side of the main street with a generous, enclosed front porch and lots of comfortable wicker furniture. It is the home of Mr. Kenneth Day and his dog, Pudgy, and for someone looking for some authentic "down east" atmosphere, Mr. Day would be hard to top. He's about as laconic a man as I have ever met.

However, while I helped him make a bed he told me that people were always talking about how clean the rooms were and many of his guests have been returning for many years. Children are quite welcome and the beach is nearby.

Breakfast is not served here, but as Mr. Day says, there are several nearby restaurants where a good breakfast is offered.

The downstairs living room is right out of a New England sampler with a piano and lots of music and lots of photographs of the Day children and grandchildren.

I think the Moorelowe would be a lot of fun. However it *was* a bit disillusioning to discover that Mr. Day, who is a sort of walking advertisement for the state of Maine, was actually born and raised in Colrain, Massachusetts!

THE MOORELOWE, Route 1A, York Harbor, ME 03911; 207-363-2526. A 7-room guest house (3 rooms with private baths). Breakfast not offered. Open June 1 to Sept. 30. York Beach, boats for fishing and pleasure trips nearby; tennis and golf within 10-min. drive. Convenient to all southern Maine attractions. No credit cards. Mr. Kenneth Day, Proprietor.

Directions: Use the York Exit from I-95. Follow 1A thru village into York Harbor.

For Lodging rates, see Index.

NEWAGEN SEASIDE INN
Cape Newagen, Maine

At the seaward tip of Southport Island, the Newagen Seaside Inn is a place where the exciting, rocky coast of Maine, so longed for by many of our West Coast readers, may be experienced in all of its awesome beauty. Several paths on the broad lawns lead to the ocean, or a sheltered cove with a saltwater swimming pool, or docks where there are working lobster boats and ducks and seabirds.

The island's known history dates back to a meeting between a British captain, Christopher Levett, and the Indian, Sagamore, in 1623. Indians destroyed the fort and settlement fifty years later.

Although I had seen the brochure in advance, the Newagen was somewhat larger than I had expected. The main inn, built in the early '40s, is in the style of a Colonial mansion with four square pillars at the entrance. It has twenty-five bedrooms, with private baths and a living room with a large fireplace. There is a smaller building with ten bedrooms and baths "down the hall," called the Little Inn, that offers bed-and-breakfast accommodations.

The Newagen is on the European plan, except for bed-and-breakfast rates available to guests in the Little Inn, and breakfast, lunch, and dinner are served in the traditional dining room. Innkeeper Heidi Larsen tells me everything is homemade, including breads, rolls, and cakes. There are summer staff shows at least twice a week, much enjoyed by the guests.

She showed me a little gazebo out on the rocks—"a beautiful place to get married," she said. In fact, she and her husband, Peter, were married there themselves!

NEWAGEN SEASIDE INN, Southport Island, Cape Newagen, ME 04552; 207-633-5242 (summer); 633-5558 (winter). A 48-guest-room (private and shared baths) full-service inn on the tip of a small island beyond Boothbay Harbor. European plan, mid-June to mid-Sept., serving breakfast, lunch, and dinner. B&B rates available in the Little Inn. Salt-water swimming pool, lawn games, nature trails on grounds. Charter sailing, rowboating, and fishing from inn's dock. Golf and tennis nearby. Ideal for children. No pets please. Heidi and Peter Larsen, Innkepers.

Directions: From Rte. 1, follow Rte. 27 south through Boothbay Harbor, cross the drawbridge and continue around the island about 5 mi. to inn entrance.

For B&B rates, see Index.

OCEAN REEFS LODGE
Chamberlain, Maine

I was taking the shortcut from Waldoboro to New Harbor, Maine, near Pemaquid Point, when I happened to notice this pleasant little waterside bed-and-breakfast opposite Long Cove. It's a Maine lodge with a partly closed-in front porch, which provides an excellent view of the constant parade of water traffic. There are dozens of bobbing lobster pots, and you can watch the lobstermen come and pull them up to see if there's anything in them

This is the rockbound coast of Maine, on a secluded road—an ambience that I must confess is hard to find.

Ocean Reefs has four rooms, each with its own private bath, and two cabins with a private bath in the house. It's not very fancy, but it's a great place for just getting off by yourself and being quiet and doing a little fishing, if you care to, or reading lots of books, or watching the cormorants diving for fish or floating on the surface of the Cove. There are even seals in the vicinity, off Ross and Haddock Islands nearby.

One can watch the Atlantic waves break over the reefs and make day trips to Camden, Reid State Park, Bailey's Island, Boothbay Harbor, and so forth. It's not far from L.L. Bean.

Ocean Reefs Lodge has been operating for nine summers; however, I'd like to suggest that anyone planning a trip there telephone in advance. Pre-season reservations should be handled by mail. By the way, a continental breakfast is included in the room rate.

OCEAN REEFS LODGE, P.O. Box 105, Rte. 32, Chamberlain, ME 04541; 207-677-2386. A 6-guestroom bed-and-breakfast waterside lodge on a secluded Maine Coast road, with an unusually pleasant view and situation. Open from mid-June to mid-Oct. Fishing, swimming and boating, and Maine coast attractions nearby. Be sure to telephone in advance.

Directions: Leave Rte. 1 at Damariscotta and follow Rte. 130 to Rte. 32 at New Harbor, then turn north.

For B&B rates, see Index.

OLD FORT INN
Kennebunkport, Maine

Kennebunkport is a Maine waterside town that still retains the atmosphere it had when clipper ships sailed from its shores. The lovely old sea captains' houses remain on its beautiful streets, and its winding river makes a real New England adventure.

The Old Fort Inn is a luxurious adult resort nestled in a secluded setting within walking distance of the ocean. Each of the colorful and beautifully decorated rooms has its own kitchen facilities, and maid service is provided.

Outdoor recreational facilities include a large fresh-water swimming pool, a private tennis court, and shuffleboard. Golf courses are only a few minutes away.

A continental breakfast served in the attractive lodge is included with the cost of the rooms.

OLD FORT INN, Old Fort Ave., P.O. Box M, Kennebunkport, ME 04046; 207-967-5353. A 16-guestroom resort-inn in Kennebunkport, within walking distance of the ocean in a historic Maine town. Includes a continental breakfast, and a full kitchen is provided with each guestroom. Daily maid service. Lodge and antique shop. Open from May 1 to mid-Dec. Heated pool, tennis court, shuffleboard on grounds. Bicycles, golf, salt-water swimming and boating nearby. Not comfortable for children under 7. No pets. Sheila and David Aldrich, Innkeepers.

Directions: Take Exit 3 (Kennebunk) from the Main Turnpike. Take left on Rte. 35 and follow signs through Kennebunk to Kennebunkport. Take left at traffic light at Sunoco station. Go over drawbridge and take first right on Ocean Ave. Take Ocean Ave. to the Colony Hotel; turn left in front of the Colony, go to the Y in the road, go right ¼ mi. on left.

For B&B rates, see Index.

OLDE GARRISON HOUSE
Cape Porpoise, Kennebunkport, Maine

Cape Porpoise, located just a few miles beyond Kennebunkport, is a real honest-to-goodness fishing village with a very paintable harbor, salt air, and gulls swooping down over returning fishing boats. Captain John Smith named it in 1614 for a school of porpoises he saw playing in the bay. What other small village boasts a plaque at the pier commemorating the repulse of the mighty British in 1782 by a small band of determined townspeople bent upon being masters of their own fate? Here at Cape Porpoise you'll find beauty, serenity, vistas, history, legends, deeds, and dire happenings.

There are no dire happenings at the Olde Garrison House overlooking the beautiful tidal cove in the front and a tidal marsh in the rear.

It is owned by Lyman Huff, who is a working lobsterman, and his wife, Louise, both of whom are natives of Cape Porpoise. They live in the house next door, leaving guests at Old Garrison House very much to themselves.

Built in 1730, the house has very pleasant bedrooms and a simple kitchen where guests may use the refrigerator, toasters, and stove for light breakfasts. "Our guests seem to like it that way," Louise said, as she showed me through. "We have many people who have been returning for several years. There are four restaurants nearby and many more in Kennebunkport, only two miles away."

In a time when it's hard to find a community that is not overrun with commercialism, Cape Porpoise has managed to hold its own, even though *some* travelers have found it.

OLDE GARRISON HOUSE, Cape Porpoise, Me. 04014; 207-967-3522. A 7-bedroom Cape Cod-type house overlooking a tidal cove in an unspoiled section of Kennebunkport. Two rms. with private baths; 5 rms. share 2 baths. Open from late May to Oct. 15. Advance reservations advised. Guests have the use of refrigerator and toaster and may boil water for breakfast. Many restaurants nearby. Sightseeing in historic, authentic fishing village, bicycle rentals, lobster boat tours nearby. All diversions available in Kennebunkport. No children under 10. No pets. No credit cards. Louise and Lyman Huff, Proprietors.

Directions: Follow Rte. 9 north from Kennebunkport for about 2 miles to Community Library in Cape Porpoise. Leaving Rte. 9, go straight on Pier Rd. and find Olde Garrison House on the left.

For Lodging rates, see Index.

THE PENTAGOET INN
Castine, Maine

Travelers hastening pell-mell across Maine on U.S. 1, between Bucksport and Ellsworth, little realize that to the south lies the eastern Penobscot Bay region, which has intriguing back roads, beautiful ponds, tidal basins, sequestered villages, historic landmarks, silversmiths, blacksmiths, wood carvers, and outdoor recreation of all kinds.

I'd suggest that the reader write to either the Pilgrim's Inn in Deer Isle, Maine, or Pentagoet Inn in Castine, for a special map showing all of the roads and enticements of this fascinating peninsula.

Castine is on the west side of one end of Route 175 and Route 166, thirty minutes from Route 1. In addition to being a fishing village and a stop on the famous Windjammer cruises, it is also the home of the Maine Maritime Academy and the location of the Pentagoet Inn.

Situated just one square from the town harbor, this gracious Victorian inn has a welcome warmth and dedicated sense of hospitality personified by its innkeepers, Lindsey and Virginia Miller. They have supplemented the turn-of-the-century atmosphere with appropriate furniture and decorations and a few fillips of their own.

A full breakfast is served daily and features freshly baked-everyday muffins, homemade breads for toast, and a choice of eggs, blueberry pancakes, and french toast. Virginia places freshly brewed coffee outside each guest's room each morning before breakfast. Although rates are based on the modified American plan, bed-and-breakfast rates are available.

THE PENTAGOET INN, Castine, ME 04421; 207-326-8616. An 18-guestroom inn in a seacoast village on the Penobscot peninsula, 36 mi. from Bangor. Some rooms with shared baths. Breakfast and dinner served to travelers by reservation. Open April to Jan. Tennis, golf, swimming, backroading, village strolling nearby. Lindsey and Virginia Miller, Innkeepers.

Directions: Follow I-95 north to Brunswick and use Rte. 1 exit. Follow Rte. 1 to a point 3 mi. past Bucksport. Turn right on Rte. 175 to Rte. 166 to Castine.

For B&B rates, see Index.

PILGRIM'S INN
Deer Isle, Maine

It may be stretching it a bit to drive the thirty miles from coastal Route 1 south into the Blue Hill Peninsula to reach Deer Isle and Pilgrim's Inn, but be assured that for anyone fortunate enough to book an overnight room, it is well worth the trip.

The thirteen guest rooms are mostly quite large and little changed from Colonial days. Rooms feature richly hued pine floorboards, a woodstove, a queen-size bed, antiques, old wooden furniture, and water views. Eight rooms have private baths. The common room and the taproom have enormous fireplaces, and both the front parlors and the taproom have the original 1793 pine paneling.

Meals are served in the converted barn from mid-May to mid-October. There is always a full breakfast with a single menu that changes daily. Omelets, freshly baked pastry, and blueberry pancakes are very popular. The maple syrup is genuine, the flowers are fresh and the hospitality is warm and friendly. Although rates are based on the modified American plan, bed and breakfast is offered to the passing pilgrim.

PILGRIM'S INN, Deer Isle, ME 04627; 207-348-6615. A 13-guestroom inn (some shared baths) in an island village on the Blue Hill Peninsula on the Maine coast. Modified American plan, May 17 to Oct. 20, includes hearty breakfast and a gourmet dinner. In season outside dinner reservations accepted. B&B rates available. A 3-day minimum stay is required in August. Ten-speed bicycles available. Golf and tennis available for inn guests. The Deer Isle area is replete with all types of cultural and recreational advantages, including fishing, sailing, hiking, and browsing. Jean and Dud Hendrick, Innkeepers.

Directions: From Boston, take I-95 to Brunswick exit. Take coastal Rte. 1 north past Bucksport. Turn right on Rte. 15, which travels to Deer Isle down the Blue Hill Peninsula. At the village, turn right on Main Street (Sunset Rd.) and proceed one block to the inn on the left side of the street, opposite the Harbor.

For B&B rates, see Index.

THE SQUIRE TARBOX INN
Westport Island, Maine

Although Westport Island, which is on Maine's coast, is only eight miles from U.S. Route 1 at Wiscasset, it actually feels very much farther out of the way.

There are two types of guests at this inn: those who have learned that it's such a pleasant place to remain for a few days, and those who are en route to or from northern Maine, New Brunswick, Prince Edward Island or Nova Scotia.

The oldest part of this inn dates from 1763. Nine guest rooms have been furnished with simple antiques for a cozy "upcountry" feeling. Three of them have private baths. A large hearth with original bake ovens, floors, beams, and wainscoting set the tone for this sedate Colonial farmhouse.

The continental breakfast served in the dining room, or on the porch on sunshiny mornings, includes homemade breads and cakes.

The one principal difficulty for the bed-and-breakfast guest who may be rushing off to the Northeast or back to the city is the great temptation to stay at the Squire Tarbox for extra days.

THE SQUIRE TARBOX INN, Westport Island, R.D. #2, Box 620, Wiscasset, ME 04578; 207-882-7693. A 9-guestroom (6 rooms with shared baths) restored Colonial farmhouse on Rte. 144 in Westport, 8 mi. from Wiscasset. Modified American plan. All lodgings include continental breakfast. Breakfast served to houseguests only. Open from May 15 to end of Oct. Exploring, towns, beach, and harbors nearby. No pets. Bill and Karen Mitman, Innkeepers.

Directions: Take Rte. 1 north from Brunswick to Rte. 144, 7 mi. north of Bath. Follow Rte. 144 to Wiscasset-Westport Bridge. Inn is located 6 mi. south of bridge on Westport Island.

For B&B rates, see Index.

SURRY INN
Surry, Maine

On a beautiful, sunny day in June, I visited this neat little inn on Contention Cove in Maine's Blue Hill area, and was pleased to find that Peter Krinsky has made a very welcome country inn out of this home, which was originally built in 1834 and once served as a lodging for steamship and stage passengers from Boston and Bangor. Its rolling lawns slope down to a private beach on the cove, near the old steamship landing.

There are eight very attractive, light and airy guest rooms in the main house, as well as five in another cottage, many of them with a view of the Cove. They are furnished with an assortment of Maine upcountry furniture, some decorated with stenciling. There is stenciling around the window and door frames in one guest room, something I've never seen before. The pattern is repeated on the top of a painted chest.

Peter went to some lengths to assure me the Surry Inn is a full-service inn, not only serving breakfast to houseguests, but also a rather extensive dinner to the public. I noted that the reviewer from the *Maine Times* has given it very good marks for freshly baked crusty bread and several main dishes, including scallops Niçoise. I'd like to go back some time and try the medallions of pork in ginger cream.

I'm delighted to report that the Surry Inn, bright as a new penny, has found a dedicated innkeeper and should flourish for many years to come.

SURRY INN, P.O. Box 25, Surry, ME 04648; 207-667-5091. A 13-guestroom (most with private baths) country inn on the water about 5 mi. from Ellsworth on the Penobscot peninsula in the Blue Hill area. Open year-round. Breakfast is included in room rate. Dinners served every night. Conveniently located to enjoy all of the many recreational, cultural, and historic attractions in the area. Able to accommodate children over 5. No pets. Peter Krinsky, Innkeeper.

Directions: From the south, follow Rte. 1 north; 7 mi. north of Buckport, turn right onto Rte. 176 and follow it to its end. Turn left onto Rte. 172 and be at the inn in 2½ mi.

For B&B rates, see Index.

TOPSIDE
Boothbay Harbor, Maine

The subtitle for this place is "What a View," and from my vantage point looking out from the top floor of this three-story summer hotel at Boothbay Harbor, I could certainly re-echo the sentiments. It was truly an impressive view of the harbor, the fishing boats, sailboats, and moorings.

All of the bedrooms in the main building are cheerful, clean, and bright, and many have a water view. They all have private baths and each room is equipped with a four-cubic-foot refrigerator. Rooms are in other large cottages scattered around the rather spacious lawns with large porches that also share the view of the harbor.

Breakfast is not served at Topside; however, morning coffee is offered and there are several restaurants within walking distance recommended by the management.

TOPSIDE, McKown Hill, Boothbay Harbor, ME 04538; 207-633-5404. A 9-guestroom summer hotel/motel located at a high point overlooking Boothbay Harbor. Open from May 15 to mid-Oct. Conveniently located for all of the recreational and cultural attractions. No pets. Rates particularly attractive after Labor Day. Mr. & Mrs. Newell J. Wilson, Owners/Managers.

Directions: From U.S. 1 follow Rte. 27 to Boothbay Harbor through the village and look for a sign on the left that says "McKown Hill."

For Lodging rates, see Index.

THE WATERFORD INNE
East Waterford, Maine

The Oxford Hills in southwestern Maine is another one of those very rare places which have not really been discovered as yet. It's just slightly off the regular tourist path, and as a result there's a wonderful unspoiled feeling about the forests, rolling fields, pleasant lakes, and small hidden villages that add to the fun of backroading.

The Waterford Inne sits atop a hill with sweeping views down the valley and to the ridge beyond. The house was built in 1825 and the five original bedrooms have been augmented by four rooms in a wing leading out to a handsome red barn.

The keepers of this inn are a mother and daughter from Oradell, New Jersey, Barbara and Rosalie Vanderzanden, for whom the inn is a second career.

The inn is open year-round, with the exception of eight weeks, beginning March 1. There is good cross-country and downhill skiing in this area.

A good night's sleep in the peaceful Oxford Hills usually generates hearty appetites which are more than satisfied with the full breakfasts which are prepared by Rosalie and served by Barbara.

THE WATERFORD INNE, Box 49, East Waterford, Maine 04233; 207-583-4037. A 9-room farmhouse-inn in the Oxford Hills section of southwestern Maine, 8 mi. from Norway and South Paris. Closed Mar. 1 to April 30. Breakfast and dinner served to travelers by reservation. European plan. Within a short distance of many recreational, scenic and cultural attractions in Maine and the White Mountains of New Hampshire. Cross-country skiing and badminton on grounds. Lake swimming, golf, rock hunting, downhill skiing, hiking, canoeing nearby. No credit cards. Alcoholic beverages not served. Well-behaved pets welcome. Rosalie and Barbara Vanderzanden, Innkeepers.

Directions: From Maine Turnpike: use Exit 11, follow Rte. 26 north approximately 28 mi. into Norway, then on Rte. 118 west for 8 mi. to Rte. 37 south (left turn). Go ½ mi., turn right at Springer's General Store, up the hill ½ mi. From Conway, New Hampshire: Rte. 16 to Rte. 302 east to Fryeburg, Me. Take Rte. 5 out of Fryeburg to Rte. 35 south, thence to Rte. 118, which is a left fork (with Rte. 35 going right). Continue on Rte. 118 east, past Papoose Pond camping area, then watch for right turn onto Rte. 37. Go ½ mi. to Springer's General Store. Take immediate right turn, ½ mi. up hill.

For B&B rates, see Index.

ROBERT MORRIS INN
Oxford, Maryland

The town of Oxford has a history far in advance of the Revolutionary War and it's always a marvel to me that this little village has managed to stave off the encroachments of contemporary living, such as the fast-food restaurant and the chain motel. I daresay it is much the same as it has been for the last 150 years, and even more. It is also accessible by a tiny auto ferry.

The Robert Morris Inn is on the banks of the Tred Avon River and was built prior to 1710 by ships' carpenters, using wooden-pegged paneling, ships' nails, and hand-hewn beams.

In addition to lodgings in the main building, guests are accommodated in the Lodge, located a short distance away on a point of land overlooking the bay. There are other accommodations in waterfront buildings as well, and some rooms have private porches overlooking the Tred Avon.

A full, à la carte breakfast is served in the warm-hued Tap Room, and features a great many unusual dishes, such as a seafood omelet, Eastern Shore scrapple, sausage, corn muffins, and toasted high-fiber granola.

Anyone wishing accommodations in the high summer season should reserve by March or April, even for midweek stays. If possible, arrive in time for dinner, it's worth it.

ROBERT MORRIS INN, Oxford, Md. 21654; 301-226-5111. A 36-room (28 rooms with private baths; 8 rooms with shared baths) village inn in a secluded Colonial community on the Tred Avon, 10 mi. from Easton, Md. European plan. Breakfast, lunch, and dinner served to travelers daily. Open year-round except Christmas. Tennis, golf, sailing, swimming, and bicycles nearby. No pets. Kenneth and Wendy Gibson, Innkeepers.

Directions: From Delaware Memorial Bridge, follow Rte. 13 south to Rte. 301 and proceed south to Rte. 50, then east on Rte. 50 to Easton. From Chesapeake Bay Bridge, follow Rte. 50-301 to Rte. 50 and proceed east to Easton. From Chesapeake Bay Bridge Tunnel, follow Rte. 13 north to Rte. 50 and proceed west to Easton. From Easton, follow Rte. 322 to Rte. 333 to Oxford and inn.

For B&B rates, see Index.

AUTUMN INN
Northampton, Massachusetts

Northampton is a beautiful, rather engaging town located on the banks of the Connecticut River and is a gateway to many intriguing travel possibilities. Route I-91, the north and south highway from New York to Vermont, intersects with Route 9 which leads eastward through Amherst, Brookfield, Ware, and Worcester, and west to Williamsburg, Goshen, and the Berkshires. It's a community where there is a very pleasant blending of "town and gown" since it is the home of Smith College. Four other colleges and prep schools are also nearby.

There couldn't be a better setting for the Autumn Inn than where it is located in the quiet residential area of Northampton, almost a part of the Smith campus. There are pleasantly landscaped grounds on all sides and a welcome heated swimming pool in the rear.

Innkeepers Vince and Irene Berger have really put a great deal of their own lifestyle into the Autumn Inn. For one thing they both are very much interested in art, and many of the bedrooms have prints, lithographs and collotypes by Norman Rockwell, Eric Sloan, Raymond Hull, and David Lee.

Particular care has been taken in furnishing the bedrooms, and each is done in a different theme. Five rooms are furnished entirely with furniture from the Hitchcock chair and furniture factory in Connecticut. Another room has furniture from Heywood Wakefield in Vermont. Every bedroom has a private bath and an individually controlled temperature.

An à la carte breakfast is served in a pleasant dining room, and the menu offers a variety of appetizing items, including country pancakes served with melted butter and maple syrup, french toast, and various egg dishes. There is a tempting luncheon menu, too.

AUTUMN INN, 259 Elm St., Northampton, Massachusetts 01060; 413-584-7660. A 30-room inn located in one of western Massachusetts' most gracious towns. Breakfast and lunch served every day of the year. Smith College, The University of Massachusetts, Amherst College, Hampshire College, Mt. Holyoke College, Deerfield Academy, and Williston Academy, all within a short drive. Swimming pool. Downhill and xc skiing nearby. No pets. Vince and Irene Berger, Innkeepers.

Directions: From I-91 take the exit marked "Northampton Center" (Exit 18) turn west on Rte. 9 through the center of the town and look for a red brick building on the north side of the street.

For Lodging rates, see Index.

BAY BREEZE GUEST HOUSE
Monument Beach, Cape Cod, Massachusetts

I would imagine that most of the visitors to Cape Cod cross over one of the two bridges and then follow Route 6 out toward Provincetown, heading for the villages and communities on the south shore. Others turn south toward Woods Hole to catch the ferries to the islands.

An alternate possibility is to follow Route 28A to Monument Beach Village to get a taste of what Cape Cod was like at the turn of the century at the Bay Breeze Guest House.

You'll know you're in the right place when you get to the old railway station at Monument Beach and there, just across the tracks, is a rambling old guest house which is kept each summer by Joe Rogers, a former teacher and education counselor who says he's retired to work here harder than ever.

It's a big house where families formerly spent the summertime. Now Joe has turned it into a comfortable old guest house where there are complete kitchen facilities. You can borrow the dishes, have space in the refrigerator, and cook three meals a day if you really want to. There's also a bath and shower downstairs when you come off the beach.

The feeling here is of being in grandmother's house with bric-a-brac galore. The walls and ceilings are all tongue and groove, and the wall hangings are in the same genre.

Some of the bedrooms face the bay and accommodate three or four beds. It's a nice place for a family to spend a few days because it's just a few steps to the semi-private beach and a large grassy area for baseball and frisbee throwing.

This is a quiet and more serene aspect of Cape Cod.

BAY BREEZE GUEST HOUSE, P.O. Box 307, Monument Beach, Cape Cod, Ma. 02553; (summer) 617-759-5069 or (spring) 617-275-7551. A 7-bedroom guest house (share 3 bathrooms). Open from June through October. No meals served, but kitchen facilities and refrigerator are available. Convenient for all of the Cape Cod cultural, recreational, and historic attractions. Semi-private beach nearby, particularly safe for children. No pets. No credit cards. Joseph and Mildred Rogers, Proprietors.

Directions: Cross the Bourne Cape Cod Canal bridge, take right at the rotary at the end of the bridge and follow Shore Rd. to Monument Beach.

For Lodging rates, see Index.

THE BRAMBLE INN
Brewster, Cape Cod, Massachusetts

The little country road that leads from Mid-Cape Highway over to Brewster is a real pleasure. It's known locally as Harwich Road because it goes from Brewster to Harwich on the South Shore. I suppose in Harwich it's known as the Brewster Road. For the interested traveler, it's also known as Route 124.

Off this road, there are many lovely homes, pleasant views, a fruit and vegetable stand, some great bike trails, and the Lake Pleasant General Store, an experience in itself.

Since my last visit to the Bramble Inn, there have been some changes. Ruth and Cliff Manchester are the new owners, and Cliff explained some of the differences to me. "The dining room has changed completely. All of the rooms have been redone, with a little bit more formal atmosphere. We now have a four-course prix fixe dinner menu that varies almost nightly."

The lodging rooms at the top of the stairs have flowered wallpaper, antiques, country furniture, and share two baths. There is a definite tilt to the doors and floors, adding to the fun. There are five additional lodgings, three with private baths, in the 1849 House just two doors away.

The inn's sunny porch is the setting for breakfast, featuring fresh fruit, homemade muffins, and coffee or tea.

THE BRAMBLE INN, Rte. 6A, Main St., Brewster, Cape Cod, MA 02631; 617-896-7644. A 7-guestroom village inn in the heart of one of Cape Cod's North shore villages. Lodgings include continental breakfast. Dinner served Tues. thru Sun. Open year-round. Swimming, sailing, water sports, golf, recreational, and natural attractions within a short drive. Adjacent to tennis club. Small, intimate inn does not meet needs of most children. No pets. Cliff and Ruth Manchester, Innkeepers.

Directions: Take Exit 10 from Rte. 6. Follow Rte. 124 to Brewster to the intersection of Rte. 6A (4 mi.). Turn right, ¹⁄₁₀ mi. to inn.

For B&B rates, see Index.

BROOK FARM INN
Lenox, Massachusetts

Sitting and listening to the birds in a garden with trees and plantings that create the effect of a woodland glade can sometimes give you all the "escape" you need. Brook Farm Inn has several pleasant groupings of outdoor furniture in just such a setting, along with a hexagonal-shaped swimming pool.

The tall yellow house with its peaked roof, dormers, porches, and bay windows is everything one would expect of a Victorian "summer cottage." The high ceilings, tall windows, fireplaces, and spacious rooms provide a perfect background for the many antique furnishings Betty and Bob Jacob have collected over the years.

Bearing witness to the wide interests of the innkeepers are the baby grand piano, the stereo with a wide collection of everything from Mozart to Sondheim, and the books in fine old glass-fronted bookcases, among which are 500 volumes of poetry.

Floral is the word for the eight guest rooms on the second and third floors, with pretty wallpapers and fabrics. The bridal suite is delightful with wing chairs, a working fireplace, an antique mirror, and a little step stool to reach the high canopied bed.

Breakfast might include fresh-squeezed orange juice, strata, french toast with strawberries, scrambled eggs and sausages, sourdough pancakes, and spinach soufflé.

BROOK FARM INN, 15 Hawthorne St., Lenox, MA 01240; 413-637-3013. A 12-guestroom (private baths) Victorian B&B in a busy, attractive village in the Berkshires. Full breakfast included in tariff. Open year-round. Minimum required stay of 3 nights on weekends in July and Aug. Heated swimming pool on grounds. Tanglewood within walking distance. Berkshire Theatre Festival, Jacob's Pillow, and all Berkshire cultural, natural, and historic attractions nearby. Children over 15 accepted. No pets. Betty and Bob Jacob, Innkeepers.

Directions: From the south, take Rte. 23 or Rte. 7 to Great Barrington, proceeding north on Rte. 7 to Rte. 7A in Lenox. At the monument in Lenox, take the street to the left of the monument and turn left immediately. Down the hill, take the first right turn onto Hawthorne St. Brook Farm is on your left. From the Mass. Tpke., take Exit 2 at Lee and follow Rte. 20 west about 4 mi. Turn left at Walker St. (Rte. 183) and continue to Lenox and the monument. Follow above directions from monument.

For B&B rates, see Index.

BULL FROG BED & BREAKFAST
South Ashfield, Massachusetts

Lucky, indeed, the traveler who finds himself on Route 116, which starts in Adams, Massachusetts, runs across part of the Berkshires into the Pioneer Valley, and continues on through Amherst. I say lucky, because it's one of the best paved back roads that I've ever encountered. For one thing it passes through the village of Ashfield, in itself a real treat, with several unspoiled little shops, including Mr. Smither's Metal Restoration Emporium, and a bona fide country store. Interestingly, the town hall steeple is of Christopher Wren design.

Continuing east on Route 116, look for the sign saying "Bed and Breakfast" at a bend on the left-hand side of the road. This is where Lucille and Moses Thibault have decided to open up the second floor of their 225-year-old farmhouse to bed-and- breakfast guests.

The house is wonderfully furnished with country things, including many splendid country antiques. The guest has a choice of a bedroom with a king-sized bed or still another bedroom with two double beds. A spacious bath with shower is shared.

When I asked Lucille about breakfast, she replied, "Anything." This translates into any kind of eggs and bacon, homemade muffins, homemade jams and jellies, or even pancakes or french toast. I'll let her explain all that to her guests.

Like the nearby Parson Hubbard House, a few miles north, this is a real bed-and-breakfast-home experience. My guess is that there will be many people who seek it out for a second visit.

BULL FROG BED & BREAKFAST, South Ashfield, MA 01330; 413-628-4493. A 2-guestroom (shared bath) bed-and- breakfast home on an exceptionally beautiful paved back road in western Massachusetts. Open all year except Jan., Thanksgiving, Christmas, and New Year's. Room rate includes breakfast; only meal served. Convenient for visits to nearby Five College area in Amherst and Northampton and easily accessible to some splendid backroading adventures. Swimming pond on grounds, shared with frogs. Babies and young children easily accommodated. No pets. No credit cards. Lucille and Moses Thibault, Proprietors.

Directions: From I-91 (north and south) follow Rte. 116 through Conway and continue on looking for B&B sign on right. From Rte. 9 (east and west) turn off on Rte. 112 at Goshen. Continue to Rte. 116 passing through Ashfield and look for B&B sign on left.

For B&B rates, see Index.

CANTERBURY FARM
Becket, Massachusetts

Nature lovers, bird watchers, hikers, and skiers would be in seventh heaven here in the woods on this 200-acre tree farm, where they might glimpse deer, turkeys, black bears, raccoons, porcupines, owls, and hawks.

A short distance off a main highway on a well-kept dirt road that is drenched in glorious colors in the fall, this circa 1780 farmhouse sits amidst giant maples, beautiful birches and pines, and a country garden of rhododendron, day lilies, and columbine.

Adele and Ralph Burgess found the house in 1940, and while they summered here, pumping their water from the well, they gradually stripped coats of paint from the wide pine floorboards and layers of wallpaper from the walls, bringing it back to its Colonial origins and adding modern conveniences. Their daughter, Linda, was married here in the garden in 1985, and now Linda and her husband, Dave Bacon, have turned the house into a bed and breakfast.

Outside views can be glimpsed through the original wavy glass of the 12-over-12 windows in the cheerful dining room, with its Early American maple furniture, hand-braided rug, and Franklin stove. Linda serves buffet breakfasts here of, possibly, a scrambled eggs and bacon dish, pancakes, or french toast, along with her homemade zucchini bread or muffins, juice, and coffee or tea.

Most guests run off to do all the things one does of a summer day in the Berkshires, but I'd be content to loll on the chaise under the pine tree, enjoying the lovely breeze, the pure air, the birds, the hum of bees. . . .

CANTERBURY FARM, Fred Snow Rd., Becket, MA 01223; 413-623-8765. A 5-guestroom (private and shared baths) circa 1780 Colonial farmhouse on 200 acres in the woods on the eastern edge of the Berkshires. Complimentary breakfast. Open year-round. Ski-touring center with ski and boot rentals, instruction, and 6 mi. of trails on grounds. Canoe also available. Applachian Trail, Jacob's Pillow, 5 summer camps, lake swimming, boating, horseback riding, tennis, 9-hole golf nearby. Tanglewood 30 min. away. No pets. Smoking in dining room only. Diane and Dave Bacon, Hosts.

Directions: From Boston, take Mass. Tpke. to Exit 2 (Lee). Turn left to Rte. 20 east and continue to Bonnie Rigg corner, turning left on Rte. 8 north for 5 mi. Fred Snow Rd. is on the left approx. 50 ft. before Cripple Creek Country Store. Make a very sharp left turn up the hill ⅕ mi. to Canterbury Farm. From NYC, take Rte. 23 to Hillsdale to Rte. 7. In Stockbridge, take Rte. 102 to Rte. 20 and proceed as above.

For B&B rates, see Index.

THE CAPTAIN FREEMAN INN
Brewster, Cape Cod, Massachusetts

Brewster in general and the Captain Freeman Inn in particular seem ideal for a family trip to the Cape. Breakwater Beach is an easy walk. There is a local Museum of Natural History and a Sealand. The general store with its potbelly stove and penny candy is just steps away from the inn, and the inn has its own swimming pool.

Captain Freeman built his elegant house in 1860, sparing no expense in adding architectural niceties such as the two-tone inlaid wood floors and imported plaster moldings. It became a guest house in 1944 and had since slipped into a discouraging condition, when John and Barbara Mulkey decided to give up the government hustle of Washington, D.C., for the quiet independence of a country inn. Their restoration is a continuing process, and the basic character of the house is being well maintained.

Children will love the trundle beds. Books and games fill the shelves of the cozy nook on the upstairs front landing, and bicycles are available for guests' use.

Continental breakfast, served on the porch overlooking the pool or inside, around an antique oak table, consists of juice, homemade muffins or coffee cake, and coffee, tea or milk.

THE CAPTAIN FREEMAN INN, 15 Breakwater Rd., Brewster, MA 02631; 617-896-7481. A 10-guestroom inn (7 private and 1 shared baths) on the green in the center of Brewster, Cape Cod, about two hours from Boston. Open year-round. Continental breakfast included in rate. No other meals served. Many good restaurants in the area. Swimming pool. Beach, museums, shops, antiquing, all nearby. Children over 12 welcome. John and Barbara Mulkey, Innkeepers.

Directions: Once on Cape Cod, take Rte. 6 (Mid-Cape Hwy.) to Exit 10 (Rte. 124). Follow Rte. 124 north to Brewster and Rte. 6A. Turn right on Rte. 6A, go 100 yards to Breakwater Rd. and turn left. The General Store is on the corner. Captain Freeman Inn is on the left.

For B&B rates, see Index.

CAPTAIN ISAIAH'S HOUSE
Bass River, Cape Cod, Massachusetts

This is one of those delightful homes built by a Cape Cod sea captain in the early 1800s. It is a gracious village guest house in an elegant old residential section of the Cape—a white clapboard home on a very quiet street a few steps from the Bass River.

The six guest rooms (four with working fireplaces) are airy and comfortable and furnished in antiques, including braided rugs, quilts, and Hitchcock chairs.

Breakfast includes at least two kinds of homemade bread, as well as blueberry buckle, a special crumb cake. Marge Fallows says, "We just leave it on the table and wander in and out of the dining room or garden chatting with people about what they are going to do as they get acquainted with each other. We're all very informal and on a first-name basis."

Like many other Americans who are guest-house enthusiasts, the Fallows traveled in Europe enough to know that for economy and comfort and meeting the locals, there's nothing like a B&B lodging. "We view ourselves as a kind of adult hostelry where guests receive more than they expect and depart feeling as though they have been visiting in a house of distant relatives who wanted them to enjoy themselves."

Captain Isaiah's House is a second career for this family, and they have found out what things work best for both themselves and their guests.

I discovered that Marge and Alden Fallows at one time had been very close neighbors of mine in the Berkshires, and it was indeed a pleasure to renew our acquaintance under such very pleasant circumstances.

CAPTAIN ISAIAH'S HOUSE, 33 Pleasant St., Bass River, Ma. 02664; 617-394-1739. A 6-bedroom guest house (4 with fireplaces) sharing 4 full baths. Breakfast is the only meal served. Open from May to Oct. Conveniently located to enjoy all of the recreational, cultural, and historical attractions in the Falmouth-Hyannis-Chatham area of the Cape. No credit cards. Alden and Marge Fallows, Innkeepers.

Directions: Take Mid-Cape Highway (Rte. 6) to Exit 8 (So. Yarmouth). Turn right and go to traffic lights on Rte. 28, cross lights, and take second left at Akin Ave. Captain Isaiah's House is on the left at the corner of Akin and Pleasant Sts.

For B&B rates, see Index.

THE CAPTAIN'S HOUSE INN OF CHATHAM
Chatham, Cape Cod, Massachusetts

Dave and Cathy Eakin are typical of many people who have fled the so-called corporate life and sought out a new career in innkeeping. They were indeed fortunate to find an exceptional house with over two acres in Chatham, one of Cape Cod's most picturesque villages.

The site was chosen in 1839 by Captain Harding for his home, and the antiques that the Eakins had been collecting for years, including many family heirlooms from their home in Yardley, Pennsylvania, found a most appropriate setting.

The bedrooms are named after the ships in which the good captain sailed, and they are now adorned with handsome flowered wallpapers and even some pictures of the captain's ships.

Besides comfortable bedrooms in the main house, there are additional accommodations in the Carriage House and in the Captain's Cottage.

Cathy does all the baking for breakfast and she explains that she puts out two or three sweet breads, including Dutch Apple Loaf. She also makes homemade blueberry muffins. Breakfast is taken in the dining room, which has a splendid view of the lovely garden.

Dave and Cathy are both sailors and they recently bought a 23-foot Seacraft Powerboat to take their guests out on when time permits.

The Captain's House is a real home-away-from-home and either Dave or Cathy are always on hand to attend to guests' special needs.

THE CAPTAIN'S HOUSE INN OF CHATHAM, 371 Old Harbor Rd., Chatham, Cape Cod, MA 02633; 617-945-0127. A 10-guestroom (all private baths) Cape Cod bed-and-breakfast inn. Additional accommodations are available in adjacent historic buildings. Open all year, but closed Dec. 1 to Feb. 15. Breakfast included in room rate. All of the historic, cultural, and scenic attractions of Cape Cod are most convenient. Beaches, golf, tennis courts, antiquing are nearby. No facilities for children under 12, except in weekly rental of Carriage House. No pets. Dave and Cathy Eakin, Innkeepers.

Directions: Follow the mid-Cape Hwy. (Rte. 6) to Exit 11 and follow Rte. 137 for 3 mi. until it intersects with Rte. 28, at which point take a left, heading toward Chatham for 2 or 3 mi. At the rotary with the Mobil and BP stations, look for a sign that says Orleans-Rte. 28 south. The inn is ½ mi. farther on the left.

For B&B rates, see Index.

CENTENNIAL HOUSE
Northfield, Massachusetts

Northfield is a very pleasant village in New England that you wouldn't find except by accident, or if by some chance you were looking for a good preparatory school for your children. The main street is really Route 63, going north and south, with pleasant 19th-century homes set well back from the roadway. There are lots of big trees and lovely gardens.

The prep school here is Northfield Mt. Hermon, which has flourished for over a hundred years and definitely sets the tone of the village. It certainly sets the tone of Centennial House, because for many years it was the residence of the president of the school. At one time it was even used as a dormitory. However, the history of the house actually goes back to 1811.

Of particular interest is a wonderful, big living room, with a marvelous fireplace, beautiful wood paneling, and heavy overhead beams, that certainly invites visits in the winter. Off the living room is an extremely comfortable summer porch, with quite a few rocking chairs overlooking the lawn and the western view.

The guest rooms are different sizes and shapes, and I particularly remember the twin-bedded room on the side with its own bath, and another very pleasant front guest room with a big brass bed and an optionally shared bath.

The continental breakfast features three kinds of homemade bread.

Northfield is just a few miles to the east of I-91, and Centennial House would make a very pleasant, surprising, and accommodating overnight stop whether you are headed for the north or back to the city. Incidentally, Route 63 is an excellent back road, continuing north, parallel to I-91 and rejoining it near Walpole. It is well worth the few minutes more to make the journey.

CENTENNIAL HOUSE, 94 Main St., Northfield, MA 01360; 413-498-5921. A warm, inviting, 6-guestroom (3½ baths) bed-and-breakfast inn in an attractive New England village. Includes continental breakfast. Open all year. Convenient for I-91 travelers. Within a few minutes of Northfield Mt. Hermon School. Skiing nearby. Marguerite L. Lentz, Proprietor.

Directions: Leave I-91 at Northfield exit, go east on Rte. 10, turn north on Rte. 63. Inn is in middle of the town across the street from fire station.

For B&B rates, see Index.

CHARLOTTE INN
Edgartown, Martha's Vineyard, Massachusetts

Like many other houses in Edgartown, which is on the far side of the island of Martha's Vineyard, the Charlotte Inn is a classic three-story white clapboard with a widow's walk.

Guest rooms are individually furnished and great care has been exercised in their decoration. All of them are very quiet and have their own private baths. There is a warm feeling of hospitality and a most romantic atmosphere. Some rooms have working fireplaces for guests to enjoy during the winter and there are quite a few four-poster beds as well.

Many people visit during the so-called off-season, when Edgartown is delightfully quiet and has fewer visitors. Guests enjoy shopping in town, walking along the beaches, bicycling to the many interesting points on the island.

The room rate includes a continental breakfast, which is served in the dining room and might include english muffins or a selection of freshly baked pastries. A full breakfast is also available.

CHARLOTTE INN, So. Summer St., Edgartown, Martha's Vineyard Island, MA 02539; 617-627-4751. A 24-guestroom combination inn-art gallery and restaurant located on one of the side streets in the village of Edgartown, just a few short steps from the harbor. European plan. Rooms available every day of the year. Continental breakfast served to inn guests. Chez Pierre restaurant open for dinner every night in season and on Fri. and Sat. in the off-season. Brunch is offered every Sun. year-round. Other island restaurants open year-round. Boating, swimming, beaches, fishing, tennis, riding, golf, sailing, and biking nearby. No pets. Gery and Paula Conover, Innkeepers.

Directions: Martha's Vineyard Island is located off the southwestern coast of Cape Cod. The Woods Hole–Vineyard Haven Ferry runs year-round and automobiles may be left in the parking lot at Woods Hole. Taxis may be obtained from Vineyard Haven to Edgartown (8 mi.). Check with inn for ferry schedules for all seasons of the year. Accessible by air from Boston and New York.

For B&B rates, see Index.

COBB'S COVE
Barnstable Village, Cape Cod, Massachusetts

The principal road from the mainland out to the end of Cape Cod (really an island) is Route 6. However, taking Route 6A, which runs along the northern shore of the Cape through Sagamore, Sandwich, Barnstable, Yarmouth, Dennis, and Brewster, rejoining Route 6 at the Orleans traffic circle, is a very pleasant and rewarding adventure.

Part of the fun would be to spend a night or two at Cobb's Cove, a very unusual bed-and-breakfast inn in the village of Barnstable.

The interior has exposed beams and beautiful wood with harmonizing accompanying colors of beige, yellow, and tan. Each of the six guest rooms has a full bath, including a whirlpool tub, a dressing room, and air conditioning. Private telephone lines are available for extended stays.

All around the house are shelves and corners filled with books and objects that indicate the eclectic interests of the innkeepers. There are groups of shells and fossils as well as minerals and gems. There are many, many books, including quite a few dealing with the natural and human history of the Cape.

When warm weather arrives at the Cape, the full breakfasts, which are individually prepared, are enjoyed on the sunny terrace. For colder weather the library is ideal. Breakfast includes fresh fruit, eggs done to order, bacon, homemade breads, biscuits, and sometimes cornbread. It's a good time to confer with other guests and map out another delightful day on the Cape.

COBB'S COVE, Barnstable Village, Rte. 6A, Cape Cod, MA 02630; 617-362-9356. A 6-guestroom secluded inn on Cape Cod's north shore. Lodgings include a full breakfast. Houseguests can arrange for dinner. Open every day in the year. Within a short distance of Cape Cod Bay and the Atlantic Ocean, the U.S. National Seashore, and Sandy Neck Conservatory, as well as many museums, art galleries, crafts shops, and other attractions of the Cape. Active sports nearby. No facilities to amuse children at the inn. No pets. Credit cards not accepted. Evelyn Chester, Innkeeper.

Directions: From Rte. 6 (Mid-Cape Hwy.), turn left at Exit 6 on Rte. 132 to Barnstable. Turn right on Rte. 6A, approx. 3 mi. through Barnstable Village, past the only traffic light and turn left just past the Barnstable Unitarian Church, at Powder Hill Rd.; then left at first driveway marked "Evelyn Chester."

For B&B rates, see Index.

COLONEL EBENEZER CRAFTS INN
Sturbridge, Massachusetts

Are you traveling on I-84 between New England and New York, or on the Massachusetts Turnpike, east and west from Boston or the Berkshires? Sturbridge is at the crossroads and hopefully you will arrive in time for afternoon tea, which is a regular feature at the Colonel Ebenezer Crafts Inn.

Assuming reservations have been made, stop first at the reception desk at the Publick House in Sturbridge to get directions to the inn which is about a mile away on top of a ridge in the residential district, away from the highway.

The inn was originally a very picturesque home built in the Colonial manner. It was named after one of the early patriots of Massachusetts, Colonel Ebenezer Crafts.

The living room really invites guests to get acquainted and there is a generously supplied bookcase and stacks of *National Geographics*, which make wonderful bedtime reading.

Each of the ten guest rooms is very light and airy and is furnished in either antiques or good reproductions.

Besides afternoon tea, guests at the inn can also enjoy dinner and lunch at the nearby Publick House as well. Old Sturbridge Village is just down the road.

The continental breakfast is one of the largest I've ever enjoyed. Besides the customary juices, there is also cranberry juice and apple cider in season. The pecan sweet rolls are made fresh every day, as are the blueberry and pumpkin muffins. In winter these are served in a cozy corner, and in the summer on the patio overlooking the swimming pool and garden. Be sure to ask for their scrumptious hot chocolate.

COLONEL EBENEZER CRAFTS INN, c/o Publick House, Sturbridge, MA 01566; 617-347-3313. A 10-guestroom bed-and-breakfast inn in a historic village 18 mi. from Worcester. Old Sturbridge Village nearby. Lodging rates include continental breakfast and afternoon tea. (Lunch and dinner available at nearby Publick House.) Open year round. Swimming pool on grounds. Tennis nearby. Buddy Adler, Innkeeper.

Directions: From Massachusetts Tpke.: take Exit 9, follow signs to Sturbridge on Rte. 131. From Hartford: follow I-84, which becomes I-86. Take Exit 3.

For B&B rates, see Index.

COLONIAL HOUSE INN
Plymouth, Massachusetts

Plymouth still lives, thanks to some entrepreneurs who have restored and recreated Plimoth Plantation where visitors are plunged into the life of Plymouth in 1627. They have also constructed *Mayflower II*, a full-scale reproduction of the type of ship that brought the Pilgrims to the New World in 1620.

I think both of these attractions considerably enhance a visit to the famous Plymouth Rock located on the water's edge in the town harbor.

The Colonial House Inn, just a short distance from Plymouth Rock, has been kept by Oscar and Olga Isaacs for thirty years. The bedrooms and public rooms have an Early American decor, and a swimming pool was added in recent years to the quiet, secluded grounds.

It's located within a short distance of all historical sites, beaches, restaurants, churches, and local entertainment.

Mrs. Isaacs informed me it is most necessary to have advance reservations, and if desired during the peak of the tourist season they should be made many weeks ahead.

Breakfast is not served, but there are several restaurants within a short distance.

COLONIAL HOUSE INN, 207 Sandwich St., Plymouth, Ma. 02360; 617-746-2087. A 5-bedroom guest house (private baths) 1 mi. south of Plymouth Center on Rte. 3A. Open year-round. No meals served, restaurants nearby. Conveniently located to visit Plimoth Plantation, the Mayflower II, and Plymouth Rock. No pets. Oscar and Olga Isaacs, Proprietors.

Directions: Plymouth is located on Rte. 3 south of Boston and north of Cape Cod. Sandwich St. is one of the main thoroughfares of the town.

For Lodging rates, see Index.

COUNTRY INN AT PRINCETON
Princeton, Massachusetts

Route 2, a portion of which has gained considerable fame as the trail used by the Mohawk Indians for many centuries before the arrival of the white man in New England, traverses the nothern part of Massachusetts, near Boston to Williamstown and beyond. It passes quite near Princeton, Massachusetts, one of those delightful villages that have remained relatively undiscovered.

Built in 1890, this gambrel-roofed Queen Anne country mansion has country gardens, rolling lawns, fieldstone walls, and granddad maples. The veranda and garden terrace overlook the pine groves and across a fifty-mile mountainous panorama to the Boston skyline.

The inn is beautifully appointed with collectors' furnishings and antiques. The atmosphere is one of some formality, but also of a great deal of warmth.

There are six very romantic and spacious parlor-rooms provided to travelers. A continental breakfast is served in the privacy of these guest bedrooms, often in front of windows with ample views of the countryside or forest.

In addition to the special ambience and decor, the inn has a restaurant that is rated as one of the top five restaurants in the Boston metropolitan area, with kudos from the *Boston Globe, Boston Magazine, Bon Appétit*, and *Gourmet*. The menu changes with the season and focuses on native New England bounty.

COUNTRY INN AT PRINCETON, 30 Mountain Rd., Princeton, MA 01541; 617-464-2030. A 6-guestroom late-Victorian mansion, 50 mi. from Boston and 14 mi. north of Worcester. Open all year except Christmas. Dinner reservations Wed. thru Sun. evenings. Sunday brunch. Closed Mon. and Tues. Near Wachusett Ski Resort, Audubon and Wildlife Society, Mt. Wachusett State Reservation. Tennis, swimming, fishing, hiking, nature trails nearby. Downhill and xc skiing 3 mi. Lodging for couples only, no accommodations for children. Sorry, no pets. Don and Maxine Plumridge, Innkeepers.

Directions: From Boston, follow Rte. 2 west to Rte. 31 south. From Conn. and Mass. Tpke. (90), follow Rte. 290 north to Rte. 190; then Exit 5 and continue on Rte. 140. At Rte. 62 turn left 4 mi., and turn right at post office and flashing light. With the town common on your left, the inn is 200 yards up Mountain Rd. on right.

For B&B rates, see Index.

THE FEDERAL HOUSE INN
South Lee, Massachusetts

In the very few years since they opened their restaurant at the Federal House Inn, Robin Slocum and Kenneth Almgren have achieved an enviable reputation for having one of the top restaurants in the Berkshires. Kenneth, who trained with the great Swiss chef Ans Benderer, has become known for his light, but masterful, touch with his menu of fourteen entrées and fourteen appetizers.

The three intimate dining rooms have a pristine quality, with their white walls, white tablecloths, lacy white curtains, and fresh cut flowers. One room is distinguished by an elegant black marble fireplace, another has a crystal chandelier, while the third has a charming French candelabra of brushed brass leaves intertwined with pink porcelain roses.

The Federal House Inn is an early 19th-century red brick building with beautiful white columns set back from the street and surrounded by large pine and copper beech trees. The bedrooms are roomy and are simply, but comfortably, furnished with bright and cheerful wallpapers and comforters and some antiques. All have private bathrooms and air conditioning. Robin notes that one room is graced with her great-great grandfather's sleigh bed.

Breakfast, included with the room charge, is served in the sunny dining room in summer and in the front dining room with a cheery fire in the winter. The fare is virtually unlimited, with fresh fruit, fresh-squeezed juice, eggs, kippers, Canadian bacon, sausage, potatoes—red flannel hash, french toast, and, of course, coffee.

THE FEDERAL HOUSE INN, Route 102, South Lee, Ma. 01260; 413-243-1824. A 7-bedroom inn (all private baths) in a quiet Berkshire community adjacent to the village of Stockbridge. Open for lodgings year-round. Summer weekends, 3-day minimum. Top-rated restaurant closed Tues. during off-season. Near all of the historic, cultural, and natural attractions of the Berkshires—Tanglewood, Berkshire Theatre Festival, Jacob's Pillow, Shakespeare & Company, Norman Rockwell Museum. Backroading, tennis, golf, swimming, boating, downhill and xc skiing nearby. Not suitable for children. No pets. Robin Slocum and Kenneth Almgren, Innkeepers.

Directions: From NYC take Taconic Pkwy. north to Rte. 23 east to Rte. 7 north to Stockbridge. Bear right on Rte. 102 east, about 1½ mi. Inn is on left. From Boston, take Mass. Tpke. west to Exit 2 in Lee; follow Rte. 102 west for 3 mi. to inn on right.

For B&B rates, see Index.

THE GOLDEN GOOSE
Tyringham, Massachusetts

There aren't very many old, sequestered, and unspoiled villages like this one in New England. Established in 1739, Tyringham is tucked into a picturesque, narrow valley between high hills with meadows and fields where cattle graze. Just four miles off the main east—west highway across the state (the Massachusetts Turnpike), Tyringham is a tiny Berkshire village that "time forgot."

Just across the road from the town hall sits the Golden Goose, resurrected from its boarding-house-for-women days by Lilja Hinrichsen, a Californian with Swedish antecedents, and her husband, Joseph Rizzo, of Italian descent. This sweet, old-fashioned house bears the imprint of the tastes of this cosmopolitan and diverse pair, starting with the four flags hung from the eaves in front of the house: the original 13-star American flag and the flags of Massachusetts, Sweden, and Italy.

Inside, there are many interesting and amusing touches in the cozy rooms, with their slanty wide-board floors. Having had antique shops in New York City, Lilja, as might be expected, has filled the house with antiques of all kinds. In the pleasant, comfortable guest rooms, there are antique washstands and dressers; one room has an Eastlake bed, another has a little school desk and seat and Lilja's hand-stenciled border around the wall. The bathrooms are modern and attractively wallpapered—one reflects Lilja's and Joe's interest in opera, with paper that is covered with reproductions of old opera playbills.

The continental breakfast, served at the long oval table with a collection of wonderful antique spindleback chairs, might be broiled grapefruit, fruit compote, melon, homemade biscuits or muffins, served with Joe's homemade marmalade or other jams, and a variety of coffees and teas.

THE GOLDEN GOOSE, Tyringham Rd., Tyringham, MA 01264; 413-243-3008. A 5-guestroom (3 private baths) cozy, mid-18th-century house on the Appalachian Trail in the Berkshire Hills of western Mass. Studio apt. also available. Complimentary breakfast and evening refreshments. Open year-round. Minimum 2-night stay in July & Aug.; 3 nights on holiday weekends. Volleyball, badminton, croquet, kites on grounds. Tanglewood, Tyringham Cobble, and all the Berkshire cultural and recreational attractions nearby. No credit cards. Lilja Hinrichsen and Joseph Rizzo, Innkeepers.

Directions: Take Mass. Tpke. and Exit 2 (Lee). Turn left to Rte. 102, and almost immediately turn left on Tyringham Rd. Continue 4 mi. to village center.

For B&B rates, see Index.

GRAY MANOR
Gloucester, Massachusetts

Gloucester, like Rockport, Essex, and Manchester, is on Cape Ann, which has 25 miles of coastline including America's oldest and most historic fishing port, 6 scenic harbors, 24 coves, and over 20 sandy beaches. Inland lie quiet, picturesque towns and dense woodlands, many of which have been set aside as public preserves.

Gray Manor is in a residential area of Gloucester on a rather quiet street. For a number of years it was, like many other Gloucester buildings, a private home. About twenty-four years ago Mrs. Madeline Gray decided to take in a few roomers, and it's been a most pleasant experience for her and Gray Manor guests ever since.

During the height of the summer season rooms of any kind are at a premium in Gloucester, and Mrs. Gray's rather modest place is a great joy with decorations and furnishings in each guest room in carefully coordinated decorator colors, air conditioning, and color TV. There are also six efficiencies with stoves and refrigerators and all the utensils that you'll need. Shopping is done at the local supermarket. Mrs. Gray has gas-fired barbecues in the backyard, as well as a large patio, for her guests' convenience. She does not serve breakfast and maintains that Charlie's Restaurant can do a much better job than she can.

Another great advantage here is that it is about a three-minute walk down the hill to a really white sandy beach that has a sort of hometown feeling about it and is a little less "touristy" than some of the others.

GRAY MANOR, 14 Atlantic Rd., Gloucester, MA 01930; 617-283-5409. A 3-guestroom (6 efficiencies) home. Some rooms have a deck. Open May 15 to Oct. 31. Within 3-min. walking distance of an excellent beach and convenient drive to several others. Near Beauport Museum and other Cape Ann attractions. Deep-sea fishing and whale watching. No pets. No credit cards. Please telephone in advance to avoid disappointment. Mrs. Madeline Gray, Proprietor.

Directions: From Boston follow Rtes. 1 and 128 north to Gloucester. At rotary go half around to second rotary, half around that rotary down the hill to a set of lights, and follow through to a second set. Then take a left on Bass Ave. and continue past Charlie's Place. Take the first road on the right, which is Atlantic Rd., and a left at the top of the hill. Gray Manor is on the corner of Atlantic Rd. and Beach Rd., parking on the side.

For B&B rates, see Index.

HAUS ANDREAS
Lee, Massachusetts

As a pleasant resort area with beautiful mountains, rushing streams, placid lakes, and delightfully cool evenings in midsummer, the Berkshires were discovered by affluent Bostonians in the 19th century. They built mansions, which they called "cottages."

Some of the atmosphere of the "cottages" has been preserved at Haus Andreas, an impressive house with extensive grounds, where Queen Wilhelmina and Princess Juliana of the Netherlands summered in 1942.

An elegant and stylish country mansion, it has broad lawns for croquet and badminton, as well as a tennis court and a heated swimming pool. The living room has a frequently played piano, a welcome fireplace, stacks of classical stereo records, and shelves of books.

Three of the six generous-sized guest rooms have their own fireplaces. All have a view of the grounds, forest, and the Berkshire hills leading up the Tyringham Valley.

The proprietors are Lilliane and Gerhard Schmid. Gerhard is from Germany and has gained an international reputation as the chef and owner of the Gateways Inn in nearby Lenox.

The continental breakfast features fresh, warm croissants and muffins, english muffins, or toast, with fresh-squeezed orange juice and coffee, and is served in the very pleasant dining room with a view overlooking the grounds.

A policy of required minimum stays is in effect for the various seasons and holidays; inquiries should be made in advance.

HAUS ANDREAS, Stockbridge Rd., Lee, MA 01238; 413-243-3298. A 6-guestroom country guest house located in the quiet outskirts of a Berkshire village. Open year-round. Tennis, heated pool, croquet, and badminton on grounds. Tanglewood, Jacob's Pillow, and the Berkshire Theatre Festival nearby. Unsuitable for children under 10. No pets. Lilliane and Gerhard Schmid, Proprietors.

Directions: From NYC via Taconic Pkwy. and Rte. 23 to Rte. 7, north through Stockbridge. Bear left at fire station, continue on Rte. 7 for 0.8 mi. Turn right on Stockbridge Rd. (unmarked) and go 1.9 mi. to Haus Andreas on the right. From Boston follow Mass. Tpke. to Lee Exit 2. Go west on Rte. 20 for 1 mi. to first stop sign. Go straight ahead up the hill 1 mi. to Haus Andreas (on the left) beyond Greenock Country Club.

For B&B rates, see Index.

THE INN AT STOCKBRIDGE
Stockbridge, Massachusetts

I'm personally quite familiar with the Inn at Stockbridge. Many years ago it was rented for the summer by some good friends of mine and I enjoyed pleasant evenings on the porch watching the sun go down and listening to the sounds of birds at eventide. On brisk evenings, my host always lit a fire in the fireplace, and the low ceiling, many books, and comfortable furniture encouraged us to much good conversation.

The scene is exactly the same today, except that Lee and Don Weitz have found a way to extend to many guests the warmth and hospitality of this big, lovely, old white house with the Grecian pillars and wonderful, large rooms.

There are seven guest rooms, some unusually large, and six-and-a-half baths. These have all been very comfortably furnished and all have splendid views of the Berkshire Hills.

Some guests might find that lazing by the pool in summer or exploring the twelve acres is as much as they care to do; others will find that the Berkshires offer a wide variety of choices for recreation and entertainment.

The gourmet breakfast that might include a soufflé or even eggs Benedict is served in the dining room or on the porch. The meal is graciously served with cloth napkins, bone china, and silver accessories. Complimentary wine and cheese is served each afternoon.

THE INN AT STOCKBRIDGE, Rte. 7, Stockbridge, MA 01262; 413-298-3337. A 7-guestroom (5 with private baths) country house about 1 mi. north of the center of Stockbridge. Closed during winter months. Lodgings include a full breakfast. Convenient to all of the Berkshire cultural and recreational attractions. A summer swimming pool on the grounds. No pets. Lee and Don Weitz, Innkeepers.

Directions: From New York City: take any of the main highways north to Stockbridge. Look for small sign on the right-hand side of Rte. 7 after passing under the Massachusetts Turnpike 1 mi. north of Stockbridge. From Mass. Turnpike: exit at Lee, take Rte. 102 to Stockbridge and turn right on Rte. 7 going north for 1 mile as above.

For B&B rates, see Index.

THE INN ON COVE HILL
Rockport, Massachusetts

Pirate treasure may have been used to build the Caleb Norwood, Jr., mansion that is now the Inn on Cove Hill. Of course, that was in 1791. However, the story of the father who died poor, but whose sons were suddenly wealthy, still lingers. Happily for those seeking the richness of comfort plus historic tradition, the three-story Federal home is a B&B, painstakingly restored and decorated with family antiques and Laura Ashley prints.

The location is perfect for those who would be in the center of artistic Rockport. Motif Number One is only steps away, and Bearskin Neck with its shops and galleries is just beyond. The view from the inn deck is enough to drive anyone to camera, if not to sketch pad or canvas and brushes. Good restaurants are within immediate walking distance; Old Garden Beach is a stroll.

In summer, breakfast is served under umbrellas in the daisy garden. In winter, trays are brought to the bedrooms. Either way, the china is English bone and the muffins fresh and home-baked.

The eleven bedrooms are both cozy and lavish with handmade quilts and afghans. Each has a small TV set and comfortable chairs. Downstairs, there is a guest living room with especially choice antique furniture and plenty of books.

Marjorie and John Pratt are world travelers as well as down-home New Englanders. This is reflected in their eclectic collection of art work, as well as the care they take of their guests.

THE INN ON COVE HILL, 37 Mt. Pleasant St., Rockport, MA 01966; 617-546-2701. An 11-guestroom (9 with private baths) bed-and-breakfast inn in the center of Rockport, walking distance to everything. Breakfast is the only meal served, but many restaurants are nearby. Closed November to mid-February. No pets. No children under 10. No credit cards. Marjorie and John Pratt, Innkeepers.

Directions: As an alternative to driving, guests can arrive by train from Boston and will be picked up at Rockport Station. By road, follow Rte. 128 (Boston's inner beltway) to its northern end, then Rte. 127 to 127A. Once in Rockport Center, 127A takes a right, becoming Mt. Pleasant St.; the inn is on your left.

For B&B rates, see Index.

THE LION'S HEAD INN
West Harwich, Cape Cod, Massachusetts

Speaking of the Lion's Head Inn, the innkeeper-in-residence on the particular day of my visit, said, "It's a romantic inn with a sense of history." A well-turned phrase if ever I heard one.

Here's a bed-and-breakfast inn that makes the most of its quiet location and historic past. The rooms all have significant names and antiques to match. For instance, in the Morning Room the Cape Cod sunlight and antiques provide the guests with a pleasant countryside feeling, and the Map Room, which was once used as a study for the original owner, sea captain Thomas L. Snow, has maps showing the oceans of the world. Captain Snow's Suite has two rooms and an adjoining bath.

The house was built in the early 1800s as what is known locally as a "Cape half-house." It's been enlarged several times over the years and has a sort of rambling feeling now.

One of the more pleasant aspects is a social hour in which the innkeepers introduce incoming guests, and plans are made by all concerned for a special Cape Cod dinner. Many guests enjoy a quiet evening of entertainment with games such as backgammon, chess, and so forth, in the living room. In one corner there is a jigsaw puzzle of a line drawing of the inn and a list of the times that some people have taken to put it together. The best time so far was nine minutes; perhaps one of the readers of this book can do it in less.

THE LION'S HEAD INN, 186 Belmont Rd., West Harwich, Cape Cod, Ma. 02671; 617-432-7766. A 5-room inn on a quiet street in a south shore village on Cape Cod. Cottages which can accommodate children available in the summer. A full breakfast is the only meal served. Near all of the Cape Cod attractions, including beaches, biking, museums, and antiquing. No credit cards. No pets. Laurie and Djordje Soc, Innkeepers.

Directions: From Rte. 6 take Exit 9 (Dennis) to the right and go about ½ mi. to stoplight. Turn left (this is marked West Harwich). Continue on this road (Upper County Road). This will converge with Rte. 28 on the line between Dennis and Harwich. Go two blocks on Rte. 28; look for Belmont Rd., on the right at the gas station. Houses on Belmont are numbered.

For B&B rates, see Index.

MERRELL TAVERN INN
South Lee, Massachusetts

The Merrell Tavern Inn, built in 1794, is an excellent example of a historic building that is being both preserved and granted a new lease on life as a bed-and-breakfast inn.

With the assistance and guidance of the Society for the Preservation of New England Antiquities (SPNEA), the owners of the inn, Charles and Faith Reynolds, have done a remarkable job of preserving the Federalist atmosphere of this former stop on the Boston-Albany stagecoach run. In recognition of their restoration of the 188-year-old inn, the Massachusetts Historical Commission has presented them with a Preservation Award.

The red brick exterior with first- and second-floor porches has remained unmarred by the passing years, and in repainting and installing new plumbing and wiring, the Reynoldses were careful to maintain the house's architectural and visual integrity.

Fabrics and original paint colors have been duplicated wherever possible, and the Reynoldses have supplemented their own collection of antiques with additional circa-1800 pieces. In addition to the four bedrooms created from the third-floor ballroom (quite a customary feature in early inns) there are five guest rooms on the first and second floors with views either of the main road passing through the village of South Lee or of the Housatonic River in the rear.

A picture in *Historic Preservation* shows Faith Reynolds serving breakfast in the original barroom, where perhaps the only remaining circular Colonial bar in America is still intact, even to the little till drawer. The original grain-painted woodwork is protected by an easement.

MERRELL TAVERN INN, Main St., Route 102, South Lee, MA 01260; 413-243-1794. A 9-guestroom (private baths) beautifully preserved and restored historic tavern in a quiet Berkshire village. Lodgings include a full country breakfast; no other meals served. Open every day except Christmas Eve and Christmas Day. Holiday weekends, 2-night minimum stay; July, Aug., 3-night weekend minimum stay. Within a convenient distance of all of the Berkshire cultural, natural, and recreational activities, including Berkshire Theatre Festival, Tanglewood, and Shakespeare and Company. No pets. Charles and Faith Reynolds, Innkeepers.

Directions: South Lee is on Rte. 102, midway between Lee and Stockbridge.

For B&B rates, see Index.

THE MORGAN HOUSE
Lee, Massachusetts

Lee, Massachusetts, is a bustling, independent-minded community located near the point where the Massachusetts Turnpike, running east and west, crosses over Route 7, one of the principal north-south roads to and from New York City.

The Morgan House has an impressive record of continuous hospitality since 1853, when it was established as a stagecoach inn. Horace Greeley, Buffalo Bill Cody, Robert E. Lee, President Ulysses S. Grant, and George Bernard Shaw all wrote their names in the register, and many of these pages are now used to paper the small comfortable lobby of this village inn. You can see them for yourself.

The inn is a three-storied, clapboard building with a second-floor gallery that is a very pleasant place to enjoy breakfast or take some refreshments at any time of the day.

Today, the innkeeping tradition is being well preserved by Beth and Bill Orford, an enthusiastic young couple who have infused this venerable old hostelry with some of their youthful zest and vigor. They have completely redecorated all of the thirteen guest rooms.

The luncheon and evening meals feature such New England fare as prime ribs of beef and New England duckling, and are served in the cozy, low-ceilinged dining room. A semi-full breakfast is offered to houseguests with hot or cold cereal, fresh fruit, home-baked breads, sweet rolls, juice, coffee, and boiling water in which you may cook your own morning eggs.

THE MORGAN HOUSE, Main St., Lee, MA 01238; 413-243-0181. A 13-guestroom village inn (1 private, 4 shared baths). Open every day including holidays. Near all of the Berkshire attractions including Tanglewood, Jacob's Pillow Dance Festival, the Berkshire Theatre Festival, South Mountain Chambe. Music Concerts, the Norman Rockwell Museum, Chesterwood, Hancock Shaker Village, and Berkshire Garden Center. Swimming, boating, canoeing, horseback riding, alpine and xc skiing nearby. No pets. Beth and Bill Orford, Innkeepers.

Directions: From Mass. Turnpike: Lee is Exit 2. From Rte. 7: follow Rte. 102 from Stockbridge to Lee.

For B&B rates, see Index.

MOSTLY HALL
Falmouth, Cape Cod, Massachusetts

Although Mostly Hall was built in 1849 by a Yankee ship captain for his New Orleans bride, there is an English country house feeling to the place. It may be the beautifully restored and maintained front garden with its rolling lawn and dogwood. Few Cape Cod houses are set so majestically back from the road.

Ginny Austin sends her guests off each morning with a full breakfast, too, though it is a good deal more imaginative than standard English fare. Ginny's french toast stuffed with cream cheese and walnuts and topped with an apricot-orange sauce so inspired one guest he has put it on the menu of his own restaurant.

There is much to do in this corner of the Cape: warm water beaches, a four-mile ocean bike path, and the ferries to Martha's Vineyard and Nantucket Islands (wonderful day trips, if not longer). Mostly Hall is right on the historic village green with the shops, galleries, and summer theater of Falmouth close at hand. Of course, you can also spend the day playing croquet, reading, or visiting with other guests on the veranda of Mostly Hall.

There are five room with private baths, plus two with shared bath, all furnished with antiques and country pieces and many personal touches.

MOSTLY HALL, 27 Main St., Falmouth, MA 02540; 617-548-3786. A 7-guestroom inn (5 with private bath) on the village green in Falmouth, Cape Cod. Approx. 90 min. from Boston, Newport, or Provincetown. Open year-round. Full breakfast included in rate. No other meals served. Located in a historic and scenic area convenient to Woods Hole and ferries to Nantucket and Martha's Vineyard. No children under 16. No pets. No credit cards. Jim and Ginny Austin, Innkeepers.

Directions: As you approach the Cape, follow signs that say Cape Cod and the Islands to Hwy. 28. Mostly Hall is 14 mi. from Bourne Bridge. Turn left on 28-S; Mostly Hall is 4th house on the right. Off-street parking in rear.

For B&B rates, see Index.

180

MUNRO'S AMERICAN HOUSE
Pittsfield, Massachusetts

If the Shakers and their furniture are of interest to you, then you will enjoy talking with Barbara and John Munro, who are closely associated with the Hancock Shaker Village on the outskirts of Pittsfield. John not only is on the board of trustees of the Shaker Village, but in his spare time is also a cabinetmaker who specializes in Shaker furniture. In fact, guests enjoy the continental breakfast sitting on the Shaker bench at the Shaker table that John built.

Set in a neat and attractive yard on a busy main thoroughfare, Munro's bed and breakfast is a homey, comfortable turn-of-the-century house with two young maple trees at the sidewalk, and a pair of lovely peony bushes flanking the steps to the front porch.

Barbara, who is a surgical nurse, told me that she and John love to go to auctions, where they have collected much of the furniture in the four guest rooms. The living room provides a pleasant place for guests to gather, with a large bay window handsomely framed by fringed curtains from the famous Country Curtains (which had its beginnings in nearby Stockbridge). There are marble-topped tables, a quaint Victorian rocker, and a TV ingeniously hidden behind a door in the corner fireplace.

John and Barbara just finished a very light and cheery breakfast room with an outside deck, which is a great place not only for breakfast but also for relaxing in the evening, looking out over the back lawn.

MUNRO'S GUEST HOUSE, 306 South St. (Rtes. 7 and 20), Pittsfield, MA 01201; 413-442-0503. A 4-guestroom (2 shared full baths, 1 private ½ bath) comfortable B&B, a few blocks from the downtown area of the Berkshires' largest town. Complimentary continental breakfast. Open year-round. Hancock Shaker Village, Bousquet Ski Area and Racquet Club, Norman Rockwell Museum nearby. Convenient to all Berkshire attractions. No pets. No credit cards. Smoking in common rooms only. John and Barbara Munro, Innkeepers.

Directions: Going north from Lenox on Rtes. 7 and 20, continue approx. 1 mi. past Berkshire Life building and Pittsfield Country Club. Watch for small sign on left side, just before large tan brick church (St. Teresa's). Turn left into driveway and continue to parking area in rear of house.

For B&B rates, see Index.

NAUSET HOUSE INN
East Orleans, Cape Cod, Massachusetts

The Nauset House Inn on Cape Cod is almost three-quarters of the way to Provincetown and within a short walk of Nauset Beach, which has some of the best surf in New England. A building of some gratifying antiquity, it is small enough for everyone to become quite friendly. The guest rooms are in the main house and the carriage house.

The owners of the Nauset House are Albert and Diane Johnson, who have brought many special touches to this old inn, including several examples of stained glass, as well as some stenciling done by their daughter, Cindy.

Furnishings in the inn are a most intriguing mixture of antiques, with some contemporary pieces providing an interesting contrast. There's also a marked involvement in various crafts, as well.

It is obvious that Diane Johnson is very fond of flowers, because they are found in profusion in every guest room and public room in the inn.

Every late afternoon, guests gather on the patio, in the fascinating glass greenhouse, or in the living room to enjoy hors d'oeuvres and refreshments. This is the time when newcomers are introduced.

On warm mornings, a full breakfast can be enjoyed on the apple-tree-shaded terrace; on chilly mornings, everyone repairs to the brick-floored dining room where there is a crackling fire.

Early risers can stroll through the grounds into the glass conservatory where coffee is available until breakfast time, when different types of omelets or french toast with maple syrup are served. Breakfast is not included in the room rate.

NAUSET HOUSE INN, P.O. Box 774, 143 Beach Rd., East Orleans, Cape Cod, MA 02643; 617-255-2195. A 14-guestroom country inn, 90 mi. from Boston, 27 mi. from Hyannis. Breakfast (not included in room rate) served to inn guests only. No other meals served. Some rooms with shared bath. Open daily from Mar. 31 to Oct. 31. Within walking distance of Nauset Beach. Riding and bicycles nearby. No children under 12. No pets. Albert and Diane Johnson, Innkeepers.

Directions: From the Mid-Cape Hwy. (Rte. 6), take Exit 12. Bear right to first traffic light. Follow signs for Nauset Beach. Inn is located ¼ mi. before beach on Nauset Beach Rd.

For Lodging rates, see Index.

THE OLD INN ON THE GREEN
New Marlborough, Massachusetts

New Marlborough is located in an unusually beguiling part of the Berkshires, and this inn is situated on a village green around which are several very venerable 18th- and early 19th-century homes, some with Palladian windows and others with pillars and pilasters. The church with the white steeple serenely oversees the scene which is highly paintable and photographable.

Writing about this tiny inn which was already 100 years old in 1869, a travel writer of the day commented: "Pleasantly situated in the hilltown of New Marlborough, travelers will find here comforts for both man and beast. Summer boarders will find the society good, the air pure, trout brooks near, the surrounding scenery magnificent, and everything provided for their accommodation and comfort."

I can well imagine that the most frequent reaction of guests walking for the first time into the kitchen of this old inn is one of complete delight. The chances are that some goodies in the bake-oven are enveloping the room with divine aromas.

There are five bedrooms sharing three baths, and everything has undergone a complete refurbishing.

One of the innkeepers, Leslie Miller, is an expert baker and has been putting her professional baking ovens to good use.

Besides the really authentic antique feeling of this inn, one of the most enticing features is the continental breakfast. There are always croissants and another type of coffee cake from Leslie's oven.

On Friday and Saturday evenings, a prix-fixe dinner is offered (by reservation only) in the newly restored tavern room, at the harvest table in the dining room, and in the private parlor.

THE OLD INN ON THE GREEN, Star Rte. 70, New Marlborough, Massachusetts 01230; 413-229-7924. A 5-room (shared baths) 18th-century tavern well-preserved and restored on green in a secluded Berkshire village. Very convenient for all of the Berkshire summer and winter recreational and cultural activities including Tanglewood, Berkshire Theater Festival, and Jacob's Pillow. Downhill and cross-country skiing. No pets. No credit cards. Open all year. Leslie Miller and Bradford Wagstaff, Innkeepers.

Directions: From the Taconic Parkway (en route from New York) use Exit 230. Follow Rte. 23 east through Great Barrington toward Monterey. Branch off on Rte. 57 and continue 5.7 mi. uphill to the New Marlborough Village Green. It is a large white building with an upper gallery.

For B&B rates, see Index.

THE OLD MANSE INN
Brewster, Cape Cod, Massachusetts

In my search for appropriate bed-and-breakfast accommodations on Cape Cod, I was delighted to find a few that were open year-round. Such is the case with the Old Manse Inn, on the north shore of the Cape in the very pleasant village of Brewster.

The white clapboard building is set off by towering trees, many varieties of flowers, and a pleasant garden table with an umbrella. Some people were just coming back from a swim and sun bathing on the beach, which is one of the things you do here in July and August. In other seasons you also go to the beach, but to walk rather than swim.

I sat with innkeeper Sugar Manchester in the typical New England living room. As she regaled me with some extremely amusing stories about innkeeping, the cat waited by the door to be petted, as she told me, by each and every guest.

This is the Manchesters' home, and there are tennis rackets, hockey equipment, a surfboard, and other signs that there are young people in the house.

There are patchwork quilts and flowery New England wallpaper in the guest rooms. Some have very attractive nonworking fireplaces. The living room fireplace is used in winter and on cool spring and fall nights.

A breakfast featuring warm muffins, juice, cereal with fresh fruit, and coffee, tea, hot chocolate, or decaffeinated is served at the long dining table where guests sit and chat. Evening meals are also available by reservation.

Among the collection of good watercolors and American primitives, there is a small sign with the aphorism, "Mingle with the Beautiful, the Famous, and the Polished."

THE OLD MANSE INN, Route 6A, 1861 Main St., Brewster, MA 02631; 617-896-3149. A 9-guestroom (private baths) inn in a picturesque Cape Cod village. Open year-round. Breakfast is included in the cost of the room. Dinner also served. Conveniently located for all of the Cape Cod historic, recreational, and cultural attractions. No pets. Sugar and Doug Manchester, Innkeepers.

Directions: Take Exit 9 from Rte. 6 left onto Rte. 134 and follow to the intersection of 6A. Turn right to Brewster.

For B&B rates, see Index.

ONE CENTRE STREET INN
Yarmouth Port, Cape Cod, Massachusetts

An old Colonial home seems an appropriate stopping place along the Old King's Highway (Route 6A) of Cape Cod. Yarmouth Port is just about midway, too, and two of the best restaurants on the Cape are within walking distance of the One Centre Street Inn.

Barbara Mutchler agrees that the neighborhood's gourmet standards contribute to the very special breakfasts she serves her guests. In addition to a select fresh fruit compote, there may be fresh apple cake, pineapple cake, or a similar home-baked delight. Her omelets come in countless variations. Since many guests are sent by local residents, arrangements may be made to invite their friends to breakfast for a modest charge.

The rooms are light and airy. The inn supplies bikes for rides down the street to Grays Beach or just around town. On the occasional rainy day, there is a pleasant fire and lots of good books. For a family holiday, it would be hard to beat either the guest quarters or the location. Antique and crafts shops are nearby, as well as the village historical sites. Yarmouth Port also has an enormous used book store, guaranteed to keep any True Reader entranced for days. At the same time, you are only minutes away from the faster-paced south shore of the Cape.

ONE CENTRE STREET INN, One Centre St. and Old King's Hwy. (Rte. 6A), Yarmouth Port, MA 02675; 617-362-8910. A 5-guestroom (3 rooms with private baths) inn located on the quiet north side of Cape Cod. Open year-round. Breakfast is the only meal served, but it is full and special. Menus on hand for the many fine restaurants nearby. Barbara and Donald Mutchler, Jack Williams, Proprietors.

Directions: Coming on the Cape across Sagamore Bridge, go about 16 mi. on Rte. 6 (mid-Cape Hwy.) to Exit 7. Turn right at the end of the exit ramp and proceed on Willow St. to Rte. 6A. Turn right again and continue approx. 1½ mi. Inn is on your left at the corner of Centre St.

For B&B rates, see Index.

PARSON HUBBARD HOUSE
Shelburne Centre, Massachusetts

The Mohawk Trail (Route 2) began as an Indian path centuries ago, and runs the sixty-three-mile distance between Petersburg, New York, and Orange, Massachusetts. It is one of the most scenic highways in the East and is particularly popular during the fall foliage season, when every accommodation has been reserved for months in advance.

Happy, indeed, is the traveler who in any season finds accommodations with Jeanne and Richard Bole at the Parson Hubbard House, a beautiful white clapboard house with a slate roof, built in 1774. The white plaster walls, blue overhead beams, and twelve-over-twelve windows, as well as the four gorgeous maples on the front lawn, set the atmosphere. Richard and Jeanne provide an accompanying spirit of hospitality and enthusiasm that rounds out the whole experience.

Two guest rooms with double beds and one guest room with a twin bed share two baths. There are augmented by most cordial sitting rooms and a Keeping Room that is the pride and joy of the house.

Jeanne's breakfasts include fresh raspberries and blueberries from the garden, baked apples done on the wood stove, truly wonderful pancakes served with maple syrup from the trees surrounding the house, and many other irresistible offerings.

By the way, the town of Shelburne Falls has the famous Bridge of Flowers, and the entire area abounds in beautiful scenic views. The Parson Hubbard House is a mere half-mile from Route 2—but so-o-o pastoral.

PARSON HUBBARD HOUSE, Old Village Rd., Shelburne Centre, MA 01370; 413-625-9730. A 3-guestroom (shared bath) guest home in a former parsonage high atop a hill, just a few minutes from Rte. 2 (the Mohawk Trail). Breakfast is only meal served. Open spring, summer, and fall. Located a short distance from historic Old Deerfield, the 5-college area, and in the summer, the Mohawk Trail Concerts. Children welcome. No pets. Please, no smoking preferred. No credit cards. Mr. and Mrs. Richard Bole, Proprietors.

Directions: Traveling west on Rte. 2, turn right at Little Mohawk Rd., and continue for ¼ mi. to Old Village Rd. (first right). Turn right; 4th house on left.

For B&B rates, see Index.

186

PISTACHIO COVE
Lakeville, Massachusetts

Here is a pleasant bed-and-breakfast place just one mile from Route 140, and only a few miles from I-195 or I-95. Set at the end of a winding driveway in a two-acre pine grove with extensive lake frontage, the house is a contemporary building with barnboard siding. The furnishings reveal a flair for decorating in the bright, homey interior.

Dana Lapolla offers her guests a warm welcome with refreshments appropriate to the season, to be enjoyed on the porch in the summer or in front of a cheery fire in the winter.

The immaculate bedrooms are outfitted with all manner of conveniences for the comfort of her guests—electric blankets, backrests, alarm clocks, intercoms, telephones, radios and color TVs with earphones, and adjustable tables for snacking or reading.

Dana's breakfasts are exceptionally hearty with eggs or quiche, a variety of sausages and ham, homemade coffeecake, or fruit compote topped with homegrown blueberries.

All holidays are celebrated with a passion with special foods and decorations. The private beach offers swimming, boating, and fishing in the summer, and skating and ice boating in the winter. A state park is just twelve miles away.

As if that isn't enough, Dana also has a private kennel where a guest may keep a pet. Pistachio Cove is listed with Pineapple Hospitality, a New England reservation service.

PISTACHIO COVE, Lakeville, Ma. (Mailing address: Box 456, East Freetown, Ma. 02717); 617-763-2383. (Also listed with Pineapple Hospitality, 617-990-1696 or 997-9952.) A 4-bedroom home with 230-ft. lake frontage on Long Pond, approx. 1 mi. from Rte. 140; 45 mi. from Boston and 10 mi. from New Bedford. Open 365 days a year. Exceptionally hearty breakfast included in room rate. Dinner may be arranged by special request. Private beach affords swimming, boating, fishing, water-skiing, and winter ice sports. Freetown State Park 12 mi. Dana Lapolla, Hostess.

Directions: From New York City, take I-95 north to I-195 east to Rte. 140 north. Take Exit 9 (County Rd.-Long Pond) and turn right, continuing on County Rd. for just over 1 mi. to black mailbox on left marked "Dana's" (in hot pink). Follow driveway approx. 500 ft. to Pistachio Cove. From Boston, take I-93 (Southeast Expwy.) to Rte. 24 to Rte. 140 south. Take Exit 9 (County Rd.-Long Pond) and turn left, continuing on County Rd. as above.

For B&B rates, see Index.

THE RALPH WALDO EMERSON INN
Rockport, Massachusetts

Massachusetts' North Shore is a most interesting combination of history and recreation. The small towns each have facts and legends in their past that bear retelling.

The Cape Ann section includes Gloucester, Essex, Manchester, and Rockport, and sea fever dominates these communities with their sun-bathed beaches, exciting rock formations, and casual disarrangement of fishing shacks and old homes.

Rockport has a fetching harbor and winding streets and a great number of year-round artists and craftsmen. The Rockport Art Association exhibits all year.

The Ralph Waldo Emerson, in Pigeon Cove in Rockport, is owned by the Wemyss family, who are also the proprietors of the Yankee Clipper. It is a traditional North Shore hotel and an expansive view of the water may be enjoyed while rocking on the broad front porch.

There is also a heated salt-water swimming pool and a most popular year-round sauna, as well as the opportunity to stroll the streets of this quiet seaside town.

The guest rooms are of a seaside-resort nature, reminiscent of the turn of the century, but with modern private baths.

RALPH WALDO EMERSON, 1 Cathedral Ave., Rockport, MA 01966; 617-546-6321. A 36-guestroom oceanside inn, 40 mi. from Boston. Modified American and European plans. Breakfast and dinner served daily from July 1 to Labor Day; B&B rates only during remainder of the year. Closed Nov. thru mid-May; open weekends in April and early May. Pool, sauna, and whirlpool bath on grounds. Tennis, golf nearby. Courtesy car. No pets. Gary and June Wemyss, Innkeepers.

Directions: Take I-95 to Rte. 128 to 127 (Gloucester). Proceed 6 mi. on Rte. 127 to Rockport and continue to Pigeon Cove.

For B&B rates, see Index.

RIVER BEND FARM
Williamstown, Massachusetts

"Home is the sailor, home from the sea..." could be the song sung by David and Judy Loomis when they return to their 1770 Georgian bed-and-breakfast farmhouse after one of their year-long schooner trips 'round the world. David is a schooner captain and Judy is an able sailor, and every so often they set out from their quiet lives in Williamstown for adventure on the high seas.

But the rest of the time, says David, they enjoy working on the continuing restoration of their center-chimney Colonial home, built by Col. Benjamin Simonds, and used as a staging area for the militiamen who went to fight the British at the Battle of Bennington.

The Keeping Room has extra-wide paneled pine walls and a huge, old brick fireplace, where the crane holds a blackened iron kettle, old iron ladles, tongs, and such. This is the setting for breakfasts of fruit and juice, homemade breads and muffins, granola, honey from the Loomis beehives, homemade jams, and milk, coffee, or tea. Two rockers in front of the fireplace and the simple lines of authentic early Colonial furnishings lend an air of peace and tranquility in this history-laden house, which is listed in the National Register of Historic Places.

Downstairs is a large bedroom with a double bed, a crocheted bedspread, braided rug, Colonial candelabra, and another large working fireplace. The downstairs bathroom is most Colonial.

Up the twisty stairs, tucked away in various nooks and crannies, are four more simple bedrooms furnished in "early attic" with double or single beds, and another bathroom with a tub, in which, David says, "some guests like to have a good soak."

RIVER BEND FARM, 643 Simonds Rd. (Rte. 7), Williamstown, MA 01267; 413-458-5504 or 458-3121. A 5-guestroom (2 shared baths) 1770 farmhouse in a quiet, classic college town in the northern Berkshire hills. Breakfast included in room rate. Closed from Thanksgiving to April 1. Williamstown Theatre Festival, museums, college cultural events, Bennington, Vt., shops and antiquing nearby. Well-behaved children accepted. No pets. No credit cards. Smoking not encouraged in guestrooms. Dave and Judy Loomis, Innkeepers.

Directions: Going north, Rte. 7 makes a left turn at intersection with Rte. 2 in Williamstown. Continue north on Rte. 7 for 1 mi. House is just beyond bridge on left. Coming from the east on Rte. 2, turn right onto Rte. 7 in Williamstown.

For B&B rates, see Index.

ROCKY SHORES
Rockport, Massachusetts

Low stone walls, a broad green lawn, a porch that invites rocking and conversation, and an excellent ocean view looking out towards Thatcher Island, to the only twin lighthouses on the Atlantic coast, are some of the hallmarks of this summertime bed-and-breakfast inn on Cape Ann.

Innkeepers Renate and Gunther Kostka have put much of themselves into this inn, and the furnishings and decorations of the living room, dining room, and bedrooms attest to their special attention and quiet good taste.

In addition to water-view bedrooms in the main house, there are several housekeeping cottages scattered throughout the property.

There's much to do for guests of all ages, including the use of several beaches, tennis courts, beach walking, and all of the interesting sights to be found in the village.

A full breakfast, which includes freshly made muffins, popovers, and cakes, is served each morning. Please make advance reservations for stays during July and August. Cape Ann is particularly pleasant during June, September, and October.

ROCKY SHORES, Eden Rd. Rockport, Ma. 01966; 617-546-2823. A waterside inn with 9 rooms and 12 housekeeping cottages. Open from Easter to the end of Oct. Breakfast is the only meal served. Conveniently located to enjoy all of the Cape Ann cultural, recreational, and historical attractions. Beach walking, swimming, sailing, tennis nearby. Excellent beaches. No pets. Renate and Gunther Kostka, Innkeepers.

Directions: From downtown Rockport, go south on Rte. 127A (South St.) 1½ mi. to Eden Rd. Turn left onto Eden Rd. for ½ mi. along ocean to Rocky Shores.

For B&B rates, see Index.

THE SALEM INN
Salem, Massachusetts

Although Salem was founded only six years after the Mayflower arrived at Plymouth and was of great importance in the seafaring history of the Colonies, it is best known today for seven months in 1692, when it was the center of witch hysteria. There are preserved and reconstructed relics of this period, but save time for the Peabody Museum with its memorabilia of the China Trade days, for Nathaniel Hawthorne's House of the Seven Gables, and for exploring the maritime historical sites.

The Salem Inn has been at the center of town for 150 years, though only recently transformed into an inn. For most of its existence, it was three separate townhouses, a fact which is reflected in its interior differences today.

There are twenty-three rooms, including two suites, eleven fireplaces, and twelve small kitchens. Since many of the rooms are quite large, cribs and rollaways may be brought in to accommodate a family. All rooms are equipped with telephone and color television.

Breakfast, lunch, and dinner are available in the Courtyard Cafe, which boasts two original brick dutch ovens.

Much is within easy walking distance of the inn. The Witch House is on the opposite corner; Chestnut Street with its beautiful Colonial homes is a block away; the museums are a five-minute stroll.

THE SALEM INN, 7 Summer St., Salem, MA 01970; 617-741-0680. A 23-guestroom (all private baths) inn in the center of Salem. Open all year. Breakfast, lunch, and dinner served to travelers. Very convenient for sightseeing, restaurants, shopping. Parking on street and in nearby municipal lot. Air conditioned. Cribs and rollaways available. No pets. Diane Pabich, Innkeeper.

Directions: The Salem Inn is located on Rte. 114 (Summer St.) at the corner of Essex. Take the Rte. 114 exit from either Hwy. 128 (Boston Beltway) or Hwy. 1 and follow signs to Salem.

For B&B rates, see Index.

SEACREST MANOR
Rockport, Massachusetts

The flag of Bermuda was flying with the American flag over the Yankee Brahmin mansion one sunny May morning. It turned out to be just one more way the innkeepers were signaling welcome to Bermudian guests, a nice gesture, though not surprising. There is a stately-home atmosphere of appropriate greeting for all who stop at Seacrest Manor. With its highly polished furniture and paneled walls, this is not Colonial Rockport, but early 20th-century North Shore coupled with English country house, a tribute to living well.

Two acres of gardens and woodland, afternoon tea by the fire, and a library full of books almost make the delights of the area superfluous. Almost, but not quite. The views from the sundeck are too appealing—on a clear day you can see Maine.

Breakfast is the only full meal served, and it is an event. Fresh fruit cup, eggs and bacon are supplemented with such house specialties as blueberry-buttermilk pancakes, Irish oatmeal with dates, and corn fritters. However reluctant to leave the charming breakfast room with its garden view, even the most dedicated sightseer can last the morning on such fare.

"Decidedly small, intentionally quiet" is the motto of Seacrest. For the unwinding guests, this is the right idea.

SEACREST MANOR, 131 Marmion Way, Rockport, MA 01966; 617-546-2211. An 8-guestroom (6 with private bath; 2 rooms with private entrance to deck as well) inn in a residential section of Rockport. Open mid-Feb. to Christmas Eve. Full breakfast and afternoon tea included in rate. No other meals served. Located in a historic and scenic area approximately one hour from Boston. No children under 16. No pets. No credit cards. Leighton T. Saville and Dwight B. MacCormack, Jr., Hosts.

Directions: From the end of Rte. 128 (Boston's inner beltway) take Rte. 127A not quite 5 mi. to Rockport. Marmion Way is on your right.

For B&B rates, see Index.

SEEKONK PINES INN
Great Barrington, Massachusetts

Here's a lovely home that was once a country estate, and before that, a large working farm dating back to the 1830s. It sits on four acres of lawn, gardens, and wild-flower meadows in an area of the Berkshires that the Indians called "the place of the Seekonk," the Indian word for wild goose.

The atmosphere could best be described as rambling and friendly. Rooms with both private and semi-private baths are available with a continental breakfast of fresh homemade muffins with homemade jam and coffee or tea. There is a larger, optional, full country breakfast available as well. The specialty of the house is pancakes made from scratch.

The guest rooms are decorated with antiques and old quilts. Several newly decorated rooms feature hand-stenciled walls and drapes. In the winter guests are invited to relax by the raised hearth in the large living room or in the summer to soak up the sun by a welcome swimming pool.

The hosts, Linda and Chris Best, both of whom are musicians, are also avid gardeners and the fresh produce that they carefully nurture is available to their guests at farmstand prices. Imagine taking fresh corn home with you!

An engaging feature of the house is a collection of watercolors by Linda Best. They enhance the living room, dining room, and the guest rooms.

Seekonk Pines Inn is located within a pleasant drive of Tanglewood, Jacob's Pillow, and the Berkshire Theatre Festival. It is also just a few moments from two major alpine ski areas and cross-country skiing is at their doorstep. Bicycles are available along with friendly advice on scenic bike routes and hiking trails in the area.

SEEKONK PINES INN, 142 Seekonk Cross Rd., corner of Rte. 23, Great Barrington, MA 01230; 413-528-4192. A 7-guestroom (some shared baths) guest home set among the pines in a beautiful meadowland, 2 mi. west of Great Barrington. Breakfast is the only meal served. Open year-round. Swimming pool and pleasant walking paths on the grounds. Conveniently located for all the cultural, natural, and recreational attractions of the Berkshires. No pets. No credit cards. No smoking. Linda and Christian Best, Hosts.

Directions: Seekonk Pines is located on the north side of Rte. 23, 2 mi. west of Great Barrington.

For B&B rates, see Index.

1777 GREYLOCK HOUSE
Lee, Massachusetts

When I first moved to the Berkshires I lived across the road from this house for about three years. Historically it is known as the oldest building in Lee, although in the years since 1777 the original structure has been somewhat disguised by Victorian additions and embellishments.

It originally belonged to one of the earliest settlers in Lee, the Bassett family, and I was often a guest of Nancy and Hurlbut Bassett's. We spent many pleasant winter evenings in front of the fireplace in the low-ceilinged beamed living room, and enjoyed sitting in rocking chairs on the sideporch in the summer.

The house is in a very pleasant parklike atmosphere with a circular drive leading up to the sideporch.

Today it is an inviting bed-and-breakfast home with a suite of bedrooms on the first and second floors. All of the rooms are very comfortably and appropriately furnished.

It's open year-round, which is an advantage for summertime visitors headed for nearby Jacob's Pillow or Tanglewood, as well as for winter skiers during Christmas and Washington's Birthday week. There is even a very convenient room to store skis and boots so they are not carried in over the lovely polished hardwood floors.

On the day of my visit, Walt Parry was making bread for the continental breakfast the next morning. He explained that he had for many years been the owner of a restaurant in Lee.

Having enjoyed many pleasant times in this historic house, it gives me a great deal of pleasure to be able to recommend it as a good bed-and-breakfast accommodation in the Berkshires.

1777 GREYLOCK HOUSE, 58 Greylock St., Lee, Ma. 01238; 413-243-1717. A 5-bedroom bed-and-breakfast home on an extremely quiet street in Lee. Most rooms have shared baths. Open year-round. A continental breakfast is the only meal served; however, there are many restaurants nearby. Conveniently located to enjoy all of the cultural, recreational, and natural attractions of the Berkshires. No pets. No credit cards. Terry and Walter Parry, Hosts.

Directions: I would suggest that upon arriving in the town of Lee, the traveler telephone the 1777 Greylock House for expert directions.

For B&B rates, see Index.

STAVELEIGH HOUSE
Sheffield, Massachusetts

"The house named itself," Marion declared, as Dorothy pointed out the name carved in the corner fireplace. Sure enough, in Olde English lettering there was the name "Staveleigh" in bas-relief in the painted oak mantel framed with Welsh tiles. Incontrovertible evidence.

Marion Whitman and Dorothy Marosy welcome their guests into a spacious, open entrance area dominated by a handsome staircase. A sitting room is on the right with the famous fireplace, and on the left is a large dining room with a generous dining table covered with a lace tablecloth. Their furnishings are drawn from family pieces, auctions, and flea markets.

Both Marion and Dorothy like to cook, and their breakfasts are legendary. They'll make just about anything, and often have puffy pancakes, crêpes, cheese stratas, various breakfast meats, homemade muffins, "...or whatever...on rainy days, we go on a baking spree," Marion laughed.

At the top of the handsome staircase is a wide landing, decorated with one of the handmade quilts from Marion's family collection and a window seat covered with more handmade quilted cushions.

The extra-wide floorboards in the bedrooms are painted to match the color scheme of the room. The blue room with pretty white antique wicker furniture from Dorothy's family has its own bath. All of the five bedrooms are nicely decorated, and have good mattresses and reading lamps, which "we think are very important," Marion declared. "And we always have fresh flowers in every guest room," Dorothy added.

A very homey, comfortable place, indeed.

STAVELEIGH HOUSE, Main St. (Rte.7), Sheffield, MA 01257; 413-229-2129. A 5-guestroom (1 private, 2 shared baths) comfortable B&B at the southern tip of the Sheffield village green in the southern Berkshires. Breakfast and afternoon tea included in room rate. Open all year except Thanksgiving Day and from Christmas to New Year's Day. Within an easy drive of all Berkshire attractions and a few miles from Connecticut border towns of Canaan, Salisbury, and Lakeville. No pets. No credit cards. Marion Whitman and Dorothy Marosy, Proprietors.

Directions: From the south, take Rte. 23 out of Hillsdale, N.Y., to Rte. 7. Turn right, approx. 5 mi. to Sheffield. From the east, take the Mass. Tpke. to Lee exit and Rte. 102. Stay on Rte. 102 to Rte. 7 south; continue through Great Barrington to Sheffield.

For B&B rates, see Index.

195

THE SUMMER HOUSE
Sandwich, Cape Cod, Massachusetts

Before arriving at the door of the Summer House, I had already admired it in the pages of *Country Living Magazine*. If you are in love with preserving and restoring old houses or just thinking of redecorating your own home, you owe yourself a stay at the Summer House to see what color and a gift for style can do.

Pamela Hunt did it all herself, too—from the puffy, white balloon curtains to the bold, oversized black-and-white checks on the breakfast room floor. Do ask to see the "before" pictures, and plan on taking lots of notes.

The Summer House is located on the Old Main Street of Sandwich, a few steps from Yesteryears Doll Museum and Dexter's Grist Mill at Shawme Pond. Seventeenth- and eighteenth-century houses and antique shops line the quiet street. Close at hand are Thornton Burgess Birthplace and Museum, Heritage Plantation, and the Sandwich Glass Museum. There are public tennis courts nearby, and Cape Cod Bay is a short walk. The Old King's Highway provides a pleasant scenic drive.

Flowers from Pamela's garden fill the house, and she is collecting period rose bushes for her garden, as much in keeping with the 1835 house as the original woodwork and hardware.

A continental breakfast of fresh fruit, home-baked pastries, and a variety of teas and coffee is served. Sugar-, salt-, and caffeine-free diets are accommodated with advance notice.

True to its name, the Summer House is open May through October. Reserve in advance for this charmer.

THE SUMMER HOUSE, P.O. Box 341, Old Main St., Sandwich, Cape Cod, MA 02563; 617-888-4991. A 5-guestroom (3 baths) guest house in the center of Sandwich Village. Continental breakfast the only meal served, but menus are available for the many fine area restaurants. Open May through Oct. Children under 12 discouraged. No pets. Pamela Hunt, Owner.

Directions: Take Exit 2 off the Mid-Cape Hwy. (Rte. 6) to Rte. 130. Turn left to Sandwich Village 1.3 mi. and bear right onto Old Main St. for 1/5 mi. to the Summer House.

For B&B rates, see Index.

THE TERN INN
West Harwich, Cape Cod, Massachusetts

Here are a few quotations from Jane Myers, describing the Tern Inn, which she and her husband, Bill, are keeping in West Harwich on Cape Cod's southern shore.

"My husband and I are among the lucky dreamers who realized our ambition when we purchased a lovely old inn on Nantucket Sound. We have renovated and refurbished it in keeping with its nearly 200-year vintage. The riff-cut wide pine floors are gleaming and the fifteen windows of the living room are sparkling; the guest rooms are fresh and bright. The daily challenge is to decide which of the muffin and hot bread recipes will become the favorite, and eventually our specialty.

"Our antiques and handmade pieces of furniture have found their proper home. But the ultimate treasure has been the fascinating variety of guests who have come our way."

After my visit, I feel there is nothing more to add, unless it be to mention the blueberry waffles, french toast, and Vermont maple syrup frequently included in the full breakfast. The inn, located about halfway out to the end of the Cape, is less than a half-mile from the beach and there is a very convenient and enjoyable bicycle trail that was formerly the old railroad right-of-way, now black-topped and running for seventeen miles from Dennis to the National Seashore.

For families with children, there are fully equipped various-sized cottages and efficiencies on the grounds, available for late spring, summer, and fall vacations.

The Tern Inn is bascially open year-round, except for a few weeks in the middle of winter. Better phone ahead to make sure.

THE TERN INN, 91 Chase St., West Harwich, Cape Cod, MA 02671; 617-432-3714. A 5-guestroom bed-and-breakfast home (private and semi-private baths) on a quiet street in a south shore village. Cottages also available. Open year-round. Full breakfast is served to inn guests. Most convenient to all of the Cape Cod natural and cultural attractions. Bill and Jane Myers, Innkeepers.

Directions: Follow Route 6 (Mid-Cape Hwy.) to Route 134 (Exit 9). Turn right on Rte. 134 and follow to Rte. 28. Turn left and follow for approx. 2.3 mi. Turn right on either River Road or Chase Street. Both lead to inn.

For B&B rates, see Index.

THORNEWOOD INN
Great Barrington, Massachusetts

Thornewood Inn certainly deserves a place among the many success stories of the reclamation of fine old houses. David and Terry Thorne saw the possibilities in the badly deteriorated building, and in their renovation have stayed close to the basic character of this vintage 1920 Dutch Colonial.

The many-windowed foyer, with its hanging plants, glass étagère, and velvet-covered settee, is but a preface to the refreshingly airy quality of the living room. With double french doors looking out over the expanse of lawn sloping down to a swimming pool, the pretty, flowered wallpaper, the baby grand piano, and the graceful arches framing a windowed hallway, the effect is both gracious and welcoming.

The neat and attractive guest rooms, all with private baths, reflect the 1920s flavor of the house with Maxfield Parrish pictures, an early 1900s cherry mahogany sleigh bed, a 1910 mahogany canopied bed in the master bedroom, and the original chickenwire tile floor with the original pedestal wash basin in one bathroom.

"Some of our most fascinating conversations have happened over breakfast," David told me. "We've had a nuclear scientist, a geologist, a systems analyst, not to mention various doctors, lawyers, and other professionals who have visited us."

Terry prepares breakfast, while David and their two teen-age daughters pitch in. Along with fruit juice, fruit cocktail, and freshly ground coffee, there might be a quiche or other egg dish, home fries, rolls or coffee cake.

THORNEWOOD INN, 453 Stockbridge Rd. (Route 7), Great Barrington, MA 01230; 413-528-3828. An 8-guestroom (private baths) 1920 Dutch Colonial B&B about 3 mi. north of Great Barrington and 6 mi. south of Stockbridge in the Berkshires. Complimentary breakfast. Open year-round except Christmas Eve and Christmas Day. On summer weekends 2-night minimum stay. Grounds abut Monument Mountain Reservation and State Forest; xc skiing and hiking from back door; swimming pool. Downhill skiing, antiquing, crafts shops, and all Berkshire cultural and historic attractions nearby. Children over 12. No pets. Smoking room available for smokers. Terry and David Thorne, Innkeepers.

Directions: From Great Barrington continue north on Rte. 7 for approx. 3 mi. Watch for inn sign on left after passing junction with Rte. 183. From Stockbridge continue south on Rte. 7. Approx. 2 mi. past Monument Mountain High School, watch for sign on right.

For B&B rates, see Index.

THE TURNING POINT
Great Barrington, Massachusetts

In earlier editions we featured a poem by a guest of the Turning Point, who referred to the breakfasts as "food worth a song." I agree. "Natural" and "creative" are the words for Turning Point breakfasts—hot cereals are made from soy, oats, rye, and wheat flakes; maple syrup is used as sweetening. There are always fresh-baked muffins or a breakfast cake. Shirley does the baking; Irving does the cooking, and he might make a frittata with asparagus just picked from the garden. Along with regular coffee and teas, there is grain coffee and a selection of herb teas, and of course, all kinds of fresh fruit and juices.

Perched on the corner of moderately-busy Route 23 and quiet Lake Buel Road, both of which lead into the bucolic woodland settings of the Southern Berkshires, the Turning Point is a short drive from the untouched country villages of Tyringham, Monterey, New Marlborough, Mill River, and Sandisfield.

The Yosts offer their guests conviviality and comfort with a cozy sitting room, where, over the Rumford fireplace, can be seen the faint antique lettering, "E. Pixley," undoubtedly the owner of the Pixley Tavern in the mid-1800s. The dining/living room has a baby grand piano and a conversational arrangement of a comfortable sofa and chairs, along with a beautiful dining table made from 200-year-old chestnut, found in the walls of the inn. This, of course, is where those incomparable breakfasts are served, under a hanging Tiffany lamp.

Bedrooms are all furnished differently; some are wallpapered, some have walls painted in Colonial colors; most have oriental scatter rugs—they all have a pleasantly harmonious feeling.

The poem probably said it all better: "...warm hearts and good beds for the night...."

THE TURNING POINT, Rte. 23 and Lake Buel Rd., RD2 Box 140, Great Barrington, MA 01230; 413-528-4777. A 7-guestroom (1 private, 3 shared baths) bed-and-breakfast inn in the Berkshires. Breakfast only meal served. Open year-round. Butternut Basin Ski Area, Beartown Mtn. xc ski trails, and Tanglewood nearby. Two- and three-night minimum during summer and holiday weekends. Well-behaved children welcome. No pets. No credit cards. Please, no smoking. Irv and Shirley Yost, Innkeepers.

Directions: From Great Barrington, proceed east on Rte. 23 to the first crossroad after Butternut Ski Area. The Turning Point is on Rte. 23 at the corner of Lake Buel Rd. and Monument Valley Rd.

For B&B rates, see Index.

UNDERLEDGE
Lenox, Massachusetts

It's always gratifying to see a magnificent old home that had been tottering on the brink of extinction brought back to its original state. Built in 1876 by financier Joseph Burden, Underledge was a comfortable, rambling summer home for many years. However, by the time the Lanoue family took it over in the 1970s, it had fallen into a pitiable state of disrepair.

Enter Ernie Lanoue and his son, Tom, who were in the business of restoration, and Marcie and daughter-in-law Cheryl. Together, after ten years of very hard work, they have returned Underledge to its gracious, elegant self.

A tree-lined drive curves up around the broad lawns to the house, which faces west to the vivid Berkshire sunsets. Spacious rooms, rich, hand-carved woods, many tall windows, thick wall-to-wall carpeting and oriental rugs, handsome fireplaces, beautiful antiques, and lovely floral upholstery, often echoed in the draperies and wallpapers, were my immediate impressions.

The spacious and immaculate guest rooms certainly offer the epitome in gracious living; several have working fireplaces, one has its own screened, sunset-facing balcony, another opens out onto the patio. The larger rooms, with queen- or king-sized beds, have private modern bathrooms, while some smaller rooms, equally attractive, share a bath. All are beautifully furnished with antiques.

A continental breakfast of freshly baked muffins, juice, and coffee is served in the solarium—breakfast room, entirely surrounded with windows looking out over the lawns and trees. A truly superior bed and breakfast.

UNDERLEDGE, 76 Cliffwood St., Lenox, MA 01240; 413-637-0236. A 12-guestroom (private and shared baths) gracious country mansion on a quiet, residential street in the Berkshires. Complimentary continental breakfast. Open year-round. Minimum stay of 3 nights on summer weekends; 2 nights on holidays. Kennedy Park with 26 mi. of hiking and xc skiing adjacent. Tanglewood and all of the Berkshire cultural, historic, and natural attractions nearby. Children over 10 accepted. No pets. Marcie and Cheryl Lanoue, Innkeepers.

Directions: From the south, take Rte. 7 to Rte. 7A into Lenox. Turn left at Cliffwood St. (opp. Mobil station), continuing to 14th house on the right. From the east, take Mass. Tpke. to Exit 2 (Lee) and follow Rte. 20 west to intersection with Rte. 183 (Walker St.). Turn left and continue into village. Proceed as above.

For B&B rates, see Index.

UNIQUE BED AND BREAKFAST
Sheffield, Massachusetts

"Everyone tells me we have a homey atmosphere," May Stendardi told me as we sat at the little round table having a cup of tea in the dining area of the Stendardis' log home. "And we do try to make our guests feel very much at home."

If the comfortable bedrooms, super-clean ceramic-tiled bathrooms, and small refrigerator for guests' use were any indication, I'd say they've accomplished their aim. In keeping with the woodsy setting among the pines at the base of 2,600-foot Mount Everett, this somewhat rustic log home has pine-paneled walls combined with pretty wallpapers, and the beds have pine headboards that blend with the decor.

Two skylights let in some sky through the high ceiling of the living room, and blue-flowered tile lines the walls behind a large thermostatically controlled wood stove in the living room. Comfortable couches and recliner chairs and a TV offer relaxation and diversion.

Guests can take their breakfasts in the sunshine on the porch instead of at the dining room table, if they prefer. They're sure to enjoy May's hearty breakfasts, which vary, but might be blueberry pancakes, sausage and eggs, home-baked biscuits, cornbread, muffins, or sweet rolls, and coffee.

May keeps lots of brochures suggesting the unlimited possibilities for recreation and entertainment in the area.

UNIQUE BED AND BREAKFAST, Undermountain Rd., P.O. Box 729, Sheffield, MA 01257; 413-229-3363. A 4-guestroom (private baths) contemporary log home among the pines at the foot of Mt. Everett in the Berkshire Hills. Complimentary full breakfast. Open year-round. Weekends and holidays and June 15 to Oct. 15, 2-night minimum. Tanglewood, Berkshire Theatre Festival, and many other historic, natural, and recreational attractions, including antiques shops and backroading. Also downhill and xc skiing nearby. No children under 12. No pets. Credit cards accepted for deposits. May Stendardi, Hostess.

Directions: From Boston, take Mass. Tpke. to Exit 2 (Lee) and follow Rte. 102 to Rte. 7. Continue south on Rte. 7 to Rte. 41 (and 23) south. Rte. 41 turns left just past So. Egremont village. Continue approx. 5 mi. Look for small sign on right. From NYC, take Taconic Pkwy. to Rte. 23 in Hillsdale. Continue past Catamount Ski Area almost 3 mi. to Rte. 41 south. Turn right and continue approx. 5 mi. Look for small sign on right.

For B&B rates, see Index.

THE VILLAGE INN
Lenox, Massachusetts

Located on Route 7, running north and south from New York to the Canadian border, the village of Lenox, settled in 1767, has thrived through several different historic and social epochs.

During one of these periods, the American Revolution, the Village Inn came into being and has operated for many years as an inn and a haven, first for Colonial travelers and then for visitors to Lenox during its famous "resort period."

Today, the area attracts music lovers, sports and nature lovers, as well as those who enjoy a stay in an inn atmosphere.

The guest rooms have an authentic New England flavor, and the low-ceilinged dining room with lovely paintings on the walls is usually abuzz with breakfast guests each morning.

This breakfast can be anything from a bowl of cereal and a muffin to belgian waffles, bacon and eggs, omelets, pancakes, or fresh fruit with yogurt. Delicious Sunday brunches and afternoon English teas are added pleasant offerings. Dinner is served Wednesday through Sunday nights.

Please take note that lodgings do not include breakfast, although breakfast is available daily, and also that the lower rates (see Index) are not offered from July 1 to Labor Day or on holidays or during the foliage season.

The Village Tavern is open nightly except Monday and offers light fare and libations and live entertainment on weekends.

THE VILLAGE INN, Church St., Lenox, MA 01240; 413-637-0020. A 27-guestroom inn in a bustling Berkshire town 4 mi. from Stockbridge, 8 mi. from Pittsfield, and 1 mi. from Tanglewood. Breakfast and afternoon tea served daily to travelers; dinner Wed. thru Sun. Open every day of the year. Lenox is located in the heart of the Berkshires with many historical, cultural, and recreational features. Swimming in pleasant nearby lakes. All seasonal sports including xc and downhill skiing available nearby. No pets. Cliff Rudisill and Ray Wilson, Innkeepers.

Directions: After approaching Lenox on Rte. 7, one of the principal north-south routes in New England, exit onto Rte. 7A to reach the village center and Church St. When approaching from the Mass. Tpke. (Exit 2) follow Rte. 20W about 4 mi. and turn left onto Rte. 183 to center of town.

For Lodging rates, see Index.

WALKER HOUSE
Lenox, Massachusetts

Here's a B&B inn that lovingly embraces classical music—in fact, even the rooms are named for great composers. The newly-arrived guest might be greeted with the rich, sonorous sounds of Telemann or Prokofiev, and from the impressive record collection and the unusual paintings on display it is obvious that Peggy and Richard Houdek certainly are lovers of the arts.

This classical Federal building was built in 1804 and is located in the center of Lenox within a very pleasant walk of the front gates of Tanglewood, where the Boston Symphony holds forth each summer.

The spacious guest rooms are decorated in styles and color schemes befitting the composers for whom they were named. All have private baths. There is a parlor of considerable size whose walls are lined with bookcases and which boasts a working fireplace and a piano. There are many cozy corners and a veranda just made to enjoy reading, conversation, and listening to music.

There are seven other working fireplaces, including one in the dining room and in five of the guest rooms. The entire house is furnished with antiques.

One of the pleasant surprises for newlyweds is a complimentary bottle of champagne with caviar and crackers.

A most generous continental breakfast, leading off with fresh juice, fresh fruit, hot croissants, blueberry muffins, and freshly ground coffee, can be taken in the dining room or on the veranda in the summer.

Afternoon tea is served to guests each day at four in the dining room; lemonade may be taken there or on the veranda during the warmer months.

WALKER HOUSE, 74 Walker St., Lenox, MA 01240; 413-637-1271. An 8-guestroom village inn in the Berkshires close to the center of Lenox. Breakfast and afternoon tea included in room rate. Open every day in the year. Complimentary bicycles are available and croquet and badminton on grounds. Tennis, swimming, downhill and xc skiing, and exceptional backroading in the area. Just a few moments from Tanglewood, the Berkshire Theatre Festival and other Berkshire attractions. Peggy and Richard Houdek, Innkeepers.

Directions: Please see the general directions to the Berkshires.

For B&B rates, see Index.

THE WEATHERVANE INN
South Egremont, Massachusetts

The Weathervane Inn is a small cluster of buildings set off the highway, with sections dating back to 1785. It is located in the lovely little village of South Egremont in the Berkshires, where there are many pre-1800 houses and a graceful church. Replete with wideboard floors, beautiful moldings, and an original fireplace that served as a heating and cooking unit with a beehive oven, the inn has a comfortable, warm atmosphere.

In addition to a large, pleasant reception room, there is a living room with a color TV, for which innkeepers Anne and Vince Murphy are building a video tape collection. Still another gathering room has a little pub corner and a grouping of sofa and chairs in front of the fireplace.

The cheery dining room with its many windows, and tables covered with white tablecloths under gay red overcloths, brightens the morning for breakfasting guests. Anne's breakfasts feature among other things blueberry pancakes, french toast, sausage, bacon, and eggs in any style, including a marvelous Brie omelet.

The eight attractively furnished country-inn bedrooms come in all sizes and shapes, and each offers something different. They are prettily decorated with quilted pictures, dried-flower arrangements, ball-fringe curtains, and, more practically, with reading lamps, books, magazines, and electric blankets.

A swimming pool offers a cooling respite on hot summer days, and there is no end of things to do in and around the Berkshires during summer and winter.

THE WEATHERVANE INN, Rte. 23, South Egremont, MA 01258; 413-528-9580. An 8-bedroom village inn in the Berkshire foothills. Modified American plan daily in summer and Thurs. thru Sun. in winter. Breakfast served to houseguests. Open year-round. Swimming pool on grounds. Golf, tennis, bicycling, backroading, hiking, horseback riding, fishing, downhill and xc skiing nearby. Tanglewood, Jacob's Pillow, Berkshire Playhouse, Norman Rockwell Museum, and great antique shops all nearby. No pets. Vincent, Anne, and Patricia Murphy, Innkeepers.

Directions: From New York City follow Sawmill River Pkwy. to Taconic Pkwy. to Rte. 23 east. South Egremont and the inn are about 2 mi. past the Catamount Ski area.

For B&B rates, see Index.

THE WEBB-BIGELOW PLACE
Weston, Massachusetts

In 1827, a prosperous time for the young and growing nation, Alpheus Bigelow Jr., built a handsome home right on the Boston Post Road. Caring owners since have added to its charm, until today the preserved Federal period house, surrounded by lawns and flowers, is more a picture than ever, as well as a perfect example of a great B&B bonus, the historic property open to guests.

I reminded Jane Webb of the strangers who used to come to her door claiming ancestral connections just to have a look inside. "Even now I want people to telephone first," she laughed.

The Webb-Bigelow Place is set on three acres in Weston's National Registered Historic District, adjacent to an 800-acre town forest great for hiking or cross-country skiing. There is off-street parking on the circular driveway and a swimming pool on the grounds. In addition to being a short drive away from Walden Pond, Concord, and Lexington, Weston has interesting remnants of its Colonial past and some of the most beautiful residential streets in Massachusetts. Sudbury's Wayside Inn is just down the road a few miles.

This is a particularly prime location for visiting area colleges: Wellesley, Brandeis, and Regis are ten minutes away; Harvard, Radcliffe, M.I.T., and Boston College, half an hour.

There are three large guest bedrooms on the second floor, each with working fireplaces and one with twin beds. Two have a connecting bath, which makes a particularly nice arrangement for a family. Guests have their own comfortable living room downstairs with fireplace, TV, and plenty of good books. The house is furnished with antiques.

A full breakfast is the only meal served, but there are many restaurants nearby.

THE WEBB-BIGELOW PLACE, 863 Boston Post Rd., Weston, MA 02193; 617-899-2444. A 3-guestroom, 2-bath B&B, 15 mi. from Boston. Breakfast only. Open year around. Sightseeing, antiquing, hiking, x-country, golf, nearby. Own swimming pool. Prefer non-smokers. Jane and Bob Webb, Hosts.

Directions: From Massachusetts Turnpike (I-90) take Exit 15, drive north on Rte. 128 (I-95) one exit (Exit 49). Drive west on Rte. 20 for 3.2 mi. House is on Weston-Wayland line, north side of Rte. 20, enclosed by stockade fence. Enter by driving through the gateway.

For B&B rates, see Index.

WESTMINSTER VILLAGE INN
Westminster, Massachusetts

Approaching Westminster Village Inn on Route 2, one could have the impression that it is a motel. However, rest assured, it is a most attractive non-motel motel.

Guest rooms are in a series of relatively recently built buildings, resembling an Early American style. Each of the thirty-one dwellings is in a different Colonial color and no two of them are alike. There are some with gambrel roofs; some contain two or three sets of lodgings; all are in a woodland setting that is further enhanced by a welcome swimming pool. All the rooms have a very pleasant atmosphere, and are furnished with reproductions of Early American furniture. My room had a fireplace and was extremely attractive.

An à la carte breakfast, not included in the price of the lodgings, is served every morning, and a simple dinner is served Monday through Thursday. Guests at the inn receive a discount at the nearby famous Old Mill Restaurant, which is also under the same proprietorship.

Westminster is located between Fitchburg, Leominster, and Gardner, and is on the extension of the famous Mohawk Trail, which was used by the Indians for centuries before the arrival of the American tourist. The Westminster Village Inn and the Old Mill will prove a most pleasant surprise.

WESTMINSTER VILLAGE INN, Route 2, Westminster, MA 01473; 617-874-5911. A 31-guestroom cluster of Early American-style lodgings tastefully situated in a grove of trees on the south side of Route 2. Breakfast not included in room price. Other meals offered at inn and also at the Old Mill Restaurant nearby. Open every day except Christmas. Swimming pool on grounds. Convenient for golf, tennis, skiing, and the Mt. Wachusett Theater nearby. The Fosters, Proprietors.

Directions: Westminster Village Inn is just east of Westminster on Rte. 2. It is 50 mi. west of Boston.

For B&B rates, see Index.

WINDAMAR HOUSE
Provincetown, Cape Cod, Massachusetts

I had almost despaired of finding some good, quiet accommodations in Provincetown, which has grown substantially in many respects since my early visits a number of years ago.

A very discreet sign provides an appropriately low-key introduction to this double white house with narrow white clapboards and black shutters, a brick walk, and a beautiful garden in the rear.

The interior is equally fetching, and the owner obviously has excellent decorating sensibilities, as is evidenced by the furnishings and adornments throughout the house and in the harmonizing tones of brown, beige, and white in the hallways and a matching Afghan named Geraldine.

Guest rooms are distinctively decorated with fine antiques and paintings, with views of Cape Cod Bay in the front and the garden in the rear.

I confess I'm unable to do proper justice to the Windamar House with this limited space, but may I suggest that you write for a descriptive and absolutely truthful brochure.

The Windamar is more than I had hoped to find in Provincetown.

WINDAMAR HOUSE, 568 Commerical St., Provincetown, MA 02657; 617-487-0599. A 6-guestroom (3 baths) Cape Cod home located at the tranquil east end of Provincetown. Two apartments with kitchen conveniences. Open year-round. Continental breakfast is included in the price of the room. Quite convenient for a stroll to the center of the village and also for swimming and sunbathing on the beach, sport fishing, dune taxi rides, tennis, golf, riding, sailing, and bicycling. No pets. No credit cards. Pickup service to and from the airport. Bette Adams, Proprietor.

Directions: Follow Rte. 6 to the very end of Cape Cod and turn left at the first Provincetown exit. Turn right on Commercial St. (one-way) and look for Windamar House on the right.

For B&B rates, see Index.

WINDSOR HOUSE
Newburyport, Massachusetts

The Windsor House in Newburyport was built in 1787 as both a residence and a ship's chandlery. The kitchen was the original shipping and receiving room and there's a series of trapdoors that open up to the third story of the house, where the original hoist wheel is located.

The brick wall of the fireplace separates the warehouse sections from the living section. The post and beam construction throughout the entire house was done by ships' carpenters, the same men who built the clipper ships. There are six guest rooms, of which three have their own private bathrooms. The other three share one bathroom.

Guests gather around the long table in the high-ceilinged kitchen to enjoy a full English breakfast, consisting of homemade biscuits, eggs cooked with fresh herbs from the Windsor House garden, and homemade sausage. The wild beach plum and rose hip jellies are delectable and the coffee has been specially blended to meet the innkeepers' own taste.

WINDSOR HOUSE, 38 Federal St., Newburyport, MA 01950; 617-462-3778. A 6-guestroom inn located in the restored section of Newburyport. Open year-round. Breakfast served to all guests; dinner by 3-day minimum advance reservation. Three mi. from Plum Island, the Parker River Nat'l. Wildlife Refuge, and ocean beaches. A short walk from the restored 19th-century retail area, restaurants, and museums. Also nearby: deep sea fishing, whale watching, swimming, art galleries, antique shops, family ski area, horseback riding, and year-round theater. Trundle beds and crib available for children. Parents must provide for infant care. Small dogs welcome. Judith Crumb and Jim Lawbaugh, Innkeepers.

Directions: From Boston and Maine: From I-95 use exit to Rte. 113, turn right onto High St. (Rte. 1A) and proceed 3 mi. to Federal St., turn left. Inn on left across from Old South Church (Rte. 1A is scenic drive from either Boston or New Hampshire).

For B&B rates, see Index.

THE INN AT UNION PIER
Union Pier, Michigan

Many cooks chase guests out of the kitchen. But at this lakeshore inn, they're welcome.

That's good, because it's easy to gravitate to the spacious back room, where there are chairs for sitting and chatting around the large kitchen table. Here ceiling fans spin lazily, wafting breakfast fragrances. Windows overlook the lawn, where in summer guests are likely playing volleyball or croquet. "On winter days, we keep soup on the stove and homemade bread on hand," says proprietor Madeleine Reinke. That's especially welcome after a day of cross-country skiing.

Madeleine runs the inn with help from her husband, Bill. Located in a casual neighborhood just a short walk from Lake Michigan, the inn's several buildings, originally part of a lakeshore resort, are painted a nautical blue, trimmed in white, and connected by walkway decks. A hot tub for eight sits on one of the decks; another has space for an outside breakfast. Inside, the nine guest rooms are decorated with clean, spare lines, often featuring light pine. Several even have Swedish ceramic wood stoves with grates that open to show the flickering flames.

The inn changes its breakfast fare seasonally. Summer is accompanied by quiche and fresh strawberries with popovers. Come fall and there are baked apples with large muffins: honey-bran, cinnamon-apple, banana-nut. Winter sees hefty sliced potatoes with sausage patties. And spring brings a light repast of grapefruit and melons, bread pudding, and bacon.

The inn has several canoes and bicycles for the borrowing, as well as equipment for lawn sports. Elsewhere, activities are those of the lakeside: fishing, swimming, boating, windsurfing. And for guests who want simply to doze, Madeleine has hung a hammock between two trees.

THE INN AT UNION PIER, P.O. Box 222, 9708 Berrien, Union Pier, MI 49129; 616-469-4700. A 9-guestroom (private baths) circa 1929 renovated lakeshore inn in the southwest corner of Michigan. Full breakfast included. Open year-round. Two-night minimum on weekends. Lawn hammock, decktop hot tub, croquet, and volleyball available at inn; area activities include swimming, fishing, biking, hiking, canoeing, windsurfing, winery tours, and antiquing. Children over 12 welcome. No pets. Bill and Madeleine Reinke, Innkeepers.

Directions: From I-94, take Exit 6 onto Townline Rd. Go approx. 1/2 mi. to Red Arrow Hwy. and turn right; continue another 1/2 mi. and turn left on Berrien. The inn is down the street on the left.

For B&B rates, see Index.

MCCARTHY'S BEAR CREEK INN
Marshall, Michigan

This inn has so many sweet touches, it's hard to choose which ones to describe.

Perhaps the footbridge, crossing the tiny creek. Or maybe the look of its white fences set crisply against the green lawns. Or the shaggy burr oaks, towering over the backyard barn. Or just the way it sits high on a hill, a gracious fourteen acres on the outskirts of town.

All of it was built in the 1940s by Robert Maes, a wealthy agricultural inventor. Michael and Beth McCarthy converted it to a country inn in 1985, adding plenty of choice details. Each of the seven guest rooms, for example, includes a reading lamp, chairs, and little radios inset with clocks. Many have delicate watercolors by local artist Maureen Reed, plus antiques and cherished family belongings that the McCarthys have collected throughout the years. Beth McCarthy has also thoughtfully set out colorful little sewing baskets for the guest with that loose button or drooping hem.

Breakfast, served on the porch, is displayed on a handsome Dutch cupboard of bird's-eye maple. It includes mason jars full of granola and cornflakes, pitchers of juice and milk, baskets of fruit, bowls of hard-boiled eggs, and plates of doughnuts, toast, or sweet breads. Guests help themselves before sitting down to individual tables, overlooking the handsome grounds. On the morning of my visit, each table sported a bouquet of bright yellow flowers that son Tim, 9, had found by the creek.

Downtown Marshall boasts a wealth of historic architecture. But the inn itself offers much to do, too. Inside, there are plenty of magazines and games. Outside, the grounds are perfect for a hike through the fields to the forest. Daughter Carey, 12, will show little visitors her rabbit in the barn; Tim will take them to the ducks by the creek. Tours of a neighbor's farm, complete with plow horses and dairy cows, are available upon request.

MCCARTHY'S BEAR CREEK INN, 15230 C Dr. North, Marshall, MI 49068; 616-781-8383. A 7-guestroom (private baths) country estate on 14 acres on the outskirts of town. Lodgings include breakfast. Closed Dec. 23, 24, and 25. Hiking, sleighrides, hayrides, and tour of neighboring farm available upon request. Mike and Beth McCarthy, Proprietors.

Directions: From I-69, take Exit 36 to Marshall. After you exit, turn west onto Michigan Ave. Almost immediately, turn left onto 15-Mile Rd., and then, almost immediately, right onto C Dr. No. The inn will be on your left.

For B&B rates, see Index.

THE RAYMOND HOUSE INN
Port Sanilac, Michigan

On the morning of my visit, this three-story brick house with gingerbread trim was filled with spring sunlight and a sweet offshore breeze from Lake Huron.

It was the open floor-to-ceiling windows that did the trick. Lace curtains and crisp white woodwork only added to the airiness of the place, built in 1871 by Uri Raymond, one of Port Sanilac's original settlers and tradesmen. The Raymonds kept the house in the family for 112 years. Only recently did they sell it to the bed and breakfast's current proprietor, Shirley Denison. "Everybody thinks I named the house after my husband, Raymond," Shirley says. Instead, of course, it's named for the family that maintained it so long.

The house is furnished in stylish Victorian. The front parlor boasts a bay window, plenty of decorative tableware, and ancestral portraits in antique frames. The old-fashioned dining room has a plate rail lined with English Aynsley china, and it's here that Shirley serves a continental breakfast, which includes fresh-baked rolls.

The six guest rooms all have their own baths. In the third-floor attic is an antique shop full of wonderful old things: poking around, I saw a butter churn, pantaloons, old rug beaters, dishes, linens, quilts, and much, much more. The shop is open on Saturday and Sunday afternoon, or by request.

At the time of our visit, Shirley, a potter, was planning an art studio for the former woodshed, just off the kitchen. There, at her wheel, she hopes to craft the ornate, highly glazed figurines, vases, and bowls that have become her trademark.

THE RAYMOND HOUSE INN, 111 S. Ridge St. (M25), Port Sanilac, MI 48469; 313-622-8800. A 6-guestroom (private baths) Victorian brick home with white gingerbread, built in 1871 in a historic port town on Lake Huron. Complimentary continental breakfast. Open May 1 through Oct. 31. Charter boats, fishing, swimming, sailing, bicycling, and golf nearby. Children over 12 are welcome. No pets. Restricted smoking. No credit cards. Shirley Denison, Proprietor.

Directions: From I-94 at Port Huron, Mich., take M25 north about 30 mi. into Port Sanilac. The Raymond House is at the corner of Ridge (M25) and Cherry Streets.

For B&B rates, see Index.

ROSEMONT INN
Douglas, Michigan

Oddly enough, the vacationing possibilities of the Saugatuck-Douglas area of Michigan were discovered by a pleasure party of Chicagoans. The host was Stephen A. Morrison, one of the first settlers of the village, and the highlight of their vacation was being serenaded by the Saugatuck Silver Coronet Band. The year was 1880, the inauguration of this part of Michigan as a vacation spot.

Through the years many thousands have followed the little group, enjoying the bounties of nature and the relaxing pleasures. The town had grown originally as a result of the lumber business, but when the timber supply was exhausted, fruit became the big business, and today, the climate, the beauty of the countryside, and the friendly atmosphere have made it into a popular holiday region.

The Rosemont, a Queen Anne Victorian building originally built in 1886 as a tourist inn, has retained much of its original country feeling. The screened porch with hanging plants is a delightful spot on which to enjoy the cooling lake breeze. In addition to the waters of Lake Michigan, innkeepers Ric and Cathy Gillette have a heated pool on the grounds, which are shaded with big maples.

There are fourteen bedrooms with Victorian furnishings, spool and canopy beds, and many different kinds of quilts. All have private baths. Most have fireplaces and views of the lake through the trees.

THE ROSEMONT INN, 83 Lake Shore Drive, P.O. Box 541, Douglas, Mi. 49406; 616-857-2637. A fourteen-bedroom lakeside bed-and-breakfast inn in a pleasant residential section of Douglas. Continental breakfast the only meal served. Open all year. Swimming pool on grounds. Conveniently located for all of the many recreational advantages of the area. No pets. Ric and Cathy Gillette, Innkeepers.

Directions: Just south of Saugatuck off I-196. Head toward lake and Lake Shore Dr.

For B&B rates, see Index.

STAFFORD'S BAY VIEW INN
Petoskey, Michigan

These "American Style" accommodations include a great many restored and preserved Victorian mansions. Stafford's Bay View Inn, located in the well-known Bay View section of Petoskey, is a prime example. It is vintage gingerbread at some of its very best.

Bay View is a summer resort community, which has grown up around a program of music, drama, art, and religious lectures and services. The early residents built Victorian homes that are scattered throughout Bay View today, and the programs are still going on.

The furnishings in the parlors and guest rooms of this inn reflect the changing periods of its history. It's sort of like visiting great-grandmother's house.

The full breakfast, included in the room rate, features hot inn-baked rolls, served as you are seated in the bustling, cheerful dining room, followed by your selection of tempting entrées.

STAFFORD'S BAY VIEW INN, Box 3, Petoskey, MI 49770; 616-347-2771. A 23-guestroom resort-inn on Little Traverse Bay in the Bay View section of Petoskey. Breakfast, lunch, and dinner served daily to travelers. Open daily mid-May through Oct., Thanksgiving, and Christmas, and daily during the winter sports season. Lake swimming and xc skiing on grounds. Golf, boating, fishing, hiking, and alpine skiing nearby. Pickup service provided from Pellston Airport on request. Stafford and Janice Smith, Judy Honor, Innkeepers.

Directions: From Detroit: take Gaylord Exit from I-75 and follow Mich. Rte. 32 to Rte. 131, north to Petoskey. From Chicago: use U.S. 131 north to Petoskey.

For B&B rates, see Index.

THE VICTORIAN INN
Port Huron, Michigan

This historic mansion is a stroll away from the Black and Saint Clair Rivers, linked to Lake Huron. Here colorful shipping vessels and leisure craft ply the waters. In July, the annual boat races from Port Huron to Mackinac also start here.

Guests who come for such events—or for any other pleasure offered by this tidy port city—can relax over dinner, back at the inn. The three-story building, with its gables and wraparound porch, was built by a city retailer as a private residence in 1896. Ed and Vicki Peterson and Lew and Lynne Secory bought it in 1983 with the idea of restoring it as a fine inn that would offer both food and lodging. "We wanted the city to see an adaptive use of a historic building," says Lynne Secory, also one of the inn's chefs.

On the first floor the couples developed three intimate dining rooms with three to six tables each. There, such interesting meals as pickerel wrapped in phyllo pastry or truffled chicken in champagne are served. Guests who await seating can gaze at the huge fireplace and dried flower arrangements set against a color scheme of peach and green. On the second floor are four guest rooms. Two of the rooms have private baths; two share one bath, including a sink and clawfoot tub.

Each room has some special touch, such as a stained-glass window or a canopied bed or fireplace. The inn is willing to serve dinner in any of the rooms, Lynne says.

That's where breakfast is served, too. Guests are asked the previous evening when they would like to eat, any time between 6 A.M. and 10 A.M. At the requested hour, a knock comes at the door. Outside stands a tray with white linen napkins and silver tea service, freshly-baked muffins in a little basket, and a goblet of orange juice. Coffee steams before a bouquet of flowers.

It's a pleasant way to greet the morning.

THE VICTORIAN INN, 1229 Seventh St., Port Huron, MI 48060; 313-984-1437. A 4-guestroom (private and shared baths) Victorian mansion in a port city in eastern Michigan on Lake Huron. Complimentary continental breakfast. Restaurant open for lunch and dinner Tues. and Sat., except on major holidays. Open year-round. Walk to downtown Port Huron, also a gateway to Canada via the Bluewater Bridge; shop, watch the boats, visit the museum, attend special events such as the Port Huron to Mackinac boat races. No pets. Michael Potter, Innkeeper.

Directions: From I-94, take Exit 271. Follow Hwy. 69 east to 7th St. Turn left; inn is 4 blocks at the corner of 7th and Union.

For B&B rates, see Index.

WICKWOOD INN
Saugatuck, Michigan

Saugatuck, just a few miles south of Holland, is on the eastern shore of Lake Michigan. It reminds the visitor of a New England coastal village with its many sailboat masts, tall shade trees, and attractive Victorian homes.

Residents of Michigan and Chicago have long known that the wide sandy beaches of Lake Michigan provide excellent vacation and holiday fare for everyone, with fishing, swimming, golfing, tennis, and other warm weather activities. Winter is also popular, with cross-country skiing.

Oddly enough, I learned that the Wickwood Inn was inspired by one of my favorite London hotels—Dukes. Sue and Stub Louis, in converting this very attractive building to ten guest rooms with private baths, succeeded in saving some of the most desirable original features.

The library, which is reminiscent of an English gentleman's club, is all in mahogany with a high gloss finish. Passing through the french doors at the end of the living room, guests step down into the sunken garden room with a brick floor, cedar walls, vaulted, beamed ceiling, shuttered windows, and trees and flowering plants everywhere.

The guest rooms, each of which is distinctively furnished, have dressers, armoires, nightstands, and settees made of pine, walnut, and cherry. They are models for inn sleeping quarters.

Continental breakfast, including fresh-squeezed orange juice and hot homemade coffee cake awaits each guest. At teatime, hors d'oeuvres are offered, and an elegant brunch is served on Sunday.

There is a final touch. The association with Dukes is further enhanced by a London taxicab, which is available for limited livery service.

WICKWOOD INN, 510 Butler St., Saugatuck, MI 49453; 617-857-1097. A handsomely decorated 10-guestroom bed-and-breakfast inn (fully air conditioned) situated in one of Michigan's most attractive resort villages on the shore of Lake Michigan. Open year-round. Two-night minimum stay on weekends during summer. Continental breakfast is only meal served. Most conveniently located for all of the recreational advantages of the area. No children. No pets. Sue and Stub Louis, Innkeepers.

Directions: Saugatuck is located just off I-196, 2½ hrs. from Chicago. From the south, take Exit 36. From the north, take Exit 41.

For B&B rates, see Index.

DOWN TO EARTH LIFESTYLES
Parkville, Missouri

Everything may be "up to date in Kansas City," but there's still old-fashioned hospitality at Bill and Lola Coons' bed and breakfast home. Conveniently located just fifteen minutes from Kansas City International Airport, on an eighty-five-acre ranch, complete with cattle, horses, and wild geese, this home offers serene country lodgings, plus easy access to many attractions and points of interest.

However, most of Bill and Lola's guests have come there primarily for the peace and privacy of a "getaway" haven. The Coonses named their rustic ranch-style home "Down to Earth Lifestyles" because it is an "earth contact" home, designed for super energy efficiency. From the front view, one would never guess that the back wall of the structure is built into the ground. The rooms on that side of the house are amply lit by large skylights.

All four of the guest rooms are spacious double bedrooms, furnished with country and antique pieces, including handmade quilts dating from the 1800s on the beds. Each room has a radio, TV, and phone, private bath, and a shared shower between each pair of rooms. The large family room boasts a huge free-standing fireplace and both an organ and a piano, on either of which Lola will gladly play requests.

The breakfast menu proves to be an array of delightful choices— egg-ham-broccoli-cheese strata, omelets, fruit-filled crêpes, a typical Missouri breakfast of sausages with biscuits and gravy, waffles or pancakes, breads, muffins, coffee cakes, and jams and jellies. These offerings are all homemade and served family style when and where the guests prefer, which could be the dining room or kitchen or the pool-side patio or on a bed tray.

As you can see, the Coonses go all out to make their guests feel welcome and at home.

DOWN TO EARTH LIFESTYLES, Route 22, Parkville, MO 64152; 816-891-1018. A 4-guestroom bed-and-breakfast home on the outskirts of Parkville, 15 min. from KCI Airport. Breakfast is included; optional lunch and dinner. Several restaurants are nearby. Open year-round. Swimming pool, farm animals, jogging trails on grounds. Jesse James home, Truman Library and home, antiquing, shopping, golf, fishing, boating, within 45-min. drive. Children welcome. No credit cards. Bill and Lola Coons, Hosts.

Directions: From KCI Airport take I-29 to exit for Hwy. 45 or 64th St. Head west 5.2 mi. to "K" Hwy. and turn right, .4 mi. to North Crooked Rd. Turn right and proceed .4 mi. to the inn sign on left.

For B&B rates, see Index.

ST. GEMME BEAUVAIS
Ste. Genevieve, Missouri

Interstate 55 sweeps down from the north through St. Louis and then roughly follows the course of the Mississippi River through Missouri into Arkansas and Tennessee and continues to New Orleans. A little over an hour south of St. Louis lies the village of Ste. Genevieve.

Ste. Genevieve is a living historic community and not an artificially created "tourist attraction." Most of the 18th- and 19th-century structures are still occupied as homes and businesses, and maintained with pride by their owners as living entities. Their original appearance can be enjoyed from the outside by visitors even when such buildings are not opened for tours.

Visitors are indeed fortunate to be able to spend a night and enjoy a splendid breakfast at the Inn St. Gemme Beauvais which has been associated with the same family for many years. Mr. and Mrs. Norbert Donze have made the old home into an old-fashioned inn with large comfortable bedrooms and such new-fashioned things as private baths, air conditioning, and telephones.

The dining room has beautiful walnut ladderback chairs, Belgian lace curtains, a marble fireplace, fine china, and graceful stemware. The bedrooms have a collection of many kinds of Victorian antiques, including marble-topped bureaus, high-backed beds, and old-fashioned flowered wallpaper. There are eight different suites in the inn and each has at least two rooms; most have two double beds.

Breakfast has a definite French style with ham-filled crêpes made with a special sauce, spiced or chilled fruit, orange juice, blueberry muffins, and lots of good hot coffee.

Take a moment to leave the interstate and spend an overnight visit at this fascinating, beautifully preserved reminder of America's heritage along the Mississippi.

ST. GEMME BEAUVAIS, 78 N. Main St., Ste. Genevieve, Mo. 63670; 314-883-5744. An 8-room village inn about 1½ hrs. from St. Louis. Modified American plan includes breakfast only. Breakfast served daily. Lunch served Mon. thru Sat. Open year-round. Closed Thanksgiving and Christmas Day. Golf, hunting, and fishing nearby. No pets. Frankye and Boats Donze, Innkeepers.

Directions: From St. Louis, south on I-55 to Hwy. 32. Exit east on 32 to Hwy. 61 to the Ste. Genevieve exit.

For B&B rates, see Index.

AMOS A. PARKER HOUSE
Fitzwilliam, New Hampshire

If Fitzwilliam didn't exist you'd have to invent it. . .that is if you were in search of the absolute, positive, quintessential New England village. It is nestled at the foot of Mount Monadnock, "the single most-climbed mountain in North America."

And the quintessential "elegant but cozy getaway" is the meticulously restored 18th-century homestead, called the Amos A. Parker House—"the house that Amos bought" in 1780. Parker was a prominent judge who was known for his poetry.

Proprietor Freda Houpt has poetically and lovingly restored the house and its extension. The original house now serves as one oversized barn-sided parlor-cum-reading-and-game-room, replete with woodburning fireplace. Each room, with polished plank floors covered with oriental rugs, is furnished in American or English antiques. One four-postered guest room is enlivened with a pink and green romantic stencil by master stencilist Jeannie Serpa. Two of the guest rooms have private baths, and those that don't are supplied with luxurious terry robes; there are two sets of fluffy towels and two pillows for every guest.

Mrs. Houpt prides herself on her "rule free" house; there are four common rooms in all. At the sunset hour mulled cider or iced tea and home-baked pastries are served. The breakfast, which begins with a fresh fruit centerpiece platter, might feature a spinach soufflé with Newburg sauce or praline-sauced french toast. Guests sit at the refectory table or, in season, might eat on the deck, which overlooks voluptuous gardens, with the mountains for a backdrop. Handsome handcrafted copper lampposts line the gravel driveway. At the side of the house is every antique buff's delight—one of New England's few remaining "liberty poles." Hewn from a tree, it was attached to the house to announce to the world that the homesteader was a colonist!

AMOS A. PARKER HOUSE, Box 202, Fitzwilliam, NH 03447; 603-585-6540. A 5-guestroom handsomely restored 18th-century homestead set on 3 acres of manicured gardens in a charming country village. Complimentary breakfast and afternoon refreshments. Open all year. Public tennis courts nearby. Bird watching, hiking, biking, antiquing, alpine and xc skiing. Within walking distance of Rhododendron State Park. Easy drive to Northfield—Mt. Hermon, Cushing Academy, and other preparatory schools, as well as Keene State College and Franklin Pierce College. Freda B. Houpt, Proprietor.

Directions: From I-91, exit at 28-A, Northfield, Mass. onto Rte. 10. At Winchester turn onto Rte. 119 into Fitzwilliam.

For B&B rates, see Index.

THE BEAL HOUSE INN
Littleton, New Hampshire

The Beal House Inn has been a New Hampshire landmark since 1833 and a famous White Mountain inn for over fifty years. It is a classic white two-story Federal building with green trim and is rather prim and proper, but with a touch of humor—something like an elderly maiden aunt slipping you a wink on the sly.

This touch of humor is particularly evident in the most cheerful interior, and starts in the parlor where there are all kinds of knickknacks, a large woven portrait of the Beal House and a number of stereoscopic views of the White Mountains. I understand that these viewers used to be made in Littleton during the 19th century. The first thing I learned was that most of the beautiful antiques in all of the public rooms and guest rooms are an extension of the very attractive antique shop.

There are flowered wallpapers, many delightful decorations, brass beds, and canopied, four-poster, and spool beds in the guest rooms. These are connected by funny little staircases (I saw a Raggedy Ann doll perched on one step) and twisty passageways. The whole atmosphere conveys the feeling of a visit to New England of the past.

The à la carte breakfast menu is posted on the wall of the dining room and includes fresh fruit, fruit juices, scrambled eggs with your choice of ham, bacon, or sausage, or waffles with the same choices, and the house specialty, fresh hot popovers. A light breakfast is included in the cost of the room.

On the many clear days that are prevalent in this part of New Hampshire, there is a view from Littleton of the famous Presidential Range with its glorious peaks that seem to march clear up to the heavens. I was there on a late winter afternoon when all of them were glowing domes in the brilliant afternoon sunshine.

THE BEAL HOUSE INN, 247 West Main St., Littleton, NH 03561; 603-444-2661. A 14-guestroom (12 with private baths) village inn located on the edge of the White Mountains. Open year-round. Breakfast served every day by the fire. Christmas and New Year celebrations. The Old Man of the Mountains, Franconia Notch State Park, downhill skiing and xc skiing all within a short distance. This is the highly scenic portion of New Hampshire. Doug and Brenda Clickenger, Innkeepers.

Directions: From I-93 take Exit 41 into town and turn left (west) on Main St. The inn is on the right on the western edge of Littleton.

For B&B rates, see Index.

THE CAMPTON INN
Campton Village, New Hampshire

Campton is at the western end of the Waterville Valley, one of the great ski areas, not only of New Hampshire, but of the Northeast. The Campton Inn is on a quiet street on Route 175 and just about two minutes from I-93. This is the great north-south traffic artery spanning the length of New Hampshire, and it is the main way to get to the White Mountains.

The building is an old farmhouse, considerably rehabilitated in recent years. One of the main features is a very efficient and handsome wood stove that heats more than half of the house from its location in the rather spacious front parlor.

Furnishings in both the public rooms and the bedrooms are, for the most part, a mixture of antique and country, but there is a rather warm, comfortable, old-fashioned feeling about this house, which extends through many periods of decorative design.

Breakfast is served in the dining room and, when weather permits, on a pleasant outdoor terrace. The full country breakfast changes each morning.

During the snow time, both cross-country and alpine skiers find their way to Waterville Valley, but this pleasant old-home B&B would be an excellent place to stop during other seasons as well.

THE CAMPTON INN, P.O. Box 282, Rte. 175, Campton Village, NH 03223; 603-726-4449. A 10-guestroom (1 private bath; others share baths) bed-and-breakfast inn. Breakfast is the only meal served; however, advance reservations can be made for dinner. Open all year. Most convenient for skiing at Waterville Valley and White Mountains. Cross-country trails nearby. Many summer scenic attractions. Children welcome. No pets. Arlene and Bill Roberts, Innkeepers.

Directions: Take Exit 28 from I-93 north, turn east and follow the signs for Rte. 175. Turn left and proceed 1/2 mi. Inn is on the left.

For B&B rates, see Index.

CHENEY HOUSE
Ashland, New Hampshire

If you're going to be traveling on I-93 up through the middle of New Hampshire to the White Mountains, it would serve your aesthetic sensibilities well to plan a stopover at this little gem of a Victorian house that has been turned into a very tidy bed-and-breakfast inn by Mike and Daryl Mooney. I first met Mike when he was on the front desk at the Whitehall Inn in Camden in 1972. Now he has what so many country inn staff members desire most—his own inn.

I toured the house admiring the extremely well-furnished bedrooms with such fetching touches as old patchwork quilts. Everything has been beautifully preserved or restored, including the floors and staircase. Then the three of us sat on the back porch enjoying a cup of tea and I could see a farmer working in the fields on a pleasant sunny day in June.

Waterville Valley Ski Area is just 25 minutes away and guests receive passes to a small sandy beach on Little Squam Lake.

Breakfast could be popover pancakes with eggs, or muffins, or a pastry. It can be taken out on the back porch on sunny days.

The houses and the atmosphere of this area are vestiges of earlier, happier days that have all but disappeared. I imagine that it would be very nice here at twilight, and during foliage time it would be marvelous.

CHENEY HOUSE, P.O. Box 683, Ashland, N.H. 03217; 603-968-7968. An elegant 3-bedroom bed-and-breakfast inn in the Lake and White Mt. region of New Hampshire. Breakfast the only meal served. Open every day from May through October. Public tennis courts within walking distance; sandy beach rights on Little Squam Lake, 1 mi. Conveniently located for all the recreational, natural, and historical attractions of central New Hampshire. No pets. No credit cards. Mike and Daryl Mooney, Innkeepers.

Directions: Take Exit 24 from I-93 (Ashland) and turn left after Ashland Insurance building into Highland St. The inn is the 10th house on the right-hand side. You can't miss it because it is the most imposing structure on the street.

For B&B rates, see Index.

COLBY HILL INN
Henniker, New Hampshire

Route 202 used to be the most popular way to get from some of the eastern urban centers to the heart of New England in New Hampshire and Maine. Today it's easier (but less intriguing) to follow I-89 and then follow Route 202 to Henniker and the Colby Hill Inn.

Henniker is the home of New England College, and B&B guests at the inn quite frequently are likely to find members of the faculty or parents of visiting or prospective students also enjoying themselves here.

The ceilings are low, the walls are hung with oil paintings and prints, and the furnishings are country antiques. A grandfather clock ticks away in one corner.

Lodging rooms are typical of country New England; many have candlewick bedspreads, hooked rugs, old bowl-and-pitcher sets, and some of them have shared bathrooms.

The inn has a delightful swimming pool sheltered by an ell formed by two huge barns. I can personally attest to the fact that it is most welcome on hot days.

Homemade sourdough pancakes head the breakfast menu, which also has eggs that were probably gathered just a few moments after dawn. Dinner is also offered every night but Monday.

As you can see by the list of recreational and cultural attractions, the Colby Hill Inn offers a delightful prospect for an overnight stay or even longer.

COLBY HILL INN, Henniker, N.H. 03242; 603-428-3281. A 12-room inn on the outskirts of a New Hampshire college town. European plan. Four rooms share two baths. Breakfast served to house guests only. Dinner served to travelers Tuesdays through Sunday, except Thanksgiving, Christmas, and New Year's Day. Open year-round. Swimming pool on grounds. Tennis and xc skiing one short block; alpine skiing 3 mi., golf, canoeing, hiking, bicycling, and fishing nearby. No children under 6. No pets. The Glover Family, Innkeepers.

Directions: From I-89, take Exit 5 and follow Rte. 202 to Henniker. From I-91, take Exit 3 and follow Rte. 9 through Keene and Hillsborough to Henniker. Turn right at blinking light in the center of town. At the Oaks, W. Main St., ½ mile west of town center.

For B&B rates, see Index.

THE CORNER HOUSE INN
Center Sandwich, New Hampshire

Center Sandwich is one of those intriguing New Hampshire villages that one stumbles onto rather than drives to. It's one that particularly appeals to me because of the lovely collection of New England houses, churches, general stores, and excellent craft center.

Oddly enough, I have been stopping off to visit the Corner House Inn briefly for several years. It's on one of my regular routes in search of inns and B&Bs.

This time I was very pleasantly surprised by some significant changes that had been made at the inn, and I was impressed by its cheerful and homelike air. The old barn had been converted into an additional dining room and the atmosphere seemed rather contemporary and fresh.

I found lots of green plants, comfortable furniture, a downstairs parlor, an old spinning wheel and flax, antiques, and near-antique furniture.

The breakfast is full-size with a set main dish, either omelets or french toast or pancakes, and so forth. It is served in the very pleasant dining room within the inn itself.

Lunch and dinner are also served.

THE CORNER HOUSE INN, Jct. Routes 109 and 113, Center Sandwich, N.H. 03227; 603-284-6219. A 4-bedroom village inn (1 private bath and 3 rooms share 1 bath). Breakfast served only to houseguests, lunch and dinner served to the public. Open year-round. Closed Christmas and Thanksgiving for lunch and dinner. Excellent stopover or place to stay for more than one night to use as a center for touring the New Hampshire lakes and nearby mountains. Don Brown and Jane Kroeger, Proprietors.

Directions: From I-93 use Exit 24, follow Rte. 3 to Holderness and Rte. 113 to Center Sandwich.

For B&B rates, see Index.

CRAB APPLE INN
West Plymouth, New Hampshire

Set beside a small brook in the midst of some very attractive lawns and gardens, with an intimate view of the surrounding mountains, the Crab Apple Inn is an 1835 brick building of preeminently Federal design. It is located in the beautiful Baker River Valley at the gateway to the White Mountain region.

Guests are quite likely to be greeted by a friendly Lhasa apso named Pekoe, who accompanies everyone on a tour of the four guest rooms, two of which have private baths.

The present owners, Bill and Carolyn Crenson, offer a warmth and hospitality guests have come to associate with B&B's. Their many interests are reflected by an extensive library, including art, literature, and history, and a waterfowl collection.

The bedrooms, as indeed the entire house, have beautifully finished wide pine floors, and great care has been taken to furnish them with appropriate beds and other furniture. The wallpaper is definitely New England. Down comforters are offered for extra warmth and luxury, as are other amenities.

A typical breakfast, taken either alfresco on the brick patio or in the dining room, might be fruit juice, fresh fruit, an herb and cheese omelet, blueberry or zucchini nut muffins, and coffee or tea.

The inn's location near Holderness School and Plymouth State College is quite convenient for parents of prospective students. The area, close to mountains, rivers, and lakes, offers infinite possibilities for all kinds of recreational activities.

CRAB APPLE INN, RFD 2, Box 200B, West Plymouth, NH 03264; 603-536-4476. A 4-guestroom bed-and-breakfast village inn, 4 mi. west of Plymouth and just a few miles off I-93. Open all year. A full breakfast is included in the room rate. Conveniently located as a touring center for the New Hampshire Lake District or the White Mountains with rivers and ski areas. Local antique and crafts shops nearby. Bill and Carolyn Crenson, Innkeepers.

Directions: From I-93 take Exit 26; go 4½ mi. west on Rte. 25. The inn is on the left-hand side.

For B&B rates, see Index.

DEXTER'S INN
Sunapee, New Hampshire

Dexter's Inn, high on top of the hill overlooking Lake Sunapee, is a place where there is some activity for almost everybody to enjoy. Many guests stay for quite a few days and even a couple of weeks at a time. The principal activity in the summer is tennis, so everyone should be advised to bring the right equipment.

The guest rooms place the accent on bright and gay colors in wallpaper, curtains, and bedspreads. The rooms of the main house are reached by using the funny little hallways that zigzag around wings.

It's possible to stay at Dexter's under the European plan, which includes the B&B rates, in May, June, and September only. At other times, it is under the modified American plan, including breakfast and dinner.

Guests can enjoy the full New Hampshire breakfast in bed or in the dining room. Frank Simpson boasts that there are always hot blueberry muffins every day as well as fruit, a full range of cereals, pancakes, or french toast or eggs. The aroma of the sausage and bacon brings guests to breakfast early every morning.

DEXTER'S INN AND TENNIS CLUB, Box R, Stagecoach Rd., Sunapee, NH 03782; 603-763-5571. A 17-guestroom country inn in the western New Hampshire mountain and lake district. Mod. American plan; B&B plan available in May, June, and Sept. only. Breakfast, lunch, and dinner served to travelers by advance reservation; closed for lunch and dinner on Tues. during July and Aug. Lunches served only July, Aug. Open from early May to mid-Oct. Three tennis courts, pool, croquet, shuffleboard, 12½ mi. of hiking trails on grounds. Limited activities for children under 12. Pets allowed in Annex only. No credit cards. Frank and Shirley Simpson, Innkeepers.

Directions: From north & east: use Exit 12 or 12A, I-89. Continue west on Rte. 11, 6 mi.—just ½ mi. past Sunapee to a sign at Winn Hill Rd. Turn left up hill and after 1 mi. bear right on Stagecoach Rd. From west: use Exit 8, I-91, follow Rte. 103 east into N.H.— through Newport, ½ mi. past Junction with Rte. 11. Look for sign at "Young Hill Rd." and go 1½ mi. to Stagecoach Rd.

For B&B rates, see Index.

FOLLANSBEE INN
North Sutton, New Hampshire

Interstate 89 is a pleasant and practical way of going to northern Vermont, eastern New Hampshire, and even on to Montreal. A late afternoon start from Boston via I-93 will get the traveler to Exit 10 at North Sutton in time for a very pleasant dinner and comfortable overnight lodgings at the Follansbee Inn in North Sutton.

The village is on Route 114, which runs between Henniker and New London, and is enhanced by the presence of beautiful Kezar Lake.

Sandy and Dick Reilein have been working very hard to put this building and all of the country-hotel-style bedrooms into very good shape. Cleanliness is certainly one of the watchwords.

Several of the individually furnished rooms have good views of the lake, which at the time of my visit was covered with snow and good for cross-country skiing, Sandy pointed out that there were many combinations of double and single beds in each of the bedrooms. One bedroom had a bath with a great old tub that was certainly big enough for two, and there are several connecting rooms that are handy for people traveling with children.

Incidentally, the inn is a very convenient place to stop if you're bringing children up for interviews at Colby-Sawyer College in New London or Proctor Academy in Andover.

There's a full country breakfast included in the room charge, with an assortment of juices, eggs, bacon or sausage, puffed pancakes or french toast, served in a very pleasant dining room with bright, cheerful colors.

FOLLANSBEE INN, North Sutton, NH 03260; 603-927-4221. A 23-guestroom (private and shared baths) country inn on the shore of Kezar Lake in central New Hampshire in one of the scenic resort areas of the state. Closed parts of Nov. and April. Dinner not served Sun. or Mon. Hiking, backroading, xc and downhill skiing nearby. Children over 8 welcome. No pets. No smoking. Sandy and Dick Reilein, Innkeepers.

Directions: Take Exit 10 from I-89 and follow North Rd. to Rte. 114. Turn right and the inn is behind the church in North Sutton. From I-91, exit at Ascutney, Vt. Follow Rte. 103 to Rte. 11, east to Rte. 114 and then south to North Sutton.

For B&B rates, see Index.

HAVERHILL INN
Haverhill, New Hampshire

I'm constantly amazed at the discrimination and taste reflected in some of the really handsome homes of the region built by the men and women who came to the Connecticut River Valley 150 years or more ago. On Route 10 beginning at Lyme, there are a series of villages that have an enchanting early-19th-century American character. In Orford, for example, there are the famous "ridge homes" built between 1773 and 1839 by the professional and business men of the town. Some of them are Bulfinch-style houses built around 1815, designed by Asher Benjamin, who was an associate of the famous Boston architect, Bulfinch.

Continuing north on Route 10, the towns are Piermont and Haverhill, where I found the attractive proprietors Stephen Campbell and Katharine DeBoer. Steve is a computer consultant and a tremendous man in height and accomplishment; although somewhat more diminutively fashioned, Katharine is an extremely gifted concert soprano.

Their beautiful, white 1810 home is set in its own grove of trees off the highway, and immediately impresses the visitor with its warmth and hospitality.

There are four bedrooms of unusual size with period furnishings, working fireplaces, and ample bathrooms. The views are of the meadows and forests nearby.

Conversation around the breakfast table is bound to include the unusual group of antique shops both on the New Hampshire and Vermont side of the Connecticut River, and many guests are interested in the extensive backroading available in both states.

One of the nicest trips is to go north on New Hampshire's Route 10 to Woodsville; then cross over to what becomes Route 5 south on the Vermont side, and continue south, crossing back over on the bridge at Thetford.

HAVERHILL INN, Box 95, Rte. 10, Haverhill, N.H. 03765; 603-989-5961. A 4-bedroom, elegant, early-19th-century home now offering bed and breakfast. Open year-round. Equally convenient to both New Hampshire and Vermont for exceptional backroading and located near many communities for outdoor recreation. Stephen Campbell and Katharine DeBoer, Proprietors.

Directions: From I-91, suggest getting off at Hanover and following Rte. 10 north.

For B&B rates, see Index.

HICKORY STICK FARM
Laconia, New Hampshire

I have been visiting Hickory Stick Farm for many years, not only to enjoy the company of the innkeepers, Scott and Mary Roeder, but also to savor the house specialty—roast duckling. The birds are roasted at low temperatures for eight hours and then refrigerated. As orders are received, they are placed in a very hot oven for fifteen to twenty minutes, which produces a golden brown bird with crisp, delicious skin.

The entrance to this old converted farmhouse is through a lovely old-fashioned door leading into a beamed, low-ceilinged room with a brick fireplace. The floors are of brick or stone, and there are antique and gift items scattered about in several rooms preceding the entrance to the restaurant. Mary Roeder's stenciling on some of the walls is after the manner of Moses Eaton, Jr., who used to travel around southern New Hampshire in the early 1880s as a journeyman stencil artist.

Scott and Mary very recently have made arrangements to provide two attractive guest rooms in the inn. These will be available during the restaurant's entire summer season, and also during the remainder of the year, except when Scott and Mary are on short vacations. Breakfast is also provided to houseguests.

HICKORY STICK FARM, R.F.D. #2, Laconia, N.H. 03246; 603-524-3333. A hilltop country restaurant 4 mi. from Laconia in the lake country of New Hampshire. Two attractive lodging rooms with breakfast available most of the year. Restaurant open from Memorial Day to Columbus Day. Dinners served from 5:30 to 9 P.M. Sunday dinner served all day from noon to 8 P.M. Extended hours during fall foliage season—call ahead. When closed, dinner available to houseguests by prior arrangement. The Shaker Village in Canterbury is nearby, as well as the Belknap recreational area and other New Hampshire attractions. Scott and Mary Roeder, Innkeepers.

Directions: Use Exit 20 from I-93. Follow Rte. 3 toward Laconia approx. 5 mi. over bridge over Lake Winnisquam. A short distance past this bridge, turn right on Union Rd. immediately past Double Decker, a drive-in restaurant. Follow Union Rd. 1½ mi. and around a 90-degree curve to the right. Immediately turn left. Inn is up the hill on right. From Laconia, go south on Rtes. 3 and 11 (do not take Rte. 106) and turn left on Union Rd. (about ½ mi. past the Belknap Mall) and follow signs.

For B&B rates, see Index.

THE INN AT CHRISTIAN SHORE
Portsmouth, New Hampshire

A journey along the New England seacoast in search of America's past should by all means include a stop at Portsmouth, New Hampshire, if for no other reason than to visit Strawbery Banke (sic). A maritime community museum, preserving some of the early homes of Portsmouth and named for the profusion of wild berries found on the shores by the first settlers, Strawbery Banke evokes the way of life of sea captains, coopers, stage drivers, maritime tradesmen, and merchants.

Four homes are authentically restored and furnished in the styles of different time periods. A total of thirty-five buildings stands within the ten-acre area, making this one of the few urban outdoor museums of its kind.

The Inn at Christian Shore, a restored Federal house built around 1800, provides the overnight visitor with an ideal ambience for visiting Strawbery Banke. Just a few years ago it was almost a total disaster, but the innkeepers began the rewarding task of painstakingly restoring it. I believe "cozy" would be one of the first words that comes to my mind. All of the five guest rooms have been furnished with a mixture of antiques, reproductions, and decorations as close to the Federal style as possible. There are several fireplaces, including one in the sitting room, where the atmosphere is most agreeable for making new friends. Guests are frequently shown photographs of the building while it was being restored.

Breakfast, served in the low-ceilinged dining room, always begins with fresh fruit in season, including melon or grapefruit served with honey, and there are sweet breads, all types of eggs, steak, or pork tenderloin, home fries, various types of breakfast vegetables, and freshly ground coffee.

THE INN AT CHRISTIAN SHORE, 5 Northwest St., Portsmouth, NH 03801; 603-431-6770. A 5-guestroom (some shared baths) Federal home in a history-laden city in the southeast corner of New Hampshire. Breakfast is the only meal served, but there are several well-known restaurants within a short distance. Open every day. Strawbery Banke, Theater-by-the-Sea, and the Young Fine Arts Galleries nearby. No credit cards. Charles E. Litchfield and Louis G. Sochia, Proprietors.

Directions: From Boston take Exit 5 from I-95 to Portsmouth rotary. Follow Rte. 1 north to Maplewood Ave. Exit ramp to downtown Portsmouth. Headed toward downtown, the inn is the sixth house on the left. Sign in front—parking behind building.

For B&B rates, see Index.

THE INN AT COIT MOUNTAIN
Newport, New Hampshire

Newport was once a summer haven for the well-to-do families of
Boston and New York. By railroad and then by lake steamer, vacationing families would arrive, trunks laden, for a season of boating,
swimming, fishing, hiking, and picnics. Built in 1790 as a farmhouse, the Inn at Coit Mountain, an 18-room Georgian mansion,
was subsequently purchased in 1878 and used as a summer "cottage" by descendants of Austin Corbin, the man who built the Long
Island Railroad and was responsible for a New York landmark
synonymous with summer—Coney Island.

There are five guest rooms at the Inn at Coit Mountain, two of
which have fireplaces; one is a handsome, airy two-room suite. A
twin-bedded room is on the first floor.

The common room is an enormous oak-paneled library, dominated by a nine-foot-high granite fireplace. Breakfast is served on
chintz-covered tables in a cheery dining room with a charming
corner fireplace. There is a choice between a standard "country" or a
"gourmet" breakfast, but each features homemade breads and fresh
fruit, in season, from the inn's garden. The gourmet breakfast offers
such things as pecan waffles with honey butter, sherried creamed
eggs with mushrooms, or apricot crêpes.

Innkeepers Judi and Dick Tatem will offer their guests dinner
when prior arrangements are made.

The Dartmouth—Lake Sunapee area is now recognized as a four-
season resort area, as famous for its alpine and Nordic skiing as for
its warm-weather sports. The recently opened Hood Art Museum at
Dartmouth and an equestrian center equipped for indoor and outdoor polo games and Grand Prix horse shows offer other diversions.

*THE INN AT COIT MOUNTAIN, HCR 63 Box 3, Rte. 10, Newport, NH
03773; 800-367-2364 or 603-863-3583. A 5-guestroom (some
shared baths) elegant Georgian mansion in the Dartmouth—Lake
Sunapee district. Breakfast included in room rate. Dinner available by prior arrangement. Open year-round, 365 days. Swimming,
boating, trout fishing, hiking, bicycling, horseback riding, alpine
and xc skiing nearby. Oldest summer stock theater, cultural activities, and art museum on the campus at Darmouth. Child's crib
available. No pets, but kennel facilities nearby. Dick and Judi
Tatem, Innkeepers.*

*Directions: From Boston: take I-89 to Exit 13. Follow Rte. 10 toward
Newport. From New York: take I-91 to Exit 8 and follow Rte. 103 east
into Newport. Take Rte. 10 north 2 mi.*

For B&B rates, see Index.

THE INN AT CROTCHED MOUNTAIN
Francestown, New Hampshire

During the 1920s and '30s before the construction of the various interstate highways, when taking an automobile for more than one night was called "touring," U.S. Route 202 was one of the most popular roads for traveling through New England.

The New Hampshire portion includes a very pleasant journey through the Mount Monadnock region and a slight detour at Bennington will bring the traveler to Francestown and the Inn at Crotched Mountain.

The inn is situated in a 150-year-old, ivy-colored Colonial building 1,300 feet above sea level.

If nothing else, I can assure the reader that the view from this inn is well worth a side trip. It is enjoyed from a great many guest rooms, as well as from the dining room, living room, terrace, and swimming pool.

Although the full à la carte breakfast is served in the dining room, guests may take their plates to the patio on sunny mornings and enjoy a beautiful view of truly inspiring mountains. Besides the usual offerings of eggs and bacon, there are particularly tasty french toast and eggs Benedict.

THE INN AT CROTCHED MOUNTAIN, Mountain Rd., Francestown, NH 03043; 603-588-6840. A 14-guestroom mountain inn (5 rooms with private baths) in southern New Hampshire 15 mi. from Peterborough. European plan; breakfast not included in rates. Open from mid-May to Oct. 31; from Thanksgiving to the end of the ski season. Breakfast and dinner available to travelers in summer; breakfast or dinner, during winter and fall (telephone for reservations and exact schedule). Within a short distance of the Sharon Arts Center, American State Festival, Peterborough Players, Crotched Mtn. ski areas. Swimming pool, tennis courts, volleyball on grounds. Golf, skiing, hill walking, and backroading in the gorgeous Monadnock region nearby. No credit cards. Rose and John Perry, Innkeepers.

Directions: From Boston: follow Rte. 3 north to 101A to Milford. Then Rte. 13 to New Boston and Rte. 136 to Francestown. Follow Rte. 47 for 2½ mi. and turn left on Mountain Rd. Inn is 1 mi. on right. From New York/Hartford: I-91 north to Rte. 10 at Northfield to Keene, N.H. Follow 101 east to Peterborough, Rte. 202 north to Bennington, Rte. 47 to Mountain Rd. (approx. 4½ mi.); turn right on Mountain Rd. Inn is 1 mi. on right.

For Lodging rates, see Index.

THE INN AT DANBURY
Danbury, New Hampshire

I had a hard time finding Danbury on the map of New Hampshire, although it's not really that far from I-93. It's just a little distance north of New London.

In the middle of several different New Hampshire resort areas, Danbury is east of Lake Winnipesaukee and not far from Newfound Lake and Lake Sunapee. Even at that, the town is off the beaten path and not heavily traveled.

The Inn at Danbury was originally a house built around 1850. There were about six of these houses built along the road in the village at that time, but this one apparently went far out by putting porches on the second floor.

The inn has two different types of lodging rooms; five rooms are traditional farmhouse guest rooms with an interesting assortment of auction-sale kinds of beds, bureaus, tables, and so forth. The other type of accommodation is three dormitories, where up to twenty people can be comfortably accommodated.

Guests come to the Inn at Danbury in the wintertime for good downhill and cross-country skiing. It's a reasonable drive to several areas. In the summer the main activity is bicycling, and the inn's services include a bike shop, rental bikes, instruction, and guides. Also there is hiking, mountain climbing, fishing, boating, swimming, craft shows, and antiques.

Breakfast is a real Yankee feast that includes home fries, french toast, pancakes, eggs any style, country sausage, bacon, toast, and as the innkeepers assured me, "You can have any and all of these that you like."

There's nothing pretentious about the Inn at Danbury, and it certainly impressed me as a very comfortable, friendly place.

THE INN AT DANBURY, Route 104, Danbury, NH 03230; 603-768-3318. A 5-guestroom inn with additional dormitory space located in the resort section of central New Hampshire near several downhill and xc ski areas. Closed Nov., April, and most of May. Full breakfast included with lodgings. The evening meal also offered. Bike shop, rental bikes, instruction and guides available. No pets. No credit cards. George and Joan Issa, Innkeepers.

Directions: From I-93 take Exit 17 and follow Rte. 4 west to Rte. 104. Inn is ½ mi. beyond junction in the center of Danbury.

For B&B rates, see Index.

THE JOHN HANCOCK INN
Hancock, New Hampshire

Travelers who are fond of sampling New England's charms will find the John Hancock Inn a most pleasant diversion during the portion of their trip that includes the Monadnock region of southern New Hampshire.

The village of Hancock, which is accessible by several gentle "roller coaster" roads, has a handsome village green, a resident gazebo, and an ancient church and town hall. The houses are of early- and mid-19th-century vintage and the tree-shaded streets seem almost too good to be true.

Although the John Hancock Inn was named for the famous signer of the Declaration of Independence, Mr. Hancock never visited it himself. It is the oldest continuously-operating village inn in New Hampshire.

The Early American decor features primitive paintings, braided rugs, and a multitude of authentic antiques. The wide floorboards, fireplaces, and the very beams that have held this building together since 1789 are still much in evidence.

The John Hancock is well known for the Mural Room, which has murals created in the 19th century by Rufus Porter, depicting scenes of the nearby countryside.

An à la carte breakfast offers a wide choice of fruits, juices, eggs, griddle cakes, and coffee.

Interesting diversions abound in the area, with crafts shops, summer theater, music concerts, and contra dancing.

THE JOHN HANCOCK INN, Hancock, NH 03449; 603-525-3318. A 10-guestroom village inn on Rtes. 123 and 137, 9 mi. north of Peterborough. In the middle of the Monadnock Region of southern N.H. European plan. Breakfast, lunch, and dinner served daily to travelers. Closed Christmas Day and one week in spring and fall. All kinds of cultural events throughout the year. Antiquing, swimming, hiking, alpine and xc skiing nearby. Glynn and Pat Wells, Innkeepers.

Directions: From Keene, take either Rte. 101 east to Dublin and Rte. 137 north to Hancock or Rte. 9 north to Rte. 123 and east to Hancock. From Nashua, take 101A and 101 to Peterborough. Proceed north on Rtes. 202 and 123 to Hancock.

For Lodging rates, see Index.

LOVETT'S BY LAFAYETTE BROOK
Franconia, New Hampshire

Franconia, New Hampshire, off I-93, is a place that is held in reverence by lovers of downhill skiing in North America. It was to this area that some of the great early European ski instructors migrated a number of years ago, and here that American downhill skiing really had its beginning.

Lovett's by Lafayette Brook, to use the full name, was one of the earliest ski resorts, although the main house actually dates back to 1784.

Many of the guests have been returning for years, their fathers and mothers having come before them. In many ways, it's like a club.

Besides skiing, other seasons in Franconia have many delights which include antiquing, summer theater, horse shows, flower shows, auctions, and country fairs. The ski lifts are also run during the summer and autumn, providing the guests with spectacular views of the great White Mountains.

The full breakfast served at Lovett's before continuing a journey, or on a winter's morning before some skiing on Cannon Mountain, or in the summer for a day of rest, relaxation, and backroading, is a real White Mountain experience. Besides all types of juices and hot porridge served with maple syrup or brown sugar, if desired, there's a choice of roast beef hash with a poached egg, shirred eggs with fresh mushrooms, fried cornmeal mush, shirred eggs with eggplant, sour cream cheddar cheese omelet, and four different kinds (including parsnip) of pancakes. Breakfasts are an additional $5.00 each.

LOVETT'S BY LAFAYETTE BROOK, Profile Rd., Franconia, N.H. 03580; 603-823-7761. A 32-room country inn in New Hampshire's White Mountains. Modified American plan omits lunch, although box lunches are available. Breakfast and dinner served by reservation to travelers. Open daily between July 1 and Oct. 11 and Dec. 26 and April 1. No pets. Two swimming pools, xc skiing, badminton, lawn sports on grounds. Golf, tennis, alpine skiing, trout fishing, hiking nearby. Mr. and Mrs. Charles J. Lovett, Jr., Innkeepers.

Directions: 2½ mi. south of Franconia on N.H. 18 business loop, at junction of N.H. 141 and I-93 South Franconia exit. 2¾ mi. north of junction of U.S. 3 and 18.

For Lodging rates, see Index.

234

LYME INN
Lyme, New Hampshire

New Hampshire and Vermont *are* different, although I'm not certain I can explain why. I would suggest that the traveler on I-91 leave this splendid highway and take Route 5 in Vermont, going in one direction, and on the way back, Route 10 in New Hampshire. Both are equally stimulating, and it's possible to see how the architectural modes in the two states differ.

The Lyme Inn rests at the end of a long New England common on Route 10, just ten miles from Hanover, New Hampshire, the home of Dartmouth College.

The ten guest rooms with private baths and five with shared baths have poster beds, hooked rugs, hand-stitched quilts, wide pine floorboards, stenciled wallpaper, wing chairs, and all types of beautiful antiques. There is no entertainment provided for young children.

The spacious front entranceway, used as a summer porch, has a most impressive collection of white wicker furniture.

The main dishes on the dinner menu include lamb chops, hunter style veal, Wiener schnitzel, and hassenpfeffer.

A full breakfast is included in the cost of the room, and might feature fried or scrambled eggs or french toast, along with fruit juices, fresh fruit in season, blueberry muffins, and coffee.

Even for one night, be sure to reserve well in advance.

LYME INN, on the Common, Lyme, NH 03768; 603-795-2222. A 15-guestroom (some shared baths) village inn, 10 mi. north of Hanover on N.H. Rte. 10. Breakfast included in room rates. Open year-round. Dinner served Wed. thru Mon. to travelers. Closed three weeks following Thanksgiving and three weeks in late spring. Convenient to all Dartmouth College activities, including Hopkins Center, with music, dance, drama, painting, and sculpture. Alpine and xc skiing, fishing, hiking, canoeing, tennis, and golf nearby. No children under 8. No pets. Fred and Judy Siemons, Innkeepers.

Directions: From I-91, take Exit 14 and follow Rte. 113A east to Vermont Rte. 5. Proceed south 50 yards to a left turn, then travel 2 mi. to inn.

For B&B rates, see Index.

235

MOOSE MOUNTAIN LODGE
Etna, New Hampshire

Moose Mountain Lodge is really one of a kind. Built in the late 1930s, mostly of logs and stones gathered from the surrounding forests and fields, the lodge perches high on the western side of Moose Mountain. The broad porch extending across the entire front of the house has views of the rolling New Hampshire countryside and of famed Vermont peaks in the far distance.

The atmosphere is indeed rustic, with twelve real "up-country" bedrooms, enhanced by colorful quilts, comfortable beds, and many, many flowers.

Bed and breakfast is available during the summer and fall only. During the winter, Moose Mountain Lodge is well known as a cross-country ski center, and a full American plan is in effect, including breakfast, lunch, and dinner.

The summer months find guests hiking, swimming, canoeing on the Connecticut River, visiting Dartmouth and Hanover, and sitting on the porch, watching the birds.

The fall foliage season weekends are almost always entirely booked; however, Tuesdays, Wednesdays, and Thursdays are wonderful times to take a vacation for a few days, and the early New Hampshire fall starts about the last weekend of September.

Moose Mountain Lodge is also part of a Connecticut River "canoeing-inn-to-inn" summer program.

MOOSE MOUNTAIN LODGE, Etna, NH 03750; 603-643-3529. A 12-guestroom (5 shared baths) rustic lodge a few miles from Hanover, New Hampshire. Open June thru Oct.; late Dec. thru March. Bed and breakfast available only during summer and fall. Winter rates include breakfast, lunch, and dinner served only to houseguests. Many wonderful New Hampshire and Green Mountain attractions and recreational and cultural advantages nearby. No pets. Peter and Kay Shumway, Innkeepers

Directions: If arriving for the first time, stop in Etna at the Etna Store and telephone for directions.

For B&B rates, see Index.

PHILBROOK FARM INN
Shelburne, New Hampshire

Philbrook Farm Inn, within sight of Route 2, is the personification of New Hampshire. It is filled with New Hampshire prints, paintings, and photographs, some of them really irreplaceable. There are many, many books about New Hampshire, and many have been written by former guests.

There is a great tradition of "taking in guests" at this venerable White Mountain farm. It all started many years ago and Connie Leger and Nancy Philbrook are the fourth generation of Philbrooks carrying on the family tradition.

"Many of our guests have been coming back for so many years they know the kitchen almost as well as we do," said Connie, "and they love to come down and peel the potatoes or cut the beans and shell the peas and just sit and visit."

The guest rooms are farmhouse in nature and always immaculate.

Breakfast, with the morning sun lighting up the fields and mountains, is served in the old-fashioned dining room with the highly polished wood floors. There is a choice of fruit juice, hot or cold cereal, a choice of eggs and bacon, and toast made from homemade bread. On Sunday morning there are homemade fish balls and cornbread, as well—a real farm breakfast.

PHILBROOK FARM INN, North Rd., Shelburne, N.H. 03581; 603-466-3831. A 20-room country inn in the White Mountains of northeastern N.H., 6 mi. from Gorham and just west of the Maine/N.H. line. American & mod. American plans available. Open May 1st to October 31st; December 26th to April 1st. Closed Thanksgiving, Christmas. Pets allowed only during summer season in cottages. Outdoor swimming pool, shuffleboard, horseshoes, badminton, ping-pong, croquet, pool table, hiking trails, xc skiing, snowshoeing trails on grounds. Horseback riding, golf, hiking, backroading, bird watching nearby. No credit cards. Nancy C. Philbrook and Constance P. Leger, Innkeepers.

Directions: The inn is just off U.S. Rte. 2 in Shelburne. Look for inn direction sign and turn at Meadow Rd., cross R.R. tracks and river, turn right at crossroad onto North Rd., and the inn is down the road a piece.

For B&B rates, see Index.

PINKHAM NOTCH CAMP
Gorham, New Hampshire

Here is bed-and-breakfast quite unlike anything I have discovered previously. The Pinkham Notch Camp is a world apart. The only skyscrapers in this neighborhood are the peaks of the White Mountains; the only distraction is the roaring of Glen Ellis Falls and Crystal Cascades; the only glaring light, that of the sunrise over Wildcast Ridge.

The camp is located eight miles north of Jackson on Route 16, just two and a half miles below the timber line. It is in the heart of the White Mountain National Forest at the base of Mount Washington and a short distance from Tuckerman Ravine, the Alpine Garden and countless other scenic attractions.

The motto here is "Latchstring always out." There are accommodations for up to 107 people in two-, three-, and four-bunk rooms, with showers and bathrooms on each floor. As for meals, there is all you can eat at breakfast and dinner—all homemade and served family-style at long tables.

Here, the primary entertainment is the outdoors, with a network of hiking trails, back-country ski and snowshoeing trails, and there is a helpful staff for information and advice.

The camp is at the apex of the Appalachian Mountain Club Hut System, which maintains eight back-country huts along the Appalachian Trail at intervals of one-day hikes.

If this has whetted your appetite for a different kind of bed-and-breakfast experience, I suggest that you write or call for further information. You might even want to join the Appalachian Mountain Club, 5 Joy Street, Boston, Massachusetts 02108; (617-523-0636)—members enjoy reduced rates.

By the way, you don't have to be a hiker or a skier to enjoy the camp accommodations. You can arrive and depart by car and just sit and bask in the sun without ever setting foot on a trail.

PINKHAM NOTCH CAMP, (Appalachian Mountain Club), Rte. 16, Box 298, Gorham, NH 03851; 603-466-2727. A splendid mountain camp facility in the heart of the White Mountains. Breakfast, trail lunches, and dinner served daily to guests and public. Lodging rate includes breakfast. Various discounts available. Open all year. Unlimited opportunities for hiking and skiing. Variety of evening events presented. Wonderful for families. No pets. No credit cards; personal checks accepted.

Directions: Rte. 16 runs north and south in New Hampshire. Pinkham Notch Camp is just a few miles above North Conway.

For B&B rates, see Index.

SIX CHIMNEYS
East Hebron, New Hampshire

The eight-mile-long Newfound Lake, "one of the cleanest in the world," dotted with marinas and stocked with trout and salmon, is synonymous with "camp-for-the-kids." Five private camps, a number of preparatory schools, and the campus of Plymouth State College are all nearby.

Records about the cozy Six Chimneys in East Hebron, an almost two-hundred-year-old square-faced house that perches on a knoll, are kept in the Hebron library. As a stop on the popular run between Concord and Haverhill, the coach house was originally dubbed "The Tavern."

Indeed, the low, beamed ceilings are reminiscent of eased boots and relaxed chats around the open hearths. There is frequently a fire dancing in the dining room when guests sit at the handsome Spanish chestnut refectory table for a hearty breakfast. It starts with juice or fruit; the large fresh eggs come from resident hens. Some days there are blueberry or pumpkin muffins; local Hebron maple syrup drenches the french toast. It is always served on heirloom English china and sparkling sterling silver.

There are four "common rooms," each with a slightly different ambience—one filled with games and books, another, "the summer parlor," prim and Victorian.

All six guest rooms are newly papered with matching coverlets and curtains. The door latches are the original hardware, old trunks serve as luggage racks, and the floors have that wonderful, authentic tilt. The shared baths, on the other hand, are thoroughly modern, with stall showers. Two of the guest rooms are in an ell which was, in days gone by, used for the stagecoach drovers. These rooms are slightly smaller but very cheerily decorated in Colonial prints.

SIX CHIMNEYS, Star Rte. Box 114, North Shore Rd. and Rte. 3A, East Hebron, NH 03232; 603-744-2029. A 6-guestroom restored 18th-century coaching stop now a comfortable inn a few miles south of the White Mountains on the shore of Newfound Lake. Complimentary full breakfast. Open all year. Hiking and xc skiing from the door. Natural spectaculars such as the Old Man of the Mountain, Mt. Washington, and the Polar Caves; also golf, fishing, boating, swimming, summer stock theater, hunting, skiing, and ice fishing are nearby. Close to camps and secondary schools. No children under 6. No pets. Peter and Lee Fortescue, Hosts.

Directions: From I-93, take Exit 23 and continue on Rte. 104 west 5 mi. to Bristol; then 9 mi. north on Rte. 3A to the intersection of Rte. 3A and North Shore Rd. in East Hebron.

For B&B rates, see Index.

SOUTHWORTH'S BED & BREAKFAST
Sugar Hill, New Hampshire

Sugar Hill, New Hampshire, is indeed an exceptional town for several reasons. First, because of its really idyllic location high in the mountains in northern New Hampshire on Route 117 between Franconia and Lisbon. And its residents have always been known for being singularly independent, a fact that was vividly borne out when the village broke off from Lisbon a few years ago to become a separate community.

Perhaps this is just the right atmosphere for David Southworth and his wife, Amy, as attractive a young couple as you will find anywhere, who moved here from Pittsburgh a few years ago to start a whole new lifestyle. David is self-employed nearby and Amy pretty much takes care of their trim little New Hampshire farmhouse during the daytime.

The house, a white clapboard with green shutters and a few added dormers, is located across the road from the Sugar Hill Meeting House and Sweet Pea Farm. At the time of my visit, almost the entire house had been redecorated, including the parlors and the three bedrooms which share one bath. The rooms are all done in a country fashion with pleasant, bright colors.

In addition to their collection of memorabilia, Amy and David have equipped a TV and game room with a variety of games and loads of books for on-the-premises entertainment.

Sugar Hill is within just a few minutes of Cannon Mountain Ski Area and there is plenty of cross-country skiing in the area, as well as a 9-hole golf course. It is a convenient, attractive place to stay in any season.

SOUTHWORTH'S BED & BREAKFAST, Route 117, Sugar Hill, N.H. 03585; 603-823-5344. A 3-bedroom, trim bed-and-breakfast home high in the mountains of northern New Hampshire. Homestyle accommodations with shared bath; continental breakfast included in room rate. Open all year. Convenient for all mountain attractions, including hiking, skiing, boating, fishing, tennis, and golf. Bruce and Judy Southworth, Owners; David and Amy Southworth, Proprietors.

Directions: From I-93 take Franconia exit, follow Rte. 117 to Sugar Hill. From I-91 take Wells River, Vt. exit; continue on Rte. 302 to a point above Lisbon and turn right on Rte. 117 to Sugar Hill.

For B&B rates, see Index.

STAFFORD'S IN THE FIELD
Chocorua, New Hampshire

Stafford's in the Field is that highly sought-after inn "at the end of the road." It's like being in a very big farmhouse, and all of the parlors, the lodging rooms, and the dining room have a wonderful 19th-century farmhouse feeling.

It's fun to sit on the porch and look out over the fields to the woods beyond. There are deer, rabbits, foxes, and game birds sharing this wonderful country, and once in awhile someone sees a small bear.

Mt. Chocorua is just a few miles away and only a short distance farther are the great peaks of the White Mountains where there is good fun and recreation in both summer and winter.

Although this inn has a special B&B rate available to our readers, I would suggest that when making reservations arrangements should be made also to enjoy dinner, because Ramona Stafford is a true gourmet cook and perhaps the traveler will be lucky enough to be there on an evening when spare ribs cooked in maple syrup are on the menu.

A full breakfast is served, usually including blueberry pancakes served with maple syrup from trees on the property. At various times there are apple muffins, Mexican specialties, omelets, baked apples, fritters, and other unusual treats, and almost always there is a homemade hot cereal. On warm mornings breakfast is served under the maples in the garden.

STAFFORD'S IN THE FIELD, Chocorua, N.H. 03817; 603-323-7766. A 12-room resort-inn with cottages, 17 mi. south of North Conway. Some rooms in inn with shared baths. Modified American plan at inn omits lunch. B&B rate available. Open all year. Bicycles, tennis, and xc skiing on the grounds. Summer theater, square dancing, golf, swimming, hiking, riding, and fishing nearby. No pets. The Stafford Family, Innkeepers.

Directions: Follow N.H. Rte. 16 north to Chocorua Village, then turn left onto Rte. 113 and travel 1 mi. west to inn. Or, from Rte. 93 take Exit 23 and travel east on Rtes. 104 and 25 to Rte. 16. Proceed north on Rte. 16 to Chocorua Village, turn left onto Rte. 113 and travel 1 mi. west to inn.

For B&B rates, see Index.

THATCHER HILL INN
Marlborough, New Hampshire

There is a 92-year-old, five-story red barn on the Thatcher Hill property that lures photographers and painters alike. An old white silo further attests that these sixty acres were once a working farm.

Now the fully renovated farmhouse, built in 1794, has seven guest rooms, each with a private bath; one room is totally handicap-accessible. There is also a wheelchair ramp at the side door.

The atmosphere at Thatcher Hill is old-fashioned: antique sewing machines serve as tables; there are Victorian parlor chairs; a five-foot-tall, eighty-year-old music box stands in one sitting room; and another wind-up music box plays Strauss waltzes on its original discs. Guests are welcome to play on the handsome carved walnut parlor organ.

All the guest rooms are spotlessly clean. The beds are covered in quilts and coverlets made by Marge Gage. She and her husband, Cal, whose family owned this homestead for generations, spent a full year on renovations. The original pine floors have been stripped and waxed. The modernized baths have claw-footed tubs painted in gay primary shades and the luxury touch of heated towel bars!

One of the guest rooms is furnished in that amusing Adirondack style, called "twig furniture." Another can be used as a suite, with two bedrooms and a sitting room. There is a delightful small porch overlooking the barn and fields, where one guest set up his field glass to watch for Halley's comet.

Games, television, a VCR, and game tables are available to all the guests. A separate breakfast room, cheery with its separate pinewood tables, is where guests gather for the morning meal—a continental breakfast featuring home-baked muffins and breads.

THATCHER HILL INN, Thatcher Hill Road, Marlborough, NH 03455; 603-876-3361. A 7-guestroom (private baths) sunny farmhouse set on 60 rural acres in southern N.H. Complimentary hearty continental breakfast. Open all year. Snowshoeing and xc skiing on grounds. Near Keene, with summer theater and Colony Mill Marketplace, Monadnock Music Festival, Apple Hill Chamber Players, and Mt. Monadnock, famous for hiking and climbing. More than 200 ponds and lakes in the area. No children under school age. No pets. No smoking in bedrooms. Marge and Cal Gage, Innkeepers.

Directions: From NYC: I-91 to Exit 3, Brattleboro, Vt.; Rte. 9 east to Keene; Rte. 101 east to Rte. 124 in Marlborough, and south to Thatcher Hill Rd. From Boston: West on Rte. 2 to Rte. 140 north to Rte. 12 north to Keene, and then Rte. 101 east to Marlborough.

For B&B rates, see Index.

WHITE GOOSE INN
Orford, New Hampshire

The first eye-catcher at the White Goose Inn is the Colonial Revival porch that encircles the trunk of a huge old elm with a waist-high, pristine white railing. (The tree was injured in a storm and cut to the roof line more than twenty years ago.) The next most noticeable feature is the cleanliness and perfect order—from the manicured lawn surrounding the spring-fed pond to the neat flower-beds in the midst of the eight-acre property.

The White Goose Inn has a *House Beautiful* decor. There are oriental rugs on highly polished original wood floors, delicate European antiques, like a lady's fruitwood desk, and sturdy Hitchcock pieces, like a deacon's bench and country trunks, and some Colonial farm implements (a long-handled rake) used as wall hangings.

The cheery dining room has an oversized braided rug and a working fireplace. Breakfast, which is served there or on the porch in good weather, consists of fruit salad using fruits in season, fresh (usually bran) muffins, with eggs any style, and french toast, which is the excuse to serve local maple syrup.

There is one large guest room with a double bed on the first floor. An often requested room appropriate for "getaway" couples or honeymooners has two double beds and a claw-footed tub in its private bath. The ceilings are eaved, and the windows overlook the brook and the pond.

The town of Orford with its famous seven Ridge houses is a photographer's dream. The inn is used on the New England bicyclers' tour. For class reunions Dartmouth alumni use the inn and reserve one year in advance. There are also numerous prep schools and campuses in the vicinity, so I would definitely advise making a telephone call well ahead.

WHITE GOOSE INN, Route 10, P.O. Box 17, Orford, NH 03777; 603-353-4812. A 9-guestroom (private and shared baths) Colonial inn near Dartmouth College, about 15 mi. north of Hanover. Complimentary full breakfast. Open all year. Dartmouth ski center with alpine and xc skiing, Appalachian Trail, hiking, biking, canoeing, horseback riding, various cultural activities at Hopkins Center/Hood Museum of Dartmouth College; Saint Gaudens National Historical site in nearby Cornish. Excellent restaurants in area. No children under 8. No pets. Manfred and Karin Wolf, Innkeepers.

Directions: From I-91 take Exit 15 (Fairlee). Cross the bridge and take Rte. 10 south for 1 mi.

For B&B rates, see Index.

WOODSTOCK INN
North Woodstock, New Hampshire

So you are between New York and Canada on Route I-93 and it's getting a little late in the afternoon—time to think about some nice cozy place to stay overnight and a hefty breakfast in the morning. Isn't it interesting that you happen to be within telephoning distance of the Woodstock Inn?

Snuggled on the lower slopes of the White Mountains, this 100-year-old-Victorian home has now been fully restored by its chef and owner, Scott Rice, and his wife, Eileen. Each room is comfortably furnished in a Victorian style with twin and double beds and is especially convenient for families. This is old-style country hospitality, and the baths are down the hall. Across the street, in a 120-year-old building, are ten additional rooms, all with private baths.

One of the most interesting features of this little inn is the glassed-in porch with additional tables for breakfast, lunch, and dinner. The chairs are old movie-house seats—this is the first time I have ever seen them used for this purpose. The atmosphere is enhanced with many hanging plants.

Dinner, featuring duck, veal, beef, and seafood entrées, as well as breakfast and lunches, is served daily.

Because Woodstock is near several ski areas, as well as the spectacular White Mountain scenery, innkeeper Rice has provided many additional package plans, but all of the rates include breakfast, which is served to the public until noon.

The latest news is that they have created a pub-type restaurant and lounge out of Lincoln's original train station, which was moved and added onto the main house last spring.

WOODSTOCK INN, P.O. Box 118, Main St., North Woodstock, NH 03262; 603-745-3951. A 16-guestroom (shared and private baths) in-town inn. Open all year. Breakfast included in room rate. Lunch and dinner served to travelers. Conveniently located for all of the White Mountain attractions, including Franconia Notch, Kancamagus Highway, Crawford Notch, Loon Mt. Gondola, Cannon Mt., and Waterville Valley. Not suitable for very young children. No pets. Scott and Eileen Rice, Innkeepers.

Directions: Leave I-93 at Loon Mt. exit (Rte. 112), North Woodstock. Inn is just a short distance west on Rte. 3.

For B&B rates, see Index.

COLLIGAN'S STOCKTON INN
Stockton, New Jersey

The beautiful Delaware River valley, north of Philadelphia, separates New Jersey and Pennsylvania in about as beautiful and fascinating a way as could be imagined. The area is rich in history, dating even before Washington's famous crossing of the Delaware during the Revolutionary War. Later on, canals were built on each side of the river and many small river towns grew up around the resulting profitable trade.

One such town is Stockton, New Jersey, and one of the earliest continuing accommodations has been on the site of the present-day Stockton Inn, which dates back about a hundred and fifty years.

The stone walls of the inn have a wonderful weathered look, and the mansard roof indicates the Victorian addition in later years.

This is the inn made famous during the thirties by the Rodgers and Hart melody, "There's a Small Hotel," and the famous wishing well is still very much in evidence.

Although today's Stockton Inn is better known as a restaurant serving an international cuisine, there are eleven guest rooms including eight suites with fireplaces, available for overnight-and-longer guests. A continental breakfast of fruit juice, cheese, yogurt, sweet roll, and coffee or tea is offered with the room rate.

COLLIGAN'S STOCKTON INN, Route 29, Stockton, NJ 08559; 609-397-1250. Outside N.J.: 800-368-7272. A traditional inn located in a Delaware River village. Lunch and dinner served every day. Continental breakfast included in room rate. Open all year except Christmas Day. All of the scenic and cultural attractions of nearby Bucks County, Pa., and New Jersey are within a very short distance. No pets. Todd Drucquer, Innkeeper.

Directions: From New York City: Take New Jersey Turnpike south to Exit 10, then follow I-287 north of Somerville, exiting to Rte. 22 west. Go 2½ miles and then take Rte. 202 south, past Flemington to the Delaware River. Use the last exit in New Jersey marked "Rte. 29, Lambertville and Stockton." Go 3 miles north on 29 to Stockton. From Philadelphia: Follow I-95 north to the Delaware River. Cross the Delaware to the first exit in New Jersey marked "29 Trenton/Lambertville." Follow 29 north through Lambertville, approximately 17 miles to Stockton.

For B&B rates, see Index.

CONOVER'S BAY HEAD INN
Bay Head, New Jersey

I visited Bay Head for the first time a number of years ago and I enjoyed an overnight visit with Carl and Beverly Conover at Conover's Bay Head Inn, just one block from the beach. It is a three-story typical Jersey Coast home with a very pleasant front porch overlooking the main street, as well as second-floor porches on the front and rear. A carriage house in the rear is available from September 15 to June 1.

It's obvious that the innkeepers have had a lot of fun visiting antique and tag sales, because the twelve lodging rooms are all furnished with some interesting pieces, and also boast matching spreads and ruffled pillows. Beverly's mother crochets the washcloths and she also does the dress scarfs and doilies in bright colors.

Breakfast is taken in the dining room or on the porch. The oranges used for the freshly squeezed juice have probably been sent north from Florida by Beverly's parents, and breakfast also includes such tempting offerings as bran muffins, blueberry-corn muffins, carrot muffins, Hungarian nut crescents, fruit kuchen, and coffee cake. Carl pitches in and, for an additional charge, will make bacon and eggs during the season, although they are included in the room rate from October to end of April.

CONOVER'S BAY HEAD INN, 646 Main Ave., Bay Head, NJ 08742; 201-892-4664. A 12-guestroom (some shared baths) inn in a conservative town on the New Jersey Coast. Continental breakfast included in room rate during the season; full breakfast in off-season. Croquet, paddleball, and horseshoes on the grounds; swimming, sailing, fishing, tennis, golf, and racquet sports nearby. Open Feb. 15 to Dec. 15. Closed Christmas and New Year's. No pets. Beverly and Carl Conover, Innkeepers.

Directions: Take Exit 98 off Garden State Parkway to Rte. 34 to Rte. 35 south. Follow signs to Pt. Pleasant Beach. Bay Head is the next town. Rte. 35 is Main Ave. in Bay Head. From Philadelphia, take Rte. 195 to Rte. 34, and then 35 south. By rail: take the North Jersey Coast Line from Penn Station and arrangements can be made to be picked up at the Bay Head Station.

For B&B rates, see Index.

246

THE KENILWORTH
Spring Lake, New Jersey

This is very much like a little Bristish seaside resort hotel except that it is far superior to many I've seen cheek-by-jowl in places like Brighton and Hastings.

To add to the English flavor, I was shown about by the manager, Ivy Mason, who is herself from England.

Located on Ocean Avenue, the Kenilworth is just a few steps across the road from the Spring Lake boardwalk and a private sandy beach.

The twenty-five guest rooms, a few of which have private baths, have a seaside-resort atmosphere with 19th-century furniture. It's all very pleasant and homey.

One of the rooms overlooks the famous Spring Lake private croquet club where enthusiasts from all over the world come to play in tournaments.

A generous continental breakfast is the only meal served and it includes all kinds of fresh fruits, cereals, bagels, danish, and doughnuts.

Spring Lake is a community where many people have lovely summer homes and have been able to exist in harmony with very pleasant and conservative guest houses and small hotels. If I lived in New York City I would certainly come here on many pleasant winter weekends to bundle up and walk on the beaches and boardwalk, and to get the smell of the salt air and enjoy the lovely atmosphere and quiet. Of course it's very popular in the summer.

THE KENILWORTH, 1505 Ocean Ave., Spring Lake, NJ 07762; 201-449-5327. A 25-guestroom (12 with private baths) Victorian ocean-front hotel located in a conservative resort community on the northern New Jersey coast. Open year-round. Breakfast included in cost of room. Private beach. Convenient to all resort activities. No pets. No credit cards. Ron and Ivy Mason, Proprietors.

Directions: Leave Garden State Parkway at Exit 98 and proceed to Rtes. 34 and 524. Follow Rte. 524 to Ocean Ave. and turn right.

For B&B rates, see Index.

THE MAINSTAY INN
Cape May, New Jersey

Cape May, along with Marshall, Michigan, enjoys the distinction of being one of the best-preserved and restored Victorian communities in North America. The tree-shaded streets of the historic district contain marvelous Greek Revival, Gothic, Queen Anne, Italianate, and mansard architecture, often with several styles combined. It is a composite picture of Victorian dignity and elegance, Southern charm and hospitality, and a scattering of Colonial simplicity.

One of the most handsome examples is the Mainstay, a lovely guest house kept by Tom and Sue Carroll, who are among the leaders in the effort to keep Cape May a place "set apart."

The house has had a most interesting history since it was built in 1872 as an elegant gambling club. It was sold in 1898 to a sedate Philadelphia family, who added the back wing and entertained some of the great and near-great of Philadelphia society during the many years that followed.

Today, the dining room, living room, and all the guest rooms contain an outstanding collection of Victorian antiques. They are the subject of much "oohing and ahing" on the daily house tour.

From mid-June to mid-September, a full breakfast is served in the formal dining room with homemade dishes, such as strawberry crêpes, quiches, and soufflés. In midsummer a lighter breakfast, consisting of fruit juices, cereal, coffee, tea, and homemade coffee cakes, is served on the broad porch.

THE MAINSTAY INN, 635 Columbia Ave., Cape May, NJ 08204; 609-884-8690. A 12-guestroom inn in a well-preserved Victorian village one block from the ocean. Breakfast served to houseguests. Open every day April thru Nov. Boating, swimming, fishing, bicycles, riding, golf, tennis, and hiking nearby. Not suitable for small children. No pets. No credit cards; personal checks accepted. Tom and Sue Carroll, Innkeepers.

Directions: From Philadelphia take the Walt Whitman Bridge to the Atlantic City Expy. Follow the Atlantic City Expy. to exit for Garden State Pkwy., south. Go south on the Pkwy. which ends in Cape May. The Pkwy. becomes Lafayette St.; turn left at first light onto Madison. Proceed 3 blocks and turn right onto Columbia. Proceed 3 blocks to inn on right side.

For B&B rates, see Index.

THE NORMANDY INN
Spring Lake, New Jersey

The Normandy is located in the residential north section of Spring Lake, a town that proudly proclaims its Irish heritage. The inn is within one block of the bathing beach, pavilion, and pool. There's a large front porch where you may wish to relax and read the newspapers or a good book, and the bedrooms are larger than usual and air conditioned.

It's a many-layered Victorian house, built in 1888 and cited by the Spring Lake centennial committee.

The owner-innkeepers, Michael and Susan Ingino, have captured that Victorian feeling with period furnishings. There is a nine-foot gold leaf oval mirror in the side parlor and an eight-foot walnut bed in one of the guest rooms. Throughout the inn there are many antique clocks that Michael has collected over the years.

A hearty country breakfast is served in the dining room, and there is a closed-in porch with a refrigerator for guests to use. There are many fine restaurants nearby for dinner.

THE NORMANDY INN, 21 Tuttle Ave., Spring Lake, NJ 07762; 201-449-7172. A 20-guestroom Victorian inn in a quiet community on the north Jersey seacoast. All but three rooms have private baths. Open year-round. A full breakfast is included with the price of the room. Located ½ block from ocean and boardwalk. Convenient to all of the Jersey coast recreational and entertainment activities. No credit cards. Michael and Susan Ingino and daughter, Beth, Innkeepers.

Directions: From Garden State Pkwy. take Exit 98 and follow Rte. 34 to first circle. Go ¾ of the way around the circle to Rte. 524 and follow this to the ocean. Turn right on Ocean Ave. one block and right again on Tuttle.

For B&B rates, see Index.

THE WOOLVERTON INN
Stockton, New Jersey

The Woolverton Inn is an elegant stone manor house set amidst formal gardens and stately trees, just a few minutes from the Delaware River, in the rather conservative village of Stockton, New Jersey, across the river from Bucks County, Pennsylvania.

It's an unusual blend of both 18th- and 19th-century architecture, having been built in 1793 and later remodeled by Maurice Woolverton, whose family held the property from 1850 to 1939.

In 1972 the property was purchased by George and Ann Hackl, who decided to turn it into an inn.

Each of the ten guest rooms has been furnished with most tasteful antiques and each one expresses an early-American individuality.

Guests enjoy home-baking for breakfast and afternoon tea, which, by the way, is a very welcome break after a day spent exploring nearby Bucks County and the Delaware River Valley or perhaps walking along the river towpath.

THE WOOLVERTON INN, R.D. 3, Box 233, Stockton, NJ 08559; 609-397-0802. A 10-guestroom pastorally oriented inn on the east side of the Delaware River, within just a few moments of historic Bucks County, Pa. Open year-round. Breakfast is the only meal offered on a regular basis and is included in the price of the rooms. Bicycles, bocci, horseshoes, and croquet on grounds. Swimming, tubing, canoeing, tennis, golf, and wonderful history-laden back roads, including visits to Washington's Crossing nearby. No children under 14. No pets. David Salassi, Innkeeper.

Directions: From New York City: Take New Jersey Turnpike south to Exit 10, then follow I-287 north of Somerville, exiting on Rte. 22 west. Go 2½ mi. and then take Rte. 202 south, past Flemington to the Delaware River. Use the last exit in New Jersey, marked "Rte. 29, Lambertville and Stockton." Go 3 mi. north on 29 to Stockton and turn right on Rte. 523, up hill ¼ mi. to a sharp left-hand turn—the inn sign. The inn is the second driveway on the right. From Philadelphia: Follow I-95 north to the Delaware River. Cross the Delaware to the first exit in New Jersey, marked "29 Trenton/ Lambertville." Follow 29 north through Lambertville, approx. 17 mi. to Stockton.

For B&B rates, see Index.

GRANT CORNER INN
Santa Fe, New Mexico

When news of the extraordinary breakfasts served guests at the Grant Corner Inn began to circulate in Santa Fe, a curious thing happened. Outsiders asked if they could come, too. Please. So now, with a day's notice, you can breakfast here in front of the fire or on the veranda, depending on the season, even if you're not lucky enough to cadge a bedroom for the night.

New Mexican favorites (huevos rancheros; green chile crêpes) are offered with such house specialties as spinach omelet, cherry blintzes, Dutch Babies, and stuffed french toast. On Valentine's Day, the french toast is heart-shaped; but any day, the juice is fresh-squeezed, the coffee fresh-ground, the breads and jams home-made.

Although no other meals are served, the Walters will put together an elegant picnic lunch to accompany you on day trips to the backlands of this enchanting region. In town, you can leave your car in the off-street parking area and walk to a dozen fine restaurants, as well as the shops and museums of the Plaza, heart of Santa Fe.

Louise and Pat Walter rescued the spacious old townhouse from oblivion and put their considerable designer talents together to produce a real charmer. No two guest rooms are alike, but all are handsomely decorated with antiques, and there are fresh flowers throughout the house year around. The portrait smiling approval from the mantel is of Jack Stewart, founder of Arizona's famed Camelback Inn and Louise's father.

GRANT CORNER INN, 122 Grant Avenue, Santa Fe, NM 87501; 505-983-6678. A 13-guestroom (7 with private baths) bed-and-breakfast inn in downtown Santa Fe. Breakfast only meal regularly served. Closed January. Sightseeing, restaurants, shopping nearby. Louise and Pat Walter, Innkeepers.

Directions: From I-25 to St. Francis, drive west. Turn right on Alameda, left on Guadalupe, right on Johnson. Inn is on corner of Johnson and Grant with own parking lot on left side of Johnson.

For B&B rates, see Index.

LA POSADA DE CHIMAYÓ
Chimayó, New Mexico

You have to take a dirt road for the last mile to La Posada, and just as you are beginning to mutter, "This had better be good," you arrive, and it is. It is delightful even on muddy-road days, because that means a fire burning cheerily in the corner fireplace of your own sitting room and maybe a chance to browse through the house books before getting into heavy sightseeing.

Chimayó is the first of the Spanish villages on the High Road to Taos, famous for its weavers of rugs and blankets, its chile peppers, its 1816 mission church, and a restaurant, Rancho de Chimayó, which brings Santa Feans twenty-five miles for the fine New Mexican cuisine.

Authentic northern New Mexican also describes La Posada. The two-apartment guest house is a real adobe with brick floors and viga ceilings. Decor and furnishings are regionally "tipico" and so is the hearty breakfast Sue Farrington gives her guests. You can expect local sausage served with incredible stuffed french toast or possibly an egg, cheese, and green chile casserole, an open-face omelet, Chimayó red chile over eggs and potatoes, chile rellenos, and a variety of home-baked coffee cakes.

Chimayó is a small but interesting village. There are four fine weaving shops where all kinds of local crafts in addition to excellent Spanish weaving may be purchased or special-ordered.

At La Posada you are well located for visits to the Indian pueblos of San Ildefonso, Nambé, Santa Clara, San Juan, and Pojoaque and only an hour away from the archaeological sites at Puye, Tsankawi, and Bandelier National Monument.

LA POSADA DE CHIMAYÓ, P.O. Box 463, Chimayó, NM 87522; 505-351-4605. A two-suite (each with sitting room, bedroom, bath) bed-and-breakfast guest house in a small village on the High Road to Taos. Open year-round with advance reservation necessary. Breakfast only. Good restaurant nearby; shops and sightseeing, too. The Santuario Church is famous for its architecture and curative "mud." Hiking, skiing, and exploring. Sue Farrington, Owner.

Directions: From Espanola (22 mi. north of Santa Fe and 45 mi. south of Taos), take NM76 east for 8 mi. Just across from Manzana Center, turn left (north) at "El Chimayó Weavers" sign; follow that road, always staying to the right *when the road forks, for approx. 1 mi. to La Posada.*

For B&B rates, see Index.

THE PLAZA HOTEL
Las Vegas, New Mexico

Don't confuse this Las Vegas with the Nevada version. Las Vegas, New Mexico, is older, smaller; infinitely less commercial and more historic. The Plaza Hotel has led the way in the historic rehabilitation of the Old Town section, where once the desperados of the Old West made this the roughest, toughest town in a rough, tough region. Shades of Doc Holliday, Billy the Kid, Big Nose Kate!

After the West was won, the Plaza Hotel became the location for many silent films; following that, the hotbed of New Mexico politics. The hotel is now a wonderful example of the best in historic preservation and rehabilitation with handsome period furnishings. Even the old plaza, at its doorstep, has been taken back to the late 1800s and restored.

The fine dining room has made the hotel so popular with local ranchers, guests should make reservations for dinner when they reserve their rooms. It is open for breakfast, lunch, and Sunday brunch, as well as the evening meal.

The Plaza is on the National Register of Historic Places, and the town has nine designated Historical Districts. You can visit the Teddy Roosevelt Roughrider Museum (there were more roughriders from New Mexico than any other state), tour the back country, and even see the wagon ruts left by the users of the old Santa Fe Trail, just outside of town.

THE PLAZA HOTEL, 230 on the Old Town Plaza, Las Vegas, NM 87701; 505-425-3591. A 38-guestroom inn (all private baths) on the old plaza in a historic town 60 mi. east of Santa Fe. Open all year. Breakfast is not included, but a Plaza Special of two eggs, hash browns, and biscuits is only $1.50. Excellent full-service dining room. Arrangements made for tours to nearby historic sites such as Fort Union, as well as genuine ranch round-ups. Children under 6 are free in same room with parents. Facilities for the disabled. Katherine and Wid Slick; Lonnie and Dana Lucero, Proprietors.

Directions: Exit from I-25 at the University Exit (Exit 345), turn left over the hwy. and follow the Plaza Hotel signs to Plaza/Bridge. The Plaza Hotel is on the northwest corner of the plaza. Coming from Taos on Hwy. 3, continue into town. Turn right at the intersection of 7th St. and National, and follow signs. Las Vegas, NM, is a stop for Amtrak Chicago-Albuquerque, so convenient for a stopover by train as well as automobile.

For Lodging rates, see Index.

PRESTON HOUSE
Santa Fe, New Mexico

Poet Peggy Pond Church used to play "Sardines" in Preston House with the children of early owners. "A Queen Anne-style house has lots of wonderful hiding places," she reminisces.

It also has leaded glass windows, a red plush window seat on the landing, and many distinctive architectural features that have been enhanced by the deft restoration and original paintings of present owner, artist/designer Signe Bergman. The hundred-year-old home, much a part of Santa Fe's Anglo history, has a carefully selected library to put you right in the mood to learn more. Yet its garden setting is an easy walk to the far older Plaza and the far newer galleries, shops, and restaurants. Centuries overlap in Santa Fe.

Preston House opened in 1981 as Santa Fe's first contemporary B&B, achieving instant reputation in a distinct departure from the big tourist/convention-oriented hotels. With only six rooms, it is always booked well ahead.

Breakfast, served in the sunny dining room overlooking the garden, is basically continental with American-style variety: assorted fresh fruits, fresh-squeezed juice, home-baked goodies like maple-bran muffins and fresh apple cake, a selection of teas and very good coffee. On cool mornings, a fire burns briskly in the corner fireplace.

Two of the bedrooms also have fireplaces, and one will accommodate three guests. Preston House combines pleasant informality with late-nineteenth-century grace. Easy to see where even a famous poet would remember every corner.

PRESTON HOUSE, 106 Faithway St., Santa Fe, NM 87501; 505-982-3465. A 6-guestroom (4 with private baths) bed-and-breakast inn 3 blocks from the Plaza. Breakfast only. Open year-round with advance reservations necessary. Restaurants, sightseeing, galleries, shopping nearby. Children under 12 not encouraged. No pets. Signe Bergman, Owner.

Directions: From Albuquerque take I-25, Old Pecos Trail exit. Turn right on the Paseo de Peralta, right on Palace, and left on Faithway. Since the Plaza is the central point in Santa Fe, you might just aim for that, then follow Palace St., 3 blocks east to Faithway. Preston House is on your right, end of the street.

For B&B rates, see Index.

254

ADELPHI HOTEL
Saratoga Springs, New York

Walking through the lobby of the Adelphi Hotel feels like stepping through a time warp into the Gilded Age. The dark, rich woods, ornate mirrors, antique paintings, potted palms, and over-stuffed sofas, settees, and chairs re-create the ambience of Saratoga's heyday.

Sheila Parkert and Gregg Siefker fell in love with the defunct 1877 hotel the first time they saw its dilapidated three-story Italianate facade. Now, several years and countless hours of hard work later, the hotel stands as a lone and stunning example of the grand hotels that once proliferated in this legendary town.

All of its three stories of rooms reflect Sheila's and Gregg's attention to the minutest of details and to the Victorian theme, with elegant draperies, fabric wall coverings, period paintings and photographs.

A continental breakfast can be taken in bed, in the second-floor sitting room, or outside terrace. There is a delightful courtyard where luncheons and light suppers are served, as well as an impressive dining room where dinner is available in July and August. Sometimes there are impromptu late-night concerts, when a few members of the New York City Ballet orchestra gather on the raised platform in one corner of the dining room and play a little chamber music.

Today, with the Saratoga Performing Arts Center, the famed Saratoga racetrack, and the state-run mineral baths, this area teems with activity during the summer months, and, of course, during the fall foliage season.

ADELPHI HOTEL, 365 Broadway, Saratoga Springs, NY 12866; 518-587-4688. A 28-guestroom (all private baths) elegant Victorian hotel in the center of town. Open May 1 to Dec. 1. Continental breakfast included in room rate. Lunch and dinner served to the public during July and August only. Rates are considerably higher in Aug. Saratoga Performing Arts Center (summer home of New York City Ballet and Philadelphia Symphony Orchestra), Saratoga Raceway, harness racing, Saratoga State Park with mineral springs and baths, tennis, swimming, golf, antiquing, backroading nearby. Sheila Parkert and Gregg Stefker, Innkeepers.

Directions: From I-87, take Exit 13N. Continue 3 mi. to downtown district. Hotel is on the left.

For B&B rates, see Index.

ASA RANSOM HOUSE
Clarence, New York

With goggles in position, and eyes straight ahead, travelers speeding across the New York State Thruway will never see Clarence, New York, more's the pity. This is the oldest town in Erie County. The first settler was a young silversmith by the name of Asa Ransom, who had been plying his trade in the fur trading posts on the shores of Lake Erie.

Today, Mr. Ransom would be very surprised to know that his two-story log cabin, which served as a hostelry, would still be commemorated by the Asa Ransom House, a very handsome place, indeed, well known to people who live in the vicinity for its excellent meals, and already sought after by the road-wise bed-and-breakfast traveler.

There are four totally different guest rooms, each with a name to suit its own personality. All have been delightfully furnished by innkeepers Bob and Judy Lenz.

The full breakfast, served in the dining room, features a special breakfast pie, which is a deep casserole containing smoked corned beef and potatoes, and topped with scrambled eggs and melted cheese. If that isn't quite enough, there are freshly made muffins and lots of fresh fruit.

Please note that the Asa Ransom House is closed Friday and Saturday because of the religious beliefs of Bob and Judy. The inn is open on Sundays.

ASA RANSOM HOUSE, Rte. 5, Clarence, NY 14031; 716-759-2315. A 4-guestroom village inn, approx. 15 mi. from Buffalo near the Albright Knox Art Gallery, the Studio Arena Theatre, the Art Park, Lancaster Opera House, and Niagara Falls. European plan. Dinner served Mon. through Thurs. 4 to 8:30 P.M.; Sun., 12 to 8 P.M.. Jackets required. Lunch is available on Wed. only. Closed Fri and Sat. Tennis, golf, fishing, swimming nearby. Limited amusement for children under 12. No pets. No credit cards. Bob and Judy Lenz, Innkeepers.

Directions: From the New York Thruway traveling west, use Exit 48A-Pembrook. Turn right to Rte. 5 and proceed 11 mi. to Clarence. Traveling east on the N.Y. Thruway, use Exit 49; turn left on Rte. 78, go 1 mi. to Rte. 5, turn right and continue 5¼ mi. Coming from the east via Rte. 20, just east of Lancaster, N.Y., turn right on Ransom Rd., go to end and turn left.

For B&B rates, see Index.

BAKER'S BED AND BREAKFAST
Stone Ridge, New York

Many a snug little bed-and- breakfast establishment, shunning the continental breakfast, turns in exactly the opposite direction and serves a sumptuous many-course morning meal that is reminiscent of the full English breakfasts served in the Cotswolds and the Lake Country of England. Such a place is Baker's Bed and Breakfast, where a frittata or puffy Finnish oven pancakes with maple syrup are more likely to be the rule than the exception, and shirred eggs with a snappy cheddar accompaniment might also be augmented by delicious, thin strips of sautéed venison. I particularly remember the super-delicious rolls.

However, there's more to Baker's than merely breakfast. There's a wonderful atmosphere of intellectual curiosity and involvement, not only with all of the arts—music, dance, painting, sculpture, and crafts—but also a definite affinity with nature and its many moods and offerings.

An interesting sidelight is a hot tub in a solar greenhouse attached to the dining room. For those of our readers in the East who have never had the pleasure of sinking luxuriously into this West Coast innovation, perhaps Baker's would be a good place to start.

There are five bedrooms sharing two baths, and the decor reflects an interest both Linda Delgado and Doug Baker have in the many varieties of both American and English furniture.

BAKER'S BED AND BREAKFAST, R.D. 2, Box 80, Stone Ridge, NY 12484; 914-687-9795. A 5-guestroom 1780 stone farmhouse (2 baths) in Ulster County's Rondout Valley, with views of the Shawangunk Mtns. Open year-round. Full breakfast with lodgings. De Puy Canal House restaurant, antique shops, Delaware and Hudson Canal Museum, Woodstock art colony, Lakes Mohonk and Minnewaska minutes away. Birding, bicycling, hiking, fishing, tennis, golf, xc and downhill skiing nearby. No children under 12 except Sun. to Thurs. Smoking permitted beside the fire or on the porch. No pets. No credit cards. Linda Delgado and Doug Baker, Proprietors.

Directions: Leave the New York State Thruway at Exit 18 and follow Rte. 299 to Rte. 32, turning right and continuing to Rte. 213. Proceed west through High Falls and turn left on Rte. 209. Take the second left to Old King's Highway; Baker's is on the right.

For B&B rates, see Index.

THE BALSAM HOUSE
Chestertown, New York

The best way really to enjoy all the many recreational and culinary delights of the Balsam House is to spend two or three days; however, if you are traveling the Northway (I-87) between Montreal and New York City, and the day is getting longer and you're a little weary of the miles, turn off for about twelve miles into the beauty of the Adirondacks and the Balsam House. Here, you can enjoy a sumptuous dinner, a comfortable bed, and a full breakfast at this newly refurbished and renovated Victorian hotel.

The Balsam House sits among the evergreens on a knoll above the private and clear sparkling waters of the Friends Lake. Dominating the building is a central tower with a mansard roof flanked by two gables. It is a type of architecture that is often seen on Prince Edward Island.

The front porch has handsome wicker chairs, and stepping into the lobby is like a visit into the late nineteenth century. As is the case with many buildings of that vintage, there are numerous nooks and crannies and recessed windows. The beds have grandmother spreads, feather pillows, and each of the twenty guest rooms has a private bath.

At dinnertime, the country French cuisine created by the Belgian chef (formerly chef saucier of the Four Seasons Restaurant in New York City) will be a very pleasant surprise, indeed, and there may be a little entertainment afterward as well.

I suspect that the other recreational blandishments, including fishing, white-water rafting, hiking, canoeing, horseback riding, bicycling, golf, and the like, will delay your return to the main road, but I'm also certain you will agree it was well worth it.

THE BALSAM HOUSE, Chestertown, NY 12817; 518-494-2828 or 494-4431. An elegant 20-guestroom resort inn in the Adirondack Mountains, just a short distance from I-87. Open all year. B&B and MAP rates available. Canoeing, sailing, rowboating, fishing, and lawn games on the grounds. Hiking, white-water rafting, tennis, horseback riding, bicycling, golf, hunting, and other joys of the Adirondacks are easily accessible. Mike and Kathy Aspland, Innkeepers.

Directions: From I-87, take Exit 23 (Warrensburg) to Rte. 9 north. Procced approx. 4 mi. to Rte. 28 (veer left) and continue for exactly 3 mi. to Potterbrook Rd. Turn right for 4 mi. to the Balsam House.

For B&B rates, see Index.

THE BARTLETT HOUSE INN
Greenport, Long Island, New York

The permanent residents of outer Long Island's North Fork will probably insist that there is something special about their little part of the world. "Our villages are different from those on the South Fork," is one person's opinion. "I think we are more natural; there is a little less hoopla over here, and there is just as much to do off- as on-season, but it is always rather quiet."

I'm sure those are some of the reasons why John and Linda Sabatino decided to convert this very attractive old-fashioned Victorian house in Greenport into a bed-and-breakfast accommodation.

Throughout the house are evidences of John's real love of wood and woodworking. The well-preserved original embellishments of this house, including the parquet flooring, must have appealed to him immediately, and he has augmented them with his own touches.

The inn is located in a residential portion of Greenport, which is, by the way, the ferry terminus for the trip to Shelter Island, and just a few minutes away from Orient Point, where the ferry leaves for New England.

The guest rooms remind me of my aunt's house back in Elmira, New York. Five have private baths and the others have large, shared bathrooms. The house used to be a convent and was empty for eight or ten years. One of the features in the living room is the carved Corinthian columns. There are two working fireplaces.

The continental breakfast is served in the dining room and Linda is especially careful to keep a supply of as much fresh fruit as possible, with which she makes simple cobblers from time to time. Both Linda and John are walking encyclopedias of information on all of the amusements and recreation on the North Fork.

THE BARTLETT HOUSE INN, 503 Front St., Greenport, L.I., NY 11944; 516-477-0371. A 9-guestroom (private and shared baths) bed-and-breakfast home in the Greenport residential area. Open all year. Conveniently located for all eastern Long Island recreational attractions. Near Orient Point ferry terminal for trips to New England. Linda and John Sabatino, Proprietors.

Directions: From New York take exit on L.I. Expwy. Greenport is the principal village on the Long Island North Fork.

For B&B rates, see Index.

BASSETT HOUSE
East Hampton, Long Island, New York

For as long as I can remember, "the Hamptons" have been a sought-after holiday objective for many people who live in the New York City area. On the outer end of Long Island's South Fork, the Hamptons offer much to discover, including miles of ocean, sound, harbor, and pond. An endless variety of natural beauty coupled with cultural sophistication make the Hamptons an area of stimulating contrasts. Pine, oak, and hickory forests with generous amounts of laurel, blackberry, and dogwood make it a wonderful place for bird watchers. East Hampton also has excellent summer theater and many galleries.

Michael Bassett's Bassett House fits right in with the eclectic mood of the Hamptons. It is furnished in what he calls country antiques, and there are several very interesting pieces scattered around, including railroad semaphores, lots of campy photographs, paintings, and prints—and everything is carefully placed in a way that contributes to a relaxed atmosphere so that it doesn't overwhelm the viewer.

Most of the guest rooms are quite large and interestingly furnished.

A full breakfast is served, and Michael will also do a special dinner if you are in the mood.

BASSETT HOUSE, 128 Montauk Highway (Box 1426), East Hampton, L.I., NY 11937; 516-324-6127. A 12-guestroom (7 baths) tidy little inn on the western end of East Hampton. Open all year; 3-night minimum stay only on weekends late June, July, and Aug. Most convenient for all of the outer Long Island recreational and cultural attractions. Michael Bassett, Innkeeper.

Directions: The inn is located 1.5 mi. west of the center of East Hampton village on Rte. 27 (Montauk Highway).

For B&B rates, see Index.

BEEKMAN ARMS
Rhinebeck, New York

The Beekman Arms shares the reputation of being the oldest continuously operating inn in America with Longfellow's Wayside Inn in South Sudbury, Massachusetts. It is located in Rhinebeck, New York, deep in the beautiful Hudson River Valley, and is most convenient for some of the exciting attractions in the Rip Van Winkle area. The inn is an American landmark and began life as a fort, built to withstand attacks from unfriendly Indians.

During the Revolution, George Washington and his staff enjoyed the inn's hospitality, and later, Franklin Roosevelt, who lived close by at Hyde Park, wound up every campaign for both governor and president with an informal talk from the porch.

It is fitting that an inn with such historical integrity should also have a guest house connected with it that is one of the architectural jewels of the Hudson Valley. It was designed and built by Alexander Jackson Davis for the first owner, Henry Delamater, in 1844. The house has been in an excellent state of preservation and remains one of the few early examples of American Gothic residences still in existence. It is reputed to be the first batten-and-board home built in the United States.

The seven guest rooms in this early Victorian mansion have been furnished with taste and care and with particular attention to authentic detail.

A simple continental breakfast is offered at the Delamater House; however, a full à la carte breakfast, including omelets of all kinds, eggs Benedict, and croissants, is featured at the Beekman Arms.

Bookings for Delamater House, as well as for the inn itself, are arranged directly through the Beekman Arms.

BEEKMAN ARMS, Rhinebeck, NY 12572; 914-876-7077. A 13-guest-room village inn with an adjacent 7-room guest house, 1 mi. from Amtrak Station in Rhinecliff. Breakfast, lunch, and dinner served to travelers daily. Open year-round. Short drive to F.D.R. Library and Home in Hyde Park, Vanderbilt mansion, World War I Aerodrome. European plan. Golf, tennis, swimming nearby. No amusements for young children. Charles LaForge, Innkeeper.

Directions: From N.Y. Thruway, take Exit 19, cross Rhinecliff Bridge and pick up Rte. 199 south to Rte. 9. Proceed south on Rte. 9 to middle of village. From Taconic Pkwy. exit at Rhinebeck and follow Rte. 199 west 11 mi. to Rte. 308 into village.

For Lodging rates, see Index.

BIRD AND BOTTLE INN
Garrison, New York

Bed and breakfast in an inn that probably played host to Benedict Arnold and other shadowy figures of the American Revolution? Yes, but only between Sunday and Thursday. See the Index for special rates at this time.

The Bird and Bottle goes back to the mid-1700s, when it was a stagecoach stop on the New York-to-Albany route. Its nearness to West Point undoubtedly made it a meeting place for many plots and counterplots.

Today, the Colonial atmosphere of narrow clapboards, low ceilings, and rich paneling is preserved and enhanced with such beautiful decorations as period wallpapers, pewter, old paintings, duck decoys, and many wooden accessories.

Canopied or four-poster beds and woodburning fireplaces carry the Colonial theme into the guest rooms, all of which have private bathrooms.

Lunch and dinner are served daily, and Sunday brunch is served year-round. So the culinary delights may persuade the bed-and-breakfast guest to stay even longer.

Breakfast is selected before retiring from a menu that includes fresh orange juice or other juices, a grapefruit half, seasonal melon, eggs, sausage, and imported jams and jellies.

BIRD AND BOTTLE INN, Garrison, NY 10524; 914-424-3000. A 4-guestroom country inn, rich in antiquity, located on Rte. 9, a few miles north of Peekskill, N.Y. Open year-round. B&B rates available Sun. thru Thurs. Lunch and dinner served daily. Sunday brunch served year-round. A short distance from Boscobel Restoration, U.S. Military Academy at West Point, and Sleepy Hollow Restorations. Ira Boyer, Innkeeper.

Directions: From NYC: cross George Washington Bridge and follow Palisades Pkwy. north to Bear Mtn. Bridge. Cross bridge and travel on Rte. 9D north 4½ mi. to Rte. 403. Proceed on Rte. 403 to Rte. 9, then north 4 mi. to inn. From I- 84, take Exit 13 and follow Rte. 9 south for 8 mi.

For B&B rates, see Index.

CAPTAIN SCHOONMAKER'S BED AND BREAKFAST
High Falls, New York

It may come as a surprise that this section of New York's Catskill and near-Catskill mountains has so much Revolutionary War history. Washington's headquarters were in nearby Newburgh, and there are beautiful old stone buildings, built even before the break with the mother country—many have been declared historic places.

Such an award has been made to Captain Schoonmaker's, built by an officer in Washington's army in 1760 and, according to the citation, "fortified and used as a place of refuge during the war." With a front wall of hand-planed boards, which is typical of Hudson Valley Huguenot dwellings ("best face forward"), the remaining three sides are finished in stone.

Sam and Julia Krieg are the hosts at this cheery and restful accommodation. There are many different levels and several different combinations of beds and baths in the main building and in the renovated barn. Some rooms offer cozy working fireplaces. There are more guest rooms in a recently acquired historical landmark building that once housed the lock-tender for Lock #17 on the Delaware-Hudson Canal.

Because breakfast is included in the tariff, it might be well to note that many different surprises are offered. In addition to a cheese-dill soufflé, scallion cheese quiche, bacon, scrapple, sausage, and freshly baked bread, still warm from the oven, there are scalloped honey apples, chilled cranberry juice, apricot strudel and, at the time of my visit, a walnut-apple-and-raisin confection.

Julia explained that Captain Schoonmaker's does not offer dinner because the area is replete with restaurants. "We provide menus and are happy to telephone with our guests' reservations, if it will help," she added.

CAPTAIN SCHOONMAKER'S BED AND BREAKFAST, R.D. 2, Box 37, High Falls, NY 12440; 914-687-7946. A 12-guestroom (6 baths) bed-and-breakfast inn located in a snug old farmhouse and renovated barn. Open all year. Breakfast is the only meal served. Golf, tennis, swimming, hiking, tubing, horseback riding, and fascinating backroading nearby. The facilities are a bit confining for small children. No pets. No credit cards. Sam and Julia Krieg, Hosts.

Directions: From the New York State Thruway (I-87) take exit 18 (New Paltz) and drive west on Rte. 299. Turn right on Rte. 32 in New Paltz, then left on Rte. 213 thru Rosendale to High Falls.

For B&B rates, see Index.

CHRISTMAN'S WINDHAM HOUSE
Windham, New York

I've lost track of the number of times that I've traveled on Route 23 in the northern Catskills and passed this extremely attractive Greek Revival building. However, until last spring it was closed each time I passed it.

This time I stopped and to my most pleasant surprise discovered that it was operated by Stanley and Roberta Christman, the aunt and uncle of Laura and Barbara Stevens, inkeepers at the Greenville Arms. I've also met Roberta's mother who has been a hotel keeper in the Catskills probably longer than anyone else.

Roberta says of the Windham House, "We have had many people coming back for years and years. We will not necessarily have many rooms available in the high season, around July and August, but in June or September we will be happy to accommodate the overnight traveler and provide dinner."

The original house was built in 1805 and at one time was a drovers' inn. It is the oldest continuously operating inn on the mountaintop. Last year it was included in the Greene County Historical Society's tour of old Windham homes.

Pasture and woodlot accommodate a two-mile hiking trail, and a renovated loft in the barn furnishes even more recreation. Swimming and tennis facilities are also available.

Fertile fields, once a part of the prosperous farm, have been converted into a full-sized nine-hole golf course that borders the Batavia Kill and is adjacent to one of the mountains for which the Catskills are famous.

Breakfast includes pancakes or french toast with maple syrup made right from the trees on the property, among other things. Lunch and dinner are also offered.

CHRISTMAN'S WINDHAM HOUSE, Windham, NY 12496; 518-734-4230. A 38-bedroom 19th-century Greek Revival inn in the northern Catskill Mts. Open from late May to mid-Oct. and early Dec. to mid-April. Breakfast included with lodgings; lunch and dinner available. Swimming, tennis, 9-hole golf course, 2-mi. nature trail, pond for boating on grounds. Recreation room with pool table, pingpong, etc. Windham ski area, horseback riding, back-roading nearby. No pets. Stanley and Roberta Christman, Innkeepers.

Directions: From N.Y. Thruway take Exit 21. Turn west on Rte. 23 and continue to Windham.

For B&B rates, see Index.

THE FRIENDS LAKE INN
Chestertown, New York

Innkeepers Sharon and Greg Taylor explain that this once-famous mountain hostelry was standing empty and forgotten when they found it.

These two ambitious young people are particularly well suited to innkeeping because they're both quite capable of making major and minor repairs to the inn. They worked together on the considerable major rehabilitation and they also share the duties of the kitchen.

I was particularly impressed with the bright bedrooms overlooking the lake. They were furnished with gay wallpaper and typical Adirondack country-inn furniture, some of which had been gathered from older inns that had gone out of existence on Friends Lake. Sharon pointed out that one of the quilts belonged to her great grandmother.

Wintertime guests ski Gore Mountain or enjoy many miles of cross-country skiing. At other seasons there's rafting on the Hudson, climbing the nearby peaks, enjoying summer water sports on the lake, and especially long, quiet walks in the mountains.

There are fourteen guest rooms, some with lake views. Some guest rooms have shared bathrooms. The veranda across the front of the inn has a splendid view of the Adirondack scenery.

Although most guests will be staying under the modified American plan, bed-and-breakfast guests will also be welcome, and a hearty North Country breakfast is included in the room rate.

Besides a definite "back country" atmosphere at Friends Lake Inn, there's a feeling of youthful expectancy and optimism that radiates from both of the young, attractive innkeepers.

THE FRIENDS LAKE INN, Friends Lake Rd., Chestertown, NY 12817; 518-494-4751. A 14-guestroom (6 private baths) restored mountain inn in the heart of the Adirondacks. Housekeeping cottages available. Modified American plan; B&B rate available. Dinner served. Open year-round. All of the area's historic, natural, and cultural activities are within a convenient drive. No pets. Sharon and Grey Taylor, Innkeepers.

Directions: From the south: take Exit 23 from I-87. Go north 4 mi. on Rte. 9 to Rte. 28. Follow Rte. 28 to the Glen, 5 mi. Just before the Glen, turn right on Friends Lake Rd. The inn is 4 mi. ahead on the left. If you have any problems, just ask someone. Everyone knows the Friends Lake Inn.

For B&B rates, see Index.

GARNET HILL LODGE
North River, New York

Garnet Hill Lodge is a rustic resort high in the Adirondack Mountains on 13th Lake, and is centered around the Log House, built in 1936.

Lodgings are in individual guest rooms, very clean and neat; all have private bathrooms. Six of the newly renovated rooms in the Log House have balconies overlooking the lake and the mountains.

There's a great deal of recreation and outdoor activity at Garnet Hill Lodge in all seasons of the year. In the wintertime the snow frequently is up to the roof of the porch. This encourages a great deal of cross-country skiing, snowshoeing, and downhill skiing nearby.

In summertime there is sailing, canoeing, fishing, swimming, backroading, and wonder walks in the woods where beaver, deer, hares, loons, blue herons, foxes, weasels, and raccoons share the sylvan confines.

Garnet Hill Lodge guests are served an Adirondack Mountain breakfast, which offers a choice of just about everything imaginable, including home-baked breads. The morning view from the dining room and porch is splendid.

For the traveler passing through the Adirondacks, Garnet Hill Lodge would make an excellent overnight stop. Fortunately, a most enticing full dinner with several entrées is also served.

GARNET HILL LODGE, 13th Lake Rd., North River, NY 12856; 518-251-2821. A 19-guestroom rustic resort-inn high in the Adirondacks, 32 mi. from Warrensburg. Open year-round. Mod. American and European plans available. Breakfast, lunch, and dinner served to travelers. Swimming, boating, hiking, fishing, and xc skiing on grounds. Downhill skiing, long-distance hikes, and beautiful Adirondack drives nearby. The area has many museums, arts and crafts centers, and historical points. No pets. No credit cards. Taxi service provided to bus stop 30 mi. away. George and Mary Heim, Innkeepers.

Directions: From the Northway (I-87) take Exit 23 and follow Rtes. 9 and 28 north 4 mi. Take left fork (Rte. 28) 22 mi. to North River. Take second left (13th Lake Rd.) 5 mi. to Lodge. For more explicit directions, write for brochure.

For B&B rates, see Index.

THE GOULD
Seneca Falls, New York

For many years I have strongly recommended Route 20 as an alternate east-west route in New York State. It passes through some of the most verdant farm country in North America and the region is blessed with a rich history.

One of the more interesting communities is Seneca Falls, famed as the birthplace of women's suffrage—the First Women's Rights Convention was held there in 1848. Two of America's leading suffragettes, Elizabeth Cady Stanton and Amelia Bloomer, lived there, and it is the home of the newly created "National Women's Hall of Fame," currently honoring women of the past and present for their contributions to the arts, athletics, education, government, the humanities, philanthropy, and science.

For years there wasn't a place to stay in Seneca Falls, but now Mr. and Mrs. George Souhan have opened the Gould, on the corner of State Street and Route 20.

The entrance is through a revolving door. To the right is a formal dining room and on the left is the local pub. There's lots of decorative glass, still another low-ceilinged, less-formal dining room with some original paintings.

There are six suites and three bedrooms and baths. Furnishings are a blend of textured woods, contemporary wall-hangings, Picasso posters, rather gaily colored pillows, and a contemporary feeling that belies the basic exterior of the Gould. There are telephones, cable TV, and air conditioning. Continental breakfast is provided at an additional nominal charge.

I was delighted to find the Gould, and I'm quite enthusiastic about the opportunity it provides the pleasure and business traveler for overnight or longer stays in this quiet, conservative, western New York village.

THE GOULD, 108 Fall St., Seneca Falls, NY 13148; 315-568-5801. A small restored hotel with 6 suites and 3 guestrooms (private baths). Open year-round. Breakfast is available at an additional cost. Lunch and dinner served throughout the week; Sun. brunch. Dining room closed Christmas Day and 4th of July. Very convenient for drives in the wine country and visits to many of the Finger Lakes. Just a few miles from the New York State Thruway. Not suitable for children under 12. Mr. and Mrs. George Souhan, Innkeepers.

Directions: Seneca Falls is between Syracuse and Rochester on Rte. 20.

For rates, see Index.

GREENVILLE ARMS
Greenville, New York

The Greenville Arms is located in the foothills of the northern Catskill Mountains and has been operated by the Stevens family for thirty years. It is a Victorian country home, with several interesting porches, cupolas, gables, and hidden corners. The grounds are well shaded with tall trees and beautifully landscaped with bushes and shrubs. The atmosphere here can best be described as homey and inviting.

Across the stream behind the main building, there is a large, beautiful lawn with a swimming pool, swings, and lawn games. The inn's carriage house, with nine bedrooms and a spacious living room, overlooks the pool area. During the summer, horses graze in a nearby pasture.

The inn is open spring, summer, and fall with trout fishing, hiking, bicycling, golf, tennis, horseback riding, antiquing, and country auctions nearby. Its location in the Hudson River Valley provides the perfect opportunity to explore a region rich in history and in natural beauty.

Guests who enjoy walnut and strawberry pancakes with locally made maple syrup, eggs Benedict, or special omelets are in for a real treat.

GREENVILLE ARMS, Greenville, NY 12083; 518- 966-5219. A 20-guestroom Victorian country inn in the foothills of the northern Catskill Mountains, 25 mi. south of Albany, 120 mi. north of New York City. Modified American or bed-and-breakfast rates available mid-April through mid-Nov. Children are welcome. Pets accommodated in nearby kennels. No credit cards. Laura and Barbara Stevens, Innkeepers.

Directions: Exit NY Thrwy. at 21B (Coxsackie-New Baltimore). Turn left on 9W south 2 mi. to traffic light. Turn right on Rte. 81W 13 mi. to Greenville. Turn left at traffic light. Inn is second house on right. Via Taconic Pkwy., exit at Ancram on Rte. 82W over Rip Van Winkle Bridge and follow Rte. 23 to Cairo. Turn right on 32N, 9 mi. to Greenville.

For B&B rates, see Index.

HILLSIDE BED & BREAKFAST
Cazenovia, New York

The central New York State Finger Lakes district is well known to New York State residents but is always a surprise to people from out of state. This unusual geography was created by the melting of the glaciers many millions of years ago, leaving many lakes, some of which have dried up. The result is that driving east and west on Route 20 there is a kind of roller coaster effect going up to the top of a hill and down into a valley.

Hillside Bed & Breakfast is a Cape Cod-style house just off Route 92 and close to Route 20, the scenic route through New York State. It is comfortably furnished in Early American antiques and is open for guests the year 'round. There are two upstairs bedrooms, both neat as a pin, sharing one bath. One is a twin-bedded room with very pleasant white quilts, and the other has a double bed with stenciling on the walls.

Merilyn Glass, the hostess, is a graduate of the Culinary Institute of America who owns and operates her own catering service. She and her husband, Jeff, established this B&B in September 1984. Merilyn serves breakfasts of home-baked breads, muffins, coffee cake, and hot or cold cereals, along with fresh fruit, juices, and coffee or tea.

There are hiking trails, beautiful views of the rolling hills, and cross-country skiing out the back door. Downhill skiing is just ten minutes away. Cazenovia Lake is three miles east and has a public access area.

HILLSIDE BED & BREAKFAST, c/o Merilyn Glass, Box 304, Cazenovia, NY 13035; 315-655-3033 or 655-9881. A 2-guestroom (shared bath) most comfortable bed-and-breakfast home a few miles from Cazenovia, New York. Breakfast is included in the room rate and is the only meal served. Open year-round. Hiking trails, xc skiing on premises. Downhill skiing, tennis, lake swimming and other seasonal recreation nearby. No credit cards. No pets. Merilyn and Jeff Glass, Hosts.

Directions: From Cazenovia go west on Rte. 20. At end of lake turn right to Rte. 92 north. Go 3.3 mi. and take a left at Bethel Rd. Hillside Bed & Breakfast is first house on left.

For B&B rates, see Index.

HOUSE ON THE HILL
High Falls, New York

The Catskill Mountains as a resort and vacation area came into their own during the last part of the 19th century, although artists, as well as people fascinated with the outdoors, discovered it much earlier.

The area is quite extensive and offers year-round recreation, including skiing, swimming, golfing, fishing, and hunting. The Catskills have hosted and entertained visitors for generations, and of course are already a legend in their own time as the proving grounds for many of today's entertainers.

In that sense, High Falls, New York, in Ulster County is quite different from the Catskill image. Located on Route 213, going from Rosendale to Stone Ridge, on the banks of Roundout Creek and the Delaware and Hudson Canal, High Falls has a few stores, but nothing flashy. The well-known Depuy Canal House is here.

The House on the Hill fits right into this ambience, set back in its own little park of evergreens and maples. It's possible to sit on the front porch of an afternoon and watch the occasional car on the highway. Guests' bedrooms are on the second floor and feature some very handsome quilts that came from southern Illinois where Sharon Glassman grew up. There is one bathroom for four of the country-style bedrooms, and the fifth room has a private bath.

Shelly Glassman is in charge of breakfast, which features crêpes and different treatments of eggs, depending on Shelly's mood, and is served in the farmhouse dining room in a little glassed-in corner in summer, or in the rustic country kitchen with expansive seasonal views.

The spacious grounds also include a duck pond complete with ducks, as well as a badminton set and a barbecue for guests who like to do their own.

HOUSE ON THE HILL, Box 86, Route 213, High Falls, NY 12440; 914-687-9627. A 5-bedroom guest house circa 1825 in the middle of a pleasant Hudson Valley hamlet. Five bedrooms share two baths. Open year-round for bed-and-breakfast from Thurs. night through Sun. night. Walk to antique shops, swimming, and gourmet dining at the Depuy Canal House and Top of the Falls restaurants. No credit cards. Sharon and Shelly Glassman, Innkeepers.

Directions: From New York State Thruway use Exit 18 (New Paltz). Turn left on 299 into New Paltz and right on 32 north to Rosendale, then left on 213 to High Falls.

For B&B rates, see Index.

THE MERRILL MAGEE HOUSE
Warrensburg, New York

Although for years a well-kept secret shared only by a privileged few, the Adirondack Mountains in New York State are fast becoming the focus of many vacationers who are seeking out some of the few areas that have not been discovered.

Interstate 87 (the Northway) carries the expectant traveler deep into the heart of the Adirondacks, and Warrensburg, just above Lake George, is a small town that provides a view of some of the unique architectural features and folkways of this vast natural area.

Tucked behind a very high white picket fence, the Merrill Magee House, literally beside the bandstand in the middle of the village, is much the same today as it was a century ago. The house abounds with lovely antiques, original wallpapers, glowing fireplaces, and a most inviting atmosphere.

Luncheon and dinner are served here, and one of the Carrington children (there are six) is the chef.

There is a tiny, proper English pub connected with the inn, which is most appropriate because Mr. Carrington is English.

One of the most welcome surprises is a swimming pool in one corner of the parklike grounds.

THE MERRILL MAGEE HOUSE, at the Bandstand, 2 Hudson St., Warrensburg, NY 12885; 518-623-2449. A 3-guestroom village inn (sharing 1 bath) at the southern gateway to the Adirondacks. Breakfast included in room rate. Lunch and dinner served daily. Dining room open daily during July and Aug.; closed Mon. the rest of the year. Open year-round. Swimming pool on grounds. Convenient to all of the Adirondack area's natural and cultural attractions, including hiking, golf, boating, fishing, Saratoga Raceway, and major downhill and xc ski areas. No pets. The Carrington Family, Innkeepers.

Directions: From I-87 take Exit 23, proceed on Rte. 9 to middle of town. The inn is on the left.

For B&B rates, see Index.

THE MILL-GARTH
Amagansett, New York

There really is a windmill at the Mill-Garth, although it is a smaller replica of the original one built in 1797 that was destroyed by fire.

This 19th-century farmhouse and surrounding five secluded cottages have been turned into homey, but sophisticated, accommodations. Just a short distance from the ocean, on a quiet country road, the bucolic setting is complete with spacious lawns, beautiful trees, ivy-covered fences, and many flowers.

All of the rooms are handsomely furnished, and each has its own fully equipped kitchen. The cottages have such names as the Dairy House, which has a studio living room with a skylight; the Gazebo, octagonally shaped, with a paneled living room and dining area; the Carriage House, with a fireplace and a studio living room that opens out on a private patio.

One of the vacation villages a little beyond the Hamptons on Long Island, Amagansett is most conveniently situated for fishing, boating, golfing, antiquing, and walking on the beaches.

I was delighted to discover that the Mill-Garth has an additional advantage: it is open all year, and this part of Long Island can be especially attractive during the spring and fall. In winter it is a perfect hideaway for a weekend. It is necessary to reserve minimum stays of seven days during July and August. I'd make reservations for those periods as early in the year as possible.

THE MILL-GARTH, Windmill Lane, Amagansett, L.I., NY 11930; 516-267-3757. A splendid 11-apartment hideaway just north of Montauk Highway in one of outer Long Island's most historic villages. Each accommodation has its own kitchen. Open year-round. Very convenient for all of the outer Long Island cultural and recreational attractions. Burton and Wendy Van Deusen, Proprietors.

Directions: Turn left off Montauk Hwy. (Rte. 27) upon entering Amagansett. It is plainly marked.

For Lodging rates, see Index.

THE MILLHOF INN
Stephentown, New York

Travelers on Route 22 to upper New York State have to digress only one mile to stop here. The word "millhof" really means mill-house, and this building, located in Stephentown, New York, right on the Massachusetts–New York State border, was actually used as a sawmill for many years.

Innkeepers Frank and Ronnie Tallet have made numerous alterations and additions, but the basic structure remains the same, and with its hand-carved and colorfully decorated railings and window shutters it is similar to many small *pensions* that I have visited, particularly in Germany's Black Forest.

The European Alpine theme extends throughout the inn and particularly to the guest rooms, each of which is individually decorated and furnished with plants, books, and magazines. Some have fireplaces.

Additional enticement at the Millhof is its inviting swimming pool and the fact that there is hiking, skiing, backroading, and all of the famous Berkshire recreational attractions nearby, including the Tanglewood Music Festival each summer.

The Europa Dining Room or the Garden Deck, depending upon the weather, is where guests enjoy a complimentary continental breakfast or a full à la carte breakfast, including homemade jams, stoneground wheat cakes, omelets, and other things from the garden in season.

THE MILLHOF INN, Route 43, Stephentown, NY 12168; 518-733-5606. An 11-guestroom central-European-style country inn, 14 mi. from Pittsfield, Mass., and 12 mi. from Williamstown, Mass., on the NY/Mass. border. European plan. (Breakfast included in room rate.) In wintertime, breakfast is served every morning, and dinner is served on the weekends and during holiday weeks by reservation. In the summer, breakfast and lunch are served daily to guests only. Open every day from May 26 through March 31. Swimming pool on grounds. Hiking, skiing, backroading, and all of the famous Berkshire recreational and cultural attractions nearby. No pets. Frank and Ronnie Tallet, Innkeepers.

Directions: From New York: exit the Taconic Parkway on Rte. 295. Travel east to Rte. 22 north. Turn east at Stephentown on Rte. 43. The inn is one mile on the left. From Boston: exit Mass. Turnpike at B3, New Lebanon. North on Rte. 22 to Rte. 43, etc.

For Lodging rates, see Index.

THE REDCOAT'S RETURN
Tannersville, New York

When Tom and Peggy Wright took over the Redcoat's Return in the fall of 1972 they converted it into an English country inn. Tom, originally from London, has not only been the chef, turning out prime ribs with Yorkshire pudding, poached fillet of sole, roast duck à l'orange, steak and kidney pie, but also the carpenter, enlarging rooms and adding bathrooms. "I would stop hammering and sawing," he said, "and run downstairs and check the sauce and test the roast."

The Redcoat's Return is in the center of the Catskill Game Reserve. There is a wealth of recreational activities available to the guests in every season of the year. Activities include hiking trails, golf, swimming, tennis, and horseback riding nearby. There's downhill skiing in Cortina Valley, Hunter Mountain Ski Bowl, and Windham Mountain.

There are twelve rooms, all of them with wash basins—and the changes have now provided private bathrooms for several more rooms.

There's no skimping on breakfast here—it starts off with fresh orange juice and several different choices including blueberry pancakes, french toast, and any style of eggs with bacon or sausage.

THE REDCOAT'S RETURN, Dale Lane, Elka Park, NY 12427; 518-589-6379. A 12-room English inn approx. 4 mi. from Tannersville, NY, in the heart of the Catskill Mts. Within a short drive of several ski areas and state hiking trails. European plan. Lodgings include breakfast. Dinner served daily except Thursdays; no lunches served. Open from Memorial Day to Easter. Closed 3 wks. in Nov.; reopen for Thanksgiving and winter season. Please call for details. Hiking, nature walks, trout fishing, croquet, skiing, swimming, golf, ice skating, riding, tennis nearby. Tom and Peggy Wright, Innkeepers.

Directions: From N.Y. Thruway, going north, use Exit 20; going south, use Exit 21. Follow 23A to Tannersville; turn left at traffic light onto Country Road 16. Follow signs to Police Center, 4½ mi. Turn right on Dale Lane.

For B&B rates, see Index.

THE ROSE INN
Ithaca, New York

I was driving north from Ithaca along the shore of Cayuga Lake, and there on the top of a small hill was a gorgeous mansion with the easily recognizable, graceful lines of a mid-19th-century Italianate home. I decided this must be the Rose Inn, and turned into the driveway. As I drew closer I was most favorably impressed by the many porches and full-length windows that came into view.

Innkeepers Sherry and Charles Rosemann told me that the Rose Inn is known locally as "the house with the circular staircase." Although the house had been built in 1851 and included a cupola, it wasn't until 1922 that a master craftsman appeared who could complete the circular staircase that extends two stories up into the cupola. The stairway is built of priceless Honduras mahogany.

High ceilings, the warm glow of woods from indigenous American trees long gone, and antique furnishings provide an elegant but most comfortable setting. Sherry Rosemann puts it well, "When callers ask us about the atmosphere of the inn we tell them we have an elegant country mansion that is both intimate and relaxed."

The five guest rooms have been furnished with pride and love to preserve the mid-19th-century ambience. There are large bath sheets, velour robes, fresh flowers, and excellent beds and linens.

Guests get a good start on the day, thanks to the complimentary full breakfast. Hand-squeezed orange juice, the Rose Inn's own blend of coffee, and homemade jams and jellies are always featured, along with the fresh fruits of the season, German apple pancakes, french toast, or eggs Benedict.

The joys of visiting the Finger Lakes District are well known to many travelers; the Rose Inn is also just a few minutes from Cornell University, making it an excellent stopping place for prospective students and their parents.

THE ROSE INN, 813 Auburn Rd., Rte. 34, P.O. Box 6576, Ithaca, NY 14851; 607-533-4202. A 10-guestroom elegant New York State mansion just a few moments from Cornell University. Breakfast included in room rate; dinner offered by advance reservation. Open all year. Finger Lakes attractions, including Cayuga Lake, wineries, and college campuses nearby. No children under 10. Arrangements for pets. Charles and Sherry Rosemann, Innkeepers.

Directions: From N.Y. State Thruway, take Exit 40 and Rte. 34 south about 36 mi. The inn will be on your left before arriving in Ithaca. From I-81, use Exit 11 (Cortland) to Rte. 13 to Ithaca. Take No. Triphammer Rd. right, 7.4 mi. to inn.

For B&B rates, see Index.

ROYCROFT INN
East Aurora, New York

It had been some years since my last visit to the Roycroft Inn, and as soon as I arrived on what is known as the Roycroft campus, I discovered many very pleasant surprises.

The Roycroft concept was actually the inspiration of Elbert Hubbard, writer, lecturer, innovator, philosopher, and author of *A Message to Garcia*. In 1895, Mr. Hubbard brought skilled artisans together at Roycroft. These "Roycrofters" became famous for their printing, book binding, leather crafts, text illumination, modeling, hand-wrought metal and furniture, and their products were sold worldwide until 1938 when Roycroft was closed.

The spirit behind the Roycroft renaissance is Kitty Turgeon, who has rekindled the entire Roycroft feeling, not only by restoring many of the crafts and artisans' shops, but also in the renewal of the Roycroft Inn.

It is in the inn that our interest lies at this time. Oriental rugs have been placed in the main dining rooms where snowy white linens cover the tables, accented by bright red napkins. Lovely centerpieces have been fashioned in the Roycroft shops and various other decorative features bear the traditional Roycroft symbol. Many of the handsome pieces of Roycroft furniture owned by people in the community have been returned to the inn, and much restoration has been done to beautify and preserve the elegant atmosphere.

All of this has been woven into the Roycroft Inn by Kitty and Robert Rust, who shares her great enthusiasm and love for things Roycroft.

There are seventeen bedrooms, some with shared baths; many with the distinctive Roycroft furniture, which has increased in value considerably during the past few years. A complimentary continental breakfast is served to inn guests. Luncheon and dinner are served every day.

ROYCROFT INN, East Aurora, NY 14052; 716-652-9030. A 17-guestroom (most with private baths) village inn. Continental breakfast is included with the room rate. Lunch and dinner served daily. Closed Christmas Eve. Convenient to enjoy all of the Roycroft arts and crafts, including antiques, galleries, weavers' shop, pottery studio, and a splendid Roycroft gift shop. No pets. Kitty Turgeon, Innkeeper.

Directions: Going west on the New York State Thruway, take the Pembroke exit. Go south on Rte. 77 to Rte. 20A (18 mi.). Turn west into the main street of East Aurora, and left onto South Grove.

For B&B rates, see Index.

SEAFIELD HOUSE
Westhampton Beach, New York

If you have a trip to the outer end of Long Island in mind, may I suggest that you put off your excursion until after the summer season is over? The traffic in and out of the city can be absolutely murderous in midsummer, and restaurants and other attractions are unusually crowded.

It is only a coincidence that Seafield House, a bed and breakfast in Westhampton Beach, is open from September 15 until May 15. It is a beautiful home, lovingly preserved by Mrs. Elsie Collins, filled with her antiques and personal touches that include Victorian lounges, a caned rocker, hurricane lamps, an antique pine apothecary chest, Shaker benches, Chinese and English porcelain, and other eclectic furnishings harmonized to create the casual, country-inn atmosphere.

The two suites are attractively furnished, with beds outfitted with handmade coverlets and quilts. Each suite has a sitting room and its own bath.

Mrs. Collins' full breakfast includes homemade coffee cake and fresh-squeezed orange juice. When guests check in there is a glass of wine or a cup of hot tea or coffee waiting for them, and when they leave, they always get a little loaf of cranberry bread or a jar of jelly.

There is plenty to do in Westhampton during the off-season, including visiting museums, bird watching, beach walking, antiquing; and indoor tennis courts and Guerney's International Health Spa are an hour away.

SEAFIELD HOUSE, 2 Seafield Lane, Westhampton Beach, NY 11978; 516-288-1559. A two-suite pleasant private home converted to bed-and-breakfast accommodations between Sept. 15 and May 15, when breakfast is the only meal offered. Swimming pool and tennis court on grounds and ample opportunity for outdoor recreation nearby. No credit cards. No pets. Mrs. Elsie Collins, Hostess.

Directions: From New York City take L.I. Expy. to Wm. Floyd Pkwy. and proceed to Rte. 27 and Sunrise Hwy. to Westhampton. Take a right turn to Six Corners (2nd traffic light) then make a left on Mill Rd. to end, which is Main St. Another left on Main St., and Seafield Lane is second street on right.

For B&B rates, see Index.

THE SEDGWICK INN
Berlin, New York

Those of us who live within a pleasant drive of the Sedgwick Inn think of it as an excellent place for lunch or dinner; however, the traveler on Route 22 is very pleasantly surprised to find that this inn also has some excellent bed-and-breakfast accommodations.

The inn is situated on twelve acres in the beautiful Taconic Valley on the western side of the Berkshire Mountains, and dates back to 1791 as a part of the Van Rensselaer land tract. Incidentally, the indentures hang in the reception room of the Colonial main house.

The building has served as a stagecoach stop, a summer house for a prominent New York City family, and for many years was renowned in the area as the Ranch Tavern.

A part of this pleasant experience is the Antique Shop, housed in a beautiful one-room building designed in the neo-classic style of the early 19th century, dating back to 1834. An old carriage house has been converted into an art gallery where old prints, modern paintings, sculpture (including some by innkeeper Edie Evans) and stained glass are on exhibit.

Breakfast, included in the room rate, is served on a glass enclosed dining porch facing an English garden.

The luncheon and dinner menus are short but appetizing. Three dinner entrées are offered, and the menu changes twice weekly, with such offerings as filet mignon, beef carbonnade, Yankee pot roast and sole Veronique. Area diners often speak glowingly of the soups and desserts.

THE SEDGWICK INN, Rte. 22, Berlin, NY 12022; 518-658-2334. A 5-guestroom (private baths) country inn almost midway between Tanglewood, Shaker Village, and Williamstown. European plan. Breakfast, lunch, and dinner served daily, except Mon. Open all year. Conveniently located to enjoy all of the recreational and cultural activities of the Berkshires. Motel accommodations also available. Bob and Edie Evans, Innkeepers.

Directions: The inn is located on Rte. 22 between Petersburg and Stephentown, New York.

For B&B rates, see Index.

THE 1770 HOUSE
East Hampton, Long Island, New York

East Hampton is one of the jewels of outer Long Island. Its sedate streets, arched overhead with swaying trees, and the beautiful Colonial homes and well-ordered and fashionable shops have an ambience of their very own. The John Drew Theater, open for much of the year, is one of the oldest and most prestigious in the Northeast. One of the most enjoyable experiences is to visit during the winter months and dress warmly to walk the broad beaches and thrill to the surf.

My place to stay in East Hampton is the 1770 House, kept by Miriam and Sid Perle, along with their son, Adam, and their daughter and son-in-law, Wendy and Burton Van Deusen.

The house has 18th-century origins and has served over the years as a general store, a dining hall for boys from the Clinton Academy next door, a private home, and a public inn. Today, the wood-paneled library with its cozy fireplace offers a pleasant meeting place for guests, and the seven guest rooms are furnished with good antiques and have wide-plank floors and a homelike atmosphere.

By all means plan to arrive in time for dinner, but be certain that you've made a reservation. The menu features a complete meal with the exception of dessert, and main courses are a good showcase for Miriam's considerable talents. She conducted a cooking school for twelve years.

Her breakfast menu might include scrambled eggs wrapped in ham or french toast and bacon with raspberry sauce, accompanied by homemade muffins, scones, or croissants, fresh juice or fruit, and coffee.

1770 HOUSE, 143 Main St., East Hampton, Long Island, NY 11937; 516-324-1770. An elegant 7-guestroom village inn near the eastern end of Long Island. Open all year. Dinner served Fri. thru Wed. in season; Fri. and Sat. off-season. Minimum stays of 3 and 4 days required in July and Aug. Convenient to many cultural and recreational diversions, including antiquing and backroading. Available by public transportation; consult innkeepers. Not comfortable for children under 14. No pets. The Perle Family, Innkeepers.

Directions: From New York City: take the Long Island Expressway to Exit 70, and then turn south to Rte. 27 east, which is the main street of East Hampton. The inn is located diagonally across the street from Guild Hall.

For B&B rates, see Index.

THE SHERWOOD INN
Skaneateles, New York

Skaneateles, New York, located on Route 20 at the head of one of the Finger Lakes bearing the same name, is one of the beauty spots of New York State. The exceptionally pure water makes it ideal for all summer sports. On the Fourth of July and Labor Day weekend the scene is considerably enlivened by sailing regattas.

The Sherwood Inn overlooks the waters of the lake, and all but just a few of the fifteen bedrooms enjoy the inspiring view. The Honeymoon Suite is decorated in shades of blue, the pattern of the quilt on the four-poster canopied bed matches both the draperies and the wallpaper.

Breakfast is served in the cheerful lobby of the inn whose broad windows also overlook the ever-changing scene on the Lake. Besides the ever-present coffee pot, there is orange juice, hot homemade muffins and breads and a choice of breakfast beverages.

Travelers moving across New York State on the New York Thruway would do well to turn onto Route 20 and enjoy a restful evening and happy stay at the Sherwood Inn in Skaneateles.

THE SHERWOOD INN, 26 West Genesee St., Skaneateles, NY 13152; 315-685-3405. A 15-room village inn on the shores of Lake Skaneateles in the Finger Lakes district of New York State. Continental breakfast included in room tariff. Lunch and dinner served daily to travelers. Open every day except Christmas. Tennis, swimming, golf, and indoor winter ice skating available nearby. Near Everson Museum, Barrow Art Gallery, and William Seward House. Ellen Seymour, Innkeeper.

Directions: From New York State Thruway use Weedsport exit and follow Rte. 34 south to Auburn (6 mi.). Turn east on Rte. 20, 7 mi. to Skaneateles. Inn is located in center of village.

For B&B rates, see Index.

SOUTH MEADOW FARM LODGE
Lake Placid, New York

If you're into cross-country skiing in the winter and lots of walking, hiking, backroading, reading, talking, eating, and general jollification in summer, then Betty and Harry Eldridge and their daughter Anne, their twin daughters Katie and Noni, and son Alan at the South Meadow Farm Lodge are certainly for you.

The first person I met was Alan and he couldn't have been more accommodating, showing me through their very fascinating home that is dominated by a common room with a cathedral ceiling, soaring windows, and a huge fireplace. Some of the bedrooms are located in a loft underneath the rafters of this most impressive room, and there are curtains between them, but no walls. There are two conventional bedrooms also available.

There are lots of windows, and throughout the house there's a wonderful feeling for textures and gay colors. It's the kind of house in which two people make it possible for their four children to be alert and tuned in to the world of ideas. There is a loom in one corner, a piano, stacks of games in another, magazines of all kinds, at least three cats, and much more.

Olympic cross-country ski trails cross the farm and they are excellent for skiers, runners, and walkers. Harry, an enthusiastic licensed Adirondack guide, is available for treks into the High Peaks region.

The full farm breakfast is included in the price of the lodging. Dinner is also available, and it is whatever the family is having.

SOUTH MEADOW FARM LODGE, Cascade Rd., Lake Placid, N Y 12946; 518-523-9369. A 5-bedroom contemporary farm-lodge in the Adirondacks with Olympic cross-country ski trails crossing the property. Shared bath. Open year-round. Closed Christmas. Full breakfast included with lodgings. Family-style dinner available. Within minutes of Cascade Mt. and Marcy Mt. trails; ½ mi. east of Olympic bobsled and luge runs. Excellent cross-country skiing, snowshoeing, hiking, nature walks, running, swimming on grounds and nearby. Betty and Harry Eldridge, Lodgekeepers.

Directions: From N.Y.C., take Northway (I-87) to Exit 30 and follow signs to Lake Placid (Rte. 73.) 7 miles west of Keene, look for pale blue sign on left for South Meadow Farm Lodge and follow signs and dirt road. The lodge, a gray contemporary building, is visible from the turn.

For B&B rates, see Index.

SPRINGSIDE INN
Auburn, New York

One of the most pleasant journeys in New York State is along Route 20, which runs between Albany and Buffalo, and one of the places to stop on the "B&B route" is the Springside Inn in Auburn, New York, at the head of Owasco Lake, one of the prettiest of the Finger Lakes.

This area is rich in entertainment and recreation of all kinds in all seasons. Fall foliage is reflected in the crystal waters of the lake and there is a variety of scenic roads and picturesque vantage points. Waterfalls, State parks, historical homes, and much history is woven into the fabric of nature's backdrop.

Each of the lodging rooms at the Springside Inn is decorated to give a different feeling. One is in shades of pink with a pink bedspread and matching curtains. A friendly rocking chair is in the front window overlooking the lake. Another room has twin beds, Victorian furniture, and lamps with red bows. A room on the top floor is done in shades of beige and yellow with formal valances at the window, a Tiffany-type lamp, hooked rugs, and twin beds.

Although the inn has attractive B&B rates, it is especially well known in the area as an excellent restaurant.

The porch and lounge, each of which shares a view of the placid pond in front of the inn, also provide an ideal setting for the continental breakfast, which might be homemade blueberry, apple, or zucchini muffins and assorted fruits. Breakfast is on a "help yourself" basis.

SPRINGSIDE INN, 41 West Lake Rd., Auburn, NY 13021; 315-252-7247. A 7-room country inn, 1 mi. south of Auburn with a view of Owasco Lake. In the heart of the historical Finger Lakes. Lodgings include continental breakfast. Some rooms with shared bath. Open every day, except Christmas. Kitchen closed Memorial Day, July 4, and Labor Day. Boating, swimming, bicycles, golf, riding, alpine and xc skiing nearby. Bill Dove and Family, Innkeepers.

Directions: From N.Y. Thruway, take Exit 40 and follow Rte. 34 south through downtown Auburn to Rte. 38. Follow Rte. 38 south to traffic circle at lake and take 2nd exit right at West Shore of Oswasco Lake. Drive ¼ mi. to inn.

For B&B rates, see Index.

THE STAGECOACH INN
Lake Placid, New York

Here's a bed-and-breakfast inn whose owners have a show business background. Peter Moreau is a playwright, actor, director, and producer. His wife, Sherry, is an actress. The inn is a fitting dramatic setting for two such interesting and vibrant people.

The only remaining Adirondack Mountain landmark from the romantic stagecoach days of the 19th century, the inn's dramatic cathedral-ceilinged living room, with its impressive fireplaces and posts and beams in yellow Adirondack birch, is furnished with interesting pieces that obviously belong.

The guest rooms have a wonderful "out of the woods" feeling and are extremely warm and comfortable. There are books everywhere and inviting rocking chairs on the broad front porch, where one could read for hours.

Some very interesting and well-known guests have stayed at the inn, particularly during the 19th century, including the famed Adirondack photographer, Seneca Ray Stoddard, who spoke glowingly of his stay at the "North Elba Hotel," the name of the inn in those days. It was also a summer retreat for Chancellor James R. Day of Syracuse University.

Richard Henry Dana, the author of *Two Years Before the Mast* and *How We Met John Brown*, also used the inn as a base when he visited the Adirondacks.

Visitors here can use the inn as a hub and enjoy the entire Adirondack State Park, which embraces an area almost as large as the state of Vermont and has forty-six mountain peaks over 4,000 feet high. Peter is well qualified to advise the novice hiker and walker about the many day-trips, including a visit to the various sites which were used in the Winter Olympics.

THE STAGECOACH INN, Old Military Rd., Lake Placid, NY 12946; 518-523-9474. A 7-guestroom (private and semi-private baths) historic Adirondack inn. Full breakfast served. Open year-round. Conveniently located to enjoy all of the considerable recreational attractions in the Adirondack Mtns., including swimming, tennis, indoor ice skating, golf, hiking, walking, downhill and xc skiing. No credit cards. H. Peter Moreau, Innkeeper.

Directions: From the Northway follow Rte. 73 past the Olympic ski jumps and look for Old Military Rd. on the left.

For B&B rates, see Index.

THE WHITE INN
Fredonia, New York

Fredonia is a bustling little town, usually connected with nearby Dunkirk, a port on Lake Erie. It has a very pleasant town square with benches and trees and also a gazebo. Fredonia is the site of one of the several branches of the University of the State of New York, where many cultural and sporting events are open to the public.

Fredonia is basically a Victorian town, and slowly but surely the businesses on the main street are removing their modern facades and allowing the pure Victorian architecture underneath to shine forth. Part of the town is listed in the National Register of Historic Places.

Certainly the restoration of the White Inn is proving most beneficial to travelers and townsfolk alike.

The first thing I observed was a hundred-foot-long veranda on the front, shaded by two ancient maple trees planted in 1821 by one Squire White, for whom the inn has been named.

The inn is certainly the center of town activity. The two owners, David Palmer and David Bryant, philosophy teachers at the Fredonia State University, have put a great deal of time, effort, and money into this first-class renovation. David Palmer's wife, Nancy, who has a degree in art history from the University of North Carolina, is the decorator.

The bedrooms are light and airy and probably larger than average.

Incidentally, the White Inn was one of the charter members of the Duncan Hines organization many years ago, and today three dining rooms provide a congenial setting for all meals. Lunch and dinner are served seven days a week and hotel guests receive a complimentary breakfast.

The White Inn, just a few minutes from the New York State Thruway, will make an excellent overnight or even longer stay on the far reaches of western New York State.

THE WHITE INN, 52 East Main St., Scenic Rte. 20, Fredonia, NY 14063; 716-672-2103. A 20-guestroom village inn (all private baths) on the main street in Fredonia. Open every day, all year. Quite convenient for visits to nearby Chautauqua and other western New York State cultural and recreational attractions. No pets. David Palmer and David Bryant, Innkeepers.

Directions: From New York State Thwy. take Exit 59, follow Rte. 60 to Rte. 20; turn right to the inn.

For B&B rates, see Index.

WILLIAM SEWARD INN
Westfield, New York

In 1982, after a stint at Jackson Lake Lodge in the Grand Tetons and Caneel Bay Plantation in the Virgin Islands, innkeepers and antique buffs Bruce and Barbara Johnson bought the William H. Seward house, built in 1821 at the eastern rim of Lake Erie. Seward, as any student of American history can recall, was secretary of state under Abraham Lincoln and famous for his purchase of Alaska from Russia.

Seward remodeled the once modest cottage, giving it the air of a Greek Revival mansion. The Johnsons have restored the house, which had fallen into disrepair over the years, remodeling and enlarging it, and naming it the William Seward Inn.

Each guest room is a jewel dominated by an antique four-poster bed topped with a puffy comforter. A spacious front room with a view of the lake is actually a suite, often reserved for newlyweds, with a queen-sized bed.

Bruce, an antique dealer, specializes in four-posters and also collects all sorts of antique furniture, which he will sell.

Original antique chairs and a Sheraton sideboard grace the cheery bay-windowed dining room, with walls covered in a period blue-and-white pattern, where Barbara's full breakfasts are served.

Fresh fruit juice and fruit are likely to be followed by one of Barbara's favorites—smoked swiss cheese and ham sandwiched in french toast or her puffy plantation pancakes, baked in individual ramekins and served with maple syrup. Eggs Benedict come topped with a sour cream sauce and fresh-snipped parsley.

There are no televisions or phones in the rooms, but a TV is in the first-floor library, where there are bookcases full of reading materials. A lovely front parlor with beautiful tall windows is also open to guests.

WILLIAM SEWARD INN, South Portage Rd., Westfield, NY 14787; 716-326-4151. A 10-guestroom (private baths) bed-and-breakfast inn overlooking the eastern rim of Lake Erie in western New York State. Full, cooked-to-order breakfast included in room rate. Closed Christmas Day only. During summer, 2-night minimum. The famed Chautauqua Institution 15 min. away; 35 min. from Peak 'n' Peak and Cockaigne ski slopes; 1 hr. from Buffalo. Westfield is an antiques lover's paradise with 17 shops to tempt the collector. No children under 12. No pets. No credit cards. Bruce and Barbara Johnson, Innkeepers.

Directions: From N.Y. Thruway, take Westfield exit and turn left to N.Y. Rte. 394; continue 4 mi. to drive on right at foot of knoll.

For B&B rates, see Index.

THE BAIRD HOUSE
Mars Hill, North Carolina

This bed-and-breakfast inn has so many attractive features that I'm not quite sure what to mention first.

Supposing we start with breakfast. While we were rocking on the front porch overlooking a part of the campus of Mars Hill College, innkeeper Yvette Bluhm explained that breakfast is sausage balls, apple fritters, orange juice, and coffee. It is served in the dining room, kitchen, or on the back terrace.

She was enthusiastic about the Southern Appalachia Repertory Theater, just a short distance away. They have a playwrights' conference here once a year and select a play for a world premiere. One play a year is on an Appalachian theme and the others are Broadway hits. During the summer it is a state theater, and during the remainder of the year the college drama department presents plays.

There are five guest rooms furnished and decorated in the traditional manner with poster beds and usable fireplaces. An inviting parlor provides the opportunity to visit with either the owner or other guests.

I'm delighted that the proprietor of Baird House wrote me a letter and that eventually I found my way to Mars Hill. Although it's the only place to stay in town, it would be a credit to any community.

BAIRD HOUSE, 121 Main St., Mars Hill, NC 28754; 704-689-5722 or 704-689-4542. A 5-guestroom (some shared baths) bed-and-breakfast accommodation in a quiet college town about 20 min. north of Asheville. Breakfast is included in the lodging rate and is the only meal served. Open year-round. Mars Hill is a convenient distance from Grandfather Mountain, Biltmore House and Gardens, the Appalachian Trail, the Great Smoky Mountains National Park, Mount Mitchell, and many other western North Carolina attractions. The area abounds in wonderful vacation opportunities. No credit cards. Yvette Bluhm, Innkeeper.

Directions: Mars Hill is west of Rte. 19-23, which runs north out of Asheville. Turn towards town center and watch for sign to turn left for Baird House at the first light.

For B&B rates, see Index.

BLUE BOAR LODGE
Robbinsville, North Carolina

This is truly an unusual experience. Originally built as a hunting lodge, it is reached by a dirt road that runs for some distance alongside Lake Santeetlah. It is a small secluded hideaway nestled in a hollow of the Nantahala National Forest.

The guest rooms have pine-paneled walls and are very pleasant. Guests gather in the lobby and living room, which is dominated by a huge fireplace and two boars' heads. There's a little trout pool almost within casting distance of the side porch.

Mountain nights mean a crackling fire even in July and August, and guests relax among the rustic furnishings or catch up on their reading.

During the day they can swim or sun on the shores of beautiful Lake Santeetlah, boat or canoe along the 108 miles of shoreline, and catch their own small- or large-mouth bass, walleye, panfish, muskie, or channel blue cat. There is also trout in the well-stocked pond, where guests may catch their own dinner.

Both breakfast and dinner are included in the rates. Dinner is served at 6 P.M., and is one main entrée served family style, and breakfast is a full mountain breakfast.

BLUE BOAR LODGE, Joyce Kilmer Forest Road, Robbinsville, NC 28771; 704-479-8126. A 7-guestroom lodge in the woods, high in the Great Smoky Mountains, just a few minutes from the main entrance to Joyce Kilmer National Forest. Open April 1 to mid-Oct. for summer guests, and mid-Oct. until just after Christmas for hunting only. Hunting, fishing, swimming, birdwatching, hiking, rafting, nature walks, and marvelous backroading in the Great Smokies. No pets. Roy and Kathy Wilson, Proprietors.

Directions: Follow Joyce Kilmer Forest Rd. 10 mi. from Robbinsville. Look for turn-off on right and follow signs on woods road.

For rates, see Index.

BUTTONWOOD INN
Franklin, North Carolina

The town of Franklin is surrounded by 420,000 acres of the Nantahala National Forest with such recreational opportunities as hiking, fishing, hunting, rafting, white-water canoeing, horseback riding, and camping. There are also facilities for skiing, golfing, tennis, and other sports. The good people in Atlanta, Charlestown, and Savannah are well acquainted with this mountain area of North Carolina, which is beautiful in all four seasons.

The Buttonwood is a small country inn with four guest rooms located next to the Franklin Golf Course.

The original residence was a small cottage built in the late 1920s between the 5th and 7th greens. A new wing retains the same rustic charm and now accommodates the inn's guests.

Dogwood and rhododendron bloom abundantly during the spring and a spacious lawn with a view of the mountains is enjoyed by the guests.

Completely surrounded by tall pines, the small and cozy Buttonwood will appeal to the person who prefers simplicity and natural rustic beauty. It provides comfortable lodgings for the overnight traveler and also for those wishing to make their stay longer. There is a cheerful apartment available by the week or month.

Homemade breakfast offerings include sour cream coffee cake, ginger muffins, and lemon butter, served along with sausage ring, scrambled eggs, baked apple, juice, fresh fruit, and coffee.

The Buttonwood was one of the most pleasant surprises that I have encountered in my search for B&B's.

BUTTONWOOD INN, 190 Georgia Rd., Franklin, NC 28734; 704-369-8985. A 4-guestroom (one suite) bed-and-breakfast home adjacent to the Franklin Golf Course. Complimentary full breakfast. Open late May to Nov. Located in the beautiful Great Smokey region of western North Carolina with all the natural, cultural, and recreational advantages. No pets. No credit cards. Liz Oehser, Proprietor.

Directions: From Dillard, Georgia, drive north to the outskirts of Franklin, N.C., on Rte. 441 (Business). Immediately look very sharply on the left for a very small sign saying "Buttonwood Inn." If you pass the entrance to the Franklin Golf Course, you've gone too far.

For B&B rates, see Index.

HAVENSHIRE INN
Hendersonville, North Carolina

Driving between Hendersonville and Brevard, I saw a sign for the Havenshire Inn and turned off on a black-topped road that followed the course of a river through some very pleasant meadowlands. It felt longer than the posted two miles, but—ah well—it was the first week of June, the laurel was out in beautiful profusion, the sun was shining, and the birds were singing.

Now, in a verdant, rolling valley, I saw a large redwood-and-cedar house greatly resembling an English country manor—the Havenshire Inn. The curved road wound its way through lush lawns and I discovered that the front of the inn looked out over the valley of the French Broad River. There were many beautiful pine trees and a wonderful air of tranquility.

From my first glimpse, I felt this was going to be exceptional, and it was. I walked onto an unusually large screened-in porch, where guests enjoy breakfast, and into a high-ceilinged center hallway with impressive chandeliers. Each of the six guest rooms, along with a guest cottage, is handsomely furnished and enjoys lovely views of the grounds and countryside. Kay Coppock was kind enough to lead me down the garden path just a few paces to Bowman's Bluff, overlooking the river, and of course it has a legend about an Indian maiden. The wonderful sweeping lawns and the house itself are bordered by a brown rather than white, horse fence, behind which horses graze. They are quite friendly and enjoy being patted.

Havenshire Inn was an unexpected surprise for me, and I was delighted to find a bed and breakfast with such an unusual ambience and ample amusement and recreation nearby.

HAVENSHIRE INN, Rte. 4, Box 455, Cummings Rd., Hendersonville, NC 28739; 704-692-4097. A 6-guestroom (some shared baths) bed-and-breakfast inn on a handsome estate between Hendersonville and Brevard. Breakfast is the only meal served and is included in the room rate. Open April 1 thru Oct. 31. Conveniently situated to enjoy all of the many recreational, cultural, and historical attractions in the area, including the Brevard Music Festival and the Vanderbilt Mansion in Asheville. No facilities to amuse small children. Kay Coppock and Cindy Findley, Innkeepers.

Directions: Look for inn sign off Rte. 64 between Horseshoe Bend and Etowah; follow Rte. 4 (Cummings Rd.) a little over 2 mi. and look for inn on right.

For B&B rates, see Index.

NU-WRAY INN
Burnsville, North Carolina

The Nu-Wray is known throughout the southern highlands as the inn where a bell rouses everyone at 8 A.M. and a similar tolling at 8:30 beckons all of the houseguests, and any other lucky people who happen to be passing through, for a fabulous breakfast.

Burnsville is in the heart of Yancey County, which contains the highest peak east of the Rockies. It's a mountainous country ranging in elevation from 1,700 to 6,300 feet.

At the Nu-Wray there are old-fashioned door keys and every guest returns his to the old-fashioned key rack in the lobby. There's a big fireplace at one end and many, many antiques of all kinds.

There are guest rooms on the two upper floors of this village inn in the mountains, and all of them have remained unchanged during the many years that I've been visiting.

The full à la carte breakfast is enjoyed by all guests seated around wonderful long tables with white tablecloths. There are platters of scrambled eggs, country ham, grits, red-eye gravy, applesauce, hot biscuits, apple butter, great pots of honey, and tubs of fresh country butter. Everyone is introduced and soon there's lots of talking, laughter, joking, and perhaps the making of new friends.

Dinner is served in the same manner, with everybody sitting around the long tables and falling to with a will summoned by the bell.

THE NU-WRAY INN, Burnsville, NC 28714; 704-682-2329. A 32-guestroom village inn on town square on Rte. 19E, 38 mi. northeast of Asheville. A few miles from Mt. Mitchell. European plan. Lodgings available year-round. Breakfast and dinner served every weekday to travelers. Noon dinner served on Sundays only. Dining room open daily mid-April to Dec. 1. Golf, swimming, hiking, and skiing nearby. Betty Wray Souders, Innkeeper.

Directions: From Asheville, go north on Rte. 19-23 for 18 mi., then continue on 19. Five mi. from Burnsville, 19 becomes 19E. From the north via Bristol or Johnson City, Tenn., take Rte. 19-23 to Unicoi. Turn left on 107 to N.C. State Line. Take 226 and turn right on Rte. 197 at Red Hill to Burnsville.

For B&B rates, see Index.

THE ORCHARD INN
Saluda, North Carolina

This inn has made considerable progress since my first visit a few years ago, when it was in the final stages of rehabilitation. Then, it was little more than an enthusiastic gleam in the eyes of Ann and Ken Hough, who are experienced restorers of old houses.

Now, it combines country farmhouse warmth with plantation elegance, but the most memorable feature is the view overlooking the fascinating undulations of the Warrior Mountain Range. It is spectacular at any time of day or year.

The building was built early in the 1900s by the Southern Railway Company, providing railroad clerks and their families a summer mountain retreat. It has now been taken over and completely renovated by the Houghs, who have created a minor miracle in getting it into such tiptop shape.

The eighty-foot glassed-in dining room has an unobstructed view, which is shared by many of the eight guest rooms.

Lunch and dinner are available by reservation. Gentlemen are requested to wear jackets at dinner.

THE ORCHARD INN, Box 725, Saluda, NC 28773; 704-749-5471. An 8-guestroom mountaintop (2,500 feet) inn in western North Carolina. A short distance from Tryon. Open year-round. Breakfast included with room rate. Lunch and dinner available. Antiquing, hiking, wild flower collecting, birdwatching, and superb country roads abound. No credit cards. Ann and Ken Hough, Innkeepers.

Directions: From Atlanta come north on I-85 to I-26. Inn is two miles off I-26. From Asheville take I-26 south to Exit 28.

For B&B rates, see Index.

RAGGED GARDEN INN
Blowing Rock, North Carolina

The full name of this very pleasant, in-town accommodation is the Ragged Garden Inn & Restaurant, and after I had a good chat with Joe Villani, I realized that his background, first at Sardi's in New York and then later at other restaurants of his own in Connecticut and Florida made cuisine a very important part of the popularity of the inn.

He explained that the menu is basically northern Italian, although there are also many continental and American dishes. Part of our conversation was in the kitchen, where he was making homemade fettucini.

An imposing porte cochere ushers the guest into this rather grand old house, built at the turn of the century. It is surrounded by roses, rhododendrons, and trees, and is centrally located, permitting guests to enjoy art galleries, boutiques, the parks and attractions of Blowing Rock.

There are five very pleasantly decorated guest rooms, available for overnight and longer stays.

Blowing Rock is the highest town in North Carolina at 4,200 feet, and derives its name from a blowing rock overhanging the Johns River Gorge. The sheer rock walls form a flume, and when the wind sweeps down, a strong force is created, and a light object will blow back each time it is tossed out into the gorge.

The Ragged Garden Inn is indeed a dream come true for Joe Villani and his wife, Joyce. They are very personable and considerate people, and the inn reflects a warm and welcoming atmosphere.

RAGGED GARDEN INN & RESTAURANT, Sunset Dr., P.O. Box 1927, Blowing Rock, NC 28605; 704-295-9703. A 5-guestroom inn (all private baths) in North Carolina's delightful mountain country. Room rate includes breakfast. Dinner served nightly except Sunday. Open mid-April to mid-Nov. Conveniently located to enjoy the many recreational and cultural attractions in this area. Not suitable for young children. Joe and Joyce Villani, Innkeepers.

Directions: Ragged Garden Inn is located 1 block off Main St. in Blowing Rock.

For B&B rates, see Index.

THE RED ROCKER INN
Black Mountain, North Carolina

For the first-time visitor, western North Carolina is jampacked with surprises. One of the best is the Red Rocker Inn in the town of Black Mountain at the entrance of the eastern Great Smoky Mountains. I learned about it through a letter from a former classmate at Bucknell University, Louise Brosius Hurd. She said, "The warm personality of the host, the special quality of the food, and the charm and imaginative decor of the bedrooms all add up to a unique and delightful experience."

Louise, you were right. Fred Eshleman, who, incidentally, taught at the Muncy, Pennsylvania, high school (relatively near Bucknell) for ten years, explained that the bedrooms were decorated "with humor."

When he and his wife, Pat, first acquired the property, it had twenty-one bedrooms and one bath down the hall. In providing more bathrooms, they placed free-standing bathtubs in some of the bedrooms, cleverly concealed behind curtains. There are many other extremely clever touches, including the decorations in one bedroom that consist entirely of the awards won during Fred Eshleman's tenure as a teacher. A great, oversized red rocker sits on the front lawn.

Food, however, is one of the important features of the Red Rocker. I happened to be there during lunch hour, and the looks of anticipation on the part of the continuous stream of ladies and gentlemen were enough to convince me that I was on the right track. The evening meal is served family style with a changing menu every day.

It's worth noting that special modified American plan rates are in effect before and after the high season.

If you don't have a sense of humor before you visit the Red Rocker, you'll have one after you leave.

THE RED ROCKER INN, 136 N. Dougherty St., Black Mountain, NC 28711; 704-669-5991. An 18-guestroom (most with private baths) country inn in a small, relaxed mountain community. Open May 1 to Nov. 1. Breakfast not included in room rate. Conveniently located to enjoy the many cultural and recreational attractions in the area. Advance reservations suggested for evening meals. Pat and Fred Eshleman, Innkeepers.

Directions: Leave Rte. 40 at Black Mountain Exit 64, 17 mi. east of Asheville. Come into town, turn left at the main intersection, go one block, turn right at Dougherty St., and look for inn.

For B&B rates, see Index.

WOMBLE INN
Brevard, North Carolina

In her book, *Music Festivals in North America* (Berkshire Traveller Press), author Carol Rabin says, "'The Summer Cultural Center of the South' is the proud claim of the Brevard Music Center. Nestled in the Smoky Mountains and the Pisgah National Forest in Transylvania County, thirty miles south of Asheville, is the little North Carolina community of Brevard. Most of the year the rural town is quiet and serene, but Brevard begins bustling in June when over 300 students and 125 faculty come to the Brevard Music Center."

She continues, "The main thrust of the center is on education and performance by young students who are enrolled in an intensive seven-week course, but much emphasis is placed on the festival performances as well. There are over forty-five different programs offered during the season, ranging from symphonic and chamber works to opera, light opera, choral works, and solo recitals."

Fortunate, indeed, are guests who can enjoy the hospitality of the Womble Inn during the festival season. It is a very pleasant red brick building with wrought-iron decorations and a second-floor gallery facing Main Street.

The guest rooms and parlor are very homey in nature and most attractive. Some of the guest rooms have two double beds and some have singles. There are many family portraits of young people everywhere and, as one would imagine, a very good piano.

Although the Womble Inn is undoubtedly booked well in advance during the festival season from the first of July until mid-August, it is open every day all year. Breakfast is served in your room on a silver tray or in the dining room with a big picture window looking out over the residential area of the town, and guests often browse in the large, very clean kitchen.

WOMBLE INN, 301 Main St., Brevard, NC 28712; 704-884-4770. A 6-guestroom (all with private baths) bed-and-breakfast inn located in the beautiful Great Smoky Mountains of North Carolina. Open all year. In season, dinner is served several nights a week. Brevard Music Festival July 1 to mid-Aug. Immediately convenient to enjoy the many attractions of the Pisgah National Forest. No credit cards. Beth and Steve Womble, Inkeepers.

Directions: Once in Brevard you can't miss Main St.; continue north and look for inn on left-hand side.

For B&B rates, see Index.

BLOSSOM TYME
Gambier, Ohio

You'll discover more than lodging at Dean and Marie Dulaney's Blossom Tyme, just outside the picturesque village of Gambier, Ohio, home of Paul Newman's alma mater, Kenyon College.

Besides a bed and breakfast at their 30-year-old home overlooking the Kokosing River Valley, they operate a greenhouse and gift shop, where they offer classes in a mind-boggling assortment of crafts, including everything from spinning wool on the "walking" spinning wheel to basketry, chair caning, calligraphy, or quilting (it's Amish country, so quilts are big). If you happen onto their home in late August, you'll encounter a minicraft festival on the Dulaneys' back four acres.

Warm pine paneling, Colonial furniture, and several antiques create a friendly feeling in the living room, where guests are welcome to spend their time—in winter, in front of a crackling fire.

Sharing a bath, there are two cozy guest rooms, each with a double bed; one a brass-and-iron bedstead covered in a white popcorn crocheted spread. The quilts were made by Dean's aunt; fresh flowers greet guests, and beds are turned down at night with mints on the pillows.

Breakfasts may be juice, fruit, blueberry buckle, coffee or herb teas, or heartier, if guests prefer, with french toast and sausages, served according to guests' own schedules.

A covered patio in back is framed by arching trees and is an inviting spot to relax and read.

Nearby Kenyon College has a lovely campus, with a Gothic church and other historic buildings of interest.

BLOSSOM TYME, 10728 Kenyon Rd., Ohio Rte. 308, Box 54, Gambier, OH 43022; 614-427-2876 or 427-3300. A 2-guestroom (shared bath) ranch house outside the picturesque college town of Gambier, 4 mi. east of Mt. Vernon and 1 hr. from Columbus. Continental or full breakfast included in room rate. Open all year except the weekend before Thanksgiving and the week before Christmas. The rolling hills and rich farmland offer hunting and camping, and there is fishing, canoeing, and sailing on the Kokosing River. No children under 5. No pets. Smoking outside only. Dean and Marie Dulaney, Hosts.

Directions: From Mt. Vernon, Ohio, take Rte. 229 east 4 mi. to Gambier. Take Ohio Rte. 308 about ½ mi. to Blossom Tyme on the right. Or from Mt. Vernon, take U.S. Rte. 36 east to Ohio Rte. 308; turn right. Blossom Tyme is ½ mi. on the left.

For B&B rate, see Index.

PORTAGE HOUSE
Akron, Ohio

Tantalizing aromas of Jeanne Pinnick's limpa rye or wheat breads wafting from the oven may greet you at Portage House, a gracious Tudor-styled home built in 1917, in what was originally a prestigious area of Akron. The Perkins Mansion, home of the founding family of Akron, and the John Brown House are just down the block. Before 1825 the area was the portage route between two river systems, and in 1785 it was the western boundary of the United States.

Jeanne serves her own jams and sausages at breakfast, the patties made from beef raised on a Kansas farm she and her husband, Harry, own. Breakfast is full or continental, according to the wishes of guests. It may be served in the sunny formal blue dining room furnished in traditional mahogany or around the friendly center island in the modernized kitchen.

Furnishings in the guest rooms, with good, solid beds, hearken to the 1920s, with full-length mirrors on the closet doors. Each room has its own alarm clock on the nightstand, a box of tissues, monogrammed toothbrushes, plenty of fluffy towels, and convenient luggage racks. Temporary cots and movable cribs accommodate families.

The Pinnicks live in the former ballroom on the third floor, so the second and first floors are for guests, with books and magazines and a spinet piano (no television except in the kitchen).

With advance notice, Jeanne serves a home-style complete dinner or lunch; complimentary snacks are available on arrival if desired, and there is fresh fruit, always.

Harry is a physics professor at nearby Akron University; he and Jeanne opened their home to guests four years ago.

PORTAGE HOUSE, 601 Copley Rd., Ohio Rte. 162, Akron, OH 44320; 216-535-9236. A 5-guestroom (1 private bath, others shared) in the Rubber City. Complimentary continental or full breakfast. Lunch and dinner available with advance notice. Closed Dec. and Jan. Blossom Music Center, summer home of the Cleveland Symphony; Stan Hywet Hall, former home of the rubber baron, Frank Seiberling; Hale Farm and Western Reserve Village; Cuyahoga Valley Natl. Recreation Area; Quaker Square; E. J. Thomas Performing Arts Hall; and Canton Football Hall of Fame all nearby. Jeanne and Harry Pinnick, Hosts.

Directions: Take I-77 north or south to Copley Rd./Ohio Rte. 162 exit. Portage House is 2 mi. east from the exit, on the right (south) side of the street.

For B&B rates, see Index.

VICTORIAN BED AND BREAKFAST
Columbus, Ohio

When I arrived, opera star John Reardon had just checked out of Marjorie and Gary Jones's bed and breakfast, having starred in the Columbus Opera production of *Man of La Mancha*. Nobel Prize winners have stayed here, too, while visiting the professors at nearby Ohio State University.

"It is not a homogenized American lodging," said Marjorie, of York, England, speaking of the 105-year-old Queen Anne hostelry that has been on the cover of *Columbus Home Magazine* and is listed in the National Register of Historic Places.

Retired British Army career man, Gary, and his wife toured the world, living in the Far and Middle East while he was on assignments. They came to the United States in 1980 and bought the three-story gabled mansion, tucked in Victorian Village on the north side of Columbus. Since Marjorie had shipped twenty-two crates of antique furniture, more objets d'art than the average curio shop, silks, satins, velvets, and laces from England, the best way to show them off was to open a bed and breakfast.

Stepping inside the 24-foot-high foyer is like being on a movie set. Paintings reach from floor to twelve-foot ceilings on all three floors; every nook and cranny, tables, shelves, windowsills, and even floors are crammed with bric-a-brac and collections of teapots, cups and saucers, snuff boxes, butterflies, plates, plaques, and animals. There are real animals, too—seven Chinese emperor dogs and one Siamese cat.

Marjorie serves English breakfasts in the formal dining room until 10 A.M., starting with fresh fruit in a crystal bowl, followed by dry cereals, porridge in winter, bacon, eggs, tomatoes, mushrooms, fried bread, toast, english muffins, lemon and orange marmalade, and "United States grape jelly." After 10, breakfasts are continental, except for honeymooners staying in the bridal suite.

One bemused houseguest called the Victorian Bed and Breakfast "a world in a world."

VICTORIAN BED AND BREAKFAST, 78 Smith Place, Columbus, OH 43201; 614-299-1656. A 3-suite historic Queen Anne home in Victorian Village on the north side of Columbus. Breakfast included in room rate. Open every day. A short walk to Ohio State University. Children accepted. No pets. Marjorie and Gary Jones, Hosts.

Directions: From I-71 north, take the 5th Ave. exit and turn right. Turn right on High St., then left on Smith Pl. to the corner of Dennison. From I-71 south, take 5th Ave. exit, turn left, and proceed as above.

For B&B rates, see Index.

THE WHITE OAK INN
Danville, Ohio

An uphill-downhill drive on the two-lane "scenic route" led to the White Oak Inn, rising like a bright white oasis in the spring twilight. The imposing 1918 farmhouse with its high gambrel roof and full-length porch was framed by grand old trees just beginning to bud. From oaks on the thirteen acres, George Crise built the spacious house in the oil-drilling and farming community of Danville, across from the rippling Kokosing River, in hopes that his three sons would live there when they grew up, but they didn't.

The property, however, was still owned by a seventy-year-old daughter-in-law of Crise when Joyce and Jim Acton bought it in 1985. After much remodeling, rewiring, and refurbishing, the Actons settled in and opened their home to guests. A few guests were gathered in front of the raised hearth, chatting, sipping wine, and nibbling on cheese and crackers when I arrived. Joyce introduced everyone by name as she invited me to join them. Several turn-of-the-century rocking chairs comprised part of the conversation grouping, and on a couple of tables, people had been playing board games.

Dinner was served family-style in the former parlor, now the dining room, across the center hall. Next morning, as the sun streamed through the patterned curtains, Joyce served a hearty breakfast, with freshly baked pastries and fluffy french toast made from her own baked bread.

Guest room doors featuring grapevine wreaths with plaid bows and brass plaques open to antique-furnished rooms, each in a different mellowed native wood. Fresh flowers, starchy white ruffled curtains at the windows, candlewick bedspreads, and patchwork quilts on the high, firm beds are homey touches.

THE WHITE OAK INN, 29683 Walhonding Rd., Danville, OH 43014; 614-599-6107. A 6-guestroom (private and shared baths) peaceful and quiet farmhouse in the midst of 13 acres of farmland near the Kokosing River, 15 mi. east of Mt. Vernon, Ohio. Complimentary full breakfast. Dinners by advance reservations. Closed Thanksgiving, Christmas, and New Year's. Roscoe Village, a restored Ohio Canal town with shops, museum, and restaurants, 25 mi.; 60 mi. from Columbus. Well-behaved children are welcome, and provisions may be made for pets. No smoking. Joyce and Jim Acton, Innkeepers.

Directions: From I-71, take Mt. Gilead/Fredericktown exit, left to Ohio Rte. 96 to Fredericktown. Turn right on Ohio Rte. 13 to Mt. Vernon. From Mt. Vernon, take U.S. Rte. 36 to Millwood, 1 mi. east of U.S. Rte. 62. Bear left on Ohio Rte. 715, 2 mi. to the inn on the left.

For B&B rates, see Index.

THE WORTHINGTON INN
Worthington, Ohio

The Worthington Inn is one of Ohio's original stagecoach stops, built in 1831 by a Connecticut Yankee who had come to Ohio to seek his fortune. Down through the years the inn changed hands and sported new names several times. The years and circumstances took their toll on the structure so that by late 1982 the building was in such poor condition that had not the present owners bought it, it would have been torn down within a year.

Beginning in 1983, the building was completely renovated and restored, and it is now listed in the National Register of Historic Places. The stately, three-story inn with a mansard roof is painted in typical Victorian colors and houses three dining rooms, a wine cellar that has a medieval dungeon door, twenty-three guest rooms, party and meeting rooms, and a grand ballroom on the third floor with a cathedral ceiling, from which hangs a massive, sparkling Czechoslovakian crystal chandelier.

Carpeted guest rooms with private baths and Greek Revival woodwork of native woods are individually decorated in different color schemes and themes. They are handsomely appointed in Hepplewhite, Sheraton, Victorian, or turn-of-the-century antiques; some of the towering beds still have rope mattresses, but their original three-quarter length has been extended to accommodate taller people. Each room also has a television, easy chairs, and a complimentary split of champagne.

Beds are turned down at night, and complimentary continental breakfasts—freshly baked croissants, pastries, juice, fresh fruit, and coffee—are brought to the rooms in the morning. Lunch and dinner are served to the public daily, with a menu that emphasizes American nouvelle cuisine as well as regional specialties.

THE WORTHINGTON INN, 649 High St., Worthington, OH 43085; 614-885-2600. A 23-guestroom (private baths) original stagecoach inn restored in 1983 and listed in the Natl. Register of Historic Places. Complimentary continental breakfast. Lunch and dinner served to the public. Open every day. Downtown Columbus 12 mi. away; German Village, a restored community with restaurants and boutiques and the Center for Science and Industry; and Ohio State Univ. nearby. Art Boone, Manager.

Directions: From north: Take I-71 south to Rte. 270 west; follow to first exit (Worthington/Delaware). Continue south 2 mi. to inn, 1 block south of Rte. 161. From south: Take I-71 north to Rte. 270 west; proceed as above. From east and west: Take I-70 to Rte. 270 north; proceed as above.

For B&B rates, see Index.

CAMPUS COTTAGE
Eugene, Oregon

I drove about a hundred miles out of my way to visit Ursula at the Campus Cottage, and it was well worth it.

Ursula explained that the cottage was built in 1922 and purchased in 1981 especially for the purpose of establishing Eugene's first bed-and-breakfast place. All of the renovations retained the original mid-1920s character. It is located just off the campus of the University of Oregon.

Ursula is an attractive, contemporary-minded woman whose many interests are reflected in the books and paintings in the house. Also she obviously has a keen enthusiasm for interior decorating.

There are three bedrooms; one, "The Suite," is the original master bedroom with a queen-sized brass bed, a sitting room with a twin Jenny Lind bed, and a bathroom with a large bathtub/shower combination. Another is a cozy south-facing guest room with a queen-sized pine bed and down-filled reading chair. The private bath has a cedar-lined shower. The third guest room, with a bay window, overlooks the garden and has a private entrance.

A full breakfast is served in the dining room or guest's room and could include any of Ursula's repertoire of delicious egg dishes. There is a deck overlooking a small garden to the rear, where breakfast may also be enjoyed.

Eugene is a pleasant university town, and if your travels take you there, I think you will enjoy the Campus Cottage.

CAMPUS COTTAGE, 1136 E. 19th Ave., Eugene, OR 97403; 503-342-5346. A 3-guestroom tiny bed-and-breakfast inn just a few blocks from the Univ. of Oregon campus. Open year-round. Bicycles provided. Older children welcome. No pets. No credit cards. Ursula Bates, Proprietress; Susan Stevens, Innkeeper.

Directions: From the south, leave I-5 at Exit 192 and proceed to Franklin Blvd. Ignore first turn to left; continue on Franklin Blvd. a few blocks; turn left at Univ. of Oregon sign and proceed down Agate St. (not marked) to 19th Ave., through the university grounds with the stadium on the right. Turn right on E. 19th and go 3½ blocks to inn, which is between two fraternity houses. From the north, leave I-5 at Exit 194; follow all Univ. of Oregon exit signs to Broadway. Turn right on Patterson, left on 19th Ave., and proceed 6½ blocks to the inn.

For B&B rates, see Index.

CHANTICLEER INN
Ashland, Oregon

For many years the main reason to go to Ashland was the Oregon Shakespearean Festival, which, after modest beginnings, now presents the works of the Bard from as early as late February to the end of October. There are three different playing areas, including a beautiful outdoor theater, a 600-seat indoor stage, and a smaller, intimate theater as well. In addition to Shakespeare's plays, there are offerings by other playwrights and a program of classic films.

While I bow to no man in my admiration of the theater, I must say that the Chanticleer Inn, situated in a residential part of Ashland, now provides an even more enticing reason to visit this beautiful section of Oregon.

In a community that is rapidly gaining a reputation for bed-and-breakfast places, the Chanticleer stands out. Jim Beaver, a former reporter for NBC radio in San Francisco, and his wife, Nancy, a former personnel manager, have created a very special place.

The first thing that impressed me was the friendly living room with an open-hearth fireplace that is often so welcome at the end of the day. There are shelves loaded with books and magazines, and an atmosphere that encourages good conversation, whether it be about the play or about a day skiing at Crater Lake.

Individually decorated guest rooms, all with their own baths, have queen-sized beds and fluffy comforters.

The full breakfast could include cheese-baked eggs, fresh squeezed orange juice, blueberry muffins, and freshly ground coffee served in the attractive sunroom. The Chanticleer is an "inn for all reasons."

CHANTICLEER INN, 120 Gresham St., Ashland, OR 97520; 503-482-1919. A 7-guestroom (private baths) bed-and-breakfast inn overlooking Bear Creek valley and Cascade foothills. Open every day all year. A short walk from the Oregon Shakespearean Festival, Lithia Park, and many shops and restaurants. Rogue River white water rafting and Mt. Ashland's ski slopes nearby. No credit cards. Jim and Nancy Beaver, Innkeepers.

Directions: Ashland is on Rte. 5, halfway between San Francisco and Portland. Gresham St. is in the center of town, running at right angles to the main street.

For B&B rates, see Index.

CORBETT HOUSE
Portland, Oregon

With views of Mount Saint Helens, Mount Hood, and the Willamette River from two of the spacious guest rooms on the second floor, Corbett House offers informal yet elegant accommodations near the University of Oregon Health Sciences Center, Portland State University, Lewis and Clark College, Memorial Coliseum, and the downtown business and shopping area.

Parks, restaurants (many with river views), and shops in the nearby waterfront Johns Landing area offer a wealth of interesting options for dining, browsing, and sightseeing. You may also like to check out what's playing at the many local live theaters (ask Sylvia for a copy of the current *Willamette Week*, which has tons of information about local events) or at the newly refurbished Arlene Schnitzer Concert Hall.

I discovered that Sylvia provides extra amenities such as robes, hair dryers, and picnic baskets for her guests. Build your own picnic; enjoy music, conversation, or reading in the charming and comfortable common room on the main floor.

CORBETT HOUSE, 7533 S.W. Corbett Ave., Portland, OR 97219; 503-245-2580. A 3-guestroom (shared baths) bed-and-breakfast inn near downtown Portland in northern Oregon. Open year-round. Continental breakfast included in room rate. The Portland Rose Festival in June; Mt. Hood year-round recreation area 50 mi. east; Oregon coast 80 mi. west; nearby scenic Columbia Gorge with sailing, windsurfing, boating. No small children. No pets. Smoking in designated areas only. Sylvia Malagamba, Innkeeper.

Directions: From the south on I-5, take Corbett exit and turn right onto Corbett Ave. for about 1.4 mi. From the north on I-5, take Exit 299 onto Rte. 43 south (Macadam Ave.). Turn right at second traffic light (Boundary) and after 1 block turn left on Corbett. Proceed to top of bluff to inn.

For B&B rates, see Index.

THE JOHNSON HOUSE
Florence, Oregon

Florence is one of the many interesting towns located on Highway 101 on Oregon's spectacular coast. The area abounds in rivers, lakes, sea fishing, beachcombing, bird watching, historical sites, viewpoints, and, of course, the presence of the mighty Pacific Ocean.

The Johnson House in Old Town Florence is an Italianate Victorian, circa 1892, and has been restored and furnished with fine, original antiques and Early American prints. Periodic art exhibits are open to the public. The five guest rooms share four baths.

The Old Town section is being restored and has a wonderful 1925 movie house, the Harbor Theatre, a fine restaurant, a general store, and a 1905 mercantile building that is reputed to be one of the finest of its kind in Oregon. This area with its many lakes is a wintering place for swans, and it is a favorite spot for avid bird watchers.

Guests will enjoy the hearty breakfast that includes orange juice, a fruit plate, cheese, ham and eggs, homemade bread, and special, freshly ground coffee or tea.

The Johnson House would make a very pleasant overnight stop with, perhaps, a long morning or afternoon excursion to points of interest nearby.

THE JOHNSON HOUSE, 216 Maple St., P.O. Box 1892, Florence, OR 97439; 503-997-8000. A 5-guestroom (4 baths) bed-and-breakfast inn located in the historic section of Florence just a short distance from Rte. 101. Open all year. Full breakfast included in room rate. There is a wealth of Oregon coast natural attractions within easy distance. Jayne and Ronald Fraese, Proprietors.

Directions: Coming north on Rte. 101 turn right after the bridge and follow briefly, turning left on Maple St. Coming south on Rte. 101, turn left onto Maple St.

For B&B rates, see Index.

JUDGE TOUVELLE HOUSE
Jacksonville, Oregon

Judge Touvelle House is located one block off Main Street in the registered National Historic Landmark town of Jacksonville, Oregon. It is situated on a gentle rise on four acres of land, with stone walls and white post fences that enclose the large, beautiful old farmhouse, the connecting guest annex, and a three-story carriage house.

The house was built in 1856 and reconstructed in 1916 by Judge Touvelle and his bride, who had just migrated out West. The building features a wraparound outside porch enhanced by antique white wicker pieces. The only modern touches are a swimming pool and hot tub nestled among redwood and oak trees.

Referred to as the "museum by the side of the road," it is completely furnished with antiques in keeping with the elegant house. The guest rooms are furnished with marble-topped dressers and other beautiful walnut Victorian pieces. There is one guest room on the first floor that is ideal for disabled and older people; the remaining five bedrooms are on the second and third floors, and feature oriental rugs, Laura Ashley wallpapers, down comforters, a private balcony, and two nonworking fireplaces.

Breakfast, served on beautiful china with silver cutlery, features croissants or waffles or hot fruit strudel, as well as fresh fruit in season, and of course coffee or tea. Fresh raspberries and blackberries in cream are served in season.

JUDGE TOUVELLE HOUSE, Box 988, 435 No. Oregon St., Jacksonville, OR 97530; 503-899-8223. A 6-guestroom (1 private bath) elegantly decorated Victorian home in a Historic Landmark town in southern Oregon. Open year-round. Complimentary full breakfast. The Peter Britt Musical Festival in July and Aug.; Shakespearean Festival in nearby Ashland, and many outdoor activities: hiking, fishing, rafting, downhill and cross-country skiing. No children. No pets. No credit cards. Nick and Verona Clark, Innkeepers.

Directions: From Medford, take Rte. 238, which becomes California St. in Jacksonville. Proceed down California St. to Oregon St., turn right for 1 block. Judge Touvelle House is on the left near a historic cemetery.

For B&B rates, see Index.

MARJON BED AND BREAKFAST INN
Leaburg, Oregon

The idyllic setting of Marjon Bed and Breakfast Inn is just 24 miles from Eugene, on the banks of one of the most beautiful and spectacular rivers in Oregon—the McKenzie. The inn is surrounded by nature's splendor: towering trees, crystal clear rivers, lush woodlands, and majestic mountains.

The inn nestles on the edge of the McKenzie River and from the beautiful living room, one looks past flowers, ferns, and trees to the river and beyond. The overall decor of this magnificent contemporary house is oriental; however, the master suite, with a 7' x 12' bed, is done in white French provincial furniture and overlooks both the river and a secluded Japanese garden. The second guest room, slightly smaller, is light and airy with oriental decor, and has a unique "fishbowl" shower that overlooks the river.

A full gourmet breakfast, included in the price of the room, featuring exotic juices, soufflés or omelets, fruit, and hot breads, can be eaten either in the dining room or on a covered terrace overlooking the river. Guests can relax or venture through two acres of grounds, where there are landscaped gardens and wooded riverside trails that wind through feathery ferns, azaleas, and rhododendrons, across a plank footbridge, past hidden seating areas, and down to a floating deck for an intimate view of the river.

Countess Margaret Olga Von Retzlaff Haas—otherwise known as Margie Haas—explained that she has set a goal. "I want the prestige of being known throughout the United States as having one of the most beautiful and elegant breakfast inns." She has plans to add four more rooms—what a beautiful and romantic inn....

MARJON BED AND BREAKFAST INN, 44975 Leaburg Dam Rd., Leaburg, OR 97489; 503-896-3145. A 2-guestroom beautiful, contemporary house on the bank of the spectacular McKenzie River 24 mi. from Eugene. Open every day, all year. Rates include a full breakfast. Drop-in arrivals welcome, but reservations are recommended. Trout fishing, rafting, and nature sightseeing on grounds. Golf, water and snow skiing, boating, guided raft trips, mountain climbing, and endless hiking trails nearby. Restaurants within short driving distance. No children. No pets. Margie Haas, Proprietress

Directions: From Eugene, Oregon, proceed east on Hwy. 126 for approx. 24 mi. Turn right on Leaburg Dam Rd., cross bridge, drive 1 mi. to inn on your left.

For B&B rates, see Index.

METOLIUS RIVER LODGES
Camp Sherman, Oregon

Located in the heart of the famous Metolius Recreation Area, this lodge offers the unique advantage of a setting on the banks of the cold, spring-fed, crystal clear waters of the Metolius River. Guests can fish for rainbow, brown brook and Dolly Varden trout just a few paces from the door.

The lodge offers a variety of accommodations, from sleeping rooms with refrigerators to fully equipped, two-bedroom housekeeping lodges, many with fireplaces. Rates include continental breakfast and firewood. During the summer season, barbecue kettles and charcoal are provided. The library on the grounds has a plentiful supply of books for adults and children, along with games and puzzles. A general store, laundromat, and post office are within a short walk.

The lodges are near several well-known mountains in the Cascade Range—Black Butte, Three Sisters, Mount Washington, and Mount Jefferson. The area is famous for downhill and cross- country skiing. Within a short distance horseback riding and golf (in season) can be enjoyed. Hiking trails begin just outside the door.

METOLIUS RIVER LODGES, P.O. Box 110, Camp Sherman, OR 97730; 503-595-6290. A mountain lodge with 12 accommodations (10 have kitchens) on the Metolius River in central Oregon, 38 mi. from Bend. Continental breakfast is included in room rate. Open every day, all year. Activities on grounds include fly fishing, hiking, photography, and bird watching. Downhill and xc skiing, horseback riding, and golf nearby. Pets allowed during spring, fall, and winter only. Pick-up at Redmond/Bend Airport can be arranged. Byron and Lee Beach, Proprietors.

Directions: From Bend, take Rte. 20 northwest for 32 mi., exit at the Camp Sherman-Metolius River Junction. Go 5.5 mi. to Camp Sherman store. The lodges are 100 yards upstream.

For rates, see Index.

THE MORICAL HOUSE
Ashland, Oregon

At the time of my first visit to the Morical House, the carpenters, road menders, and gardeners were all at work and Phyllis Morical was on the scene making sure that everything was going according to her plans. For instance, the paneling of the old staircase had been taken right down to the natural wood, and the effect in the Victorian atmosphere is splendid. The stained-glass windows and detailed woodwork, too, were receiving needed attention.

Each of the five guest rooms has been decorated in a turn-of-the-century motif with appropriate antiques and homemade comforters, and each has a private bath. All of the guest rooms have a view of the Cascade Mountains in the distance, as well as views of the lawns and adjacent gardens, which have over 100 varieties of colorful and fragrant trees, shrubs, and flowers.

A full breakfast, including fresh-baked goods, is served in the dining room or on the porch, and a light afternoon refreshment is a welcome touch.

The Morical House is a fifteen-minute walk to the theaters of Ashland's well-known Shakespeare Festival which runs from the end of February through October.

Incidentally, things are very busy here during the height of the festival, between the first of June and the middle of September, and weekends, even in the spring and fall, are packed, so it is well to reserve in advance.

THE MORICAL HOUSE, 668 No. Main St., Ashland, OR 97520; 503-482-2254. A 5-guestroom bed-and-breakfast inn located in scenic, south-central Oregon. Breakfast is the only meal served. Open year-round. Bent grass putting green on grounds. Conveniently located for guests to enjoy the many cultural, natural, and historical attractions nearby, including the Shakespeare Festival. Joe and Phyllis Morical, Innkeepers.

Directions: Ashland is in southern Oregon on Rte. 5. The Morical House is on Main St., at the north end of the town.

For B&B rates, see Index.

THE PRINGLE HOUSE
Oakland, Oregon

When the Pringle House opened its doors in April, 1984, it became the first approved bed and breakfast in Douglas County. A beautiful, two-story, Queen Anne-style Victorian house, it stands on a rise at the end of the main street in this registered National Historic village (population 850).

From the Pringle House sign, a cast iron relic from an Englishman's fireplace, to the Victorian gingerbread, painted in five colors, to the flower gardens, bird baths, and walkways, and, eventually, to the gazebo, this bed and breakfast is a picture out of the past.

Jim and Demay Pringle are the happy, caring innkeepers who accomplished this transformation almost single-handedly. The interior is decorated appropriately with antiques, wallpaper, chandeliers, stained glass windows, and oriental rugs on the polished floors.

The study betrays Jim's past. It contains a piano, record collections, books, and photographs on the wall depicting marching bands and choirs under his direction. You guessed it, Jim has been a music teacher for almost thirty years.

The two guest rooms have been decorated with antique beds and bureaus, beautiful quilts, coordinated wallpaper, and oriental rugs. A hundred-year-old quilt on one bed is described by Jim as an anthology of feather stitching with hundreds of different stitch patterns. The "his and hers" bathroom is shared.

Bring a good appetite, as the special breakfast is huge, offering fruit juice, coffee, tea, milk or hot chocolate, fresh baked breads or croissants, cheese, fruit in season with yogurt dressing or cream, crème caramel, or perhaps a house specialty.

THE PRINGLE HOUSE, 114 N.E. 7th St., P.O. Box 578, Oakland, OR 97462; 503-459-5038. A 2-guestroom (shared bath) Victorian bed-and-breakfast inn 1 hr. south of Eugene in a National Historic Register village. Open all year. Historic walking tour, city museum, antique shops, hiking, wildlife safari, backpacking, and fishing nearby. Older children only. No pets. No credit cards. Checks accepted with bank guarantee. Smoking in designated areas only. Demay and Jim Pringle, Innkeepers.

Directions: From Eugene going south, drive approx. 55 mi. to Exit 138, proceed 1.5 mi. to Oakland, continue up Locust St., the main street. The Pringle House is at the end of the street on the corner of 7th and Locust. From Roseburg driving north, drive approx. 18 mi. to Exit 138, then proceed with instructions above.

For B&B rates, see Index.

SPINDRIFT
Bandon, Oregon

Ocean lovers will enjoy the breathtaking beauty of the Oregon coast at Spindrift bed and breakfast. This lovely home is perched on a bluff just forty feet above a long, sandy beach that is framed by massive offshore rock formations. Floor-to-ceiling windows and a large deck, with direct beach access, offer views of changing surf, sea animals, and glorious sunsets.

Hosts Don and Robbie Smith have given the house a pleasantly unique feeling with antiques (many from Don's grandparents) and books that hint of Don's many years as a librarian. Their bedroom contains one of Robbie's weaving looms. Don, who looks like a New England sea captain (he was born and reared in Maine), enjoys winemaking.

There are two guest rooms. The floor-to-ceiling corner window in the Seaview Room is spectacular, with a panoramic view of the ocean. The room has a private bath, fireplace, and queen- sized bed with a down quilt. French doors open onto the deck and a ramp has been added for the disabled.

The second bedroom, the Surfsound, is smaller and does not have an ocean view, but is restful with twin beds and down quilts. The bath is shared.

Breakfasts at Spindrift are hearty, and include eggs cooked any way, breakfast meats, or even seafood in season, popovers, fresh fruit, and fresh-brewed coffee.

SPINDRIFT, 2990 Beach Loop Rd., Bandon, OR 97411; 503-347-2275. A 2-guestroom inn (1 private bath) by the sea, 25 mi. south of Coos Bay on the southern Oregon coast. Full breakfast and afternoon refreshments included. Open every day all year. Fishing, crabbing, clamming, hiking, horseback riding, golfing nearby. Many interesting shops to explore—the famous Cranberry Sweets Manufacturing Co.; Bandon Cheddar Cheese factory. No pets. Don and Robbie Smith, Innkeepers.

Directions: From north (Hwy. 101): Continue south past 11th St. traffic lights for approx. 1 mi. Turn right (west) on Seabird Dr. to Beach Loop Rd. Turn right (north), and Spindrift is 2nd house on the left. From south (Hwy. 101): Watch for Seabird Dr. then follow above directions. From east (I-5): Exit at Rte. 19, south of Roseburg. Follow signs on Rte. 42 for Bandon, entering Bandon from north. Follow directions above "from North."

For B&B rates, see Index.

STEAMBOAT INN
Steamboat, Oregon

Route 138 proceeds east out of Roseburg, Oregon, into the mountains, following the course of one of the famous wild rivers of Oregon, the Umpqua. The road points upwards almost immediately.

Here, up in this wonderful, wild country, I found Jim and Sharon Van Loan and the Steamboat Inn. Although it is on the road to Diamond and Crater lakes, and is a major east-west route to Highway 97, most people who find their way here for either overnight accommodations or dinner, or both, have heard about it in advance.

Originally, this inn attracted people who came for the steelhead fishing on the North Umpqua River. However, in recent years many non-fishermen and their families have discovered that this is a very exciting hideaway with an appeal for every member of the family. There's good swimming and backpacking and hiking trails. But most of all, there's a wonderful feeling of being literally embraced by nature.

Each of the eight guest rooms has a breathtaking view of the river that is enhanced by a broad veranda. Nestled among the towering firs, the inn is about two hours by car from airports at Eugene or Medford.

One of the big attractions here is dinner. It is served each night of the summer about a half hour after dark and in the winter about seven o'clock. It is by reservation only and the cabin guests have automatic reservations. Sharon Van Loan's cold salmon with mustard sauce is one of the many different menu items, along with the homemade breads, that are changed each day. She relies on farmers' produce stands and people who bring fruits and vegetables from their gardens.

The Steamboat Inn is one of the most unusual places I have ever visited. You can stay for one night if you care to, but the temptation to remain on and on is very great.

STEAMBOAT INN, Steamboat, OR 97447; 503-496-3495 or 503-498-2411. An 8-guestroom rustic riverside inn in one of Oregon's most spectacular nature areas. Open all year. Breakfast, lunch, and dinner served daily; breakfast is not included in the room rate. Dinner ½ hr. after sundown in summer, 7 P.M. in winter. Fishing, backpacking, and hiking in abundance. Sharon and Jim Van Loan, Innkeepers.

Directions: From Roseburg drive 38 mi. east on Rte. 138.

For Lodging rates, see Index.

BARLEY SHEAF FARM
Holicong, Pennsylvania

Barley Sheaf Farm, in the heart of Bucks County, was a part of the William Penn Land Grant and was originally built during the time that the Lenape Indians lived in this area.

As is the case in many early Pennsylvania dwellings, there are actually two buildings; the original wooden dwelling, built in 1740, and the stone house, built probably between 1770 and 1800. Much of the feeling of Colonial antiquity has been preserved by the original wide floorboards and beautifully crafted doorways and windows.

Apparently, this has been a farm for most of its years, although there have been quite a few owners. The present proprietors, Don and Ann Mills and their family, were inspired to open a bed-and-breakfast inn by their trip to England, during which they stayed in several farm-type accommodations.

The house sits a pleasant distance from the road and is surrounded by fields and a wooded area. Of particular note is a gorgeous, irreplaceable copper beech tree, growing just outside the entrance to the house.

There are nine guest rooms of ample size and all very tastefully furnished with colorful furniture, curtains, and bedspreads. All have private baths. Some of these rooms, as well as the breakfast and living rooms, have some early American paintings.

A full farm breakfast is served on the sun porch, and almost everything is either raised or prepared right on the farm. The eggs are gathered every morning from the barn, and the bees that buzz around the bushes and flowers make the honey. There's bacon or ham and homemade scrapple, as well as freshly baked breads and homemade jams.

BARLEY SHEAF FARM, Box 10, Holicong, PA 18928; 215-794-5104. A 9-guestroom bed-and-breakfast inn, 8 mi. from Doylestown and New Hope, Pa. Breakfast only meal served. Open Jan. & Feb. weekends; then daily mid-Feb. to week before Christmas. Croquet, badminton, swimming pool, farm animals on grounds. Tennis, boating, canoeing, and horseback riding nearby. Near Delaware River, Bucks County Playhouse, George Washington's Crossing, and other natural and historical attractions of Bucks County, Pennsylvania. Recommended for children over 8. No credit cards. Don and Ann Mills, Innkeepers.

Directions: Barley Sheaf Farm is on Rte. 202 between Doylestown and Lahaska.

For B&B rates, see Index.

THE BODINE HOUSE
Muncy, Pennsylvania

The letter from David and Marie Louise Smith said in part: "Our home, known as the Bodine House, was built in 1805 and has been restored to that era both outside and inside. It is furnished with antiques and reproductions, has four working fireplaces, and is located within a National Historic District. Most of our guests agree that it is quite unique."

Well, I happened to be visiting Bucknell University for a class reunion and decided to circle around and go up through Muncy for a quick visit to the Bodine House.

My unexpected visit caught the Smiths on their way to a wedding, but I was able to see the entire house and, if anything, their letter understated its many virtues.

I was most impressed with the furnishings and with the handsome painting of Marie Louise's great-great-great grandmother. Other pieces that caught my eye were a grandfather clock, Windsor chairs, and a lovely silver service.

Breakfast consists of a choice of four juices, hot or cold cereal, eggs cooked at least three different ways, french toast, bacon, muffins, and so forth. "It's a full breakfast," David said. "We always light a fire in the dining room on chilly mornings."

Accommodations are in four guest rooms, including one twin room with a fireplace. Guests are invited to make themselves at home in the small upstairs sitting room, which has a rather extensive library of books.

It's just a few minutes off the Interstate, and within a short drive of two state parks and the Endless Mountains, with spectacular scenery and fall foliage.

THE BODINE HOUSE, 307 S. Main St., Muncy, PA 17756; 717-546-8949. A 4-guestroom (private and shared baths) village bed-and-breakfast located in central Pa. in a very quiet community between Lewisburg and Lynchburg. Complimentary full breakfast. Open year-round, except for Thanksgiving and Christmas. Conveniently situated to enjoy summer and winter activities, such as hiking, fishing, boating, swimming, auctions, antiques shops, summer theater, and xc skiing. Well-behaved children over 6 are welcome. No facilities for pets. Restricted smoking. No credit cards. David and Marie Louise Smith, Innkeepers.

Directions: Take Exit 31B from I-80 and then I-180 west towards Williamsport. Approx. 10 mi. to Muncy Main St. exit. Turn left 1 mi. to Bodine House on right.

For B&B rates, see Index.

CAMERON ESTATE INN
Mount Joy, Pennsylvania

Tucked away in the Pennsylvania farming country near Lancaster, this bed-and-breakfast stop has been designated by the Department of the Interior as a National Historic Landmark.

The mansion was built in 1805 and later became the country home of Simon Cameron, Lincoln's first secretary of war. He was also a four-time U.S. senator and ambassador to Russia.

Just four miles from Mt. Joy, the inn is set in a commodious grove of trees through which a well-stocked trout stream meanders.

There are oriental rugs and period furnishings in the parlor, dining rooms, and generously sized guest rooms, some of which have canopy beds and seven of which have fireplaces.

The proprietors are Abe and Betty Groff of the internationally acclaimed Groff's Farm Restaurant, just a few miles away.

In addition to breakfast, which is offered as part of the B&B rates, lunch and dinner is also served, with choices from a French and American country cuisine.

CAMERON ESTATE INN, R.D. 1, Box 305, Donegal Springs Road, Mount Joy, PA 17552; 717-653-1773. An elegant 18-guestroom (most with private baths) inn in a former mansion 4½ mi. from both Mount Joy and Elizabethtown. Continental breakfast included in rates. Lunch and dinner served Mon. thru Sat.; brunch on Sun. Closed Christmas. Open all year. Convenient to all of the attractions in the Pennsylvania Dutch country including museums, art galleries, and theaters. Located halfway between Gettysburg and Valley Forge. No children under 12 years. No pets. Abram and Betty Groff, Innkeepers.

Directions: Traveling west on the Pennsylvania Tpke. take Exit 21. Follow Rte. 222 S to Rte. 30 W to Rte. 283 W. Follow Rte. 283 W to Rte. 230 (the first Mount Joy exit). Follow Rte. 230 through Mount Joy to the fourth traffic light. Turn left onto Angle St. At first crossroads, turn right onto Donegal Springs Rd. Go to the stop sign. Turn left onto Colebrook Rd. Go just a short distance over a small bridge. Turn right, back onto Donegal Springs Rd. Follow signs to inn— about ½ mi. on the right.

For B&B rates, see Index.

DISCOVERIES BED & BREAKFAST
Sigel, Pennsylvania

This place really thrilled me. It is located in northwestern Pennsylvania, north of I-80, in the Cook Forest State Park area.

The house is a beautiful Victorian, built in 1880, and this is an area where extra guest rooms are called "spare rooms." In addition to an immaculately clean and well-run B&B, there is also an antiques and crafts shop with the attractive extra feature of fruits and vegetables in season.

The owners are Bruce MacBeth and his wife, Pat. He is a college professor and she is a medical technologist. They have lived here for the past twenty-eight or more years, but now that their two older children are grown and away, they thought it would be fun to have a B&B, and it has worked out beautifully.

The house has three fireplaces and the guest rooms look like the spare rooms of 100 years ago. There are many white-painted cast iron beds and beautiful carved antiques as well. I was particularly impressed with all of the many different kinds of quilts, which are also on sale in the crafts shop.

Vacationers and travelers coming to this part of the world, which abounds in so many recreational opportunities, will be glad to know that a full breakfast is offered to the MacBeth guests. Among other things, there might be a cheese omelet with home-cured bacon, hot muffins, fresh fruit, and coffee. This is served in the dining room with good china and silver or on the large, enclosed front porch.

"Discoveries" was indeed a great discovery for me. (I just couldn't resist saying that.)

DISCOVERIES BED & BREAKFAST, R.D. 1, Sigel, PA 15860; 814-752-2632. A 5-guestroom (sharing two baths) B&B located in the scenic Cook Forest and Clear Creek State Park area of northwestern Pennsylvania. Breakfast is the only meal served. Open April thru Nov. An excellent crafts and antiques shop adjoins. No credit cards. No pets. Bruce and Pat MacBeth, Proprietors.

Directions: Discoveries is located on Rte. 36, 2½ mi. north of Sigel. From I-80 used Exit 13 and follow Rte. 36 north.

For B&B rates, see Index.

EVERMAY-ON-THE-DELAWARE
Erwinna, Pennsylvania

At Evermay-on-the-Delaware overnight guests enjoy not only a breakfast included with the price of the rooms, but *afternoon tea* as well!

The inn is situated right on the picturesque Delaware River in the upper section of Bucks County, Pennsylvania, and the earliest part of the building dates to 1700. It took on new life as a hotel from 1871 to 1930, and during that time many prominent people enjoyed its hospitality, including the famous theatrical Barrymore family.

Today, it has been beautifully restored by Ron Strouse and Fred Cresson. Each of the guest rooms has views of either the Delaware or the rolling fields at the rear of the inn, and has been furnished with carefully chosen antiques. All have a very romantic atmosphere.

The public rooms and the dining room all have been painstakingly restored to create a 19th-century feeling.

Afternoon tea can be taken on the back porch or in the warm and gracious parlor. The breakfast dining room is at the back of the inn, overlooking the fields and low hills and is enhanced by Victorian stained-glass windows.

A prix fixe dinner, usually five courses with a choice of two or three entrées, is also offered at Evermay. There is one sitting at 7:30 P.M.

EVERMAY-ON-THE-DELAWARE, Erwinna, PA 18920; 215-294-9100. A 16-guestroom riverside inn in upper Bucks County. Breakfast and afternoon tea included in the room tariff. Box lunches available for houseguests. Dinner served Fri., Sat., Sun., and holidays at 7:30 P.M. by reservation. Convenient to all the Bucks County natural and historical attractions including handsome mansions, museums, and historical sites. Xc skiing, backroading, and canoeing nearby. No amusements for small children. No pets. Ron Strouse and Fred Cresson, Innkeepers.

Directions: From New York City: take Rte. 22 to Clinton; Rte. 31 to Flemington; Rte. 12 to Frenchtown. Cross river and turn south on Rte. 32 for 2 mi. From Philadelphia: follow I-95 north to Yardley exit and Rte. 32 north to Erwinna. There are several other routes also.

For B&B rates, see Index.

FAIRFIELD INN & GUEST HOUSE
Fairfield, Pennsylvania

Gettysburg is one of the great tourist objectives in North America, and deservedly so, although I have personally taken the tour of the battlefield with mixed emotions.

Be that as it may, the whole trip can be an adventure, although there are quite a few commercial intrusions; namely, motels, restaurants, and souvenir stores, named after some of the principal field commanders.

Fortunately it's possible to avoid the hurly-burly of downtown Gettysburg by staying overnight at either Hickory Bridge Farm, which I have mentioned elsewhere, or the Fairfield Inn, whose history long antedates the summer of 1863.

It was originally the plantation home of Squire William Miller who settled in Fairfield in 1755. In those days the highway was known as the "Great Road" from York to Hagerstown and the inn was a stagecoach stop as well as a drovers' tavern. It has been in continuous operation since 1823.

In 1980, the enterprising owner of the inn, David Thomas, completed restoration of another of the first homes of Fairfield, which for many years has been known as the Cunningham House. During the War Between the States the house was used as a hospital for wounded officers and it has been said that a ghost of one of them may still be in residence.

This guest house has been painstakingly furnished, mostly with antiques. There are four bedrooms in all. Some of them look out over the village street scene, and others in the rear look out at the beautiful mountains.

Overnight guests may cross the village street to the main inn where luncheon and dinner are served every day except major holidays and Sundays. It's a country breakfast, for sure, served à la carte in the dining room featuring Adams County country ham, freshly baked biscuits, and honey from local beehives. Just the sort of fortifying needed to sustain one for a tour of the historic environs.

FAIRFIELD INN & GUEST HOUSE, Main St., Fairfield, Pa. 17320; 717-642-5410. A country restaurant near Gettysburg with 4 lodging rooms available. Breakfast, lunch, and dinner served daily. Closed on major holidays, Sundays, and first week in Sept. and Feb. Dinner reservations advised. Nearby region is rich in history, including Gettysburg Battlefield. No pets. David W. Thomas, Innkeeper.

Directions: Fairfield is 8 mi. west of Gettysburg on Rte. 116.

For Lodging rates, see Index.

HICKORY BRIDGE FARM
Orrtanna, Pennsylvania

American history buffs are really in luck when they visit the Gettysburg Battlefield National Park because they have a choice of at least two places in which to enjoy overnight accommodations that are a sufficient distance from the inevitable crowds that always flock to this great American shrine.

One of them is the Hickory Bridge Farm in Orrtanna, which is hidden away back in the foothills to the west of Gettysburg.

The building is a 19th-century farmhouse furnished with period furniture including beds with lovely old quilts, beautiful old chests, braided rugs, antique dolls, and marble-topped bureaus.

Additional bedrooms are to be found just a short distance away in two cottages in the woods reached by a footpath that follows the brook.

The entire bucolic atmosphere is enhanced by a bass pond and a rustic bridge leading to a gentle island woodland, which makes a beautiful sight for guests enjoying breakfast on the outer deck of the farmhouse.

Adding to this atmosphere is a collection of turn-of-the-century farm machinery that was put back into working order by one of the farm neighbors with the help of the Hammett sons.

The farm restaurant is located in the barn across from the farmhouse. Farm-style dinners are served to guests and travelers on Saturday evening.

A full breakfast is served by innkeeper Nancy Jean Hammett and her daughter, Mary Lynn, in the dining room. In the summer breakfast is just perfect on the sunny porch overlooking the creek.

HICKORY BRIDGE FARM INN, Orrtanna, Pa. 17353; 717-642-5261. A 7-room country inn on a farm 3 mi. from Fairfield and 8 mi. from Gettysburg. Open year-round. A deposit required. A 2-night minimum stay on weekends, May 1 to Oct. 31. Full breakfast included in room rate. Near Gettysburg Battlefield Natl. Park, Caledonia State Park, and Totem Pole Playhouse. Hiking, biking, fishing, hunting, and country store museum on grounds. Golf, swimming available nearby. The Hammett Family, Innkeepers.

Directions: From Gettysburg take Rte. 116 west to Fairfield and follow signs 3 mi. north to Orrtanna.

For B&B rates, see Index.

THE INN AT STARLIGHT LAKE
Starlight, Pennsylvania

The casual tourer in northeastern Pennsylvania or the traveler using Route 17 to cross New York State by way of Binghamton, Corning, Olean, and Jamestown, will find that the short side trip from Hancock, New York, to Starlight, Pennsylvania, will reward him with a night's lodging at the Inn at Starlight Lake.

As the name implies, the inn is located beside a lake of pure, clear spring water and it is surrounded by many acres of untouched forest and farmland meadows.

The main house provides seventeen comfortable rooms, ten cottage rooms, and a three-bedroom family house, all open year-round. Boarding for pets can be arranged at a nearby kennel.

This pleasant informal atmosphere could be a welcome change for travelers with children because there are plenty of diversions beside the lake and in the game room for young people of all ages. In fact, Jack and Judy McMahon have children of their own and the inn is their home.

Because this inn is slightly off the beaten path, it is a good idea to plan to take the evening meal as well.

The sunny dining room with views of the lake is the scene of the full American breakfast, which includes homemade breads, coffee cakes, raised-dough waffles, blueberry pancakes, and always fresh-ground coffee! This is included in the bed-and-breakfast rate.

THE INN AT STARLIGHT LAKE, Starlight, PA 18461; 717-798-2519. A 30-guestroom resort-inn located 5 mi. from Hancock, N.Y. Modified American plan. B&B rate available. Breakfast, lunch, dinner served daily. Closed between Apr. 1 and 15. Swimming, boating, canoeing, sailing, fishing, hunting, tennis, hiking, bicycling, xc skiing, and lawn sports on grounds. Canoeing, hunting, fishing, golfing nearby. No pets. Judy and Jack McMahon, Innkeepers.

Directions: From N.Y. Rte. 17 exit at Hancock, N.Y. Take Rte. 191S over Delaware River to Rte. 370. Turn right, proceed 3½ mi.; turn right, 1 mi. to inn. From I-81, take exit 62 and go east on Rte. 107. Turn left on Rte. 247 to Forest City. Turn left on Rte. 171, go 10 mi. to Rte. 370. Turn right, proceed 12 mi. Turn left, 1 mi. to inn.

For B&B rates, see Index.

MAPLE LANE FARM
Paradise, Pennsylvania

I can assure those among our readers who have never visited the Pennsylvania Dutch country that they are in for a most unusual experience. The wonderful farms, so clean and neat, operated very frequently by the Amish people, and the engaging little towns and villages provide a backroading experience that has remained unchanged for over a hundred years in many cases.

In the heart of this country, I found the Maple Lane Farm, just outside of Strasburg, Pennsylvania.

Marion and Edwin Rohrer have been taking in guests for seventeen years, and one of the very attractive features about this guest house is the fact that it's across the road from the original old farm, constructed of beautifully mellowed Pennsylvania stone. Mr. and Mrs. Rohrer are delighted to have their guests visit the farm and the barn and watch the milking or take a hike in the woods. Children can even wade in the brook. There's a forty-mile view at the top of the hill.

The guest house itself is a recently built Colonial-style brick building, and all of the guest rooms are very pleasantly furnished with Pennsylvania antiques, framed needlework, and some exceptionally fine quilts.

A very pleasant parlor has been set aside especially for the use of the guests.

Morning beverage and rolls are included in the room rate and there are excellent restaurants nearby for a full breakfast.

Most guests find Mrs. Rohrer's collection of covered boxes a very interesting hobby.

MAPLE LANE FARM, 505 Paradise Lane, Paradise, PA 17562; 717-687-7479. A 4-bedroom (2 with private baths) farm guest house located just a short distance from Strasburg. Open all year. Within a short distance of many area attractions, including the Strasburg Railroad and Amish markets. No credit cards. Mr. and Mrs. Edwin Rohrer, Proprietors.

Directions: Turn south on Rte. 896 off Rte. 30. Proceed to Strasburg. Turn left on Rte. 896 at traffice light and proceed 1½ mi. out of town and turn at sign for Timberline Lodge, which is Paradise Lane.

For B&B rates, see Index.

OVERLOOK INN
Canadensis, Pennsylvania

The Overlook Inn is located high in the Pocono Mountains in northeastern Pennsylvania. The fragrant pine, blue spruce, and locust forests stretch out in all directions,and the cardinals, quail, and robins flit about in the rhododendron and mountain laurel.

All of the country inn guest rooms have baths and all have patchwork quilts and books and plants, adding immeasurably to the homey feeling. My favorite room is one that looks out over the high fields at the rear of the inn. It's such a quiet and peaceful place in the early morning.

In pleasant warm weather, the porch is an ideal place to enjoy the full breakfast. There are fresh orange juice, homemade muffins, Danish and other breakfast pastries, fruit-filled pancakes, Welsh rarebit, Pennsylvania scrapple, and homemade sausage. It's hard to leave breakfast because almost everybody starts interesting conversations.

Travelers to and from New England on I-84 can take the "Promised Land" Exit (Route 390) and be at the inn in a very short time for a pleasant overnight stay.

OVERLOOK INN, Dutch Hill Rd., Canadensis, PA 18325; 717-595-7519. A 20-guestroom resort-inn in the heart of the Poconos, 15 mi. from Stroudsburg, Pa. Mod. American plan. Breakfast and dinner served to travelers. Open every day of the year. Pool, shuffleboard, bocci, hiking on grounds; golf, tennis, alpine slide, ice skating, downhill and xc skiing, indoor tennis, antiquing, backroading, summer theater nearby. No children under 12. No pets. Bob and Lolly Tupper, Innkeepers.

Directions: From the north (New England, New York State and Canada) use I-84 and take Rte. 390 south through "Promised Land" about 12 mi. to traffic light in Canadensis. Make right-hand turn on Rte. 447 north—go ⅓ mi. to first right-hand turn (Dutch Hill Road). Inn is 1½ mi. up hill. Look for new sign on right. From New York City, take George Washington Bridge to I-80 west. Turn off at Pennsylvania Exit 52. Follow Rte. 447 north straight through Canadensis traffic light. Turn right on Dutch Hill Rd. as above.

For B&B rates, see Index.

THE PINEAPPLE INN
Lewisburg, Pennsylvania

"And the furniture in this bedroom belonged to one of the Archbishops of Canterbury."

Standing in a guest room of this Federal-style home in Lewisburg, Pennsylvania, I was certainly intrigued by Deborah North's statement. There were several dark oak English pieces, including an armoire with a stained glass door. Deborah explained that a great deal of the furniture in the Pineapple Inn is on consignment from a very meticulous wholesale antique dealer. Because much of the furniture is for sale, there is almost a moveable feast of furnishings.

The building is a lovely brick house on the corner of Fifth and Market, and in a small town that is notable for its many handsome early- to mid-19th-century dwellings, the Pineapple Inn really stands out.

The entrance from the porch is into a hallway with a lovely curving staircase to the second floor. On the right is a high-ceilinged living room with a large bay window and a baby grand piano. A display of handmade quilts was from the Upside Down Shoppe in the basement, where beautiful Pennsylvania Dutch handmade furniture, knitted items, and crafts by Susquehanna Valley people are sold.

Breakfast is served in the dining room, decorated with Williamsburg wallpaper and furnished mainly with Colonial-style pieces. Deborah describes it as a country-style breakfast rather than a gourmet breakfast because "we are able to get farm-fresh eggs and wonderful bacon at the Mennonite store about twenty miles away."

In addition to Bucknell, there are four other universities in the immediate vicinity. Lewisburg and surrounding towns are, according to Charlie North, "peppered with quaint antique shops and unusual crafts shops. From handmade furniture to quilts, old and new, it's all here, and in abundance."

THE PINEAPPLE INN, 439 Market St., Lewisburg, PA 17837; 717-524-6200. A 5-guestroom (private and shared baths) B&B in a most attractive town in central Pennsylvania. Complimentary breakfast and afternoon tea. Open year-round. Air conditioned. Five universities, many outdoor activities, antique and crafts shops nearby. No special facilities are available to accommodate children. No pets. No credit cards. Smoking is not permitted in the guestrooms. Charles and Deborah North, Innkeepers.

Directions: Lewisburg is conveniently located for both north-south and east-west travel in central Pa. It is just a few miles from I-80.

For B&B rates, see Index.

1740 HOUSE
Lumberville, Pennsylvania

Bucks County, Pennsylvania, is rich in history. It is here that Washington's army made its famous crossing of the Delaware River, and the Battlefields of Trenton and the encampment of Valley Forge are both nearby. It's possible to stay in Bucks County for two or three days just to follow the historically oriented back-road tours.

The 1740 House is located on the Delaware River just a few miles from New Hope, Pennsylvania. It is conservative and quiet.

Weekend reservations must include two nights; usually these are booked well in advance. Dinner is served between 7:00 and 7:30 P.M. in a small dining room overlooking the canal and river, and it is necessary for everyone—even houseguests—to have advance reservations.

Guest rooms are located in the main house and also in several outbuildings along the canal side. All are furnished with exceptional care and taste.

All the rooms have terraces or balconies with lovely views of the tree-lined and sometimes ivy-covered embankment sloping down to the river. There is a pleasantly furnished cozy living room and a welcome swimming pool for the warm weather.

Harry Nessler refers to the morning meal as a buffet breakfast. with orange juice, coffee, cold cereal, scrambled eggs, danish, croissants, english muffins, jam, and homemade bread.

1740 HOUSE, River Rd., Lumberville, Pa. 18933; 215-297-5661. A 24-room riverside inn, 6½ mi. north of New Hope, in the heart of historic Bucks County. Lodgings include breakfast which is served to houseguests daily; dinner served daily except Sundays by reservation only. Open year-round. Pool and boating on grounds. golf and tennis nearby. Harry Nessler, Innkeeper.

Directions: From N.Y.C., travel south on N.J. Tpke., and take Exit 10. Follow Rte. 287 north to another Exit 10. Proceed west on Rte. 22 to Flemington, then Rte. 202 south over Delaware Toll Bridge. After an immediate right U-turn onto Rte. 32N, drive 5 mi. to inn. From Pa. Tpke., exit at Willow Grove and proceed north on Rte. 611 to Rte. 202. Follow Rte. 202 north to Rte. 32 and turn north to inn. From Phila., take I-95 to Yardley-New Hope Exit, follow 32N through New Hope and 7 miles to inn.

For B&B rates, see Index.

SOCIETY HILL HOTEL
Philadelphia, Pennsylvania

Typifying the term "urban inn," the Society Hill Hotel is located on Third and Chestnut Streets in the midst of Independence National Historical Park, the federal development that sparked the revitalization of Society Hill and the old section of the city. These areas today have become an attraction to over three million visitors per year.

Known affectionately as "Philadelphia's smallest hotel," the Society Hill Hotel is within two blocks of Independence Hall, Franklin Court, Penn's Landing, and is diagonally across the street from the Federal Visitors Center.

The twelve guest rooms have been decorated with brass double beds, beautiful antiques, and fresh-cut flowers, and six of them are two-room suites.

The restaurant, designed in light woods, stained glass, and greenery, contributes to the congenial and casual atmosphere, and the huge windows give patrons a spectacular view of the park.

The breakfast served in each room is fresh-squeezed juice, coffee or tea, and warm croissants or coffee cake with butter and jam. A Sunday brunch is offered in the restaurant and includes Belgian waffles, eggs Benedict, and steak and eggs.

Bed-and-breakfast has arrived in Philadelphia in a manner that even Benjamin Franklin would applaud.

SOCIETY HILL HOTEL AND RESTAURANT, Third & Chestnut Sts., Philadelphia, PA 19106; 215-925-1394 (restaurant: 925-1919). A 12-guestroom urban hotel in the heart of Philadelphia. Air conditioning, color TV, and private baths. A continental breakfast is served in the room every morning. Open year-round. Within walking distance of many of the important cultural, recreational, and historic attractions of the Old City. Kate C. Hopkins, Innkeeper.

Directions: From the New Jersey Tpke. take Exit 4 and Rtes. 30 & 38 across the Ben Franklin Bridge and turn left on 6th St. to Chestnut. Turn left to Third and Chestnut.

For B&B rates, see Index.

SPRING HOUSE
Airville, Pennsylvania

Thanks to my Stockbridge friend Mark Swann, the Spring House at Muddy Creek Forks in York County is a real find—an 18th-century stone house in a historic pre-Revolutionary village.

Mark described the village to me, "It's much as it was a hundred years ago with clapboard mill buildings, a creamery, and a Gothic country store. It is reached by unpaved roads, and the now-unused railroad bed of the 'Ma and Pa' (Maryland and Pennsylvania) Railroad provides splendid hiking opportunities."

The Spring House, with a history as a tavern, is the dream-come-true for Ray Hearne, who visited a number of B&Bs in England and conceived the idea of turning this beautiful old house into an inn. She restored it literally with her own hands, preserving the creaky floorboards, uncovering the stencils on some of the walls, and restoring the interior. Modern plumbing and heating have been added, but the five guest bedrooms have been furnished with featherbeds from Ireland, and additional stenciling and murals in the old-time manner have been created by artist Peggy Kurtz.

The kitchen has an old pie safe, a jelly cupboard, a coffee grinder, and a wood cook stove. Among the time-to-time offerings on the full breakfast are scrapple, local sausage, or French pancakes with hand-picked tree-ripened peaches, blackberries, or raspberries. Honey is provided from hives on the property, and all the eggs come from local chickens. Breakfast is eaten in the dining room or on the front porch overlooking the sylvan scene.

SPRING HOUSE, Creek Forks, Airville, York County, PA 17302; 717-927-6906. A 5-guestroom country bed-and-breakfast experience some distance from the madding crowd. Open year-round, except for "1 month plus" during winter. Breakfast is the only meal served, but prior arrangements can be made for dinner. Walking, swimming, fishing, canoeing, and swinging on the porch all readily available. Conveniently located for trips to all of the historical, recreational, and cultural attractions in the area, including 4 wineries. No pets. No credit cards. No smoking. Ray Constance Hearne, Innkeeper.

Directions: Because this is such a rural location, complete directions for arriving from all points of the compass would be well-nigh impossible and I suggest you call Ray Hearne. I'm certain she will put you on the right road.

For B&B rates, see Index.

STERLING INN
South Sterling, Pennsylvania

A few miles out of the way from I-84 and I-80, the Sterling Inn is on a back road in the Poconos. There is a very pleasant nine-hole putting green, a swimming area with a sandy beach, and a little pond with willow trees, which is sometimes home to a select group of ducks.

Guest rooms are in several very attractive buildings in a parklike atmosphere. They are all beautifully situated with extremely pleasant and colorful decorations. All have private baths. There are also some new, elegant Victorian suites with Franklin fireplaces.

Breakfast at this inn in the woods is a Major Project, beginning with a choice of fruit or juice and continuing on to hot or cold cereal, eggs any style and bacon or sausage; or homemade hot cakes, or blueberry hot cakes, or waffles, or french toast—all of them served with bacon or sausage. Every plate will have some fried potatoes or hash-browns, coffee cake, and, of course, lots of beverages.

Basically, this is a modified American plan resort inn, but a few B&B accommodations have been set aside for readers of this book. Please make reservations considerably ahead to avoid disappointment.

THE STERLING INN, Rte. 191, South Sterling, PA 18460; 717-676-3311 or 3338. (Toll-free from Conn., N.Y., N.J., Md., Del., Wash. D.C.: 800-523-8200.) A 60-guestroom secluded country inn resort in the Pocono Mountains, 8 mi. from I-84 and 12 mi. from I-380. Mod. Amer. plan. Reservation and check-in office closes at 10 P.M. Breakfast, lunch, and dinner served to travelers daily. Breakfast served 8-9 A.M.; lunch served 12:30-1:30 P.M.; dinner served at two seatings 6:30 and 8:00 P.M.. Jackets requested for dinner. Open year-round. Swimming, boating, 9-hole putting green, shuffleboard, all-weather tennis court, scenic hiking trails, all on grounds; also xc ski trails, game room, tobogganing, sledding, ice skating. Golf courses and horseback riding nearby. Golf packages available. No pets. Ron and Mary Kay Logan, Innkeepers.

Directions: From I-80, follow I-380 to Rte. 940 to Mount Pocono. At light, cross Rte. 611 and proceed on Rte. 196 north to Rte. 423. Drive north on Rte. 423 to Rte. 191 and travel ½ mi. north to inn. From I-84, follow Rte. 507 south through Greentown and Newfoundland. In Newfoundland, pick up Rte. 191 and travel 4 mi. south to inn.

For B&B rates, see Index.

THE BRINLEY VICTORIAN INN
Newport, Rhode Island

There are so many wonderful, small touches of Victoriana in this handsome, two-house inn, guests quickly fall under the spell of authentic 19th-century charm. There is, for example, the parlor where even the books are chosen for their century-old popularity. As for the bedrooms, no two are alike. All is circa 1870.

Fresh flowers and collectible, miniature antique lamps appear throughout the house. There are mints on the pillows. It is not surprising that many choose the Brinley for Christmas and New Year holidays as well as the summer season. You are near the Newport Art Association and the boutiques and restaurants on and off Bellevue Avenue. It is only a ten-minute walk to the waterfront. You can even stroll to the mansions.

On your way to the magnificent cottages, you will pass the old Newport Casino, also on Bellevue Avenue. Once the most complete resort in America, it now houses the International Tennis Hall of Fame and the Tennis Museum. It's a great place to pick up a souvenir for your partners at home. There is also a pleasant restaurant serving both simple and full luncheons, and an evening meal as well.

The Brinley Victorian will put you in the right frame of mind for **your meander**ings. Included in the nightly rate is a continental-plus breakfast of juice, fruit, home-baked coffee cake, cheese, and coffee, tea, or milk. After that, most of Newport is within walking distance, and you are on your own.

THE BRINLEY VICTORIAN INN, 23 Brinley St., Newport, RI 02840; 401-849-7645. A 17-guestroom (7 with private baths) guest house centrally located on a quiet street. Breakfast is the only meal served. Open year-round. The Kay Street and Bellevue Avenue area offers sightseeing, restaurants, and shopping. Parking. Children over 12 accepted. No pets. Amy Weintraub and Edwina Sebest, Proprietors.

Directions: Brinley St. is a one-way arc that can only be entered from Kay St. (across Kay St. it becomes Bull St.). The inn is on your right almost at the end of the block.

For B&B rates, see Index.

INN AT CASTLE HILL
Newport, Rhode Island

Two of the places I've suggested in Newport are owned by the same innkeepers; one is the Inntowne, and the other is the Inn at Castle Hill, which presents quite a different aspect of Newport.

Actually antedating the famous Newport mansions, the Inn at Castle Hill is built on a point where Narragansett Bay joins the Atlantic Ocean, and many of the guest rooms, as well as the dining room, offer a full view of the ever-changing panorama of sea, sky, and water.

Lodgings are in the main mansion which has retained much of the original character and many of the original furnishings, including oriental rugs and hand-crafted oak and mahogany paneling. For many years the eminent American playwright Thornton Wilder was a regular guest. These lodgings are available year-round. There are other bayside cottages, beautifully furnished and roomy enough to accommodate three people comfortably, down near the water's edge and available during warmer weather. I might add that reservations for all of these accommodations should be made well in advance.

The cheerful Sunset Room is the scene of a very pleasant continental breakfast.

The regular visitors to Newport as well as the local residents speak glowingly of the dinners which are served every day except Sunday during the period from Easter to early December.

Newport is a very busy place during the height of the season and I suggest that it may be enjoyed to the fullest around the first of September and the first of June.

INN AT CASTLE HILL, Ocean Drive, Newport, R I 02840; 401-849-3800. A 10-bedroom mansion-inn on the edge of Narragansett Bay. European plan. Continental breakfast included in room tariff. No dinner served on Sun.; no lunch served on Mon. Dining room closed from early Dec. to Easter. Guest rooms open all winter. Lounge open winter weekends. Near the Newport mansions, Touro Synagogue, the Newport Casino, and National Lawn Tennis Hall of Fame, the Old Stone Mill, the Newport Historical Society House. Swimming, sailing, scuba diving, walking on grounds. Bicycles and guided tours of Newport nearby. No pets. Jens Thillemann, Manager; Paul McEnroe, Innkeeper.

Directions: After leaving Newport Bridge follow Bellevue Ave. which becomes Ocean Dr. Look for inn sign on left.

For B&B rates, see Index.

THE INNTOWNE
Newport, Rhode Island

It's midwinter and you've either had it with skiing or else there's a shortage of snow and you're dying to get away for a short trip. May I respectfully suggest Newport, Rhode Island?

The Inntowne is a perfect complement to the rest of historic Newport. It is open twelve months of the year and is most convenient for visiting Bowen's Wharf with its many shops and boutiques, and furthermore, it's easy to drive around the Ocean Drive for a tour of the many mansions, some of which are open year-round, as is the Tennis Hall of Fame.

The Inntowne is owned and kept by Betty and Paul McEnroe, and the interior design, which is exceptionally attractive, has been created by Rodney and Ione Williams, who are also the innkeepers at the Inn at Sawmill Farm in Vermont.

Each room has been individually designed, reflecting Ione's really exquisite taste. The drapes, bedspreads, wallpapers, lampshades, and small touches have all been almost choreographed to create a beautiful decorator feeling. They are very bright and gay, just the kind of rooms that make you want to smile when you enter. All have air conditioning but no telephones or television.

The building is on Thames Street and one square from the waterfront area. It is one of the old Newport buildings that has been completely restored and at the same time has maintained the integrity of its Colonial heritage. Stepping into the lobby is like entering a very tastefully decorated living room.

Although dinner is not served, Paul and Betty will be happy to make arrangements for the evening meal at the Inn at Castle Hill or at other excellent restaurants in the Newport area.

THE INNTOWNE, 6 Mary St., Newport, R I 02840; 401-846-9200. An elegant 20-room inn in the center of the city of Newport overlooking the harbor, serving continental breakfast only. Open every day. Convenient for all of the Newport historical and cultural attractions which are extremely numerous. No recreational facilities available; however, tennis and ocean swimming are nearby. Not adaptable for children of any age. No pets. Betty and Paul McEnroe, Innkeepers.

Directions: After crossing Newport bridge turn right at sign: "Historic Newport." Drive straight to Thames Street; Inntowne is on corner of Thames St. and Mary St., across from Brick Marketplace.

For B&B rates, see Index.

LARCHWOOD INN
Wakefield, Rhode Island

Rhode Island is a state of stone walls. They come in various heights, thicknesses, and condition of repair. Roads leading through the woods between the fields are most numerous for a state that is reputedly small, and often offer some interesting historical sites as well as beautiful homes.

There is much to see and do, but perhaps one of the most impressive things about Rhode Island is the south-shore beaches which are often favorably compared with others elsewhere in New England.

The Larchwood Inn is a large manor dating back to 1831. The interior has many Scottish touches, including quotations from Robert Burns and Sir Walter Scott, and photographs and prints of Scottish historical and literary figures. One of the dining rooms has wall paintings showing farms and seascapes of southern Rhode Island.

In addition to bedrooms at the main inn, accommodations now include splendid rooms at Holly House, located just across the street from the inn itself. The building is about 150 years old and all the furniture has been carefully selected to match the ambience of the manor.

The Larchwood is a full-service inn, offering breakfast, lunch and dinner. Bed-and-breakfast devotees will be very enthusiastic about the à la carte breakfast menu, which includes everything from a dish of seasonal fruit to steak and eggs.

Wakefield is on the western side of Narragansett Bay and is a few miles from the famous bridge that leads over the bay into Newport. It is a very pleasant holiday experience.

LARCHWOOD INN, 176 Main St., Wakefield, R.I. 02879; 401-783-5454. A 19-room village inn just 3 mi. from the famous southern R.I. beaches. Some rooms with shared bath. European plan. Breakfast, lunch, dinner served every day of the year. Swimming, boating, surfing, fishing, xc skiing, and bicycles nearby. Francis and Diann Browning, Innkeepers.

Directions: From Rte. 1, take Pond St. Exit and proceed ½ mi. directly to inn.

For Lodging rates, see Index.

PHOENIX INN
Narragansett, Rhode Island

There was no sign on the stone pillars at the Gibson Avenue entrance but, map in hand, I found the Phoenix. Roses were blooming, and a boat was parked casually on one side of the driveway. Was I in the right place? Happily, yes.

The impressive shingle mansion, designed by Stanford White in the late 1800s for the New York restaurateur, Louis Sherry, was originally one of several houses ("cottages" in the local lexicon of understatement) in a family compound. When fire swept the others, this one rose from the ashes to become, in present life, a bed-and-breakfast country retreat.

Second-floor east and west wings each have two bedrooms and one bath; a smaller bedroom on the third floor has a private bath. Downstairs there is a large living room and the dining room, where breakfast is served guests in a big way. Guests also enjoy the veranda.

Fresh fruit at breakfast is followed by eggs prepared in such creative forms as shrimp and avocado omelet or eggs Benedict. There may be cheese blintzes with strawberries; ham, bacon, or sausage. Fresh baked breads are as fragrant as the newly ground coffee. All this and Wedgwood too.

Narragansett Pier is undergoing a revitalization of the shops and restaurants, as well as the popular beach area, but such things are far removed in spirit, if not in distance. The beach is close by—a mile. Newport is approximately twenty minutes over the Jamestown (free) and Newport (toll) Bridges.

PHOENIX INN, 29 Gibson Ave., Narragansett, RI 02882; 401-783-1918. A 5-guestroom bed-and-breakfast home (1 private, 2 shared baths) in a pleasant, quiet neighborhood across Narragansett Bay from Jamestown Island and Newport. Full breakfast the only meal served. Open all year. Swimming, boating, surfing, fishing nearby. Children over age 10 preferred. Joyce and Dave Peterson, Proprietors.

Directions: From the north, follow the signs on Rte. 1 to the Pt. Judith exit, which puts you on So. Pier Rd. From the south, take the Narragansett exit. You will be on So. Pier Rd. Continue to Gibson Ave. and turn right. After Westmoreland St. watch on right for stone pillars directly opposite Earles Ct. Rd. Turn in. Follow driveway bearing to your left to Phoenix Inn.

For B&B rates, see Index.

THE QUEEN ANNE INN
Newport, Rhode Island

Peg McCabe's bed-and-breakfast inn is only two blocks from the waterfront and has its own off-street parking, two factors which in themselves make it remarkable. Much more, however, awaits those who stay in this Newport rose Victorian. The rooms are done with great style, and breakfast, whether served in the reception room or in the pretty garden, is a chance to visit with an international clientele. Many are returned visitors.

Of course, Peg knows everything that is going on in Newport (past and present) and can recommend restaurants in all price ranges. Breakfast, however, is the only meal served at the Queen Anne, and might consist of fresh fruit or Portuguese sweet bread with jams, and coffee or tea.

Clarke Street is a historic street usually discovered only on foot. You may find yourself going around in circles looking for its one-way access, but once there, you can leave your car and walk to all the downtown attractions.

If you turn right outside the door of the Queen Anne and walk to the end of the block you will be on Touro Street and near the Touro Synagogue, the oldest Jewish house of worship in North America (1763). It stands beside the Newport Historical Society, which houses priceless Townsend and Goddard furniture, as well as Rhode Island pewter and silver.

At the end of a day of walking and looking, it's especially nice to have a charmer like the Queen Anne Inn waiting.

THE QUEEN ANNE INN, 16 Clarke St., Newport, RI 02840; 401-846-5676. A 12-guestroom (7 shared baths) bed-and-breakfast inn in the heart of Newport. Open "almost all year." No pets. Private off-street parking. A 2-night stay is required during July and August and on weekends all year, 3 nights on holiday weekends. No phone service between 11 P.M. and 8 A.M. Peg McCabe, Innkeeper.

Directions: Clarke is a one-way street one block long that can only be entered off Touro St., one block east of Thames St. The inn is on your left.

For B&B rates, see Index.

THE 1661 INN
Block Island, Rhode Island

Here's a good idea if you happen to be traveling on the New England coast: schedule an overnight trip to Block Island, off the coast of both Rhode Island and Connecticut. Ferries run year-round, and even during the winter there are two a day.

Fortunately, there are excellent year-round accommodations at the 1661 Inn, which is set apart from the rest of Block Island's little world on a height of land overlooking the sand dunes and the ocean.

The country-inn-type guest rooms are located in the original early 19th-century house, and in some very attractive new ocean-view rooms in the guest house that are particularly adaptable for off-season holidays.

From Memorial Day to Columbus Day, a full buffet breakfast is served, including a wide variety of fresh fruit juices, homemade muffins and breads, Rita's homemade preserves, scrambled or hard-boiled eggs, breakfast meats, especially prepared quiches, and daily hot seafood and poultry specialties. In the off-seaon, it's a mini-buffet that includes all of the above, except the hot specialties.

Caution: the 1661 Inn is fully booked during the height of the summer season, but a chance telephone call may be rewarded with a room made available by a last-minute cancellation. Other times can be fairly open.

THE 1661 INN, Spring St., Block Island, RI 02807; 401-466-2421 or 2063. A 25-guestroom (11 private baths) island inn off the coast of R.I. and Conn., in Block Island Sound. Mod. American and European plans. Open from Memorial Day thru Columbus Day weekend. Breakfast served to travelers daily. (Guest House open year-round; continental breakfast included in off-season rates.) Lawn games on grounds. Bicycling, ocean swimming, sailing, snorkeling, diving, salt and fresh water fishing nearby. Block Island is known as one of the best bird observation areas on the Atlantic flyway. Children over 10 only. No pets. The Abrams Family, Innkeepers.

Directions: By ferry from Providence, Pt. Judith, and Newport R.I. and New London, Ct. Car reservations (401-789-3502) must be made in advance for ferry. By air from Newport, Westerly, and Providence, R.I., New London and Waterford, Ct., or by chartered plane. For air information and reservations: 401-596-2460.

For B&B rates, see Index.

WAYSIDE
Newport, Rhode Island

Part of the fun in visiting the "cottages" of the very rich is imagining how it would be to spend the night in such opulence. Now if you have made reservations well in advance, you can turn into the circular driveway almost opposite the Elms and play Houseguest-for-a-Night-or-More at the Wayside.

Among those neighbors: The Elms is across the street; down the block is Chateau-sur-Mer, Rosecliff (where *The Great Gatsby* was filmed), Mrs. Astor's Beechwood, Marble House, and Belcourt Castle. The tour guides will tell you all about the scandals as well as the costs of living it up in the Gilded Age.

The Georgian-style, 1890s mansion has bedrooms so large they are sitting rooms as well, and each is individually decorated. Alas, the retinue of servants is gone, and you serve yourself a simple continental breakfast from a buffet in the lobby before starting out on foot to pay calls at the museum palaces of the neighbors.

After a day's walking, it's especially nice to be able to take a dip in the house swimming pool before heading out for dinner in one of the fine restaurants of Newport.

Oh yes, the servants' quarters are also available. Here you share the bath.

WAYSIDE, Bellevue Ave., Newport, RI 02840; 401-847-0302. An 8-guestroom (most with private baths) guest house on famous and fabulous Bellevue Avenue. Continental breakfast the only meal served. Open year-round. Swimming pool, ocean beach, mansions, restaurants, shops nearby. No pets. No credit cards. Off-street parking. Reservations should be made well in advance. Al and Dorothy Post, Proprietors

Directions: Bellevue Avenue is probably Newport's most famous street. As you drive towards Ocean Avenue, the Elms will be on your right. Watch for driveway on left marked "Wayside" (nothing so crass as house numbers in this neighborhood) and turn in.

For B&B rates, see Index.

THE WILLOWS OF NEWPORT
Newport, Rhode Island

These two adjoining townhouses in the oldest part of historic Newport were actually built 100 years apart, so when Pattie Murphy set out to restore them she left each in its own time. They are both, incidentally, on the National Register of Historic Places. Since Pattie is a True Believer in the theory that a vacation should be a fantasy, she has converted these rooms into dreamy period pieces: a Colonial Wedding Room and a Canopy Room in the 1740 house; a Victorian Wedding Room and French Quarters in the 1840 segment. The shared parlor is pink.

To keep the fantasy going, breakfast is served to guests in bed, using silver and bone china. In the evening, guests find mints on their pillows, their beds turned down, and the lights left on low. Some rooms have working fireplaces. Even your automobile gets special treatment at the Willows, as there are closed garages, as well as off-street parking next door.

Although bustling Newport is only a few minutes' walk away, this quiet and for the most part pre-Revolutionary enclave is worth a lot of wandering. Hunter House, pride of the Preservation Society, is down on the Battery, a five-minute walk.

Many of the restored houses here on "The Point" are labeled with the names of their original owners and the approximate dates of construction. Except for Hunter House, however, they are not open to the public. This is just one more reason (and not the least) you will enjoy being a genuine resident, if only for a few nights, in another place, another time. As Pattie says, "part of the fantasy."

THE WILLOWS OF NEWPORT, 8-10 Willow St., Newport, RI 02840; 401-846-5486. A 4-guestroom (all private baths) guest house in the Historic Point section of Newport. Open year-round. Breakfast-in-bed the only meal served. Close to all downtown and waterfront Newport activities. Garage parking next door. No children. No pets. No credit cards. Pattie Murphy, Proprietor.

Directions: From Rte. 95, take Rte. 138 east to Newport. Cross Newport Bridge, downtown exit right at first traffic light onto Van Zandt Ave., proceed to waterfront. Turn left at Washington St., and go 7 blocks to Willow St., turn left and continue to 8 Willow St. From Rte. 24, take Rte. 114. Turn right on Coddington Hwy. and follow signs to Newport Bridge. Go right at traffic circle onto Third St. and turn left at Washington St. Continue 7 blocks to Willow St., as above.

For B&B rates, see Index.

THE BARKSDALE HOUSE INN
Charleston, South Carolina

It was appropriate that I was introduced to the Barksdale House Inn by a soft-spoken young student from the College of Charleston, since a decade ago this was a fraternity house. Its subsequent rescue and restoration by Suzanne and Robert Chesnut, a well-known landscape architect, just proves you can't keep a good house down.

Built in 1778 by George Barksdale of Youghall Plantation as the city residence for his family, the house proved to be a survivor, outlasting most of its neighborhood vintage. Barksdale House Inn is outside the crosshatch of streets that constitute the Colonial point of historic Charleston, though convenient to shops, restaurants, and the Charleston Museum. It is, at most, a ten-minute stroll to the old market.

The rooms are beautifully decorated and furnished with antiques and designer wallpapers and fabrics. There are ceiling fans throughout, and working fireplaces and whirlpool baths in five of the ten rooms. A pleasant rear courtyard with a fountain is the setting for afternoon tea or sherry as well as for the continental breakfast. Or you may choose to have breakfast in your room, together with morning paper and fresh flowers on the tray. The inn aims to pamper its guests.

The Barksdale House Inn has a red mansard roof and has been painted a sunny yellow. "It didn't look like this when it was a frat house," my earnest guide said, then smiled. Even he recognized that as a masterpiece of understatement.

THE BARKSDALE HOUSE INN, 27 George St., Charleston, SC 29401; 803-577-4800. A 10-guestroom (private baths) Colonial townhouse luxury bed-and-breakfast inn in historic Charleston. Complimentary continental breakfast and afternoon tea. Open year-round. Located near Charleston Museum and historic houses; within walking distance to all Old Town sights. No pets. Robert and Suzanne Chesnut, Innkeepers.

Directions: The inn is on the south side of George St., between King and Meeting Sts., 2 blocks below Marion Square.

For B&B rates, see Index.

BAY STREET INN
Beaufort, South Carolina

"There go our two favorite ducks," Kathleen Roe said, waving towards the Beaufort River. "We get porpoises, too." I was on the veranda of the Bay Street Inn looking across at the bridge to Lady's Island. The tidelands dusk was long and subtle.

It wasn't easy to leave the ducks or the promise of porpoises, but I wanted to walk around old Beaufort before dark. The Bay Street Inn is perfectly located for strolling the back lanes of this important antebellum town as well as for simple relaxing and shutting out all modern-world concerns.

There are more than 100 homes in the registered Historic District that begins on "The Point" and continues on the other side of State Highway 21. That is where the waterfront park broadens into the marina and yacht harbor for the intracoastal waterway. So much to see and enjoy in the town that was once known as "Queen of the Sea Islands." The Spanish were here long before the English reached Plymouth Rock; Lafayette was a guest in the 1790s; the first Ordinance of Secession of the state was signed here, which is why Beaufort suffered such devastating consequences.

The history of the Bay Street Inn parallels the town's. It was built in 1852 as a private home, became an officers' club, a Union hospital, and is now a haven for travelers who seek comfort and authenticity with their bed and breakfast.

The Roes are Connecticut transplants who came to South Carolina in 1984. Son Gene bakes the breakfast french and sweet breads that go along with the morning juice, fruit, coffee, and tea. "The guests rave about the bread," Kathleen says. "It must be pretty good."

There are five guest rooms, all with private baths, fireplaces, and air conditioning. Though each claims a water view, the two large front rooms share the second-floor veranda and are especially choice. A basket of fruit, a decanter of sherry, and evening chocolates are frosting on the cake.

BAY STREET INN, 601 Bay St., Beaufort, SC 29902; 803-524-7720. A 5-guestroom (private baths) restored antebellum mansion on the water in historic Beaufort, midway between Savannah and Charleston. Complimentary breakfast. Open year-round. Bicycles available for touring. All restaurants, shops, museums, and historic structures nearby. No pets. Gene and Kathleen Roe, Innkeepers.

Directions: Hwy. 21 bisects Beaufort and continues across Lady's Island Bridge. Bay St. crosses at the waterfront. Turn left.

For B&B rates, see Index.

KINGS COURTYARD INN
Charleston, South Carolina

If your idea of heaven is staying in the heart of the antique shopping district, Kings Courtyard Inn is paradise enough. I was so busy window-shopping I almost missed the discreet entrance on King Street. Then, once inside the old courtyard, it took a few minutes to find the tucked-away parlor reception area.

The architecture is Greek Revival, popular in 1853, and there are unusual Egyptian details. Each of the thirty-four guest rooms has been given a different decorative treatment; some have fireplaces, one even has its own small private courtyard. During the Spoleto Festival (late May—early June) a late-night supper is served in the main courtyard, an area open to the public for breakfast and afternoon refreshments. Continental breakfast is included in the room rate, but a complete breakfast may be ordered at additional charge.

King Street was once the main roadway into old Charles Towne, and it has never lost its lineup of shops and restaurants or its attractiveness for strollers. The old covered-market area is only a block away from the inn, too. That means you can carry your purchases back to your room, enjoy a cool drink or a dip in the spa, and be ready to shop again. Of course, you can also walk to historic houses, churches, or the Dock Street Theater. If you have time.

KINGS COURTYARD INN, 198 King St., Charleston, SC 29401; 803-723-7000; outside S.C.: 800-845-6119; inside S.C. 800-922-3313. A 34-guestroom (private baths) inn on King St. in the Historic District of Charleston. Complimentary continental breakfast. Open year-round. Free off-street parking. Nonsmoking rooms available. Emily Bailey, Manager.

Directions: Inn is located on King St. just below Market St. Parking is free in the city parking lot directly behind the inn, and there is direct access to the reception from the parking area. Entrance on Horlbeck Alley.

For B&B rates, see Index.

MIDDLETON INN AT MIDDLETON PLACE
Charleston, South Carolina

To take the River Road out of Charleston is to leave antebellum town life for antebellum country life. Drayton Hall, Magnolia Plantation, and Middleton Place are three of the great showpieces saved and held in trust for fortunate visitors to the Old South. Visiting them is a mere day trip from Charleston, and it was exciting to read that Middleton Inn had opened on the grounds adjacent to Middleton Place.

Middleton Place is a marvel of an 18th-century house (1755) and garden (1741). Even the stableyards constitute a living museum of animals plus the support system of the 18th and 19th centuries: coopering, tanning, shinglemaking, spinning, candlemaking, and so forth, all in working order. Middleton Place householders signed the Declaration of Independence as well as the Ordinance of Succession. Henry Middleton was president of the First Continental Congress.

When the decision was made to build an inn on the property, authenticity of time and place was taken into consideration. The result is a complex of four completely contemporary buildings placed at different levels in the pine woods along the Ashley River.

Tennis, swimming and golf (nearby) plus horseback riding keep inn guests busy enough, but one of the real bonuses is a pass to all the attractions of Middleton Place. This makes the overnight tariff a real bargain, and your walk through the woods takes only seven minutes.

MIDDLETON INN AT MIDDLETON PLACE, Ashley River Road (Highway 61), Charleston, SC 29407; 803-556-0500. A 55-guestroom contemporary bed-and-breakfast inn adjacent to the gardens of National Historic Landmark Middleton Place, 14 mi. from Charleston. Complimentary continental breakfast; lunch and dinner available at Middleton Place Restaurant nearby. Open year-round. Tennis courts, swimming pool, nature trails. Horseback riding and golf nearby. No pets.

Directions: Follow Rte. 61 west out of Charleston and watch for signs. Entrance to Middleton Inn is on your right, ½ mi. before you reach Middleton Place.

For B&B rates, see Index.

36 MEETING STREET
Charleston, South Carolina

When you take the horse-drawn carriage ride through old Charleston, the driver always stops to point out a perfect example of "a little Charleston house" on Meeting Street. "It was built in 1740," the driver says, "and is one of the oldest clapboard buildings in Charleston."

If you are staying at 36 Meeting Street, the perfect example itself, you count yourself lucky. You might also feel great sympathy for Suzanne Redd, who had to get ready for a Preservation Society house tour scarcely three weeks after her family of five moved in. She recalls the time as both hectic and frustrating since she could not begin to make the changes she had planned in order to put the interior squarely where it belonged in the 18th century.

Now, however, bed-and-breakfast guests, as well as the house viewers who trek through for the spring, fall, and Christmas tours, can enjoy the finished product. Beds are canopied, handmade quilts folded just so, colors and prints perfectly chosen, antiques polished, and heart-pine floors glowing. No "Charleston Single House" could ask for more.

Each of the three guest suites is, in local terms, a "dependency" with direct access either to garden or piazza. Mine also had an original 1740 cooking fireplace in the bedroom, a second fireplace in the living room, and a kitchenette. Juice was in the refrigerator, homemade pumpkin bread on the counter, a bowl of fruit on the table, and all the makings of a proper breakfast at hand.

The last Royal Governor may have lived next door, but we would choose 36 Meeting Street every time.

36 MEETING STREET, 36 Meeting St., Charleston, SC 29401; 803-722-1034. A 3-suite "dependency" bed and breakfast in Charleston's picturesque, historic southernmost tip. Breakfast ingredients provided. Open year-round. Bikes to borrow or you can walk everywhere. Colonial garden. Parking available. No credit cards. David and Suzanne Redd, Hosts.

Directions: On east side of Meeting St., south of Tradd St. and two blocks north of S. Battery St.

For B&B rates, see Index.

TWO MEETING STREET INN
Charleston, South Carolina

In the 1890s, when two wealthy families were united in marriage, one father sent the young couple to Europe on a two-year honeymoon and the other had a magnificent home built for them while they were away. On their fifth wedding anniversary, Waring Carrington naturally gave Martha a pair of Tiffany glass panels to enhance further the beautiful Queen Anne-style house across from Battery Park. Do you doubt?

Great Victorian houses are rare in Charleston, but Two Meeting Street would be an architect's choice anywhere. The exquisite staircase, spacious high-ceilinged rooms, and carved oak paneling are set off by beautiful antique furniture and the personal collections of owner-restorer David Spell. Fresh flowers appear in stunning arrangements throughout the house.

The appropriately patrician continental breakfast (juices, fruit, a pastry-of-the-day, fresh-brewed coffee) is often taken out on the cool, wide piazza, but with morning sunlight through stained glass lighting up the dining room, the temptation is to linger indoors.

There are five large, distinctive rooms on the second floor, each with private bath. On the third, two rooms share two baths.

Since the house was originally a wedding gift, honeymooners and anniversary couples are particularly welcome.

TWO MEETING STREET INN, 2 Meeting St., Charleston, SC 29401; 803-723-7322. A 7-guestroom (mostly private baths) Queen Anne bed-and-breakfast mansion opposite Battery Park in historic Charleston's nicest part. Complimentary continental breakfast. Open all year. Bicycles. Victorian garden. No pets or young children, please. No credit cards. David Spell, Owner-Innkeeper.

Directions: Inn is directly across the street from Battery Park at the southern tip of Charleston peninsula.

For B&B rates, see Index.

PARISH PATCH INN
Normandy, Tennessee

If you are traveling on Route 41-A or I-24, between Nashville and Chattanooga, I have some excellent news for you. Just outside the small town of Normandy, I have discovered the Parish Patch Inn, right in the middle of a 750-acre working farm in southern Tennessee.

With waving fields of grain, a feed lot, and many cattle, the setting is unmistakably bucolic. However, there is a great deal more to be experienced than meets the eye.

The main house was built by Chuck Parish, who was, until his passing, the largest manufacturer of baseballs and bats in the world. He built the house to entertain friends, guests, and people associated with the company.

The exterior is of board and batten construction quite in keeping with this part of Tennessee. The interior, which might be described as "elegant rustic," has a living room, library, and dining room with splendid cherry and walnut paneling. There are also two kitchens, a master bedroom with a balcony and two bathrooms, and three other double bedrooms, also with bathrooms.

In the guest rooms, furniture, counterpanes, and comforters are all blended to create a marvelous feeling of relaxation and harmony. The living room, kitchens, and dining room all enjoy the views of the meadows and the orchard. There are also two cottages with additional rooms.

The overnight guest will be enticed to stay longer for the swimming, fishing, canoeing, picnicking, bicycling, and bird watching, which abound on or near the inn property.

PARISH PATCH INN, Normandy, TN 37360; 615-857-3441. A 4-guestroom (private baths) elegant bed-and-breakfast inn in the verdant Tennessee countryside. Breakfast is included in the room rate; evening meals are served to houseguests only with advance reservations. Open all year. Swimming pool. Wide variety of recreation available. Marty Ligon, Owner; Phyllis Crosslin, Innkeeper.

Directions: From I-24, take Exit 97 (Beechgrove-Shelbyville-Hwy. 64 Exit). Take Hwy. 64 west to Wartrace. In Wartrace take 269E to Parish Patch Inn (4 mi.). From Shelbyville, continue south on 41-A for 7.2 mi. and look for a left turn at the sign for Normandy.

For B&B rates, see Index.

BRIGHAM STREET INN
Salt Lake City, Utah

The restoration and redecoration of this beautiful Victorian mansion, located on the street where Mormon leader Brigham Young had lived, makes an unusual story. What started as a fund-raising designers' showcase, with each room designed and decorated by a different interior designer, ended up being the Brigham Street Inn with award-winning designer rooms.

The fact that owners John and Nancy Pace had close ties with the architectural and interior design community helped. John heads an architectural firm and Nancy has been on the board of the Utah Heritage Foundation, and their purchase of what was a dilapidated but charming old home coalesced with the idea of a designer's showcase to benefit the Heritage Foundation. After an extremely successful show in 1982 with many awards and citations, the Paces purchased all of the furnishings and opened the inn.

There are eight working fireplaces, some with the original tile facings, and there are warm woods everywhere. Golden oak wainscoting highlights the entry, and bird's-eye maple is used in the parlor for the fireplace and a custom-made coffee table, while a cherrywood facade conceals a steel support in a third-floor guest room. In the dining room, with its shuttered windows and large table where guests enjoy a continental breakfast, a 17th-century Tibetan tapestry graces one wall. Local pianists sometimes come in the evening to play the grand piano in the sophisticated living room.

The innkeepers, however, do not rest on the laurels derived from their beautiful surroundings; they provide such special touches as turn-down service, clock radios, private telephones , concealed color TVs, morning newspapers, fresh flowers, and a host of additional helpful services, all aimed at their guests' comfort and enjoyment.

BRIGHAM STREET INN, 1135 East South Temple, Salt Lake City, UT 84102; 801-364-4461. A 9-guestroom (private baths) elegant B&B in a restored and revitalized neighborhood in the heart of Salt Lake City. Complimentary continental breakfast and afternoon coffee or tea. Open all year. Air conditioning, telephones, color TV. Ski areas nearby and sightseeing in Utah's capital city. Children by arrangement. No pets. John and Nancy Pace, Owners.

Directions: From Temple Square in Salt Lake City, drive east on South Temple St. to 1135 E. South Temple.

For B&B rates, see Index.

WASHINGTON SCHOOL INN
Park City, Utah

This is a most remarkable inn, set in the mountains and winter snow country of Utah, yet only forty minutes from downtown Salt Lake City. One of the nation's prime ski centers, it offers all sorts of outdoor activities to be enjoyed in other seasons also.

Washington School was opened in 1889 and survived until 1931, when it was forced to close because of declining enrollment. It subsequently survived a variety of uses over the years, finally falling into a state of disrepair.

Innkeeper Sharon MacQuoid tells me that the beautiful old limestone rock building was purchased in 1983 and has been completely restored and refurbished. It is now listed in the National Register of Historic Places.

Rich hardwoods, locally quarried limestone, and hand-etched glass, fresh flowers, and plants add a touch of elegance, while bright wallpapers and fabrics decorate the attractive guest rooms. Color-coordinated comforters and shams are used on the various-sized beds in the fifteen guest suites, some of which have fireplaces. There's also a jacuzzi, a sauna, and a steam shower for après-ski relaxation.

A hearty breakfast, served in the pleasant dining room, might include anything from a mixed fruit bowl or honeydew melon or spinach quiche with sautéed Polish sausage or corn casserole with ham slices or sticky pecan muffins to orange-baked pears and "Dad's old-fashioned pancakes." There are recommendations for the many restaurants in the area.

WASHINGTON SCHOOL INN, 543 Park Ave., Park City, UT 84060; 800-649-2341 and 800-824-1672. In Utah: 800-824-4761. A 15-guestroom (private baths) newly built country-style contemporary inn in a resort town, 35 min. from the Salt Lake Airport. Breakfast and pre-dinner appetizers included in tariff. Open year-round, except May. Telephones, TV, whirlpool spa, dry sauna, steam shower, ski lockers, and changing room, along with TV security monitor, on premises. First-class downhill and xc skiing, fishing, golf, tennis, hiking, hot-air ballooning nearby. No-fare city bus service to ski areas and other points of interest. No children under 12. No pets. No smoking. Sharon MacQuoid, Innkeeper.

Directions: Take I-80 to Hwy. 224, which becomes Park Ave. after 6 mi. The inn is in the historic district.

For B&B rates, see Index

BARROWS HOUSE
Dorset, Vermont

If you're traveling north or south on Route 7 in Vermont let me make a suggestion: a very pleasant variation, and still in the same basic direction, is to take Route 30, beginning in the south at Manchester and ending in the north at Middlebury. This would include a ride through some most pleasant Vermont villages, such as Dorset, Pawlet, and the Mettowee Valley, past Lake St. Catherine to Poultney (the home of Green Mountain College), and north through Castleton, past Lake Bomoseen, and on to Hubbardton, Sudbury, and Cornwall. Part of the method in my madness is to suggest an overnight stop at Barrows House in Dorset, which is itself a jewel of a village.

The Barrows House is a traditional New England white clapboard building with black shutters, set considerably back from the east side with many varieties of flowers, including phlox, lilies, iris, tulips, and peonies. The entire setting is in a small park with elms, sugar maples, birches, locusts, and various evergreen trees.

One of the front parlors has a welcome fireplace and an entire wall of books. It's a comfortable place in which to relax in any season.

The guest rooms are replete with flowered wallpapers, country and antique furniture, and lots of books and magazines. There are all sizes and kinds of rooms available: some are in the several buildings clustered on the grounds; some are suites with sitting rooms; and all double rooms have private baths.

A full breakfast is served with the B&B rate, including small, light pancakes, either plain, apple, or blueberry, served with Vermont maple syrup; french toast made with homemade bread, eggs any style, and a variety of breads, homemade sourdough english muffins, fresh fruit and juices, and aromatic freshly brewed coffee and a variety of teas.

BARROWS HOUSE, Dorset, VT 05251; 802-867-4455. A 30-guestroom village inn on Rte. 30, 6 mi. north of Manchester. Modified American plan omits lunch; B&B rate on request. Breakfast and dinner served daily to travelers. Swimming pool, sauna, tennis courts, bicycles, xc skiing facilities, including rental equipment and instruction on grounds. Golf, tennis, trout fishing, and alpine skiing nearby. No credit cards. Charles and Marilyn Schubert, Innkeepers.

Directions: From Rte. 7 in Manchester, proceed 6 mi. north on Rte. 30 to Dorset.

For B&B rates, see Index.

BIRCH HILL INN
Manchester, Vermont

Travelers on U.S. 7, one of the main north-south arteries in Vermont, or Route 30, a very interesting road that starts in Brattleboro and cuts across the state in a northwesterly direction, will be delighted to find Birch Hill Inn, just a few moments away from where the two roads intersect in Manchester, Vermont.

It is a beautiful, private country home that has within recent years been converted into an intimate inn. The original part of the house was built in 1790 with harmonizing additions having been made since 1919, and today it is owned by Pat and Jim Lee who offer bed-and-breakfast accommodations, as well as lodgings on the modified American plan.

Bedrooms are characterized by country wallpaper, French prints, hunting prints by Paul Brown, and in two of the large bedrooms there are exposed beams.

A full breakfast is offered including eggs or pancakes served with either sausage or bacon, homemade muffins, and coffee.

Birch Hill has much to recommend it as a vacation accommodation with cross-country skiing, a private trout pond, and a swimming pool on the grounds. There are numerous golf and tennis facilities nearby and alpine skiing at several central Vermont areas.

Arrive in time for dinner, it's a real treat—but be sure to make reservations in advance.

BIRCH HILL INN, Box 346, West Rd., Manchester, Vt. 05254; 802-362-2761. A 5-bedroom (some shared baths) extremely comfortable country home-inn (a cozy cottage nearby) about 5 min. from downtown Manchester Center. Breakfast included in room rate. Dinner offered to houseguests by reservation only. Kitchen closed Weds. and Suns. Open after Christmas to mid-April, and May to late Oct.; 2-night minimum preferred. Swimming pool, xc skiing, trout fishing, and walking trails on grounds. Alpine skiing at major areas, as well as tennis and golf nearby; great biking. No pets. No credit cards. Pat and Jim Lee, Innkeepers.

Directions: From New York City: Taconic Pkwy. to U.S. 22. Turn east from Rte. 22 at NY Rte. 7 to Bennington, Vt. Take Vt. Rte. 7 north to Exit 4 and follow Rte. 30 to Historic 7A. At Center (7A) take Rte. 30 north 2½ mi. to Manchester West Rd. Turn left and look for inn on left, ¾ mi. From Boston: Mass. Tpke. to I-91 to 2nd Brattleboro Exit and continue to Manchester on Rte. 30 to Center at Historic 7A. Go north on Rte. 30—following above directions from this point.

For B&B rates, see Index.

BLACK RIVER INN
Ludlow, Vermont

Abraham Lincoln slept here, sort of. A framed document on a bedroom wall (the Lincoln Room) testifies that the President slept in the spindle-backed double bed that was made in Ohio in 1794. Co-owner John Garton is a woodworker who had been selected to repair the Lincoln bed. Besides the Lincoln Room there are seven titled guest rooms at the Black River Inn, four with private baths.

This Federal brick house, which sits beside the meandering Black River, was built in 1835. Floors in the main house are the original parquet. A ponderous newel post on the main staircase is of hand-carved oak; all the lighting fixtures are from the 1890s with hand-etched glass.

Ludlow is nestled at the foot of the 3,500-foot Okemo Mountain. The banks of the Black River beside the inn are covered with flowers. Waters are stocked four times yearly with trout, making this a fisherman's heaven. Buttermilk Falls, near the inn, rushes into a ten-foot-deep swimming hole, delightfully cool on a summer's day.

The emphasis at Black River Inn is "romance," in decor and ambience, and the innkeepers encourage mostly couples to come there, perfect for a honeymoon. Guests are invited to order breakfast in bed by using the bilingual (French/English) menu card to be hung outside the door before retiring. Homemade muffins or breads and juice, coffee, tea, or hot chocolate are brought steaming hot to the guest room door at the requested hour. There is a large and airy dining room for breakfast, if that is desired. Dinner is served on request to houseguests only.

The comfortable porch faces the river, nice for a quiet chat or siesta. In the common room there are plenty of books and magazines. An 1893 piano and a guitar are there for guests' use. A floor-model skyscope stands at the window facing Okemo, and from the parlor in the winter one can see the skiers.

Besides downhill and cross-country skiing there is ice skating, sledding, and a winter carnival. Ludlow has earned the title "Snow Town, U.S.A."

BLACK RIVER INN, 100 Main St., Ludlow, VT 05149; 802-228-5585. An 8-guestroom Federal brick mansion at the foot of Okemo Mountain beside the Black River. Complimentary continental breakfast. Open all year except April. Trout fishing, golf, inn-to-inn bicycling, alpine and xc skiing. No children. No pets. John Garton and Rosemary Krimbel, Innkeepers.

Directions: Take I-91 to Exit 6 (Bellows Falls) and follow Rte. 103 west to Ludlow.

For B&B rates, see Index.

CAMEL'S HUMP VIEW FARM
Moretown, Vermont

Camel's Hump is a 4,083-foot peak in the Green Mountains of Vermont, much praised by hikers who want above-treeline views for their efforts, and by photographers who see it as one of the state's most picturesque landmarks. This is the view to the west of Camel's Hump View Farm, a country inn with all the comfort and cheer you might expect in a friendly home.

The Mad River flows on the east side of the 1831 farmhouse, and there is a barnyard full of animals. Home-grown and homemade are the adjectives applied to all the good things that appear on the table here. In addition to a full country breakfast, included in the B&B rates, dinner is available (to guests only) at a modest charge.

Camel's Hump Farm is a member of the "Country Inns Along the Trail" that caters to hikers along an 80-mile section of Vermont's Long Trail. You don't have to be quite so ambitious—there are many short trails in the area where you can work up an appetite suitable for Wilma's hearty meals.

In the winter there is cross-country and downhill skiing. All year there is great sightseeing, and arts, crafts, and antique shopping in the villages. You are also near Montpelier, state capital of Vermont; Barre, with its granite quarries open to the public; and Burlington, with its famous Shelbourne Museum.

A variety of accommodations are included in the inn's eight rooms: double beds, twin beds, 4-bunk beds, all with shared baths and a family suite with private bath. There is a bright living room for guests and a dining room where meals are served family style, as well as porches, nooks and crannies. In short, a thoroughly delightful place.

CAMEL'S HUMP VIEW FARM, RFD #1, Rte. 100B, Moretown, VT 05660; 802-496-3614. An 8-guestroom (1 private, 4 shared baths) country inn in Mad River Valley, central Vermont. Full country breakfast included, plus evening meal on request to guests only. Convenient to hiking, skiing, swimming, fishing, shopping, and sightseeing. Member Country Inns Along the Trail. No smoking. No pets. Children over 10 preferred, though younger accommodated in suite. Wilma and Jerry Maynard, Proprietors.

Directions: From I-89, take Exit 9 (Middlesex) and Rte. 100B south. Camel's Hump View Farm will be on your left. From Rte. 100, watch for junction with 100B in Moretown as you drive north. You will now be going east, and the inn is on your right.

For B&B rates, see Index.

THE CAPT. HENRY CHASE HOUSE
Guilford, Vermont

Set in a rural agricultural valley that seems to have been by-passed by time, this 1798 white clapboard farmhouse is a good example of the best of Vermont country architecture.

Because it is really in the country and because there are horses, chickens, goats, and ducks, it is an excellent place for children. There are stables and horseback riding nearby.

There is a handsome old fireplace in the main living room, as well as a spinet and lots of books. There are two separate guest rooms (sharing a bath) on the second floor; for a family traveling with children, there is also an additional small guest room. It is all very homey.

In good weather, breakfast is served on the terrace, screened in on three sides, and during cold weather, in a nice little dining room off the kitchen.

The cross-country skiing is good in this area. I should imagine that it would be absolutely glorious during the winter season.

In summer there is much to do in this section of Vermont and nearby New Hampshire, and it would be lovely to return to such a quiet, pleasant atmosphere. Be sure and call ahead.

THE CAPT. HENRY CHASE HOUSE, West Guilford Rd., Guilford, VT. Mailing address: RFD 4, Box 788, West Brattleboro, VT 05301; 802-254-4114. A 2-guestroom (1 bath) bed-and-breakfast home— extra adjoining guest room available. Open all year. Breakfast only meal served. Convenient for many southern Vermont and New Hampshire cultural, recreational, and historic attractions. Closed Thanksgiving and Christmas. Patrick and Lorraine Ryan, Proprietors.

Directions: Use Exit 2 from I-91, go west on Rte. 9 toward Bennington; on the far side of West Brattleboro look for Greenleaf St. on the left next to Lou's Gulf Station. You are now exactly 6.5 mi. from the Capt. Henry Chase House. Stay on paved road until you notice a large house on the right, across street from a barn at beginning of dirt road. Capt. Henry Chase House is next place on right, past Green River Rd.

For B&B rates, see Index.

THE CHARLESTON HOUSE
Woodstock, Vermont

On a frigid January morning in 1934, Farmer Gilbert allowed the first (American) rope tow to go up his ski hill, and Woodstock hasn't been the same since.

Woodstock is famed not only for its natural beauty but also for its many handsome homesteads: elegant brick Greek Revivals; graceful, white clapboards; some gingerbread Victorians.

One of these, the Charleston House, listed in the National Register of Historic Places, is run by a charming couple who are ski aficionados and architecture buffs. Laird and Betsy Bradley have painstakingly created a luxurious inn out of a neglected homestead. They have used the rigid standard for historic restoration but have softened it with peachy pink walls, Chinese rugs, and the flowers, books, and paintings one would find in any elegant home. A striking portrait of the lissome Betsy graces the dining room behind the Queen Anne mahogany table, where breakfast is served each morning. "Laird is a trained chef, so I let him do all the cooking," Betsy remarks in soft Southern tones that explain the name of the inn. Breakfast hour is flexible, to suit the skiers' early runs, and offers specialties like seafood omelet or apple or Grand Marnier pancakes and, of course, grits.

Each of the cozy bedrooms has lots of pillows, comfy comforters, good reading lamps, and a name. Most of the beds are queen-sized four-posters, but one room, named "Good Friends," has four-poster twin beds.

The art of innkeeping is in making the guest feel at home. The Bradleys have done this with tiny bouquets placed in quiet corners, platters of fresh fruit bedside, herbal shampoos and shower caps in the bath, and an evening treat of a homemade, chocolate-dipped meringue for each guest.

THE CHARLESTON HOUSE, 21 Pleasant St. (Rte. 4), Woodstock, VT 05091; 802-457-3843. A 7-guestroom (private baths) 1835 Greek Revival homestead, 3 min. from the center of Woodstock. Complimentary full breakfast. Open Memorial Day weekend to mid-Nov. and Thanksgiving to mid-April. HBO on TV in common room. An easy drive to 6 major alpine ski areas; xc skiing close by. Golf, tennis, fishing, hiking, biking. Many art galleries and antique shops. Hood Art Museum and Hopkins Center at Dartmouth College in nearby Hanover, N.H. No children under 6. No pets. Laird and Betsy Bradley, Hosts.

Directions: From I-93 or I-91, take I-89 north to Exit 1, turning left to Rte. 4. Continue approx. 10 mi. to Woodstock Village.

For B&B rates, see Index.

THE COLONIAL HOUSE
Weston, Vermont

Travelers will find the Colonial House ideal, not only because the village of Weston is one of the prettiest in Vermont, nor because they can walk out the door, put on their cross-country skis, and start off on 150 miles of trail, but also because of the food. The Nunnikhoven family believes in feeding guests well and often.

Hikers, bikers, and skiers will find hot cider and cheese and crackers waiting in the big, comfortable living room. Tea and home-baked goodies are ready for the relax-by-the-fire crowd. There are memorable dinners prepared only for guests, with such things as Savoury Soup and Burgundy Berry Pie. Breakfasts are nothing short of amazing: five kinds of hot cereal served with butter and maple syrup; eleven ingredients to combine at will in the omelets, fresh-baked breads, berry or fruit pancakes. "We don't need alarm clocks," John says. "The fragrance of Betty's early morning baking brings everyone downstairs on the double."

There are six simple rooms with shared baths in the old inn, and a modest motel wing with private baths adds facilities, if not atmosphere. Either way, you share the Nunnikhoven hospitality, which includes advice on the sights, shopping, and outdoor activities available; the schedule of the famous Weston Playhouse in summer. They can also put you in touch with local professional hiking and ski touring leaders and arrange inn-to-inn trail trips.

THE COLONIAL HOUSE, Rte. 100, Box 138BBA, Weston, VT 05161; 802-824-6286. A 6-guestroom (2 baths) bed-and-breakfast inn (9 bedrooms with private baths in the motel) south of Weston village. Afternoon tea and/or cider included, along with breakfast, in the rate; dinners also served to guests. Open all year. Hiking and xc skiing at the door; downhill skiing nearby; all village amenities nearby, as well as the Weston Priory. No pets. Betty, John and David Nunnikhoven, Proprietors.

Directions: Take Exit 6 from Hwy. I-91, then Rtes. 103 and 11 to Rte. 100. Go north towards Weston. The Colonial House will be on your right 1½ mi. south of the village.

For B&B rates, see Index.

DARCROFT'S SCHOOLHOUSE
Wilmington, Vermont

When snow is on the ground, this is one of the most popular areas in the Green Mountain State, because there are several downhill ski areas, all within a very short distance, including Mount Snow and Haystack.

Darcroft's Schoolhouse is about four miles north of the crossroads of Routes 9 and 100, and is located on the west side of Route 100. It is indeed a former schoolhouse of sturdy construction, and today its utilitarian lines serve the purpose of housing a very pleasant bed-and-breakfast guest house.

On the first floor, where valley scholars had formerly learned their reading, writing, and arithmetic, guests enjoy a common room with a low-beamed ceiling and a raised-hearth fireplace that is big enough for everybody to gather around it and become acquainted. There is also a guest room with a private bath. Upstairs, there are two guest rooms with a shared bath, and also a sort of informal dormitory arrangement that works out well if you're traveling with kids.

Proprietress Doris Meadowcroft offers a continental breakfast every morning to guests, and kitchen privileges are also available for preparing the evening meal, should that be desirable.

DARCROFT'S SCHOOLHOUSE, Wilmington, VT 05363; 802-464-2631. An 1837 one-room schoolhouse converted to a 3-guestroom and dormitory guest house on Rte. 100 just a few miles south of Mt. Snow. Open year-round. Continental breakfast included with the price of the room and kitchen privileges offered for the evening meal. Convenient to major downhill ski areas and excellent xc skiing; also golf, tennis, swimming, antiquing, backroading, and walking. Kennel facilities for pets nearby. Doris Meadowcroft, Proprietress.

Directions: Drive 4 mi. north on Rte. 100 from the center of Wilmington and look for the sign on the left side of the road.

For B&B rates, see Index.

1811 HOUSE
Manchester Village, Vermont

It could be the home of a Colonial gentleman of means, surrounded with reminders of his English past. It could be, but it isn't. The 1811 House is an elegant bed-and-breakfast inn where guests may feel at home among the beautiful appointments—handsome American and English antique furnishings, oriental rugs, fine paintings, porcelains, and objets d'art.

Each of the eleven guest rooms, all with private baths, has been given a distinctive treatment—three have working fireplaces, several have canopied or four-poster beds. The bedroom of an earlier owner, Mary Lincoln Isham, Lincoln's granddaughter, has a marble shower and a porch overlooking the Equinox golf course. Even the bathrooms are all different. Telephones and TVs are available for the rooms, if desired.

Mary and Jack Hirst go all out on the full English breakfast they offer. Beginning with fresh-squeezed orange juice and fresh fruit in season, the menu might have anything from eggs with bacon to kippers to chicken livers, accompanied by grilled tomatoes, mushrooms, sautéed apple rings, fried bread, and home fries. The huge eggs come (within a day of laying) from a local farm, and the jams come from Clearbrook Farm in Ohio.

I could go on about the authenticity and luxury of the period decor and furnishings, or describe the reproduction of an Early American tavern with its pewter mugs, horse brasses, and carriage lamps—but more important is Jack's comment that informality is the rule, and this is the kind of place where guests can wander into the kitchen to make themselves a cup of tea, or kick off their shoes in the library and curl up with a good book.

1811 HOUSE, Manchester Village, VT 05254; 802-362-1811. An 11-guestroom beautifully restored Federal inn adjacent to the Equinox golf course in a bustling Vermont village. Full English breakfast included in the cost of the room. Open year-round. Golf, tennis, fishing, backroading, antiquing, biking, xc and downhill skiing nearby. Not suitable for children under 16. No pets. Mary and Jack Hirst; Pat and Jeremy David, Innkeepers.

Directions: From New York City: Taconic Pkwy. to U.S. 22. Turn east from Rte. 22 to N.Y. Rte. 7 and continue to Bennington, Vt. In Bennington, take Vt. Historic Rte. 7A to Manchester Village. Inn is on the village green next to the Congregational Church.

For B&B rates, see Index.

THE GOVERNOR'S INN
Ludlow, Vermont

Although this handsomely restored and preserved Victorian mansion (circa 1890) has B&B rates, it is in reality a village inn that also offers a modified American plan, including a full breakfast, afternoon tea, and dinner. B&B guests are also offered afternoon tea. Guests enjoy the magnificent hand-painted slate-and-mirrored fireplaces and crackling fires on chilly winter nights and the refreshing mountain breezes in summer. The view of Okemo Mountain from the living room is especially spectacular during the fall foliage season.

Embroidered duvets, Oriental rugs, fragrant potpourri, and Marble family antiques may be found in each of the eight guest rooms, all of which have private baths. One room is graced with a 100-year-old brass four-poster bed. Early morning Victorian tray service is also offered.

After I enjoyed one of their six-course dinners, I'd suggest that B&B guests plan on arriving in time for the evening meal. Breakfast and dinner are served in two beautifully appointed dining rooms. One has a wonderful antique Crawford wood stove. The staff wear charming handmade Victorian and Edwardian "costumes" that underscore the Victorian atmosphere that permeates the inn. Don't forget to order a gourmet picnic. It will be ready for you after breakfast in a take-along Vermont-made hamper. A bit of romance in the country.

Charlie and Deedy enjoy sharing the treasures they have collected in their world travels. Guests are likely to discover they are having tea in a cup from France or using a spoon from Egypt or sleeping under a lace coverlet from England.

THE GOVERNOR'S INN, 86 Main St., Ludlow, VT 05149; 802-228-8830. An 8-guestroom village inn (private baths) in a bustling central Vermont town. Open year-round. B&B rates available. Modified American plan includes breakfast, tea, and dinner. Conveniently located for many Vermont historical, recreational, and cultural attractions. Okemo Ski Area, 1 mi. distant; Stratton, Killington, Bromley, and others within 30 min.; also xc skiing horseback riding, biking, golf, hiking, and antiquing abound. Charlie and Deedy Marble, Innkeepers.

Directions: From I-91, take Exit 6 and follow Rte. 103 to Ludlow.

For B&B rates, see Index.

GREEN MOUNTAIN TEA ROOM
South Wallingford, Vermont

Built in 1792, this historic house was originally a stagecoach stop and tavern on the old stage road from Bennington to Rutland. Here the driver would exchange his tired horses for fresh ones, and most likely have a convivial visit in the tavern to catch up on local gossip.

Herb and Peg Barker are the hosts these days, and offer five bedrooms to overnight guests. Three of the bedrooms were created out of the former upstairs ballroom and all have been furnished in an up-country Vermont manner.

A pleasant tradition at this guest house on Route 7 is afternoon tea, which includes fifteen varieties of tea in colorful individual pots, along with homemade desserts or Vermont cheese and crackers.

If you're staying overnight you'll be tempted to stay longer after you see the view of Otter Creek from the bedrooms in the back and learn that there's trout fishing, hiking, skiing, and Appalachian Trail walks nearby.

Breakfast and lunch are served here, all with homecooked flavor.

South Wallingford is on Route 7, the direct north-south road from southern New England to Canada, wending its way up the west side of Vermont.

GREEN MOUNTAIN TEA ROOM & GUEST HOUSE, South Walling-ford, Vt. 05773; 802-446-2611. A 5-bedroom guest house in the valley of Otter Creek. Open year-round. Restaurant open 7:30 A.M.-4:00 P.M.; closed Mondays and Tuesdays. Breakfast, lunch, and afternoon tea served. Canoeing, fishing, swimming, picnicking on grounds. Backroading, skiing, antiquing, and other Vermont diversions nearby. No credit cards. Herb and Peg Barker, Proprietors.

Directions: South Wallingford is just a few moments south of Wallingford on Rte. 7.

For Lodging rates, see Index.

354

HICKORY RIDGE HOUSE
Putney, Vermont

Almost without being told you could guess this handsome brick house had been inhabited by a scholar. And so it was no surprise to learn that Hickory Ridge House, whose main section was built in 1808, had once been the home of the president of Windham College.

There is a high-ceilinged library bursting with books; in the very spacious upstairs hall sits a small harpsichord. The floors, wide-planked tamarack, a soft and rare wood, are polished to a fare-thee-well. The antique glass in the Palladian windows has the charming occasional giveaway bubble, and the guest room doors have their original latches.

The spacious guest rooms are done in interesting colors and furnished in antiques, and two of them have large working fire-places. Innkeepers Sharon and David Brostrom will provide futons when they are desired.

Putney, besides being a mecca for schools like the Putney School and Landmark, has wonderful apple orchards. Breakfast usually includes an apple, baked, sauced, or in a muffin.

A short stroll from the house is an ol' swimmin' hole and lovely vistas on the twenty-three rolling acres. There are barns to explore, and of course there are always the wonderful Vermont country roads. In winter, there is cross-country skiing right from the back door.

HICKORY RIDGE HOUSE, Hickory Ridge Rd., R.D. 3, Putney, VT 05346; 802-387-5709. A 6-guestroom (private and shared baths) handsome brick Federal house in southern Vermont, near the N.H. border. Complimentary continental breakfast. Open 365 days. Xc trails on grounds; lessons and rentals nearby. Near Landmark School and College and Putney School. Marlboro and Yellow Barn Music Festivals, community theater, hiking, biking, spa and sauna, and shopping in the numerous Putney crafts shops nearby. No pets. Sharon and David Brostrom, Innkeepers.

Directions: From I-91, take Exit 4 into center of Putney; turn left at Town Hall and continue north. Go up hill 1.7 mi. Turn left onto Hickory Ridge Rd.; 4th house on left.

For B&B rates, see Index.

HILL FARM INN
Arlington, Vermont

U.S. 7, which starts in southern Connecticut and goes north through the Berkshires of Massachusetts and on up to the very top of Vermont, is one of the principal roads in the East that leads to vacation and holiday destinations.

In Arlington, Vermont, Historic Route 7A is particularly attractive, threading its way between Mt. Equinox on the west and undulating forest and farmland on the east. In Sunderland, just north of Arlington, there is a small sign directing the traveler to the right on a country road, past the Union Church, to Hill Farm Inn with its broad, pleasant porch and dairy farm and herd in the rear.

My grandmother didn't live in Vermont, but if she had, I wish it could have been in a house like this one, owned by George and Joanne Hardy and Cathy Harper. As you step inside, a welcome feeling pervades the light and airy dining room with its sturdy wood tables decorated with pots of African violets. I didn't have breakfast, but I can imagine what a cheerful and fortifying experience it must be with oatmeal or other cereals, eggs, bacon or sausage patties, toast and homemade jams, or perhaps George's french toast or pancakes with maple syrup. And it's all included with the room rate. You might decide to stay for one of Joanne or Cathy's special dinners, which include vegetables from George's garden, homemade soups and breads and desserts, along with a hearty main dish.

The guest rooms in the main house and in the adjacent 1790 farmhouse are neat and comfortable, and a basket of apples and a jar of homemade jam welcome the newly arrived guest. Five of the eleven guest rooms have private baths.

HILL FARM INN, R.R. 2, Box 2015, Arlington, VT 05250; 802-375-2269. An 11-guestroom farmhouse with 5 rooms in guest house (5 private baths). Open year-round. Modified American plan. B&B guest may make arrangements for dinner in advance, if desired. Convenient to all of the recreational, cultural, and natural attractions in the area. Pets allowed in cabins only. Please, no smoking in guest rooms. George and Joanne Hardy and Cathy Harper, Innkeepers.

Directions: Coming north, follow Historic Rte. 7A to Arlington, and about 3 mi. north, watch for signpost on the right. (The road is just beyond "Christmas Days.") Coming south on 7A, look for road on the left just beyond "Basketville."

For B&B rates, see Index.

THE HUGGING BEAR INN
Chester, Vermont

Of all the stories Georgette and Paul Thomas tell about the inn, my favorite concerns the little girl who carried twenty bears up to her room for a good night's sleeping, then returned them all to the Hugging Bear Shoppe before 9:00 A.M., the next morning. "Absolutely within our rules, such as they are," Georgette says.

None of this paltry "Three Bears plus Goldilocks" either. There are bears at the windows, bears on the beds, bears in the chairs and one that is a life-sized floor mattress by a New York artist. All the bears are available for hugging, and the ten percent discount in the shop for inn guests lasts a full month after departure. "So many people telephone a week later and say they simply *must* have that bear." The proprietors understand the feeling.

The inn is a delightful Victorian structure, built in 1850, and later embellished with a tower and bow windows (all the better for bears to peek from). Each of the six bedrooms is different, though each has its share of bears as well as a private bath.

Breakfast is a full country repast, with whole-wheat, sunflower seed pancakes the house specialty. Honey is available, but in Vermont most guests opt for maple syrup.

Besides being a warm, fun place for adults, the Hugging Bear is going to be a part of the pleasant memories of childhood for a lot of youngsters fortunate enough to spend some magical nights in Bear Country, Vermont style. The Thomases belong to the Good Bears of the World, an international organization that provides teddy bears for children and the elderly in hospitals and homes.

Teddy puppet shows throughout the day and late afternoon refreshments are further delights for young and old.

THE HUGGING BEAR INN, Main St., Chester, VT 05143; 802-875-2412. A 6-guestroom (all private baths) bed-and- breakfast inn and shoppe on Rte. 11, 8 mi. from Springfield, Vt. Breakfast (full) the only meal served, but there are restaurants nearby. Open all year. Antique and craft stores all around; skiing nearby. Children welcome (cribs and teddy bears available). Special advance arrangements necessary for pets. No smoking. Georgette and Paul Thomas, Proprietors.

Directions: From I-91 take Exit 6. Go north on Rte. 103, which becomes Main St., Rte. 11, in Chester.

For B&B rates, see Index.

THE INN ON THE COMMON
Craftsbury Common, Vermont

The village of Craftsbury Common in Vermont's North East Kingdom was founded in 1789. It's one of Vermont's most remarkable hill towns. The most impressive feature is the Common which dwarfs the surrounding old homes, church, and Academy. A white-rail fence surrounds the Common area.

The inn is composed of three restored 19th-century houses, all handsomely wallpapered and furnished with antiques, original and folk art, hooked rugs, and colorful custom quilts. There are all varieties and sizes of rooms, some with fireplaces; many with private baths. Well-stocked bookshelves and a library of films on tape offer quiet entertainment.

Basically, the inn is on the American plan because there is all manner of sports, recreation, and entertainment available in all four seasons. However, there are a few B&B accommodations available. I would strongly advise telephoning considerably ahead in order not to be disappointed.

Big breakfasts are the order of the day, with a full measure of approval from the Colonial portraits in the dining room. It's possible to order almost anything, and the omelets are especially good.

THE INN ON THE COMMON, Craftsbury Common. Vt. 05827· 802-586-9619. A 17-room (most with private baths) resort-inn in a remote Vermont town 35 mi. from Montpelier. Modified American plan omits lunch. Breakfast and dinner served to houseguests only. Open all year. Attended pets allowed. Swimming, tennis, croquet, xc skiing, snowshoeing, on grounds. Golf, lake swimming, sailing, canoeing, fishing, xc and downhill skiing, skating, hiking, and nature walks nearby. Michael and Penny Schmitt, Innkeepers.

Directions: From Exit 7, I-89N, take Rte. 2 east to Rte. 14 north until 8 mi. north of Harwick. Watch for marked right hand turn, go 2 mi. to inn. From Canada and points north, use Exit 26 and I-91 and follow Rte. 58W to Irasburg. Then Rte. 14 southbound 12 mi. to marked left turn, 3 mi. to inn.

For B&B rates, see Index.

INWOOD MANOR
East Barnet, Vermont

East Barnet is quite a ways north in Vermont, although still south of the famous North East Kingdom. The Connecticut River separates most of Vermont and New Hampshire, but at this point veers off to the east, and travelers along Route 5, which runs parallel to I-91, are treated to the sights along the Passumpsic River.

Inwood Manor is just over the bridge at East Barnet to the east of Route 5, and was once the main site for the world's largest croquet factory. It is situated on a plateau overlooking the river and it's a very short walk to the delightful waterfalls.

The hosts here are Peter Embarrato and Ron Kaczor, who are both Vermont transplants and feel that they've finally found a home. It's obvious that they've put a great deal of work and consideration into this building whose original integrity is now preserved for many generations to come.

The nine guest rooms all have shared baths and have been furnished with early attic beds and tables and generous helpings of good humor. It is old Vermont come to life again.

It's worth noting that travelers can be accommodated for lunch and dinner if advance notice is given.

Included with the room rate is a continental breakfast featuring home-baked breads and homemade jams. A full Vermont breakfast is available at an additional charge.

The Inwood Manor is one of the inns on the upper Connecticut River that is cooperating in a canoeing program, making it possible for participants to enjoy the river and float from inn to inn spending a night in each, if desired. A telephone call or letter will fill in more details. A 2½ acre pond provides swimming in summer and ice skating in the winter.

INWOOD MANOR, East Barnet, VT 05821; 802-633-4047. A 9-guest-room inn (shared baths) in one of the most beautiful natural sections of Vermont, quite convenient to both the White and Green Mountains and all of the recreational opportunities. A light lunch and dinner are served upon advance request. Open year-round. Closed Christmas. Swimming, ice skating, tobogganing on grounds. Xc and downhill skiing nearby. No pets. No credit cards. Peter Embarrato and Ron Kaczor, Innkeepers.

Directions: From I-91 use Exit 18 (Barnet), follow Rte. 5 north and turn east on the Lower Waterford Road across the railroad tracks. Turn left at inn sign.

For B&B rates, see Index.

IRASBURG GREEN BED & BREAKFAST
Irasburg, Vermont

The upper section of Vermont has been traditionally called the North East Kingdom, and for the traveler in search of a unique type of independent remoteness some of the villages in this part of the state are choice discoveries.

Such a discovery is Irasburg, where there are some extremely interesting late 18th- and early 19th-century houses built around a village green, and where the town meeting place is the general store.

To add to the intrigue even more, the Irasburg Green Bed & Breakfast is owned by a most interesting German woman named Steffi Heuss, who has a lively sense of humor, is an excellent conversationalist, and, as the creator of silver jewelry, has a more-than-average interest in crafts. Furthermore, she maintains a very brisk business in local crafts, which are displayed throughout the house.

Steffi has three second-floor bedrooms which share the family bathroom on the first floor, so it is a good idea to bring a bathrobe. The season starts around May first and ends about the middle of October.

The breakfast is most generous with a choice of bacon, eggs, toast, juice, and coffee. This would be a good basis for the vigorous summertime activities in the area, which include swimming, hiking, fishing and golf. Steffi will serve the evening meal on request.

Irasburg is not for the traveler who has become accustomed to being pampered and spoiled by exotic accommodations. It is a slice of Vermont the way it was more than 100 years ago, but I think visitors would be most intrigued, not only with the village and the accommodations, but also with the proprietress.

IRASBURG GREEN BED & BREAKFAST, Irasburg, Vt. 05845; 802-754-6012. A 3-bedroom bed-and-breakfast home in one of the remote villages of Vermont's North East Kingdom. Full breakfast included in the cost of the accommodations. Open May 1 to mid-Oct. Plenty of outdoor activity available nearby. No pets. Steffi Heuss, Proprietress.

Directions: Leave I-91 at Orleans, follow Rte. 58 to Irasburg. House is located on village green and includes sign in front for craft shop.

For B&B rates, see Index.

THE JACKSON HOUSE
Woodstock, Vermont

George Washington didn't sleep here, but Gloria Swanson did, in 1948.

The Jackson House is a three-story Victorian mansion set on three manicured acres about a mile and a half outside Woodstock, sometimes called "the most beautiful village in America."

In 1890 Wales Johnson, a sawmill owner, decided to build the finest house in Woodstock. He used different woods in every bedroom—cherry, basswood, bird's-eye maple, oak. There is exquisite detailing in sills, doorways, and dados throughout the inn; a solid cherry bannister runs the length of the main staircase.

In a labor of love, which has taken more than two years, the present owners and innkeepers, Bruce McIlveen and Jack Foster, have refinished every wooden surface, polishing it to the original luster, and furnishing the house with antiques.

Jack proudly pointed out to me other unique touches, like the ceiling fans in each bedroom and the extra-large stall showers in every redesigned bath. Messrs. Foster and McIlveen put an emphasis on cleanliness; you feel as though you could eat off those polished floors!

Bruce filled me in on the details about food. Each morning there is a full breakfast; the menu changes daily and always includes fruit in season but with a flair, like the honeydew melon with prosciutto served with grapes and kiwi. On Sundays, when guests tend to be at their most relaxed, the breakfast is even more elaborate. French toast, Santa Fe or cheese blintzes, or eggs grisanti might be featured.

THE JACKSON HOUSE at Woodstock, Rte. 4 West, Woodstock, VT 05091; 802-457-2065. A 9-guestroom (private baths) Victorian inn in a picture-book New England village, about 15 mi. west of Hanover, N.H. Complimentary full breakfast and evening libations. Picnic lunch available. Open mid-May to Nov. and mid-Dec. to April. Books and VCR with film library on premises. Convenient to major alpine and xc ski trails; hiking, swimming, tennis, golf, fishing, horseback riding, polo matches, community theater, antiquing, and good restaurants nearby. No children under 10. No pets. No smoking. Bruce McIlveen and Jack Foster, Innkeepers.

Directions: From I-91 or I-95, take I-89 north to Exit 1 in Vermont. Turn left on Rte. 4. Continue approx. 10 mi. to Woodstock Village.

For B&B rates, see Index.

JUNIPER HILL INN
Windsor, Vermont

Juniper Hill Inn is not your run-of-the-mill accommodation. For example, stately white columns greet the visitor to this sizable mansion, which includes, among other things, fifteen guest rooms, twelve baths, and thirteen fireplaces. It was built by Maxwell Evarts, who was a descendant of one of the signers of the Declaration of Independence.

Jim and Krisha Pennino have owned the inn since 1984 and have been busy redecorating it to the way it was when the Evarts family lived here for over forty years. It is located high on a hill a mile north of town in a very private setting, amid trees that are ablaze with color in the fall, and with a commanding view of Mount Ascutney, the highest monadnock east of the Mississippi River.

It might be called a "mansion in transition," and like a really good thoroughbred racehorse that hasn't raced in a few years, it is now being brought back up to peak condition. At the time of my visit, guest rooms and baths were being redecorated and furnished with antiques the Penninos have collected.

The morning sun streams into the informal dining room where breakfast, prepared by Jim, is served. He makes apple pancakes or french toast to go with eggs, juice, and coffee or tea.

Windsor is literally the birthplace of Vermont and has the longest covered bridge in the United States. There's much to see and do of historic and cultural interest in the area.

JUNIPER HILL INN, R.R. 1, Box 79, Juniper Hill Rd., Windsor, VT 05089; 802-674-5273. A 15-guestroom (10 private baths) bed-and-breakfast mansion. Full breakfast. Open from late April to early Nov. and late Dec. to mid-March; also Thanksgiving weekend. Conveniently located for visits to the Vermont State Crafts Center, St. Gaudens National Historic Site, Mt. Ascutney ski area, and Vermont and New Hampshire back roads and antique shops. Jim and Krisha Pennino, Proprietors.

Directions: From Rte. 5 turn west on Juniper Hill Rd. (next to animal clinic); go ¼ mi. and then take left fork, signposted "Juniper Terrace."

For B&B rates, see Index.

THE LAKE HOUSE AT LAKE FAIRLEE
Post Mills, Vermont

Sunday morning breakfast at the Lake House (just a few steps from the shores of Lake Fairlee in the village of Post Mills) features delicious, made-from-scratch waffles with real Vermont maple syrup, and also homemade muffins and scones. In the summertime guests can take breakfast on the porch and enjoy the wonderfully clear Vermont air and verdant countryside.

Originally built as an inn in 1870, the Lake House's tradition of innkeeping is being continued by Charles and Betty Pemberton.

The antiques and furnishings in some of the bedrooms are really quite exceptional. I saw a platform rocker, many tufted bedspreads, and flowered wallpapers that reflect a real country feeling.

There are eleven bedrooms, two with private bathrooms, in this old Vermont country house. There are lots of opportunities to sit in the living room and become acquainted with other guests, many of whom may be staying longer than just one night. There are many activities nearby, including golf, tennis, boating, fishing, and swimming in the lake. Dartmouth College sports and cultural activities are just a few minutes away as well.

A new restaurant and tea room will provide additional meals and teatime treats.

With numerous country roads, cyclists may enjoy easy scenic rides around the shores of Lake Fairlee and Lake Morey. Scenic flights over Vermont can be enjoyed from Post Mills Airport, only a short walk from the inn. Just watching the sailplanes and airplanes come and go can be fun, too.

THE LAKE HOUSE, Rte. 244, P.O. Box 65, Post Mills, VT 05058; 802-333-4025. An 11-guestroom (2 with private bath) bed-and-breakfast inn just off I-91 a few miles north of Norwich, Vermont. Open all year. Many outdoor activities and country recreation available including bike riding, horseback riding, apple picking, downhill and xc skiing, snowshoeing, snowmobiling, and ice fishing available. The countryside has many covered bridges and leisurely drives. No pets. Charles and Betty Pemberton, Innkeepers.

Directions: From I-91 take exit No. 14 west, drive approx. 7 mi. on Rte. 113, turn right ¼ mi. beyond Baker's General Store on Rte. 244 and go exactly 9/10 mi. to the inn on the left.

For B&B rates, see Index.

LAKE ST. CATHERINE INN
Poultney, Vermont

Lake St. Catherine is another of the wonderful places in the world in which I have a proprietary interest. When my sons were growing up we spent many summers and many Thanksgivings and Christmases on the lake, which is one of the most beautiful and purest in Vermont. It is circled with a ring of low hills and the lake water provides marvelous swimming, canoeing, fishing, and sailing. We all learned to water-ski and sail on it.

That's why I was delighted when I learned from Patricia Marks and Raymond Endlich, the innkeepers of the Lake St. Catherine Inn, that although it is basically a modified American plan inn, special arrangements can be made for bed-and-breakfast guests. Be sure to indicate this when you make your reservation.

The inn is at the lakeside and has all of the water sports mentioned above.

The thirty-five guest rooms all have private baths and some of them have very pleasant lake views. It's a great place for young and old alike. One diversion that has grown in popularity in recent years is bicycle touring, which provides more intimate views of the wonderful scenery.

Besides the rooms in the main section of the inn, there are cottages that are spread out among the campuslike grounds.

On the basis of the wonderful aromas coming from the dining room, I would advise anybody staying even for one night to arrive in time for dinner.

LAKE ST. CATHERINE, Poultney, VT 05764; 802-287-9347. A 35-guestroom resort inn on beautiful Lake St. Catherine in western Vermont. All rooms have private baths. Open May to Oct. A full breakfast is included. Modified American plan, but arrangements can be made for bed and breakfast with advance notification. All of the Vermont summer and winter attractions are nearby, including excellent fishing, xc skiing, backroading, swimming, tennis, bicycling, antiquing, and the like. No pets. No credit cards. Patricia Marks and Raymond Endlich, Innkeepers.

Directions: From I-87 (Northway) take Exit 20. Go east on Rte. 149 to Rte. 4 at Ft. Ann. Take left on Rte. 4 for 4 mi. and then right on Rte. 22 (across bridge) for 9 mi. to Rte. 22-A. Turn left at flasher, and right over bridge 2 mi. to Rte. 149 at red flasher which is Granville. Turn left on Rte. 149 for 2 mi. to Rte. 30 (flasher). Turn left on Rte. 30 and proceed 6 mi. to turn-off on the left to the inn.

For B&B rates, see Index.

LAREAU FARM COUNTRY INN
Waitsfield, Vermont

"We had a country wedding last week right over there in the meadow," Susan Easley said, pointing to a particularly lush part of the forty-five green acres that belong to the inn. Lucky bride and groom, I thought, to begin married life knee-deep in daisies.

More commonly, visitors arrive to enjoy the pleasure of all four seasons in the Mad River Valley that runs north and south along the Green Mountains near Sugarbush. In winter, there are three major downhill ski areas minutes away, and that meadow is a great start for cross-country and for horsedrawn sleigh rides available through the inn. In summer, consider the fact that the Mad River runs right through the inn's front yard, and the fishing is easy. Autumn in Vermont is so special it has become a cliché, and as for spring—well, in spring there are wildflowers and fresh maple sugar.

This 150-year-old farm-cum-inn is on the State Register of Historic Buildings with a barn that is officially listed as one of the few wood stanchion dairy types left in the state.

Traveling families will find the rooms bright and sunny, each individually decorated with interesting old pieces and homemade quilts. There is a homey living room for guests, and rocking chairs on the porch. A full country breakfast is served in the informal dining room, and when you come back to the inn after a day of activity, Susan and Dan will probably offer you a nice cup of tea of après-ski hors d'oeuvres.

LAREAU FARM COUNTRY INN, Box 563, Rte. 100, Waitsfield, VT 05673; 802-496-4949. A 10-guestroom (4 with private bath) bed-and-breakfast inn in Sugarbush Valley, Vt. Full country breakfast included; dinners on occasion; picnics on request. Many excellent restaurants in the area. Open all year. Skiing, swimming, canoeing, fishing, tennis, horseback riding, shopping all nearby. Crib and rollaways available. No smoking in bedrooms. No pets. Susan and Dan Easley, Proprietors.

Directions: Rte. 100 runs north and south in the middle of Vermont. The Lareau Farm Country Inn is set back on the western side of the road, and there is a large sign. It is south of the Rte. 17 junction, ¼ mi. from the Waitsfield shopping areas.

For B&B rates, see Index.

MAPLE CREST FARM
Cuttingsville, Vermont

This is the Vermont you've always dreamed about—a farm in a stand of maple trees on a country road with a sweeping view of the valley that has been in the same family for five generations.

The parlor, bedrooms, dining room, and kitchen are like a Norman Rockwell illustration. Sharing space with dozens of family photographs, diplomas, and hundreds of well-read books and magazines are blue ribbons won by various members of the Smith family in recent years for canning, vegetables, and cattle-raising at the Vermont State Fair.

The furnishings in this farmhouse reflect the five generations that have grown up here. There are wonderful high beds, platform rockers, old prints and paintings, and many colorful quilts.

Besides the bedrooms there are also efficiency apartments with separate accommodations for children, if you prefer. Each has its own entrance leading to the lawn and the great barn where there are over a hundred cows.

Breakfast is the time when everyone sits around the big table in the kitchen and, while Donna Smith turns out endless stacks of pancakes and plates of scrambled eggs, guests share the table with members of the family, including three strapping sons.

One of the most interesting times to visit would be during maple sugaring time which starts around the 18th of March and runs for a month. Chances are there would be some cross-country skiing as well.

When you visit Maple Crest Farm be prepared to wish you could have stayed longer.

MAPLE CREST FARM, Cuttingsville, Vt. 05738; 802-492-3367. (An American Bed & Breakfast host.) A beautiful old 6-bedroom Vermont farmhouse with two efficiency apartments. Ideal for longer stays. Open year-round. A full breakfast is the only meal served; however, there are good restaurants nearby for the evening meal. Downhill and xc skiing, backroading, walking, antiquing abound. No credit cards. No pets. Donna Smith, Proprietor.

Directions: Cuttingsville is on Rte. 103 between Ludlow and Rutland. Once in Cuttingsville turn east on a country road that runs next to the green bridge in the middle of town. Drive about two miles to the top of the hill where you can see the red buildings of the farm and a sign on the side of the barn.

For B&B rates, see Index.

MAY FARM LODGE
Waterbury Center, Vermont

It was the "Antiques" sign that caught my eye from the road, then the "1790" on the house that made me turn around and pull into the parking area of the May Farm Lodge. I was traveling north on the Stowe Road (also known as Route 100) out of Waterbury, and was almost too distracted by the Green Mountain scenery to notice things close at hand. Fortunately, I glanced to the right at the serendipitous moment.

Antiques do not end at the door of the crowded shop. They spill into the kitchen, up the stairs, and through the four big bedrooms. However, you don't have to be a dedicated antiquer to enjoy these spacious, sunny quarters, to sit out on the neatly clipped back lawn, or to appreciate the full country breakfast served every morning in the dining room.

The location is excellent, too. The inn is just two miles south of the Stowe town line. Cross that and you are in an area world-famous for its skiing, dining, and shopping. There is golf, hiking, biking, theater, and either a gondola or an automobile ride to the top of Mount Mansfield for the fabulous views. There are galleries and a flea market every Sunday all summer long.

May Farm Lodge doesn't advertise or put out a brochure. Many of the returning guests were directed here in the first place by the pricey inns when they ran out of space. Alas for the big ones, they lost their customers forever to this home-away-from-home.

MAY FARM LODGE, Rte. 100, P.O. Box 161, Waterbury, VT 05677; 802-244-7306. A 4-guestroom (2 shared baths) bed-and-breakfast lodge just south of Stowe in north-central Vermont. Breakfast the only meal served, but it is a full country one. Open year-round. All restaurant, resort, and shopping facilities nearby. Off-street parking. Antique store attached. No pets. No credit cards. During foliage season (mid-Sept. to early Oct.) reserve far in advance. Rose and Joseph Lukowich, Proprietors.

Directions: Rte. 100 is the north-south road that bisects Vermont. If you are coming south from Morrisville, the inn will be on your left about 2 mi. after crossing the Stowe/Waterbury town line. If you are going north (take the Waterbury exit from Hwy. 89), start looking for the inn on your right about 4 mi. out of Waterbury. There is a sign, and the driveway is on Rte. 100.

For B&B rates, see Index.

NORTH HERO HOUSE
North Hero, Vermont

Unlike some of the places mentioned in this book that are not on the road to anywhere, North Hero, Vermont, is on the way to a great many "somewheres."

It is located on North Hero Island on Lake Champlain, just a few miles south of the Canadian border and sixty-five miles south of Montreal. The traveler-in-a-hurry can reach it from New York City in a day's drive by taking the New York State Thruway and the Northway. (See directions below.)

Once arrived, I don't know how anyone could leave without staying at least two days. The North Hero House is an early American Champlain Island inn that has been offering hospitality to travelers since the mid-19th century. It has a magnificent view across Lake Champlain to Mount Mansfield, and has motorboating, canoeing, sailing, a lakeside sauna, swimming, and fishing for the considerable varieties of finny denizens in the lake.

Comfortable guest rooms are to be found in the main house and in several waterside buildings, all painstakingly restored by the owners, Roger Sorg, and his wife, Caroline, along with their now-grown children, David and Lynn.

Guests may enjoy a full Lake Champlain à la carte breakfast of juice or fresh fruit cup, blueberry waffles or eggs with bacon or sausage, bread doughnuts with maple syrup, country-inn french toast, pancakes, or omelets.

Lunch and dinner are also served.

NORTH HERO HOUSE, Champlain Islands, North Hero, VT 05474; 802-372-8237. A 23-guestroom New England resort-inn on North Hero Island in Lake Champlain, 35 mi. north of Burlington and 65 mi. south of Montreal. European plan. Breakfast not included in tariff. Breakfast, lunch, and dinner served daily to travelers. Open from mid-June to mid-Oct. Swimming, fishing, boating, waterskiing, ice-house game room, sauna, bicycles, and tennis on grounds. Horseback riding and golf nearby. No pets. No credit cards. Roger and Caroline Sorg, Innkeepers.

Directions: Travel north from Burlington on I-89, take Exit 17 (Champlain Islands) and drive north on Island Rte. 2 to North Hero. From N.Y. Thruway (87 north), take Exit 39 at Plattsburg and follow signs "Ferry to Vermont." Upon leaving ferry, turn left to Rte. 2, then left again to North Hero. Inn is 15 min. from ferry dock on Rte. 2.

For Lodging rates, see Index.

368

THE OLD BARN INN
West Wardsboro, Vermont

It was the sign on the west side of Route 100 in West Wardsboro that first attracted my attention to this inn and caused me to back up twenty-five yards after I passed it. The sign is actually a painting into which the words, "Old Barn," have been carefully designed.

Investigation proved that this was, indeed, not only a bed- and-breakfast inn, but one that serves dinner as well. It is the result of loving attention and hard work by Denis and Kathy Smith, who manage to have the best of all possible worlds, wintering on the Florida coast, where they maintain a charter boat business and summering here in glorious central Vermont.

The inn is really a barn, built in 1797 and moved to its present location in 1935. Weathered beams and wide floor boards are complimented by antiques, old photographs of the barn in its various stages, and a twelve-foot fireplace, which is an exact duplicate of one found in the Jared Coffin House on Nantucket. There is a deck off the main sitting room affording a glorious view of this hidden valley.

Bedrooms are all furnished in a wonderful Vermontish style, accented by colorful quilts. Kathy refers to the furnishings as "early flea market."

Originally, the Smiths established a restaurant in the barn seven years ago; however, dinner guests came, loved the rooms, and wanted to remain overnight, so it was decided to add the guest bedrooms.

As far as breakfast is concerned, guests are invited to rise at their leisure, come down into the kitchen and cook breakfast themselves. Coffee has been set up in advance as well as homemade breads and juices. There are always plenty of fresh eggs and cereals so guests can fend for themselves.

It may have been the sign that attracted my attention, but I can assure the reader that it is the ambience, the spirit of friendliness and warmth, that would bring me back to this inn many times.

THE OLD BARN INN, Rte. 100, West Wardsboro, VT 05360; 802-896-6100. A 4-guestroom (sharing 2 baths) country inn in the central Vermont fastness. Make-your-own-breakfast is included in the room rate. Dinner is served. Open from the last week of June thru the third week in Oct. Conveniently located to enjoy all of the wonderful summer and fall delights of the Vermont mountains and countryside. Denis and Kathy Smith, Innkeepers.

Directions: West Wardsboro is a few miles north of Mt. Snow on Rte. 100.

For B&B rates, see Index.

PARTRIDGE HILL
Williston, Vermont

Partridge Hill is an ideal bed-and-breakfast home. It sits on the top of a hill with a commanding view of the northern Vermont countryside, Mount Mansfield, and Camel's Hump.

Roger and Sally Bryant (he is the head athletic trainer at the University of Vermont) furnished and decorated their home, including the two guest bedrooms, with quiet good taste. There are many prints, photographs, and watercolors, used to great advantage.

One room has a queen-sized bed, and the other has two single beds. Both of these share a private guest parlor, bath, and private entrance.

Sally serves a typical Vermont breakfast of orange juice, pancakes made with whole-wheat flour or french toast made with Sally's homemade bread, sausage or bacon, their own maple syrup, real cream, and real butter. Even the plates are heated.

In summer, breakfast is often taken on the deck overlooking the beautiful view to the east, and in winter, in the main dining room, where there is a fireplace.

Partridge Hill is ideal for a summer visitor, with the Shelburne Museum close by. During the winter, guests may enjoy cross-country skiing two miles down the road at the Catamount Family Center or downhill skiing at Stowe, only thirty-five minutes away.

PARTRIDGE HILL, 102 Partridge Hill, Williston, VT 05495; 802-878-4741. A 2-guestroom private bed-and-breakfast home located 8 mi. from Burlington and 25 mi. from Stowe. Open year-round. A full breakfast is included in the price of the room. Conveniently located for all the northern Vermont recreational, historical, and cultural activities. Xc skiing on grounds. No smoking, please. Roger and Sally Bryant, Proprietors.

Directions: From Burlington use the Essex Junction, Rte. 2A Exit 12 from I-89. Continue toward Essex Junction to the first traffic light. Turn right on Rte. 2 and continue 2.3 mi. to the Federated Church on the left. Turn right onto Oak Hill Rd. and continue ½ mi. Just past the Thomas Chittenden Health Center, turn right, where the road up to Partridge Hill is clearly marked with a fancy sign. Inn is at the top of the hill.

For B&B rates, see Index.

RABBIT HILL INN
Lower Waterford, Vermont

Lower Waterford, Vermont, on the edge of the North East Kingdom, is one of the most picturesque, and hence photographed, villages in Vermont. Across the street from the Rabbit Hill Inn is the village church, built in 1859, and around the corner is the 150-year-old post office that is also an "honor system" library. There is a glorious view of New Hampshire's White Mountains and many enticing outdoor activities nearby, including fishing, sailing, canoeing, nature walking, mountain climbing, and skiing, both downhill and cross-country.

The main building of the inn was built in 1825 and was located on the main route from Portland to Montreal.

All of the inn's twenty guest rooms have their own private baths, and all but two have a view of the mountains. There is a comfortable lounge, a book nook, and dining rooms.

Hearty breakfasts are included in the price of the room.

The inn is kept by the Charlton family, originally from England, who are adding new dimensions to American innkeeping.

RABBIT HILL INN, Pucker St. (Rte. 18), Lower Waterford, VT 05848; 802-748-5168. A 20-guestroom (private baths) country inn with a view of mountains on Rte. 18, midway between St. Johnsbury, Vt., and Littleton, N.H. Modified American, European plans. Breakfast is not included in tariff. Open all year except April and Nov. Breakfast and dinner served to travelers. Fishing, xc skiing on grounds. Tennis, swimming, walking, alpine skiing, sailing, backroading nearby. The Charlton Family, Innkeepers.

Directions: From I-91: Exit 19, then Exit 1 onto Rte. 18 south. From I-93: Exit Rte. 18 junction, turn north (left) on Rte. 18.

For B&B rates, see Index.

ROWELL'S INN
Simonsville, Vermont

If you are traveling on Route 11, which cuts east and west across Vermont from Manchester to the Connecticut River Valley, I hope you'll keep your eye peeled for Rowell's Inn. It is a beautiful red brick building with a three-tiered front porch and a most graceful enclosed arch on the third story. I have admired this building literally scores of times, and now I am happy to say that it is not only a historic five-bedroom country inn, but has also been placed on the National Register of Historic Places.

The interior is equally as impressive as the exterior, and rather than listing all of its virtues, including the beautiful floors, carved mantel pieces, and many family antiques, let me say that true inn lovers will be delighted even to stop in for a quick look.

The more I wandered around this inn, which started out as a stagecoach stop built in 1820 by Major Edward Simons, the founder of this tiny village, the more I felt myself being absorbed into the past of Vermont. Today, its role is being lovingly continued, probably better than ever, by Beth and Lee Davis, who became enchanted with the idea of owning an inn during a New England inn-hopping trek. I burst with pride to say that they became interested in inns as a result of reading *Country Inns and Back Roads* a number of years ago.

Breakfast is a full country repast with everything from bacon and eggs to ham and cheese soufflés, omelets, and pancakes. Something is baked fresh every morning from sticky buns to bread and muffins. A single entrée, fixed-price dinner is served to house-guests on request with advance notice.

Rowell's Inn is not only a warm, cozy country in, it's a prime example of the rewards in store for anyone who is lucky enough to find such a building and faithfully restore it.

ROWELL'S INN, Simonsville, VT 05143; 802-875-3658. A 5-guest-room (private baths) restored stagecoach stop, now a welcoming country inn. Full breakfast included in room rate. Dinner on advance request to houseguests only. Open all year, except 2 wks. in April. Convenient for the splendid recreational, cultural, and scenic attractions in both southern Vermont and New Hampshire. Major ski areas nearby. Children over 6 welcome. No pets. Beth and Lee Davis, Innkeepers

Directions: Simonsville is located between Londonderry and Chester on Rte. 11.

For B&B rates, see Index.

SAXTONS RIVER INN
Saxtons River, Vermont

The Saxtons River Inn is about midway between New York City and Montreal. It is just a few miles west of I-91, and is a most engaging stopover.

Saxtons River is an almost-hidden Vermont village where a group of people from some of our larger cities have decided to create a new lifestyle. There's a community interest in music, arts, crafts, and improving the environment.

The center for much of this activity is found in the Saxtons River Inn on the main street, right in the middle of the town. You can't miss it because it has a tower section that extends about two-and-a-half stories above the main building.

The front porch, tavern, and dining rooms always find an interesting mix of both locals and travelers enjoying the hospitality. Although there is a fascinating collection of Victoriana throughout the inn, the feeling is somewhat contemporary because of a great many art gallery posters. It is an excellent collection and I must say blends in very well with the entire atmosphere.

In her brochure, Averill Larsen, the innkeeper, points out that inns express their individuality in many ways, and in the case of the Saxtons River Inn, no two guest rooms are alike and each is individually decorated, varying in size and decor. There are nineteen altogether; eight do not have private baths. One in particular would make a very nice honeymoon room. Each of these rooms is generously supplied with a packet of information about everything that can be done in both southern Vermont and nearby New Hampshire.

A continental breakfast is served in the front dining room and is included in the room rate. Dinner is also served every night except Tuesdays.

SAXTONS RIVER INN, Saxtons River, VT 05154; 802-869-2110. A 19-guestroom (some shared baths) most interesting and casual village inn about 4½ hrs. from NYC and 2½ hrs. from Boston. Breakfast included in room rate. Dinner served every night except Tues. Most conveniently located for guests to enjoy all of the scenic, recreational, and cultural attractions in southern Vermont and New Hampshire. Children welcome. No pets. No credit cards. Averill Larsen, Innkeeper.

Directions: Leave I-91 at Exit 5, turn left off the exit ramp, travel about ¼ mi. to T intersection, and turn right. Continue 3 mi. to next T and turn left onto Rte. 121 west. This continues on into Saxtons River.

For B&B rates, see Index.

STONE HOUSE INN
North Thetford, Vermont

Here's a suggestion for the I-91 traveler on the east side of Vermont: momentarily abandon the interstate at St. Johnsbury or Norwich, follow the Connecticut River villages on the Vermont side, and see some of the loveliest sights in New England. The farms, barns, river views, and fields will enchant.

In North Thetford, Vermont, a few miles north of Norwich, the Stone House Inn is set on the river side of Route 5 in a little jog off the highway. Six guest rooms are comfortable and cheerful, with views toward the mountains, river, and pond. There's a wide screened veranda, an armchair by one of the fireplaces, and a pleasant walk through the woods alongside the pond to create a wonderful country mood.

The bedrooms are typical farmhouse style, well furnished, clean, and very inviting. The parlor has an upright piano, a fireplace, and there's ample opportunity for guests to become acquainted.

Dianne Sharkey, innkeeper, along with her husband Art, bakes great sticky buns for breakfast, and all the bread, muffins, and sourdough English muffins. These are served with coffee, tea, and fruit juice and during the summertime can be taken on the porch, which overlooks the pond.

Of even further interest is the fact that there is a canoeing program among inns located on the Connecticut River, and Dianne and Art have all the information.

STONE HOUSE INN, North Thetford, Vermont 05054; 802-333-9124. A 6-bedroom (3 shared baths) guest house located on the banks of the Connecticut River just a few miles north of Norwich, Vermont. Open every day of the year. There is much to offer in both the Green and White Mountains nearby. Within a short distance of Hanover, New Hampshire and Dartmouth College. No pets. Dianne and Art Sharkey, Innkeepers.

Directions: From I-91 take Exit #14 (Thetford). Turn right on Rte. 113 and left after one mile on Rte. 5. The inn is two miles on the right-hand side of the road.

For B&B rates, see Index.

THREE MOUNTAIN INN
Jamaica, Vermont

Our journey on Route 100, the road that runs up the backbone of Vermont, finds us still in the ski country just outside the entrance to Stratton Mountain and within twenty minutes of Bromley and Magic Mountain. Our objective is the very interesting old village of Jamaica, tucked away in this mountain fastness since at least 1780.

In the middle of the village at one of the crossroads stands the Three Mountain Inn, with a history dating back to the late 18th century. The living room has a roaring fire in the large fireplace, wide-plank pine walls and floors, and the original Dutch oven.

The innkeepers are all members of the Murray family—Elaine and Charles, and their three vivacious daughters.

The guest rooms have the hallmarks of real country Vermont, with candlewick spreads, old prints, framed needlework, and some country furniture made in one of the nearby villages.

The menu in the main dining room with pink tablecloths changes every night, and the modified American plan rates include dinner on the night of arrival and breakfast on the following morning.

Breakfast menus vary according to what is fresh and in season. Starting with June and July there are freshly picked strawberries and red raspberries. These are followed by blueberries, melons, peaches, and apples. Among the breakfast offerings there's a special recipe for light pancakes served with pure Vermont maple syrup, and also Vermont scrambled eggs served with local cheddar cheese. B&B rates are available for readers of this book.

THREE MOUNTAIN INN, Jamaica, VT 05343; 802-874-4140. A 10-guestroom village inn (8 with private baths) in the mountains of southern Vermont. Closed from the 15th of April to the 15th of May. Dinner is also served. Swimming pool on grounds. Fishing on the West River, with special fishing packages available. Downhill skiing at Stratton, Bromley, and Magic Mountains, a short distance away. Xc skiing, snowshoeing, hiking, tennis, and wonderful Vermont backroading at the doorstep. No pets. The Murray Family, Innkeepers.

Directions: From I-91 take the second exit at Brattleboro and follow Rte. 30 to Jamaica. From Rte. 7 take Rte. 5 east to Wilmington and follow Rte. 100 north.

For B&B rates, see Index.

WAYBURY INN
East Middlebury, Vermont

The Waybury Inn is a great deal more than a bed-and-breakfast inn. It's a traditional New England inn, built in 1810 at the foot of the Green Mountains as a stagecoach stop on one of the major passes through the mountains. Much of the atmosphere of almost 175 years ago still prevails and is reflected in the furnishings of the bedrooms and public rooms with their massive hand-hewn beams.

It's just down the road from the Middlebury Snow Bowl and a short distance from the Breadloaf Writers' Conference, which is held each summer. Lake Dunmore is nearby and there is lots of good Green Mountain backroading, walking, and hiking, as well as both downhill and cross-country skiing. Middlebury College is just a few miles away.

Besides breakfast, which features on occasion absolutely scrumptious blueberry pancakes, dinner and Sunday brunch are also served. The inn has a local reputation for the roast rolled leg of lamb and fresh, homemade breads, desserts, and entrées.

There are scores of nearby attractions, including the Vermont State Craft Center at Frog Hollow in Middlebury, the Sheldon Museum, the UVM Morgan Horse Farm, the Fort Ticonderoga Ferry, the New England Maple Museum in nearby Pittsford, the Vermont Marble Exhibit and Gift Shop in Proctor, Wilson Castle, and the Middlebury College campus and activities that abound there.

You'll recognize the Waybury Inn at a distance because of the beautiful maple trees, which are gorgeous during the fall foliage season.

WAYBURY INN, Rte. 125, East Middlebury, VT 05740; 802-388-4015. A 12-guestroom (private baths) traditional village inn 5 mi. south of Middlebury. Open year-round. Breakfast for houseguests only. Dinner is served daily to the public. Located just a few miles from Lake Dunmore on a mountain-pass road. Conveniently located for all of the Green Mountain recreational, historical, and cultural attractions. Hiking, swimming, fishing, downhill and xc skiing, golf, antiquing, backroading all nearby. Jim and Betty Riley, Innkeepers.

Directions: East Middlebury is just off Rte. 7 on Rte. 125, 29 mi. north of Rutland and 5 mi. south of Middlebury.

For B&B rates, see Index.

WHETSTONE INN
Marlboro, Vermont

This inn, which is right next door to a beautiful white-spired church, is one of the most photographed locations in Vermont. Marlboro is located about midway between Interstate 91 and Route 100—a very tiny village that has excellent cross-country skiing in the winter and the Marlboro Music School and Festival during the summer.

The inn was built around 1800 and was used as a tavern in stagecoach days. There are inviting living rooms with open fires and books and music. The guest rooms, most of which have private baths or lavatories, are large and cheerful. The inn sits on the top of a very high hill with a beautiful view across the valley to the east, and has a lovely little pond in the rear.

This is a four-season inn, but I must point out that during the summer Marlboro concert season and fall foliage-time, reservations are made far in advance.

The full Vermont à la carte breakfast frequently includes waffles, popovers, and pancakes. It is served in the antique dining room where there's a huge old fireplace with a crane holding an iron cauldron.

Dinner is served most Saturday nights, and with varying frequency on other nights, depending upon the season.

Innkeepers Harry and Jean Boardman make a stop at the Whetstone Inn a very memorable experience.

WHETSTONE INN, Marlboro, VT 05344; 802-254-2500. An 11-guestroom (8 with private baths) mountaintop inn located in southern Vermont. Open all year. Breakfast is not included with room. Marlboro, Hogback Mt. ski area, Vermont backroading, hiking and walking, and xc skiing available from the inn's doors. No credit cards. Harry and Jean Boardman, Innkeepers.

Directions: From I-91 follow Rte. 9 west to top of the mountains and turn left at the signs for Marlboro.

For Lodging rates, see Index.

WOODCHUCK HILL FARM
Grafton, Vermont

In an era when bed-and-breakfast homes are popping up like dandelions in the springtime, Anne and Frank Gabriel at Woodchuck Hill Farm, with sixteen years of experience behind them, can certainly be classified as veterans.

The location of Woodchuck Hill is exceptional. It is about two miles from the village of Grafton at the end of a real dirt road in a deep forest. The views of the mountains and mowings are enchanting.

The farmhouse is one of the oldest buildings in Grafton—a circa 1780 Colonial, furnished in antiques, with accommodations for as many as twenty guests. One of the special features is a large open porch with cushioned wicker furniture and hanging plants, overlooking the seventy-five-mile view of the mountains of Vermont and New Hampshire. The atmosphere is most informal and guests are always encouraged by the Gabriels to make themselves at home. The Gabriels will even serve dinner to their houseguests with advance notice.

An additional, attractive feature of Woodchuck Hill Farm is their own antique shop located in the old barn. This is filled with some of the most enticing and attractive small antique furnishings I have ever seen.

Behind the barn is a large pond surrounded by pleasant lawns—most inviting for swimming and getting a good Vermont tan—and it sometimes provides the trout for dinner.

There are guest rooms appropriately furnished in the main house as well as two additional apartments, some with fireplaces.

WOODCHUCK HILL FARM, Middletown Rd., Grafton, VT 05146; 802-843-2398. A 9-guestroom B&B home located high in the mountains near Grafton village. Open May through Nov. 1. Continental breakfast included with room. Dinner available by advance request. Afternoon tea is also offered. Exceptional backroading abounds in the area, swimming on grounds, other active outdoor sports within a short drive. Frank and Anne Gabriel, Proprietors.

Directions: From Grafton Village drive to the end of the main street, ignore right turn on Rte. 121 and continue about 200 yds. Take the right fork at the sign for Gabriels' Barn Antiques; continue about 2 mi. through forest.

For B&B rates, see Index.

THE ALEXANDER-WITHROW HOUSE
Lexington, Virginia

Lexington, Virginia, just a few minutes from I-81, is one of the most interesting and off-the-beaten path areas in the South. Besides the campuses of Virginia Military Institute and Washington and Lee University, it contains much memorabilia connected with Stonewall Jackson and Robert E. Lee.

The surrounding countryside has beautiful scenery and the Natural Bridge, a 215-foot towering limestone structure, the Blue Ridge Parkway, Goshen Pass, and Cyrus McCormick's farm and workshop are nearby.

The Alexander-Withrow House is an exquisite guest house, now included in the National Register of Historic Places. It was built in 1789, just two years after the founding of the town.

There are seven rooms and suites in the A-W House, and in the McCampbell Inn, another historic house across the street, there are now sixteen rooms. They are all beautifully furnished with antiques, private baths, and the little touches that make a country inn. Each suite has its own sitting room, bedroom, and refreshment area equipped with a hot pot and refrigerator and packets of coffee and tea.

Alexander-Withrow guests may now enjoy, compliments of the house, orange juice, freshly baked muffins, and coffee or tea from 8:30 to 10 every morning in the Great Room of the McCampbell Inn, which affords an opportunity for some pleasant conversation with other guests.

THE ALEXANDER-WITHROW HOUSE, 11 No. Main St., Lexington, VA 24450; 703-463-2044. Two historic houses with 23 elegant bedrooms and suites. Continental breakfast included. Advance reservations recommended. Open year-round. Within walking distance of Virginia Military Institute, Washington and Lee University, and the George C. Marshall Research Library. Natural Bridge, Blue Ridge Parkway nearby. Golf, hiking, Appalachian Trail, canoeing also available. No pets. Mr. and Mrs. Peter Meredith and sons, Owners; Don Fredenburg, Innkeeper.

Directions: Take any Lexington exit from I-64 or I- 81. Follow signs into Lexington. The Alexander-Withrow House is on the corner of Main and Washington Streets.

For Lodging rates, see Index.

THE INN AT GRISTMILL SQUARE
Warm Springs, Virginia

Gristmill Square is a village within a village. It is set in southwestern Virginia in a sequestered valley with hills on both sides. The brook running through the middle of the town still turns the great mill wheel, built in 1900. The Mill House is now a rustic restaurant.

Around Gristmill Square are an antique and a country store and fourteen guest accommodations, some with a kitchen, living room, balcony or sundeck, and a wood-burning fireplace. There are also double rooms and small suites.

This section of Virginia has been a playground for outdoor sports since the 1880s, and guests at the inn can enjoy tennis and swimming on the grounds as well as golf at the famous Cascades Club.

B&B guests at Gristmill Square are served a continental breakfast in their rooms.

The Waterwheel Restaurant is located in what used to be the old mill and the atmosphere is enhanced by the pervading scent of grain.

Even a hasty traveler intent on covering as many miles as possible every day will find the side trip to Gristmill Square most rewarding. I can only warn that the temptation to stay on longer is very great.

THE INN AT GRISTMILL SQUARE, P.O. Box 359, Warm Springs, VA 24484; 703-339-2231. A 14-guestroom restoration with a restaurant in a small country town in the Allegheny Mountains, 19 mi. north of Covington. European plan. Restaurant open for dinner daily Tues. thru Sun. Also open for Sun. brunch; luncheon Tues. thru Sat., May to Oct. Closed Mon. Suggest telephoning for details. Tennis courts, swimming pool on grounds. Golf at nearby Cascades or Lower Cascades. Skiing at the Homestead and Snowshoe, West Va., a little over an hour away. Skating, riding, hiking, fishing, hunting, antiquing, and backroading nearby. Children and pets welcome. Janice McWilliams and Bruce McWilliams, Innkeepers.

Directions: From Staunton, Va. follow Rte. 254 to Buffalo Gap, Rte 42 to Millboro Spring, Rte. 39 to Warm Springs. Turn left on Rte. 692 in Warm Springs. From Lexington, take Rte. 39 to Warm Springs. From Roanoke, take Rte. 220 to Warm Springs; turn left on Rte. 619.

For B&B rates, see Index.

MEADOW LANE LODGE
Warm Springs, Virginia

Meadow Lane Lodge, owned by my good friends, Cathy and Philip Hirsh, is a small bed-and-breakfast inn of gracious charm situated in the beautiful Allegheny Mountains of southwest Virginia. It is an integral part of an estate comprising approximately 1600 acres of woods, fields, and streams.

The accommodations consist of three suites and six double guest rooms all with private baths. The decor of the entire lodge is that of an earlier period of American life, coupled with all modern conveniences. The rooms are liberally furnished with lovely antiques.

A short stroll from the lodge will bring animal lovers to the barnyard and pastures where the sheep and goats graze and gambol. Chickens, ducks, guinea fowl, geese, and turkeys inhabit the old horse stalls and large stable and freely wander about in the surrounding areas. Cats and kittens mingle, as do farm dogs.

There is a full breakfast prepared by Phil. He has already made his mark as a morning chef and specializes in all kinds of egg dishes, delicious pancakes, and french toast.

Besides the tennis court, and all of the wonderful walks and rides in the mountains, and the trout fishing in the river, guests have the advantage of being close to the Cascades and Lower Cascades golf courses.

MEADOW LANE LODGE, Star Route A, Box 110, Warm Springs, VA 24484; 703-839-5959. A 9-guestroom lodge, a portion of a large estate where guests are accommodated in the main building as well as in a comfortable outbuilding. Additional lodgings are in a historic building in the village of Warm Springs. Open April 1 to Jan. 31. A full breakfast, the only meal served. Dinners are available at nearby restaurants, 10 min. away. Tennis court and excellent fishing on grounds. Also, miles of hiking and walking trails. Golf, riding, skeet and trap shooting, swimming pool nearby. Philip and Cathy Hirsh, Innkeepers; Hella Armstrong, Manager.

Directions: From Staunton, Va., follow Rte. 254 west to Buffalo Gap; Rte. 42 south to Millboro Spring; Rte. 39 west to Warm Springs. From Lexington, take Rte. 39 west. From Roanoke, take Rte. 220 north to Warm Springs and Rte. 39 west to Meadow Lane Lodge. From Lewisburg, W. Va., take I-64 to Covington; Rte. 220 north to Warm Springs. Lodge is on Rte. 39 four miles west of Warm Springs.

For B&B rates, see Index.

PEAKS OF OTTER LODGE
Bedford, Virginia

The Blue Ridge Parkway is one of the truly remarkable motoring experiences in North America. It starts at the Skyline Drive near Front Royal in northern Virginia and continues on to North Carolina. There are no commercial intrusions for the entire course of the road, and the effect of being in a completely natural setting is enchanced by the absence of guard rails.

There are just a few accommodations on this road, among which is the Peaks of Otter Lodge. Even though it is a motel, everything has been kept in harmony with nature with a very pleasant lakeside setting and a decor of natural woods and subtly blended textures, tones, and colors.

The guest accommodations are in spacious rooms with two double beds and private baths. Each has its own secluded balcony and terrace, and features a truly spectacular view.

Although the lodge is open year-round, reservations are always advisable and it is practically impossible to book a room in October during the fall foliage season. A "winter special" is available from December through March. Breakfast is available in the restaurant.

Peaks of Otter Lodge and Restaurant is an authorized concessionaire operation in the National Park System. Facilities for the handicapped are available.

PEAKS OF OTTER LODGE, P.O. Box 489, Bedford, VA 24523; 703-586-1081. A 58-guestroom motel at the intersection of Rte. 43 and Blue Ridge Parkway, 10 mi. south of I-81 and 10 mi. north of Bedford. Breakfast, lunch, and dinner served daily. Open all year. Hiking, fishing, nature trails, and exceptional mountain motoring. No pets. Reservations absolutely, positively necessary.

Directions: From Rte. 460 in Bedford follow Rte. 43 north with the Peaks of Otter in plain view. Turn north for ½ mi. on the Blue Ridge Parkway. It is located on milepost 86.

For Lodging rates, see Index.

PROSPECT HILL
Trevilians, Virginia

The "American Style" in our title also includes a few authentic southern plantation houses. Prospect Hill dates to 1732, and in 1793 additional slave quarters were added, some of which are being used as guest rooms today. Part of its history involves one of the owners, who returned from the War Between the States to find his family plantation overgrown and his slaves gone.

If the history is intriguing, the setting is even more so, for Prospect Hill begins where the boxwood hedge along the entrance-way ends. It's in the midst of an English tree garden, shaded by rare magnolias, tall tulip poplars, and giant beeches. Innkeeper Bill Sheehan says, "This is the way Prospect Hill was two centuries ago, and the way it is today."

It is within a convenient distance of Charlottesville, Monticello, and the University of Virginia campus, and just off the main high-way from Charlottesville to Richmond.

This is the place where breakfast in bed is usually the choice. On the groaning tray, brought directly into each room, there are fresh-baked french bread and croissants, breakfast soufflés, and such specialties as crêpes with fried apples, all of which are homemade. All of this is also served in the dining room.

PROSPECT HILL, Rte. 613, Trevilians, VA 23070; 703-967-0844. A 7-guestroom (private baths) country inn on a historic plantation, 15 mi. east of Charlottesville, Va.; 90 mi. southwest of Washington, D.C. Bed and breakfast-in-bed Sun. thru Tues. Mod. American plan with full breakfast-in-bed and full dinner Wed. thru Sat. Dinner served Wed. thru Sat. by reservation. Dining room closed Sun., Mon., and Tues. Breakfast always served to houseguests. Near Monticello, Ashlawn (Pres. Monroe's home), Univ. of Virginia, Castle Hill, and Skyline Drive. Swimming pool. Children welcome. No pets. Bill and Mireille Sheehan, Innkeepers.

Directions: From Washington, D.C.: Beltway to I-66 west to Warren-ton. Follow Rte. 29 south to Culpeper, then Rte. 15 south thru Orange and Gordonsville to Zion Crossroads. Turn left on Rte. 250 east 1 mi. to Rte. 613. Turn left 3 mi. to inn on left. From Charlottes-ville or Richmond: take I-64 to Exit 27; Rte. 15 south ½ mi. to Zion Crossroads; turn left on Rte. 250 east 1 mi. to Rte. 613. Turn left 3 mi. to inn on left.

For B&B rates, see Index.

RED FOX INN AND TAVERN
Middleburg, Virginia

Middleburg is in the famous horse country of Virginia and there are large estates and farms along Route 50 that have some beautiful animals grazing in the fields bordered by fences.

The Red Fox Inn and Tavern, which has been in the same building for more than 200 years, is at the crossroads in Middleburg, adjacent to some very excellent shops offering country clothes and saddlery.

There are seventeen tastefully decorated guest rooms in the Red Fox and in other buildings called the Stray Fox and McConnell House. Some have sitting rooms and 18th-century documented wallpapers and paint colors. Each room is furnished with period antiques; some have canopied beds, and most have working fireplaces.

On the second floor of the tavern there is a most attractive pine-paneled dining room with two fireplaces. This had been a lounge that was converted, by popular demand, into a dining room and is now one of the seven dining areas in which guests may enjoy their meals. Dinner is served every evening.

A continental breakfast is included in the room rate. The full breakfast, served in one of the dining rooms, features homemade buttermilk pancakes or waffles, cappuccino or espresso coffee, and a selection of country jams and jellies.

It's just forty miles to Washington and an ideal distance for a stop the night before a few days in the nation's capital.

RED FOX INN AND TAVERN, Middleburg, VA 22117; 703-687-6301. A 17-guestroom historic village inn (8 of the rooms in the Stray Fox and 5 in the McConnell House) near the Blue Ridge Mountains, approx. 40 mi. from Washington, D.C. Near Manassas Battlefield, Oatlands, and Oak Hill (President Monroe's White House). European plan. Complimentary continental breakfast included in room rate. Breakfast, lunch, and dinner served to travelers. Open every day of the year. Spectator sports such as polo and steeplechasing available nearby. No activities available for small children. Consult innkeeper for policy on pets. The Reuter Family, Innkeepers.

Directions: Leave Washington, D.C., at Rte. 66 west, to Rte. 50. Follow Rte. 50 west for 22 mi. to Middleburg.

For B&B rates, see Index.

384

SOJOURNERS BED AND BREAKFAST
Lynchburg, Virginia

Lynchburg, on the James River at the gateway to southwest Virginia and the Blue Ridge Mountains, is in a rural countryside rich in heritage and history. It is the home of Randolph-Macon Women's College and Lynchburg College, and is just a short distance from Sweet Briar College in nearby Amherst.

Sojourners is located in one of the most attractive residential areas of this small city and, in fact, when guests call to make the required advance reservations, a special map is sent with the confirmation.

The larger of the guest rooms has a double and a single bed, private bath, individual heat, TV, and semi-private entrance. The other guest room is small, with a single bed and shared bath. Actually, Sojourners is a bed-and-breakfast home, so the entire atmosphere is one of being in a home away from home.

The proprietors, Clyde and Ann McAlister, are both gracious, contemporary-minded hosts, and the conversations at breakfast or over an afternoon cup of tea could run the gamut from Algiers to Zoroaster. Both are professional genealogists.

Breakfast is a veritable feast and always has some of Ann's or Mac's homemade breads. Grits, eggs, and sausage are available on request.

Besides the natural beauty and educational establishments in and around Lynchburg, the community also has Westminster-Canterbury, a retirement home nearby, and Sojourners would be an excellent place for visitors to stay.

SOJOURNERS BED AND BREAKFAST, 3609 Tanglewood Lane, Lynchburg, VA 24503; 804-384-1655. A 2-guestroom bed-and-breakfast home in a quiet, residential section of Lynchburg, Virginia. Breakfast, included in the room rate, is the only meal served. Situated conveniently for a vacation in the Blue Ridge Parkway section of Virginia, an area rich in history. No credit cards. No pets. Clyde and Ann McAlister, Proprietors.

Directions: Please telephone between 10:00 A.M. and 6:00 P.M. or write Sojourners for full information.

For B&B rates, see Index.

WELBOURNE
Middleburg, Virginia

As trite as it may sound, visiting Welbourne is indeed like stepping into the past. Located in the Piedmount hunt country, this stately Colonial mansion, with six graceful pillars, was built in 1775. The Morison family made it their home in 1820 and have lived there continuously since then. Major additions and wings were added as late as 1870.

The accommodations are exactly what one would expect in such stately surroundings. The guest rooms are extremely large and the furniture extremely antique. There are sleigh beds, four-posters, free-standing full-size mirrors, and many pieces that could never be duplicated. The house, grounds, and gardens have a remarkable air of genteel antiquity.

Most impressive are the oil portraits of members of the Morison family who have occupied this home. Some of them are in the dress of Colonial times and others in uniforms of the War Between the States. One of them is of Major John Pelham, the boy hero of the Confederacy.

The hostess of this 600-acre farm, which is on the list of Virginia Historic Landmarks and the National Register of Historic Places, is Sally Holmes Morison, who is the fifth generation of her family. Her son, Nat, and his wife, Sherry, are also a part of the gracious hospitality. The most appropriate thing I can say is that they belong with the house.

WELBOURNE, Middleburg, VA 22117; 703-687-3201. A 7-guestroom antebellum mansion, and 3 cottages, in the heart of the Virginia hunt country a short distance from the center of Middleburg, and 30 mi. from Dulles Airport. Full breakfast is the only meal served, but there are restaurants in nearby Middleburg. Centrally located for beautiful backroading and walking. No credit cards. Mrs. N. Holmes Morison, Innkeeper.

Directions: From blinker light in Middleburg take U.S. 50 west for 3½ mi. Turn right on Rte. 611; go 1½ mi.; turn left on 743. Welbourne is 1¼ mi. on the left.

For B&B rates, see Index.

THE ASHFORD MANSION
Ashford, Washington

Mount Rainier National Park is one of the great attractions of the Pacific Northwest, so finding a historic house offering bed and breakfast only six miles from the Paradise entrance is good news for travelers. Ashford town took its name from the family who built the elegant frontier home at the turn of the century, though they called the place "Twin Brook Estate," for the streams that still cross it.

Guests get a big Northwest breakfast: juice, fresh fruit, eggs, homemade bread, crumpets, and huckleberry muffins. The variety of jams always includes wild blackberry, from fruit gathered on the side of the mountain. "You need a good start if you're going to hike in the park all day," Jan Green says.

Jan can tell you what there is to see and do in this picturesque area both in and outside the park. She can advise you on hiking trails and fill you in on the history and topography of the park. She has the menus of the local restaurants, so you can preplan dinner, while resting on the veranda or before the fireplace in the parlor, where there is a grand piano.

The mansion is off the main highway, a peaceful as well as a beautiful place to stay.

THE ASHFORD MANSION, Old Mountain Rd., Ashford, WA 98304; 206-569-2739. A 4-guestroom (shared bath) bed-and-breakfast home on the slopes of Mt. Rainier, 6 mi. from the Paradise entrance to the park. Breakfast only. Open all year. Advance reservations necessary. Restaurants, sightseeing, craft shops, hiking, mountain climbing, xc skiing, tubing, nature walks, nearby. Children should be at least 12 years old. Pets O.K. if kept outside on leash. No smoking. Jan Green, Owner.

Directions: Old Mountain Rd. is an arc that both joins and parallels busy Hwy. 706. The big white mansion sits well back from the road on the north side.

For B&B rates, see Index.

THE CAPTAIN WHIDBEY INN
Coupeville, Whidbey Island, Washington

Whidbey Island is about fifty miles north of Seattle and six miles south of Everett. It is the largest of the 172 islands in Puget Sound and is reached by ferry systems and the scenic Deception Pass Bridge. A most unusual holiday of island-hopping that can last hours or even days may be enjoyed via the ferries that travel to several different islands.

The Captain Whidbey Inn, built of the famous madrona logs, is as fetching a piece of New England as can be found west of Cape Cod.

The natural center of the inn is the living room with its massive fireplace, made of round stones. Here everyone sits around leafing through dozens of magazines and chatting. There's a fire almost every evening. The Chart Room features nautical decorations and an occasional view of an errant whale in Penn Cove.

Some of the guest rooms are upstairs in the main house overlooking Penn Cove, and others are hidden away in a number of rustic cottages built in the woods across the road, overlooking a pastoral pond.

The continental breakfast allows guests to get off to a good start with sweet rolls, english muffins, juice, coffee and tea.

By the way, the New England flavor of this Puget Sound Inn is entirely authentic, as the Stone family is from Nantucket Island, off the coast of Massachusetts.

THE CAPTAIN WHIDBEY INN, 2072 W. Capt. Whidbey Rd., Coupeville, WA 98239; 206-678-4097. A 25-guestroom (private and shared baths) country inn, 50 mi. north of Seattle, 3 mi. north of Coupeville. European plan. Breakfast, lunch, and dinner served daily to travelers. Open year-round. Boating and fishing on grounds. Golf nearby. Pets allowed in cottages only. Geoff and John Stone, Innkeepers.

Directions: Whidbey Island is reached year-round from the south by the Columbia Beach — Mukilteo Ferry, and during the summer and on weekends by the Port Townsend — Keystone Ferry. From the north (Vancouver, B.C., and Bellingham), take the Deception Pass Bridge to Whidbey Island.

For B&B rates, see Index.

CHAMBERED NAUTILUS
Seattle, Washington

Situated high on a wooded knoll in the university neighborhood, this Georgian Colonial-style inn was first the home of a University of Washington professor—it was built in 1915 for his family. An informal family atmosphere has been effectively retained by innkeepers Kate McDill and Deborah Sweet.

Common rooms on the main floor are enormous and filled with comfortable furniture grouped around a mantled fireplace. Just beyond is a roomy sun porch where I felt the urge to curl up with a book or have a short snooze.

The guest rooms, located on the second and third floors, are furnished with antiques, and the comfortable beds all have comforters. Four rooms have their own private sun porches.

I think you'll enjoy the friendly atmosphere of the university shopping area with its colorful melange of shops, tea rooms, boutiques, eateries, and, of course, students.

CHAMBERED NAUTILUS, 5005 22nd Ave. N.E., Seattle, WA 98105; 206-522-2536. A 6-guestroom (baths shared) bed-and-breakfast inn near the University of Washington. Full gourmet breakfast included in room rate. Open year-round. The Seattle Center (home of the 1962 World's Fair) with the Opera House and Bagley Wright Theatre; Pike Place Market, shops, and restaurants on the waterfront nearby. Older children preferred. No pets. Smoking in designated areas only. Kate McDill and Deborah Sweet, Innkeepers.

Directions: From north or south on I-5, take the N.E. 50th Ave. Exit and proceed east several blocks to 20th, turning left (north) 4 blocks to 54th St. Turn right (east) and go 2 blocks to 22nd Ave. and right again for 4 blocks to inn.

For B&B rates, see Index.

HAUS ROHRBACH PENSION
Leavenworth, Washington

Located in the quaint Bavarian-style village of Leavenworth, Haus Rohrbach is nestled against Tumwater Mountain, overlooking broad meadows and distant Douglas fir—forested hills. You may want to bring your skis during winter months when the meadow is knee-deep in white powder.

Many of the guest rooms and the common area below open onto wide balconies, which overflow with colorful flower boxes all summer. Functional guest rooms have handcrafted wood beds and chests, pine wainscoting, white eyelet curtains, and down comforters. You'll find that staying at Haus Rohrbach is like visiting an Old World Bavarian lodge.

Breakfast in the large common area may include Kathryn's cinnamon rolls, sour cream coffee cake, or fresh-baked breads, sourdough pancakes, omelets, and plenty of coffee and teas. I found the cheerful wood stove a toasty place to linger over a second cup of coffee with Bob and Kathryn.

HAUS ROHRBACH PENSION, 12882 Ranger Rd., Leavenworth, WA 98826; 509-548-7024. A 12-guestroom (3 private baths) European-style bed-and-breakfast inn in the Cascade Mountains east of Seattle and Everett. Full breakfast included in room rate. Open year-round. Autumn Leaf Festival in September and October; Christmas Lighting Festival early December; Mai Fest in May. Outdoor swimming pool and hot tub, ping-pong, and croquet at the inn. Skiing, tobogganing, snowshoeing, sleigh rides, hiking, white-water rafting, fishing, horseback riding nearby. Children welcome. No pets. Smoking in designated areas only. Bob and Kathryn Harrild, Innkeepers.

Directions: Drive east from Everett on Hwy. 2 over Stevens Pass (elevation 4,061 feet) to Leavenworth. At Kristall's Restaurant turn left on Ski Hill Dr. to Ranger Rd. Left on Ranger Rd. to top of hill.

For B&B rates, see Index.

ORCAS HOTEL
Orcas Island, Washington

Here's an appealing idea—how about spending a few days marooned on an island not too far removed from civilization? For this lovely experience, take the one-hour ferry ride from Anacortes (two hours north of Seattle) to Orcas Island. It's one of the green island gems among the some 175 islands that are found in the San Juan Islands.

Old brochures invited turn-of-the-century guests to vacation here while "fishing, sailing, canoeing, horseback riding, or hiking" over the island's 56 square miles and 125 miles of coastline. The early island resort offered guest rooms as well as tent sites on its original 89 acres.

Extensive restoration of the 86-year-old hotel was undertaken by the Jamiesons in 1985, after the structure was approved for the National Registry of Historic Places. The finished product is well worth a visit.

Guest rooms on the second and third floors offer antiques, "Log Cabin" quilts made by island craftswomen, Victorian hatbox wallpapers, soft carpeting, and numerous rocking chairs. Colors of pale peach, rust, cream, and brown offer a soothing background.

A continental breakfast is served in the hotel's small restaurant.

ORCAS HOTEL, P.O. Box 155, Orcas, WA 98280; 206-376-4300. A 12-guestroom (3 private half-baths) inn in the San Juan Islands, about 3 hrs. north of Seattle. Complimentary continental breakfast. Lunch and dinner served daily in restaurant. Open year-round. Parlor available for small seminars, private parties, receptions. Annual Library Fair in August; boating and sailing. Moran State Park, Mount Constitution, hiking trails, horseback riding, golf. Free moorage for boats. Quiet children only. No pets. Barbara and John Jamieson, Innkeepers.

Directions: Drive north on I-5 from Seattle to Anacortes. Follow signs to ferry terminal; take 1-hr. automobile ferry to Orcas Island.

For B&B rates, see Index.

SHELBURNE INN
Seaview, Washington

Sleep in an antique bed! Such is the claim of the ninety-year-old Shelburne Inn in southern Washington.

The twelve guest rooms are decorated in Early American comfort—bright, cheerful rooms with brass beds, braided rugs, and beautiful old quilts. There are private and shared baths.

The Shelburne Inn is a restoration of a Victorian hostelry, built by Charles Beaver as an overnight rest stop for travelers in 1896, and now listed in the National Register of Historic Places.

The caring innkeepers, Laurie Anderson and David Campiche, have carefully restored the Shelburne Inn inside and out, returning it almost perfectly to its original state. The dark green shingled exterior is crisply outlined by white trim.

The lobby is completely covered with warm, dark woods. The decor is Victorian, with English and American antiques. At the time of this writing, renovation of the first floor had just been completed. The lobby was enlarged, and beautiful stained glass windows of the Art Nouveau period, newly imported from England, fronted the street.

The Shelburne Inn's restaurant has received national acclaim. In addition to its regular meals, there are Sunday brunches. In spring, the menu may feature sautéed chicken breasts served with raspberry sauce. In fall, venison may be the choice, with fresh chanterelles from the surrounding hills. The wine list is lengthy and designed for people with a real interest in wine.

SHELBURNE INN, Box 250, Seaview, WA 98644; 206-642-2442. A 12-guestroom (5 rooms have private baths) antique-filled Victorian inn, just north of the Oregon border in a small, oceanside village. Breakfast included with room. Open year-round. Restaurant is open daily during summer; on a reduced schedule off-season. Sun. brunch. No television or telephones. Children welcome. No pets. Laurie Anderson and David Campiche, Innkeepers; Tony and Ann Kischner, Restaurateurs.

Directions: From Portland, Oregon take I-5 to Longview, Washington—turn west on Hwy. 4 to Johnson's Landing, take Hwy. 101 to Seaview, which is 15 mi. Inn is on Pacific Hwy. 103 and J St., left side—watch for large inn sign.

For B&B rates, see Index.

HOUSE OF SEVEN GABLES
Baraboo, Wisconsin

The House of Seven Gables, the private home of Ralph and Pamela Krainik, is an architectural delight. Built in 1860 by a Baraboo banker, the house boasts balustrades, finials, pendants, variously carved posts—and of course, the seven steeply pitched gables for which the house is named.

This assortment of gaily colored gingerbread, done up in shades of peach, salmon, and burgundy, has gotten the house listed in the National Register of Historic Places. It is a classic example of Gothic Revival, dubbed "Carpenter Gothic" for the chance it gave woodworkers of the period to strut their stuff.

Do-it-yourselfers will enjoy talking with Ralph Krainik, a local real estate developer who did most of the restorations himself over the twenty years the Krainiks have owned the house. At the time of my visit, Ralph was working on yet another addition: a backyard gazebo. There, summer guests will be able to enjoy the continental breakfast of fresh fruit and homemade breads baked by Pamela. In the winter, of course, breakfast is served inside in the formal dining room, with its marble-topped sideboard and high-backed chairs carved from dark walnut.

Tours of the house are given for the public upon request for three dollars. Guests of this bed and breakfast receive the tour free, however, and shouldn't miss the opportunity to see either the hand-painted mural in the family den or the folk-art stone walk outside. After the tour, guests may relax on the sun porch or in the music room.

HOUSE OF SEVEN GABLES, P.O. Box 204, 215 6th St., Baraboo, WI 53913; 608-356-8387. A 2-guestroom (private baths) home listed in the National Register of Historic Places for its ornamental early Victorian architecture. Lodgings include house tour plus generous continental breakfast. Open year-round. Nearby are the scenic bluffs of Devil's Lake State Park, Circus World Museum (located at the original Ringling Brothers' Circus winter quarters), and the Wisconsin Dells. Biking, hiking, and canoeing also available. No pets. Ralph and Pamela Krainik, Proprietors.

Directions: Take Exit 106 off I-90/94. Go west on Hwy. 33 into Baraboo. At the Ross Floral Shop, turn left and go two blocks. Turn right on 6th St.

For B&B rates, see Index.

MARYBROOKE INN
Oshkosh, Wisconsin

Marybrooke Inn is a fine partnering of two born innkeepers: Mary and Brooke Rolston. From the first smile hello to the last wave goodbye, they make guests feel especially welcome here, providing wakeup knocks, making solicitous inquiries about breakfast preferences, even offering transportation to and from the local airport, if needed.

The Rolstons bought the three-story house, built in 1895, to provide a home for weary travelers as well as for themselves. Tasteful colors of crimson, apricot, rose, and pewter grace guest rooms on the upper floors. Rooms offer handsewn comforters and fresh flowers. Full breakfast may include omelets with fresh tomatoes and chives from the Rolstons' backyard garden and sometimes, the specialty of the house—a baked apple pancake. In the afternoon the Rolstons host a sherry-or-tea hour for their guests; at night, parlor games such as backgammon or Trivial Pursuit are available in the sitting room. A piano is also there for the playing.

Area natives, the Rolstons are experts on places to go and things to do. There is, of course, Oshkosh's annual premier event: the Experimental Aircraft Association's fly-in, an aviation showcase. But the town is also home to such diverse entertainment as the Oshkosh B'Gosh clothing outlet and the Paine Art Center, plus many outdoor sports such as biking, boating, fishing, camping, hunting, skating, skiing, swimming, and snowmobiling. It is a good point of departure for all northern Wisconsin.

Whether you are coming or going from the inn, don't forget to look up at the outside second story. There you'll see the white architectural medallion that has become this bed and breakfast's graceful trademark.

MARYBROOKE INN, 705 W. New York Ave., Oshkosh, WI 54901; 414-426-4761. A 4-guestroom (sharing 2 baths) home in east-central Wisconsin. Lodgings include complete breakfast. Open year-round. Lake Winnebago and the Fox River are close by the inn; also in the area are the Paine Art Center and Arboretum and the Museum of the Experimental Aircraft Assoc. (EAA). Children over 12 welcome. No pets. No credit cards. No smoking. Brooke and Mary Rolston, Proprietors.

Directions: Take I-94 to Milwaukee, where you can pick up U.S. 41. Go north on Rte. 41 to Wisconsin 21. Head east on 21 across the Fox River. Turn right on High Ave. (first stoplight) and continue one block to New York Ave. Turn left on New York Ave.

For B&B rates, see Index.

MONCHES MILL HOUSE
Hartland, Wisconsin

This rustic retreat is less than an hour from Milwaukee. But you'd never know it from the peaceful surroundings.

Rolling hills, back-country roads, and a sleepy river frame this old fieldstone home, built in 1842 for the miller who used to grind grain on the Oconomowoc here. Now it is the private residence of Harvey and Elaine Taylor. Guests who come on Wednesdays and Fridays may decide to stay for one of Elaine's elegant luncheons, though they must plan well ahead of time to reserve a spot. Served from 11:30 A.M. to 2:30 P.M., the luncheon always includes homemade soup, garden salad, quiche, dessert, and Russian tea. Ingredients are fresh from the Taylors' garden and henhouse. They are prepared in the style Elaine learned in France.

The river begs for a good canoe, and the Taylors willingly lend theirs to guests. They are also generous with the jacuzzi, located in the family's solar house elsewhere on the estate. Tennis, biking, and hiking are available too. But the mood of Monches Mill House is such that you may just wish to curl up on the balcony with a good book. There, you can glance up every so often to rest your eyes on the river and soft, distant fields.

MONCHES MILL HOUSE, W301 N9430 Highway E, Hartland, WI 53029; 414-966-7546. A 4-guestroom (shared baths) rustic seven-acre estate on the Oconomowoc River. Complimentary continental breakfast. Open mid-May thru Dec. by reservation only. Tennis and canoeing available on estate. Nearby is Kettle Moraine State Forest with hiking and xc skiing. Elaine Taylor, Proprietor.

Directions: From I-94, exit at Hwy. 16. Leave 16 at the Hwy. E (Hartland-Merton Ave.) exit. Take Hwy. E about 5 mi. north to the village of Monches. Look for the inn by the river.

For B&B rates, see Index.

OLD RITTENHOUSE INN
Bayfield, Wisconsin

The northwest corner of Wisconsin is pinched between Minnesota on the west and that inexplicable portion of western Michigan on the east. On a peninsula stretching out into Lake Superior are the town and county of Bayfield, the Redcliff Indian Reservation, and the Apostle Islands National Lakeshore. As a vacation and resort area, it may be one of the best-kept secrets in North America.

One of the most fascinating aspects is that in this unspoiled but still accessible area, the Old Rittenhouse Inn is a model of Victorian style and elegant grace.

Although the main stress of this book is on excellent accommodations and succulent breakfasts, I just can't imagine visiting the Old Rittenhouse Inn without arriving in time for dinner.

Innkeepers Jerry and Mary Phillips told me that the house had been built in 1890 as a summer home. The basic form was there, but it was necessary to find appropriate Victorian furniture.

Guest rooms have four-poster beds, marble-topped dressers and commodes to add to the Victorian atmosphere. There are fireplaces in three of the five guest rooms, and Lake Superior can be seen from rooms facing the southeast. An à la carte breakfast is served every morning in the same dining room where the dinner menu is recited to guests each night. Among the unusual offerings are wild rice pancakes, sourdough pancakes, omelets, and freshly baked english muffins. The Old Rittenhouse is one of the few inns I have ever visited where there is a sweet course served at breakfast, which could be tortes, crêpes, or small cakes.

OLD RITTENHOUSE INN, 301 Rittenhouse Ave., Bayfield, WI 54814; 715-779-5765. A 10-guestroom Victorian inn in an area of historic and natural beauty, 70 mi. east of Duluth, Minn., on the shore of Lake Superior. European plan. Breakfast and dinner served to travelers. Open May 1 to Nov. 1 Advance reservations most desirable. Extensive recreational activity of all kinds available throughout the year, including tours, hiking, and cycling on the nearby Apostle and Madeline Islands. Not comfortable for small children. No pets. Jerry and Mary Phillips, Innkeepers.

Directions: From the Duluth Airport, follow Rte. 53-S through the city of Duluth over the bridge to Superior, Wisconsin. Turn east on Rte. 2 near Ashland (1½ hrs.), turn north on 13-N to Bayfield.

For Lodging rates, see Index.

THE RENAISSANCE INN
Sister Bay, Wisconsin

One of the very agreeable things about Door County, Wisconsin, besides the occasional glimpses of distinctive local architecture and the pleasant shoreline drives, is the fact that everything is within an easy driving distance.

For example, from Sturgeon Bay there is a choice of roads that eventually will lead to Sister Bay, and it's possible to go up one side and down the other and enjoy a very pleasant drive.

I must say that I was very much surprised to find a bed-and-breakfast inn with a Renaissance theme located in this part of the world. It has five smallish guest rooms on the second floor, all with private baths, and each room is decorated differently with European furniture and Renaissance prints. This Renaissance theme is carried out with reproductions of various well-known pieces of art by easily recognizable Renaissance artists. Oddly enough, there are also some French impressionist touches as well, mixed in with some late 19th-century American wrought-iron bedsteads.

The best one-word description for this inn is "neat." That's the first and most lasting impression I had during my visit with innkeepers JoDee and John Faller.

It was also a surprise to find that a rather intimate dining room provides guests with the evening meal, which is basically a seafood cuisine, featuring Cajun international dishes. Fresh fruit and fresh-baked coffee cake are offered for breakfast, along with eggs, french toast, and various other offerings, which change daily.

Situated in a residential area, the Renaissance Inn is within walking distance of numerous shops, galleries, boat docks and the public beach. Of course, there is much to do in Door County within convenient driving distance.

THE RENAISSANCE INN, 414 Maple Dr., Sister Bay, WI 54234; 414-854-5107. A 5-guestroom (private baths) modest inn located in the upper end of the Door County peninsula. Breakfast and dinner served daily. Open all year except for the inclement weeks of the winter. Conveniently located to enjoy the cultural and recreational advantages of Door County. No pets. JoDee and John Faller, Innkeepers.

Directions: Follow Rte. 42 to Sister Bay and turn left at the Bundas Department store. The inn is just a few rods farther on the right.

For B&B rates, see Index.

SEVEN PINES LODGE
Lewis, Wisconsin

Although overnight lodgings including breakfast are available at this sophisticated rustic lodge in the Wisconsin deep woods, I feel it only fair to warn the prospective guest that it will be very difficult to leave after a single night's stay. One of the attractions is a trout stream that meanders through the tree-shaded grounds. In fact, freshly caught trout from that stream are a main entrée on the dinner menu—and on the breakfast menu, upon request.

Accommodations at Seven Pines Lodge are in the main building, where there are five year-round guest rooms, and also in unique outbuildings that are used during the temperate seasons.

Everybody gathers around the fireplace in the living room after dinner and, among other things, there are many albums of photographs of the earlier days at this lodge, which at one time played host to Calvin Coolidge.

Although a full breakfast is available at an additional charge, I find that the continental breakfast, included in the room rate, consisting of homemade breads, Danish aebleskiver or caramel roll, juice, and coffee is quite enough for me. It is served, when the weather permits, on the porch overlooking the stream. Otherwise, it is served in the rustic dining room, where dinner is also served.

SEVEN PINES LODGE, Lewis, WI 54851; 715-653-2323. A 10-guest-room rustic resort inn (3 rooms have shared baths) in the Wisconsin woods about 1½ hrs. from Minneapolis. Open year-round. Closed Thanksgiving and Christmas Day. St. Croix Falls, Taylors Falls, National Wild River Scenic Waterway nearby. Tennis, swimming, golf, woodswalking, downhill skiing, backroading nearby. Xc ski pkgs. available. Very attractive for children of all ages since the innkeepers also have children. No pets. No credit cards. Joan and David Simpson, Innkeepers.

Directions: From Minneapolis/St. Paul: follow I35W or I35E north to US 8 at Forest Lake, Minn. East on US 8 through Taylors Falls, Minn./St. Croix Falls, Wis., to Wis. 35 north to Lewis. Turn right at gas station to T, right 1 mi. to fork in road and turn left ½ mi. to Seven Pines Lodge entrance.

For B&B rates, see Index.

398

WASHINGTON HOUSE INN
Cedarburg, Wisconsin

"Guests without baggage are required to pay in advance." That's the warning in the July 5, 1895 registry of the original Washington House, once an outpost for rugged wilderness travelers on their way north or west.

Today, this three-story inn is far more urbane. The inn boasts other amenities that early pioneers could not have imagined: complimentary chocolates, private whirlpool baths, televisions and telephones, sauna, valet services, elevator. And modern check-in techniques are standard procedure.

Yet the building, built of Cream City brick fashioned from the clay bluffs of Lake Michigan, can still spark dreams of yesteryear. The old registry is on display in the lobby. There visitors can see the original hardwood floors and marble-trimmed fireplace. The ceiling is sculpted tin. Several of the breakfast breads are based on a turn-of-the-century Cedarburg cookbook, which guests can peruse for the asking. And each of the inn's twenty rooms is named after a Cedarburg pioneer.

Check in early and you'll have time to walk the town's main street, listed as a National Historic District. A local guidebook, "Walk Through Yesterday," is helpful here. Be sure to catch the five-story gristmill, built in 1855 from limestone quarried from the riverbed of nearby Cedar Creek. After your tour, return to the inn for its 5 P.M. social hour with cheese and local fruit wines.

Guests may choose a room in either of the hotel's two sections: one done up in primitive pioneer style with pencil-post beds and patchwork quilts, pine floors, and rough stone walls, or the other, decorated in Victorian elegance with brass beds, eyelet bed-coverings, and daintily flowered wallpaper.

And oh, yes—any guest, with or without baggage, is welcome.

WASHINGTON HOUSE INN, W62 N573 Washington Ave., Cedarburg, WI 53012; 414-375-3550. A 20-guestroom (private baths) restored 1800s inn in the center of town. Complimentary continental breakfast and evening social hour. Picnic baskets available. Open year-round. Nearby are many shops (specialty retail, crafts, and antiques), historic sites, and county parks with opportunities for picnicking, fishing, hiking, and xc skiing. Bike rentals available. No pets. Judy Drefahl, Innkeeper.

Directions: From I-43, take Exit 17 into Cedarburg. Turn right on Washington Ave. in the center of town.

For B&B rates, see Index.

THE WHITE GULL INN
Fish Creek, Wisconsin

Our midwestern readers are probably very familiar with the term "Fish Boil," which is, as far as I know, a tradition limited to Wisconsin. The Fish Boil at the White Gull Inn features freshly caught lake fish, boiled potatoes, homemade cole slaw, fresh-baked bread, and cherry pie. The wood-smoked fire combined with the aroma of Lake Michigan fish creates truly gargantuan appetites. Fish Boil dinners are served every Wednesday, Friday, Saturday, and Sunday evening during the summer and fall. On non-Fish-Boil nights, the inn serves candlelight dinners from its regular menu.

The White Gull Inn is also open during the winter, when the Fish Boil is served on Saturday and Wednesday nights only.

Lest I give the impression that the only thing there is to do in Door County, Wisconsin, is to eat, let me explain that the location of Fish Creek along the shores of Lake Michigan provides ample four-season recreational activity plus a generous helping of attractions for those inclined to the theater and the arts.

During the winter season breakfast is included with the room rate. In the summer, it is additional.

THE WHITE GULL INN, Fish Creek, WI 54212; 414-868-3517. A 14-guestroom inn with 4 cottages, many fireplaces, in Door County, 23 mi. north of Sturgeon Bay. Rooms with and without private baths. Open year-round. European plan. B&B rate available in winter. Breakfast and lunch daily year-round. Fish Boils: Wednesday, Friday, Saturday, Sunday nights throughout the season. All meals open to travelers. Reservations requested for evening meals. Golf, tennis, swimming, fishing, biking, sailing, and other summer and winter sports nearby. Excellent for children of all ages. No pets. Andy and Jan Coulson, Joan Holliday, Nancy Vaughn, Innkeepers.

Directions: From Chicago: take I-94 to Milwaukee. Follow Rte. I-43 (141) from Milwaukee to Manitowoc; Rte. 42 from Manitowoc to Fish Creek. Turn left at stop sign at the bottom of the hill, go 2½ blocks to inn. From Green Bay: take Rte. 57 to Sturgeon Bay; Rte. 42 to Fish Creek.

For B&B rates, see Index.

WHITE LACE INN
Sturgeon Bay, Wisconsin

In many ways the White Lace Inn, a Queen Anne Victorian with a big, wide porch and green shingles on the third floor, is a wonderful introduction to Door County. On a quiet street in the residential area of Sturgeon Bay, it is within five blocks of the bay, and two blocks of the National Historic downtown district.

At the time of my visit, Dennis Statz who, with his wife, Bonnie, is the innkeeper, was busy working on the newest addition, the Garden House, a simple Victorian "cottage," circa 1885, behind the main house. Bonnie declared there were going to be many, many perennials planted to give it a real garden feeling. (The latest news is that over 300 have now been planted.)

As I wandered through the main house, admiring the extremely well-preserved interior woodwork, hardwood floors, and other Victorian embellishments, Bonnie explained to me that although Door County is certainly well known in the summertime for all of the water-oriented activities on the lake, cross-country skiing is extremely popular during the wintertime. Particularly on the weekends between January and March.

"Very often our guests ski for about an hour or two and then mostly just relax and read and do a bit of driving around. There's also a small downhill slope in Sturgeon Bay," she told me.

There is a total of eleven guest rooms, all with private baths. There are many antiques, flowered wallpaper, down pillows, cozy comforters and quilts, live plants, and lace curtains. There is a fireplace in each of the guest rooms in the new Garden House.

"Our breakfast is continental with muffins, juice, and coffee, and is served on plates rather than self-served. Coffee and tea are available at any time during the day."

For the first-time visitor, the White Lace Inn, like Door County, is a very pleasant surprise.

WHITE LACE INN, 16 N. Fifth Ave., Sturgeon Bay, WI 54235; 414-743-1105. An 11-guestroom (private baths) bed-and-breakfast inn in one of Wisconsin's attractive resort areas. Breakfast to guests only is the only meal served. Open year-round. Conveniently located near all of the cultural and recreational attractions in Door County. Special three- and five-day packages available during the winter. No pets. No credit cards. Dennis and Bonnie Statz, Innkeepers.

Directions: From the south take the Rte. 42-57 bypass across the new bridge, turn left on Michigan and go right on Fifth Ave.

For B&B rates, see Index.

ANNIE MOORE'S GUEST HOUSE
Laramie, Wyoming

Annie Moore's Guest House is a real gem. A post-Victorian, Queen Anne—style house, it was built around 1910 and run as a boarding house by one Annie Moore from 1935 to 1949. After extensive and exquisite renovations by the present owners, it was opened as a bed and breakfast in 1984. Until I learned of Annie Moore's, I didn't know of a single bed and breakfast in the state, much less along heavily traveled Interstate 80, so finding this charming guest house was quite a pleasant surprise.

Located in a quiet, residential neighborhood across the street from the University of Wyoming campus, with a variety of native Wyoming plants, on carefully landscaped grounds, the house is light gray-blue with darker slate-blue trim, and the effect is crisp and inviting. Inside, an abundance of windows, both stained glass and clear, as well as a few strategically placed skylights, give the Annie Moore an unusually light and cheerful atmosphere. The woodwork is all handcrafted, oriental carpets cover polished wooden floors, and a generous number of thriving houseplants are placed among the comfortable, attractive furnishings. There's a TV in one sitting room, a stereo in another, and the kitchen is open for tea and coffee throughout the day.

The guest rooms are all bright and in keeping with the exceptionally fine decor throughout the house. A large second-story sundeck is accessible from one of the bedrooms or by a spiral staircase from below.

Breakfast is served buffet-style and includes fresh muffins or rolls, yogurts, cereals, homemade maple-nut granola, special-blend imported coffee, tea, juice, and fresh fruit in season.

Out on the plains of Wyoming, Annie Moore's is an interesting and unique opportunity for very fine lodging.

ANNIE MOORE'S GUEST HOUSE, 819 University, Laramie, WY 82070; 307-721-4177. A 6-guestroom (4 shared baths) bed and breakfast. Breakfast included in lodging price. No other meal served. Open year-round. Convenient to scenic and historic areas. Not suitable for young children. No pets. Smoking limited to sitting room. Diana Kopulos, Innkeeper.

Directions: From I-80 (east or west), take 3rd St. exit into Laramie. Go north on 3rd St. for approx. 1 mi. to downtown intersection of 3rd and Ivinson. Go east on Ivinson for 6 blocks to 9th St. and take a left onto 9th. Annie Moore's is one block up, on northwest corner of 9th and University.

For B&B rates, see Index.

THE BEACONSFIELD INN
Victoria, British Columbia

Travelers seeking an elegant, urban inn must add to their itinerary the Beaconsfield, one of Victoria's award-winning downtown bed-and-breakfast inns. The home was built in 1905 by architect Samuel McClure for R. P. Rithet, as a wedding gift for Rithet's only daughter, Gertrude.

Inside the Edwardian English-style structure is a formal English library, with dark leather sofas, a red oriental rug, and the original mantled fireplace. Floor-to-ceiling bookshelves are filled with books, including a collection of bound volumes.

Each of the guest rooms has a descriptive name, such as the Blue Room and the Verandah Room, or is named for a person in history. Oscar's Room takes its name from Oscar Wilde, and its colors from his favored lavender. Lily's Room is named after Edward VII's mistress, Lily Langtry.

Guests are invited to gather in the morning for fresh fruit, an omelet, bacon or sausages, homemade scones, jams, and fresh-brewed coffee.

THE BEACONSFIELD INN, 998 Humboldt St., Victoria, B.C. V8V 2Z8; 604-384-4044. A 12-guestroom (private baths) bed-and-breakfast inn in downtown Victoria. Full breakfast included in room rate. Open most of the year. Parliament buildings and grounds, Provincial Museum (don't miss it), and famous Butchart Gardens; many tea rooms, shops, boutiques; walk along the harbor or ride in a horse-drawn carriage. Adult oriented. No pets. Smoking is discouraged. Christine Kirkham, Innkeeper.

Directions: Victoria is located on Vancouver Island and can be reached by ferries from Seattle, Port Angeles, and nearby Vancouver, B.C. (Allow plenty of time; there will be longer lines on weekends.) From downtown Victoria, take Douglas St. to Humboldt St. Turn right (west, away from the harbor) to the corner of Humboldt and Vancouver Sts., where the inn is located. Parking off the street.

For B&B rates, see Index.

FERNHILL LODGE
Mayne Island, British Columbia

At Fernhill Lodge guests will find an unexpected surprise—several acres planted in culinary, fragrant, and medicinal herbs. The Crumblehulmes grow fresh plants as well as the dried herbs. A guided tour of the gardens among the mugwort, lavender, thyme, garlic, and basil offers a unique and fascinating experience.

Each of the guest rooms is decorated in a different period—from 18th-century French and Victorian to Colonial and rustic farmhouse, each offers a pleasant haven. The clucking of the family hens may be the loudest sound you hear during your visit to Fernhill Lodge.

Breakfast entrées are prepared by Brian and may include fresh eggs from the resident chickens, fresh-squeezed orange juice, and a fruit plate. Mary may bake orange rolls or scones, which are extremely tempting. On request, Brian will prepare a special medieval, Renaissance, or Roman-style dinner.

FERNHILL LODGE, P.O. Box 140, Fernhill Rd., Mayne Island, B.C. VON 2J0; 604-539-2544. A 6-guestroom bed-and-breakfast inn in the Gulf Islands southwest of Vancouver, B.C. Full breakfast included in room rate. Open year-round. Rural island atmosphere; beachcombing, hiking, fishing, boating, sailing. Historical sites. No pets. Mary and Brian Crumblehulme, Innkeepers.

Directions: From the international border at Blaine take Hwy. 99 toward Vancouver, B.C., following signs to Tsawwassen Ferry. Take Gulf Island ferry to Mayne Island. Follow Village Bay Rd. about 1.5 mi. to Miner's Bay. Turn right at the stop sign onto Fernhill Rd. for about 1.5 mi. to lodge.

For B&B rates, see Index.

ROSE GARDEN GUEST HOUSE
Vancouver, British Columbia

With more than 200 varieties of roses, including grandiflora, tea, floribunda, and miniatures, the Beglaws enjoy showing their prize-winning garden to guests. Dwyla harvests rose petals for drying and creates perfumed sachets, potpourri, scented pillows, and be-ribboned pictures using dried miniature roses.

Travelers will find bright, cheerful guest rooms with rose wallpaper and decor, and a private entrance on the garden level. One guest room has a queen-sized bed with a cozy eiderdown, a love seat, overstuffed chair, vanity, and desk. A second guest room has twin beds.

Breakfast is wholesome at Rose Garden Guest House. Dwyla bakes whole-wheat muffins and biscuits, and often will serve eggs Benedict or blueberry pancakes along with herbal teas and coffee. If you would prefer a vegetarian breakfast, Dwyla will be happy to accommodate you—just let her know when you make reservations.

ROSE GARDEN GUEST HOUSE, 6808 Dawson St., Vancouver, B.C. V5S 2W3; 604-435-7129. A 2-guestroom (shared bath) bed-and-breakfast home south of downtown Vancouver. Full breakfast included in room rate. Open year-round. Queen Elizabeth Park will appeal to garden lovers. A plethora of golf courses, Bloedel Conservatory (tropical plants and birds), shopping centers, Stanley Park, and Grouse Mountain. There is a seabus across Burrard Inlet, site of Expo 86. Children permitted. No pets. No smoking indoors. No credit cards. Dwyla and Ed Beglaw, Hosts.

Directions: From the international border at Blaine, north of Seattle, take Hwy. 99 toward downtown Vancouver. Take the Knight St. Bridge exit to 49th Ave. Turn right on 49th Ave. and continue past 2 stoplights to Dawson St. Turn right and look for white picket fence and an abundance of roses.

For B&B rates, see Index.

PANSY PATCH
St. Andrews, New Brunswick, Canada

What a surprise this was! I visited it originally because I found a fetching little brochure for the Pansy Patch Shop, and discovered not only an enticing collection of fine furniture, antiques, rare and out-of-print books, prints, silver, glass, china, paintings, maps, quilts, baskets, primitives, and many other items, but also a very pleasant bed-and-breakfast inn.

The proprietors are Kathleen and Michael Lazare, who live in Sherman, Connecticut, in the wintertime and operate Pansy Patch during the summer.

The shop is very attractive and greatly resembles some excellent shops of the same nature that I have visited in England. The living room is filled with fine furniture, antiques, and prints. The sun porch is lined with bookcases of volumes on virtually every subject; the dining room sparkles with silver and glass, and there are maps and books in the library. Even the butler's pantry is open, with a large selection of cookbooks, books on gardening, antiques, and Colonial living.

A breakfast of homemade biscuits, muffins or rolls—especially blueberry muffins in season—with homemade jams and coffee and fresh fruit in season can be enjoyed on a terrace looking down across a beautiful lawn and into the streets of the town of St. Andrews.

There are three very tidy guest rooms on the second floor and breakfast is included in the room rate.

There is an Old Welsh quotation carved into the mantelpiece: *"Now faire betyde who here abyde / and merrie may they be and / faire befalle who in this halle / repaire in courtesie. From morne till nighte / be it darke or brighte / we banish dole and dree / come sitte besyde our hearthe tis wide / for gentle companie."*

PANSY PATCH, 59 Carleton St., St. Andrews, New Brunswick, Canada EOG 2XO; 506-529-3834. A 3-guestroom bed-and-breakfast inn situated in a delightful shop located immediately behind the Algonquin Hotel. Breakfast the only meal served. Open from June until early Oct. Most conveniently located to enjoy all of the recreational, historical, and cultural advantages of St. Andrews. Not particularly suited for children. No pets. Michael and Kathleen Lazare, Inn-Shopkeepers.

Directions: Pansy Patch is immediately behind the Algonquin Hotel.

For B&B rates, see Index.

HIGHLAND HEIGHTS INN
Iona, Nova Scotia, Canada

Many of the early settlers to Nova Scotia came from the highlands and islands of Scotland, bringing to this province their native Gaelic language and folkways. At Iona, Cape Breton, these cultural attributes are maintained, partly through the efforts of a volunteer board of Nova Scotians dedicated to retaining for posterity the whole early lifestyle of Scots, which was transplanted to Nova Scotia in the 18th century. One of their major undertakings has been the development of a 43-acre open-air museum consisting of nine historic buildings, a costumed staff trained in conversational Gaelic and local history, and a hilltop view of the four Cape Breton counties and both sections of Bras d'Or Lake.

The Highland Heights Inn was opened in 1973 on the same site as the Highland Village. It, too, overlooks Bras d'Or Lake, an internationally unique saltwater lake carved naturally from the entire central area of the island. There are twenty-six guest rooms, all with two double beds, private baths, and lake views. Old-fashioned country cooking is featured, and local salmon and oatcakes are among its specialties. This inn is listed in *Where to Eat in Canada*.

HIGHLAND HEIGHTS INN, P.O. Box 19, Iona, Cape Breton Island, Nova Scotia; 902-622-2360. A 26-guestroom pleasant personally run motel in the scenic area of Cape Breton Island. Dining room open daily from 7:30 A.M. to 9:00 P.M. Breakfast is included in room rate. Conveniently situated to enjoy fishing, swimming, boating, and hunting. Also convenient for visits to Fortress Louisbourg and the Alexander Graham Bell Museum. The Cabot Trail is just a few minutes away. Sheila and Bruce MacNeil, Innkeepers.

Directions: From Trans-Canada 105, take the Little Narrows Ferry (operating every 10 min., 24 hrs. a day) to Rte. 223 and continue 15 mi. to inn. From Sydney, turn left off Trans-Canada 125 at Leitches Creek on Rte. 223 and continue 30 mi. to inn.

For B&B rates, see Index.

INVERARY INN
Baddeck, Nova Scotia, Canada

Baddeck, on the Bras d'Or Lake on Cape Breton in Nova Scotia is an exciting nautical paradise for sailboat and yachting enthusiasts because of its sparkling clear water, many sheltered anchorages, and the superb highland scenery.

Most of the early settlers came to Baddeck from the highlands of Scotland. Gaelic language and Scottish culture are preserved here in a number of ways.

Alexander Graham Bell's life and inventions are commemorated at the museum in Baddeck and include Dr. Bell's successful efforts toward powered flight, telephone communication, early X-ray, and a first attempt to use an iron lung.

The North American traveler intent on covering the Canadian Maritimes in as quick a fashion as possible errs in not remaining at least two nights at the Inverary Inn. It takes at least a full day to traverse the Cabot Trail, which runs along next to the sea among the fishing villages, and then plunges into the Great Nova Scotia forests.

The inn is an old farmhouse with a barn, wagon house, and pine-paneled cottages on the outskirts of Baddeck, overlooking the lake. The winding paths lead through the trees past the children's playground to the bathing wharf.

It's quite a drive from the southern end of Nova Scotia or the New Brunswick–Nova Scotia border to Baddeck, so it is well to plan on enjoying an Inverary dinner.

A full Scottish breakfast of hot spiced applesauce, oatmeal porridge with brown sugar and cream, crisp fried Scottish sausage and home fries, and a basket of Scottish oat cakes and bannock, is offered as part of the B&B rate. It is served in the dining room, which itself has a most pleasant view of the lakes. It's almost the same as being in Scotland.

INVERARY INN, Box 190, Baddeck, Cape Breton, N.S. Canada 902-295-2674. A 40-guestroom (private and shared baths) village inn on the Cabot Trail, 52 mi. from Sydney, N.S. On the shore of Lake Bras d'Or. European plan. B&B rate available. Breakfast and dinner served to travelers daily. Open from May 15 to Nov. 1. Swimming pool, tennis courts, bicycles, and children's playground on grounds. Boating and small golf course nearby. Isobel MacAulay, Innkeeper.

Directions: Follow Trans-Canada Hwy. to Canso Causeway to Baddeck.

For B&B rates, see Index.

HANDFIELD INN (AUBERGE HANDFIELD)
St. Marc-sur-le-Richelieu, Quebec, Canada

The Handfield Inn is a great many things: a venerable mansion that has seen a century and a half of history; an enjoyable French restaurant; a four-season resort; and perhaps best of all, it is an opportunity to visit a French-Canadian village which has remained relatively free from the invasion of developers.

Accommodations are in rustic rooms decorated and furnished in the old Quebec style, but with touches of modern comfort including tile bathrooms and controlled heating.

The village of St. Marc is wonderfully French and when I was there I had animated communication with the village baker, he in French, I in English, while the aroma of his bread and rolls sent my gastronomic senses reeling. St. Marc stretches along the Richelieu River, and has a twin village on the opposite side called St. Charles, which is reached by ferry.

Visitors during the summer can enjoy summer theater on the converted ferry boat *l'Escale* from June 15 to September 15. There is also a marina with a 300-foot pier for pleasure boats. Visitors between March 1 and the end of April can also take part in the maple sugar parties in the nearby woods.

A full French-Canadian breakfast is served in the old-fashioned dining room. It includes homemade beans, omelettes and bacon, maple-smoked ham, buckwheat pancakes, and eggs cooked in maple syrup. Special B&B rates are available to readers of this book.

HANDFIELD INN (Auberge Handfield), St. Marc-sur-le-Richelieu (Saint Marc on the Richelieu River), Quebec, JOL 2EO, Canada; 514-584-2226. A 60-room French-Canadian country inn about 25 miles from Montreal. Different lodging plans available. Please consult with the inn in advance. Some rooms have shared baths. Breakfast, lunch, and dinner served daily to travelers. Ladies are expected to wear a skirt or dress and gentlemen, a coat at dinner. Open every day all year. All summer and winter active sports easily available. Many handcrafts, antique, and historical tours in the area. No pets. M. and Mme. Conrad Handfield, Innkeepers.

Directions: From Champlain, Victoria, or the Jacques Cartier bridges, take Hwy. 3 to Sorel, turn right at Hwy. 20. From the east end of Montreal go through the Hyppolite LaFontaine Tunnel. Rte. 20 passes through St. Julie, St. Bruno, and Beloeil. Leave Hwy. 20 at Exit 112 turning left on Rte. 223 north. Handfield is 7 miles distant.

For B&B rates, see Index.

HOTEL MANOIR d'AUTEUIL
Quebec City, Canada

In the account of my visit to Chateau de Pierre, a companion hotel to this very pleasant accommodation, I have explained in some detail why the North American visitor to Quebec City will find it a most interesting adventure. At this moment I have listed only two small hotels in Quebec City; however, the tourist bureau of the city can supply the traveler with many others, both in and out of the Old City.

The Manoir d'Auteuil is out of the more heavily traveled riverfront area of Quebec, but visitors should be warned that during the high summer season tourists from all over North America are great in number. I found it very intriguing that the atmosphere of the entire city is predominantly French, and it makes it that much more attractive to me.

The Manoir d'Auteuil is just inside the walls of the Old City, across from the Esplanade Park. In a city that has quite a few examples of Victorian architecture, it seemed rather interesting to me that Art Deco should be the prevailing theme of the decor here. I learned that one of the previous owners of the hotel had become interested in this particular style, and the present owners, the Couturier family, have preserved the circa-1930 look. Some rooms were being redecorated during my stay.

The bedrooms basically are quite comfortable in size. Mine, in particular, had a bathroom big enough for a half-court game of basketball. There are showers and tubs in every bathroom—my shower had seven water spouts.

Parking is available at a reduced rate for hotel guests in the underground public parking garage.

HOTEL MANOIR d'AUTEUIL, 49 rue d'Auteuil, Vieux-Quebec, (Quebec) QC, G1R 4C2; 418-694-1173. A 17-guestroom (private baths) small hotel within the walls of the Old City of Quebec. All rooms have color TV and direct-line telephones. Breakfast is not included in the room rate and is not served during the summer months. Most conveniently located to enjoy all of the touristic sights of the Old City. (See section on Le Chateau de Pierre.) Parking nearby. Georges-Humbert Couturier, Hotelier.

Directions: Stop at one of the many tourist information bureaus en route to Quebec City and you'll get good directions and a good map.

For Lodging rates, see Index.

LE CHATEAU DE PIERRE
Quebec City, Canada

First of all, I would like to encourage everybody to visit Quebec City. It is one of the most unusual, instructive, entertaining, and joyful experiences I've ever had. Like Victoria, its counterpart in British Columbia on the west coast of Canada, it has a wonderful, natural feeling.

Incidentally the term "Quebec" can refer either to the city or the entire province.

I cannot go into great detail here because we do want to tell our readers about Le Chateau de Pierre; however, suffice it to say that the old section of the city (Vieux-Quebec) is the big attraction. Dominated by the really tremendous Hotel Chateau Frontenac, Le Chateau de Pierre sits high up on the bluffs above the St. Lawrence River. The old streets and shops and the general atmosphere are quite like Paris, and I found the entire experience most delightful. It's a good idea to make a short stop at the Museum du Fort, which will provide an entire historical background of the city.

For a complete booklet on the region, contact: Tourisme Quebec, Ministère de l'Industrie, du Commerce et du Tourisme, Case postale 20 000, Quebec, Qc Canada G1K 7X2.

LE CHATEAU DE PIERRE, 17, Avenue Ste-Genevieve, Quebec City, Canada, G1R 4A8; 418-694-0429. A 15-guestroom (private baths) conservative, clean, Victorian-style hotel in the Old City, just a few steps from the river. Open year-round. Breakfast is not served. No credit cards. English, French, and Spanish spoken. Mme. L. Couturier, Proprietress.

Directions: Stop at one of the many tourist information bureaus en route to Quebec City and you'll get good directions and a good map.

For B&B rates, see Index.

POSADA AJIJIC
Ajijic, Jalisco, Mexico

If you were writing a mystery story set south of Guadalajara, Posada Ajijic would be the perfect prop. Not only is this small hotel, built around a garden, everyone's idea of what a Mexican inn should be, but sooner or later every American wintering along the shores of romantic Lake Chapala drops by for a meal or the music. All your canny detective would have to do is wait. In comfort.

Ajijic (ah-hee-HEEK), on the north shore of Lake Chapala, began as an Indian fishing village, but is now known for its arts and crafts. The town also has a small museum and a 16th-century church that starts ringing its bells early in the morning. The Posada dining room faces the lake, and we cannot argue with the assertion, "This is the most beautiful sunset in Mexico."

The food is remarkably good and very reasonable. The very popular Aztec Soup is usually on the menu, and the shrimp in garlic butter is worth a special trip. Sunday brunch includes a fruit plate, then either eggs Benedict, German apple pancakes and bacon, or Chilaquiles with smoked pork chops for less than four dollars.

Guest rooms have private baths, fireplaces, and either porches or patios, but everything opens to the garden. Flower-bordered paths lead to the swimming pool and dining room, and the heady fragrance of blooming citrus trees fills the air year around. The bright colors of hibiscus are repeated in rooms furnished in the colonial style and decorated with local art and textiles.

Music from the piano bar begins late afternoon every day except Sunday, while a five-piece band plays for dancing on weekend evenings. The reputation of Posada Ajijic is no mystery.

HOTEL POSADA AJIJIC, Calle 16 de Septiembre No. 4 (Box 30), Ajijic, Jalisco, Mexico C.P. 45920; (376) 5-33-95. A 15-guestroom (private baths) inn on the north shore of Lake Chapala about 30 min. from Guadalajara International Airport. Breakfast not included in room rate. Breakfast, lunch, dinner, and Sunday brunch served to travelers. Informal. Open all year. Swimming pool in garden; horseback riding, golf, theater, archeological museum nearby. Galleries and shops just steps away. Buses to Guadalajara every hour. Pets accepted. Street parking watched by hotel guard. Michael H. Eager, Manager.

Directions: From the airport or Guadalajara city, the road to Lake Chapala and Ajijic is clearly marked. Take Plaza Street exit from the highway toward the lake; continue 5 blocks. Posada is on the lakefront by the pier.

For Lodging rates, see Index.

LA CEIBA BEACH HOTEL
Puerto Morelos, Quintana Roo, Mexico

Those seeking something less conventional than the high-rise hotels and condos of Cancún can go south a few miles along the coastal highway to the hamlet of Puerto Morelos. Puerto Morelos is a typical Mexican Caribbean village, known primarily as a ferry port for the island of Cozumel.

Almost out of town and directly on the water is La Ceiba, a secluded string of relatively new duplex cottages, with a central reception-dining room-kitchen-bar and a diving shack where you can rent boats, snorkeling, fishing, and scuba gear, sign up for diving lessons, and otherwise prepare yourself for the underwater wonders of the reef, 600 yards offshore.

The place is run by a friendly young family with a helpful staff. Everything is very informal, and the food is remarkably good, specializing in ocean-fresh seafood as well as steaks and Yucatecan dishes. Breakfast is not included in the rates, but juice, sweet rolls, coffee or tea come to less than two dollars, and a full American breakfast is about four dollars. There are also small refrigerators in the rooms.

There is at present no telephone whatever at the inn, though the necessary lines are expected to be put in soon.

The sea provides the main activities, but you are well located for day trips, whether to the ruins at Tulum or the shops of Cancún.

The cottages are not luxurious. However, they are large and comfortable with attractive wall hangings and Mexican leather chairs. Each has a private bath and covered terrace; all face the sea.

LA CEIBA BEACH HOTEL, Puerto Morelos (mailing address: Box 1252, Cancún, Q-Roo, Mexico 77500); 1-800-621-6830. A 20-guestroom bungalow hotel on the beach, approx. 12 mi. south of Cancún International Airport. All rooms with private baths (showers), ceiling fans, and refrigerators. European plan. Breakfast, lunch, and dinner available. Dining room open 8 A.M. to 9:30 P.M. Good facilities and special rates for families. Swimming and wading pools. Boats and diving equipment for rent; instruction available. Pets accepted. Rosario Kimmel, Manager.

Directions: With car rented at the airport take Hwy. 307 south, following signs to Puerto Morelos. Turn left from highway toward village. Sign to La Ceiba will direct you left again on an unpaved road. The hotel is on your right. Taxi and public bus also available. La Ceiba will send their van if you let them know your arrival well in advance.

For Lodging rates, see Index.

VILLA ARQUEOLÓGICA
Cobá, Quintana Roo, Mexico

When you explore Cobá, you see it almost as the first excited discoverers did in 1897. There has been little reconstruction compared to the other major archaeological zones, though over 6,500 structures have been more or less identified.

Cobá flourished from A.D. 600 to 900, an important city at one end of the 65-mile ceremonial White Road, built and paved by people who had no pack animals and had not discovered the wheel. It contains Nohuch Mul, the highest pyramid in Yucatán, and, rarest of all in this area without surface water, four shallow green lakes.

A good paved road from Tulum to Nuevo X-Can has finally opened Cobá to visitors. It is an intriguing stop between the developed restorations at Tulum and Chichén Itzá. There is nothing manicured about Cobá. The paths are uneven, and you should be prepared to do a lot of walking.

So far, the only inn is right on the site. It is the very pleasant Villa Arqueológica, built around a flower-filled patio. A swimming pool, tennis court, spacious lounges, and even a library are among the amenities. Guest rooms are small but comfortable with large windows and built-in furniture. The dining room is quite good with a wide selection of dishes and is open for three meals. Sandwiches and salads are also available poolside.

Other villas with the same amenities are located at the Chichén Itzá and Uxmal ruins. A full American breakfast is about two and a half dollars, or you can take the very reasonable modified American plan.

VILLA ARQUEOLÓGICA, in the archaeological zone of Cobá, Quintana Roo, Mexico. (Reserve through the operating agency, Club Med, Calle Leibnitz 34, Mexico DF 11590; telephone: 533-4800. In the U.S., through your travel agent or Club Med: 800-CLUB MED.) A 40-guestroom (private baths) colonial-style inn about 110 km from Cancún. Different lodging plans available. Breakfast, lunch, and dinner served daily to travelers. Informal. Open every day all year, but the weather is best Dec. thru April. Swimming pool, tennis court, library, boutique.

Directions: From coastal Hwy. 307, turn right after Tulum Village, following signs to Cobá. Continue about 43 km. Signs are clearly posted to Cobá ruins and the Villa. You will be turning left. From inland Hwy. 180, turn at the northern end of the town Nuevo X-Can, signposted to Cobá and Tulum. The turn-off to the excavations and hotel (to your right) is at 44 km.

For Lodging rates, see Index.

HACIENDA CHICHÉN
Chichén Itzá, Yucatán, Mexico

Hacienda Chichén is one of the most historic colonial buildings in Yucatán, as well as a convenient lodging for travelers visiting the ruins of Chichén Itzá. Like so many Mexican charmers, it doesn't look like much from the road (a low yellow wall with the name of the place spelled out in slightly askew oversized letters), but don't let that put you off.

The central casa was originally built by Montejo the Younger shortly after the Conquest, using stones picked up from the ruins. Subsequent owners grew henequen, raised cattle, and hosted early explorers.

It stood abandoned when Edward H. Thompson, the controversial U.S. consul, bought the entire ruins of Chichén Itzá, including the hacienda, for $75 in the late 19th century. He rebuilt the house, and also dredged the sacred well, sending priceless artifacts home to the United States until the Mexican government intervened.

Today, guests stay in cottages and swim in the pool built for resident archaeologists by the Carnegie Foundation in the 1920s. Recently, the hacienda has been home to other teams of experts as well as a hotel for travelers. Breakfasts are sumptuous and served on the terrace of the handsome central casa overlooking the gardens. The grounds of the hacienda abut the ruins, known as Old Chichen, and are a ten-minute walk at most to the back entrance of the prime archaeological digs.

The rooms are large but simple with private bathrooms and covered terraces. You awake in the morning to the sounds of a variety of brightly plumed birds, and go to sleep lulled by the nightsong of tiny frogs. Long ago, the high priests of Itzá probably had the same experience.

HACIENDA CHICHÉN, Chichén Itzá, Yucatán. Reserve through Maya-Caribe Travel, 14 W. 95th St., New York, NY 10025; 1-800-223-4084. (In N.Y., 212-666-6620.) An 18-guestroom (private baths) historic cottage hotel in the archeological zone. Ceiling fans; some refrigerators. Breakfast, lunch, and dinner served daily. (Full American breakfast, $3.50.) Open from early Dec. to late March. Swimming pool. Botanical gardens. Julio Hoil, Manager.

Directions: Chichén Itzá is 121 km east of Mérida, off Hwy. 180. Follow signs to the archeological zone. Hacienda Chichén is on your left, opposite the Villa.

For Lodging rates, see Index.

HOTEL CASA DEL BALAM
Mérida, Yucatán, Mexico

As the capital of the state of Yucatán, Mérida is a considerable town of 500,000 people. It was founded in the early 1500s by the conquistadores, who built on top of the ruins of the ancient Mayan city of T'ho. There are very good restaurants, crafts markets, shops, architectural gems covering five centuries, a museum of anthropology, as well as free outdoor concerts or dance performances.

Casa del Balam is a relatively small hotel, just across the street from the university, two blocks from the beautiful Plaza de la Independencia, and within walking distance of all the central attractions. It is built in the colonial style around a cool patio containing trees and a fountain, and there is a swimming pool in the back.

The colonial styling is authentic and the ambience is extremely pleasant with a staff that is exceptionally courteous and responsive to requests. Guest rooms are large and well furnished with full baths and air conditioning.

The hotel has a good restaurant, serving American, Yucatecan, and Mexican food from early morning until ten at night. Breakfast is not included in the room rate, but a full American-style breakfast is only about three dollars.

Advance reservations are important since Hotel Casa del Balam is an open secret with those who write about and visit the city regularly. Incidentally, the name means "House of Jaguars."

HOTEL CASA DEL BALAM, Calle 60 No. 488, corner Calle 57, Mérida, Yucatán. Reserve through Maya-Caribe Travel, 14 W. 95th St., New York, NY 10025; 1-800-223-4084. (In N.Y., 212-666-6620.) A 52-guestroom, 2-suite (private baths), full-service authentic colonial hotel with air conditioning. Breakfast, lunch, and dinner served daily. Dining room open 7 A.M. to 10 P.M. Advance reservations essential; may be made through your travel agent. Travel agency on premises; also swimming pool. Centrally located two blocks from Plaza de la Independencia, with museum, shops, restaurants, concerts within easy walking distance. Valet pay-parking nearby. No pets. Ms. Canelaria Alonzo, Manager.

Directions: Whether you arrive from the east (Cancún) or the south (Mérida airport) you need only find Calle 60, which is one-way in the direction you need to go. Mérida is laid out on a simple grid pattern, and when you cross Calle 57, the entrance to the hotel is immediately on your right.

For Lodging rates, see Index.

CALIFORNIA GUEST HOUSE
Nelson, New Zealand

I have never been to New Zealand, but I thought it would be fun in response to two letters I have received from out-of-the way places (the other one is Alaska) to at least include a listing in this book. If any of my readers visit, I would be very much interested in hearing your opinions.

The California Guest House is presided over by two young Americans who fell in love with New Zealand as tourists. They explain that the climate in Nelson is similar to that of California's Santa Clara Valley, where they both grew up—warm sunshine day after day, very little rain, mild winters with occasional frost. Nelson is a popular tourist spot because of its sunshine and beaches and it is also on the main route around South Island.

The house is described as really lovely with twenty-four stained-glass windows, beautiful old wood paneling, three fireplaces, eleven-foot ceilings, a veranda on two sides, large lawn and gardens, and is set well back from the street in a residential area about five minutes' walk from the town center.

There are six guest rooms furnished with antiques, fluffy quilts, and flowers from the garden.

The specialty of the house is a home-baked California breakfast that includes freshly squeezed orange juice, fresh fruit, and such goodies as apple blintzes, omelets, and apricot-nut bread. Finnish pancakes with fresh fruit and pure Canadian maple syrup are also served.

The California Guest House in Nelson, New Zealand, is now open all year except July and August. I would be delighted if every reader who visits Carol and Alan would send me a postcard.

CALIFORNIA GUEST HOUSE, 29 Collingwood St., Nelson, New Zealand; (054) 84173. A 6-guestroom home in a scenic section of New Zealand on the road to the Southern Alps. A full breakfast is the only meal served. Open Sept. thru June. Carol Glen, Innkeeper.

For B&B rates, see Index.

INDEX/RATES

The rates for lodgings mentioned in this Index are intended as general guidelines only and are not to be considered as firm quotations. Naturally, with the fluctuating inflation rate and the high cost of doing business, they are subject to change.

In order to avoid any misunderstandings, when making reservations, please indicate that you wish the B&B rate. Some of the accommodations listed also have American plan and modified American plan rates.

INDEX/RATES

(This Index is arranged alphabetically by state and town. To find a specific inn, please see the following Alphabetical List of Inns. These are approximate rates for lodgings and breakfast for two people for one night and may include low, off-season rates, as well as high-season rates. In some cases, tax and service charge are additional.)

†AP or MAP

Rates are approximate for 2 people for 1 night

INN	RATE	PAGE
BOULDER, Briar Rose Bed & Breakfast	$65-$95	77
COLORADO SPRINGS, Hearthstone Inn	$58-$98	80
FORT COLLINS, Elizabeth Street Guest House	$39	79
FORT COLLINS, Helmshire Inn	$49	81
FRISCO, MarDei's Mountain Retreat	$20-$86	82
GOLDEN, The Dove Inn	$34-$55	78
GREEN MOUNTAIN FALLS, Outlook Lodge	$35-$40	83

CONNECTICUT

EAST HADDAM, Bishopsgate	$75-$95	87
ESSEX, Griswold Inn	$64	91
GREENWICH, Homestead Inn, The	$90-$150	93
GROTON LONG POINT, Shore Inne	$40-$47	98
KENT, Candlelight, The	$40**	88
KENT, Flanders Arms	$65-$75	90
NEW CANAAN, Maples Inn, The	$75	95
NORFOLK, Manor House	$60-$120	94
OLD LYME, Bee and Thistle Inn	$56-$92*	86
PUTNAM, Felshaw Tavern, The	$75	89
RIDGEFIELD, West Lane Inn	$95	99
RIVERTON, Old Riverton Inn	$48-$76	96
SALISBURY, Yesterday's Yankee	$55-$60	100
THOMPSON, Hedgerow House	$60	92
THOMPSON, Samuel Watson House	$50	97

DELAWARE

BETHANY BEACH, Sea-Vista Villa	$60	102
NEW CASTLE, David Finney Inn, The	$60*	101

FLORIDA

AMELIA ISLAND, 1735 House	$60-$65	105
CORAL GABLES, Hotel Place St. Michel	$80	104
LAKE WALES, Chalet Suzanne	$75-$95*	103

GEORGIA

SAVANNAH, Ballastone Inn	$85-$150	106
SAVANNAH, Foley House	$95-$175	107
SAVANNAH, Gastonian, The	$85-$200	108
SAVANNAH, Liberty Inn	$85-$135	109

* Breakfast additional   ** Breakfast unavailable

INN	RATE	PAGE
ILLINOIS		
GALENA, Aldrich Guest House	$50-$65	110
ILLIOPOLIS, Old Illiopolis Hotel	$20	111
INDIANA		
ANGOLA, Potawatomi Inn	$35*	114
BRISTOL, Open Hearth B&B	$45	115
INDIANAPOLIS, Hollingsworth House Inn	$65-$85	113
MADISON, Clifty Inn	$36*	114
MARSHALL, Turkey Run Inn	$36*	114
MICHIGAN CITY, Creekwood Inn	$85-$95	112
MIDDLEBURY, Patchwork Quilt B&B	$45	116
MITCHELL, Spring Mill Inn	$30-$33*	114
NASHVILLE, Abe Martin Lodge	$30-$35	114
ROCKPORT, Rockport Inn, The	$26-$39	117
SPENCER, Canyon Inn	$33*	114
IOWA		
AMANA COLONIES, Die Hiemat	$32	118
DUBUQUE, Redstone Inn, The	$48-$120*	119
DUBUQUE, Stout House	$45-$60	120
KENTUCKY		
HARRODSBURG, Beaumont Inn, The	$62-$85	121
MAINE		
BAR HARBOR, Cleftstone Manor	$50-$125	129
BATH, Grane's Fairhaven Inn	$33-$55**	135
BLUE HILL, Blue Hill Inn	$51*	123
BOOTHBAY, Kenniston Hill Inn	$45-$70	141
BOOTHBAY HARBOR, Hilltop House	$28-$42	138
BOOTHBAY HARBOR, Topside	$45-$80**	152
BROOKSVILLE, Breezemere Farm	$71-$91	125
CAMDEN, Blue Harbor House Bed & Breakfast	$30-$80	122
CAPE NEWAGEN, Newagen Seaside Inn	$50-$70	144
CAPE PORPOISE, Olde Garrison House	$42-$45‡	147
CASTINE, Pentagoet Inn, The	$85-$105	148
CHAMBERLAIN, Ocean Reefs Lodge	$45	145
DAMARISCOTTA, Brannon-Bunker Inn, The	$42-$50	124
DEER ISLE, Goose Cove Lodge	$50-$70	149
DEER ISLE, Pilgrim's Inn	$110	134
EAST WATERFORD, Waterford Inne, The	$40-$70*	153

* Breakfast additional   ** Breakfast unavailable   ‡ Kitchen privileges

* Breakfast additional   ** Breakfast unavailable

* Breakfast additional   ** Breakfast unavailable   ‡ Kitchen privileges

* Breakfast additional   Rates are approximate for 2 people for 1 night.

* Breakfast additional   † AP or MAP

INN	RATE	PAGE
NORTH CAROLINA		
BLACK MOUNTAIN, Red Rocker Inn, The	$30-$65*	292
BLOWING ROCK, Ragged Garden Inn	$65-$70	291
BREVARD, Womble Inn	$38	293
BURNSVILLE, Nu-Wray Inn	$43*	289
FRANKLIN, Buttonwood Inn	$40-$48	287
HENDERSONVILLE, Havenshire Inn	$60-$70	288
MARS HILL, Baird House	$40-$45	285
ROBBINSVILLE, Blue Boar Lodge	$70†	286
SALUDA, Orchard Inn, The	$68	290
OHIO		
AKRON, Portage House	$24	295
COLUMBUS, Victorian Bed and Breakfast	$50	296
DANVILLE, White Oak Inn, The	$45-$60	297
GAMBIER, Blossom Tyme	$35	294
WORTHINGTON, Worthington Inn, The	$95	298
OREGON		
ASHLAND, Chanticleer Inn	$69-$99	300
ASHLAND, Morical House	$65	306
BANDON, Spindrift	$50-$59	308
CAMP SHERMAN, Metolius River Lodges	$41-$71	305
EUGENE, Campus Cottage	$65-$85	299
FLORENCE, Johnson House, The	$50-$60	302
JACKSONVILLE, Judge Touvelle House	$60	303
LEABURG, Marjon Bed and Breakfast Inn	$60-$80	304
OAKLAND, Pringle House, The	$35	307
PORTLAND, Corbett House	$35-$60	301
STEAMBOAT, Steamboat Inn	$60*	309
PENNSYLVANIA		
AIRVILLE, Spring House	$50-$80	323
CANADENSIS, Overlook Inn	$85	319
ERWINNA, Evermay-on-the-Delaware	$57-$95	314
FAIRFIELD, Fairfield Inn and Guest House	$45*	315
HOLICONG, Barley Sheaf Farm	$85-$125	310
LEWISBURG, Pineapple Inn, The	$50	320
LUMBERVILLE, 1740 House	$57-$65	321
MOUNT JOY, Cameron Estate Inn	$55-$100	312
MUNCY, Bodine House, The	$35-$40	311
ORRTANNA, Hickory Bridge Farm	$59	316

* Breakfast additional   † AP or MAP

Rates are approximate for 2 people for 1 night.

INN	RATE	PAGE
IRASBURG, Irasburg Green Bed & Breakfast	$34	359
JAMAICA, Three Mountain Inn	$60-$75	374
LOWER WATERFORD, Rabbit Hill Inn	$35-$80*	370
LUDLOW, Black River Inn	$80	345
LUDLOW, Governor's Inn	$100	352
MANCHESTER, Birch Hill Inn	$72-$88	344
MANCHESTER VILLAGE, 1811 House	$70-$120	351
MARLBORO, Whetstone Inn	$45-$60*	376
MORETOWN, Camel's Hump View Farm	$44	346
NORTH HERO, North Hero House	$57-$70*	367
NORTH THETFORD, Stone House Inn	$42	373
POST MILLS, Lake House at Lake Fairlee, The	$49-$59	362
POULTNEY, Lake St. Catherine Inn	$104†	363
PUTNEY, Hickory Ridge House	$35-$55	354
SAXTONS RIVER, Saxtons River Inn	$35-$65	372
SIMONSVILLE, Rowell's Inn	$68	371
SOUTH WALLINGFORD, Green Mountain Tea Room	$20-$24*	353
WAITSFIELD, Lareau Farm Country Inn	$60-$80	364
WATERBURY CENTER, May Farm Lodge	$35	366
WEST WARDSBORO, Old Barn Inn, The	$30-$35	368
WESTON, Colonial House, The	$46-$70	349
WILMINGTON, Darcroft's Schoolhouse	$25-$60	350
WILLISTON, Partridge Hill	$50	369
WINDSOR, Juniper Hill Inn	$45-$75	361
WOODSTOCK, Charleston House, The	$78-$90	348
WOODSTOCK, Jackson House, The	$85	360

VIRGINIA

BEDFORD, Peaks of Otter Lodge	$54*	381
LEXINGTON, Alexander-Withrow House, The	$67-$82	378
LYNCHBURG, Sojourners Bed and Breakfast	$36	384
MIDDLEBURG, Red Fox Inn and Tavern	$65-$175	383
MIDDLEBURG, Welbourne	$85	385
TREVILIANS, Prospect Hill	$100-$120	382
WARM SPRINGS, Inn at Gristmill Square, The	$65-$95	379
WARM SPRINGS, Meadow Lane Lodge	$80-$95	380

WASHINGTON

ASHFORD, Ashford Mansion, The	$38-$48	386
COUPEVILLE, Captain Whidbey Inn	$60-$90	387
LEAVENWORTH, Haus Rohrbach Pension	$55-$65	389

* Breakfast additional   † AP or MAP

* Breakfast additional   Rates are approximate for 2 people for 1 night.

ALPHABETICAL LIST OF INNS

ALPHABETICAL LIST OF INNS

(For inns in specific towns and for rates, please see preceding Index.)

101 PRETENTIOUS HORS D'OEUVRES

101
PRETENTIOUS
HORS D'ŒUVRES

G.H. CROWN

Chicago Review Press

ISBN 0-914091-36-0
LC# 83-15385

Cover and interior design by Li-Eng Lee

Published by Chicago Review Press
213 W. Institute Place
Chicago, IL 60610

The author wishes to thank Bob Randall for the encouragement to write *101 Pretentious Hors d'Oeuvres* and the late Bob Mark, whose creative entertaining ideas were and continue to be a source of joy.

PREFACE

My specialty is boiling water.

Making instant coffee gives me a headache. Percolating is out of the question. The kitchen is as foreign to me as the fourth ring of Saturn.

How then, could I impress those who dropped by for a quick drink and nibble before we trotted off to our favorite Hunan Palace? That was the question that plagued me a few years ago.

I am delighted to report that the plague is over. Herewith, after several years of collecting, ferreting, and cooking, are 101 pretentious hors d'oeuvres that almost anyone can prepare (and if the list includes me, believe me, it's anyone).

Read a few and you will never slice a piece of cheese again.

CONTENTS

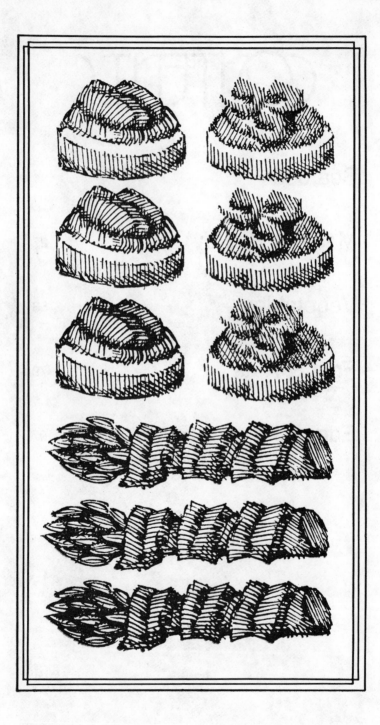

SEAFOOD

Anchovy Egg Canapes

8 tinned anchovies
4 hard-boiled eggs, mashed
1 t fresh dill, chopped
6 stuffed green olives
3 T melted butter
4 slices thin white bread
2 T mayonnaise

Combine mashed eggs and mayonnaise. Add dill to mixture and set aside. Cut two slices from the middle of each olive. Set aside. Using a cookie cutter or small glass, cut three circles from each slice of bread and toast one side. Spread egg mixture on untoasted side of each bread circle and center each with an olive round surrounded by an anchovy. Brush with butter and broil for three minutes. Serve warm.

12 Pieces

Anchovy Garlic Rounds

3 oz. cream cheese
3 T anchovy paste
1 t grated onion
1 t fresh lemon juice
1 t Worcestershire sauce
1 clove garlic, crushed
2 T parsley, chopped
3 slices thin white bread

Using a cookie cutter or small glass, cut 4 rounds from each slice of bread. Toast one side. Cool. Reserve parsley and mix remaining ingredients. Spread on untoasted side of rounds. Border each round with chopped parsley. Chill.

12 Pieces

Caviar Cakes Rene

2 oz. salmon caviar
2 large potatoes
1 small onion
1 large egg
½ pt. sour cream
¼ t pepper
¼ t salt
2 T butter
2 T vegetable oil

Peel potatoes and refrigerate overnight in water. Grate potatoes and squeeze out excess liquid. Lightly beat egg. Mince onion. Combine egg and onion with potato, add salt and pepper. Heat oil and butter in heavy skillet. When very hot, drop individual spoonfuls of mixture into skillet. Brown on both sides. Drain on paper towel. Place a teaspoon of sour cream on each cake and then a mound of caviar. Serve warm.

About 18 Pieces

Caviar Canapes

1 2 oz. jar caviar
½ t fresh lemon juice
1 finely chopped hardboiled egg
2 T mayonnaise
1 t minced onion
½ t Dijon mustard
16 tiny sprigs parsley
4 slices thin white bread

Using a cookie cutter or small glass, cut 4 rounds out of each slice of bread. Toast one side. Cool. Combine all ingredients except caviar and parsley. Spread mixture on untoasted side of rounds. Top each with a teaspoonful of caviar and garnish with parsley sprigs. Serve chilled.

16 Pieces

Potatoes Royale

12 small russet potatoes, similar in size
1 oz. Beluga caviar
½ cup sour cream
2 hardboiled egg yolks
1 T finely minced onion
1 T chopped dill

Boil potatoes until just tender. Do not over-
cook. Refresh under cold water.Peel potatoes
and trim bottoms so they will sit flat. Using a
melon scoop, make a 1″ pocket in each potato
top. Press egg yolks through a heavy sieve.
Mix sour cream, egg yolks, onion and dill. Fill
potato cavities with this mixture and top with a
mound of caviar. Chill.

12 Pieces

Clam Canapes

1 7 oz. can minced clams
½ cup cottage cheese
1 t grated onion
1 t Worcestershire sauce
   dash pepper
   Melba toast rounds

Blend first five ingredients. Spread on rounds and chill.

About 12 Pieces

Spicy Clam Canapes

1　7 oz. can minced clams, drained
3　oz. cream cheese
1　t lemon juice
1　t white horseradish
½　t Worcestershire sauce
2　drops hot pepper liquid seasoning
6　slices thin white bread

Using a cookie cutter or small glass, cut 2 rounds from each slice of bread and toast one side. Blend remaining ingredients and spread on untoasted side of each round. Broil for a few minutes and serve warm.

12 Pieces

8

Crabmeat Cheese Triangles

1 6½ oz. can shredded crabmeat
¼ lb. butter (one stick), softened
⅓ cup grated Edam cheese
4 whole English muffins

Split muffins. Combine remaining ingredients and spread on each half. Cut each half into 4 triangular pieces and broil until cheese melts. Serve warm.

32 Pieces

Crab Relish Canapes

1 6½ oz. can crabmeat, flaked
2 T pickle relish
2 T mayonnaise
½ T white horseradish
  dash salt
  dash white pepper
5 slices thin white bread

Using a cookie cutter or small glass, cut four circles from each slice of bread. Toast one side in broiler. Combine remaining ingredients, blend well, and spread on untoasted side of each bread circle.

20 Pieces

Escargot in Tomato Crowns

 1 can escargot (24 escargot)
24 large cherry tomatoes
 3 T butter
 1 small clove garlic, crushed
    salt and pepper to taste
 2 T chopped parsley

Cut the tops from the tomatoes. With a melon scoop remove the pulp and reserve. Saute tomatoes in butter for about 2 minutes, until they are slightly softened. Remove from pan. Add to pan tomato pulp, garlic, escargot, salt and pepper. Saute about 3 minutes. Place one escargot in each cherry tomato, skewer with a pick and sprinkle with parsley. Arrange on a plate and serve warm.

24 Pieces

Lobster Canapes Carryl

1 cup shredded cooked lobster meat (use a
    fresh lobster or a frozen lobster tail)
5 T butter, softened
1 t Dijon mustard
6 stuffed green olives, chopped, pimientos
    reserved
3 drops Worcestershire sauce
5 slices thin white bread
1 T chopped dill

Trim crusts from bread and cut each slice
diagonally to form 4 triangles. Toast one side.
Cool. Blend remaining ingredients, spread on
untoasted side of toast triangles. Top each
with a tiny triangle of pimiento.

20 Pieces

Salmon Caviar Nests

6 hardboiled eggs
3 T finely flaked salmon
1 T salmon caviar
2 T minced onion
4 T sour cream
12 tiny parsley sprigs

Cut hardboiled eggs in half. Carefully remove yolks, leaving whites intact. Trim bottoms of whites so they sit flat. Press yolks through a heavy sieve and combine with other ingredients. Spoon into egg whites, mounding slightly. Garnish with parsley sprigs and serve chilled.

12 Pieces

Salmon Garden Balls

¼ cup Nova Scotia salmon, flaked
6 oz. cream cheese
2 T chopped onion
½ cup grated carrot
¼ cup chopped parsley

Blend cream cheese, salmon and onion and form mixture into balls about 1″ in diameter. Combine carrot and parsley in bowl and roll cream cheese balls in mixture. Chill. Serve on picks.

16 Pieces

Smoked Salmon-Wrapped
Asparagus

2 thin slices smoked salmon
12 3″ asparagus spears
12 small sprigs dill

Steam asparagus spears for about 5 minutes,
until bright green but still firm. Refresh under
cold water, drain. Cut salmon into ½ inch by 3
inch strips and wrap around salmon candy-
cane fashion. Tuck a sprig of dill into each
salmon-wrapped spear. Chill.

12 Pieces

Sardine Butter Rounds

1 tin skinless, boneless sardines, drained
6 T butter, softened
  juice of ½ lemon
1 T chopped parsley
3 slices thin white bread

Mash sardines, adding lemon juice. Blend thoroughly with butter, parsley. Using a cookie cutter or small glass, cut three circles from each slice of bread and toast one side. Mound about 1 teaspoon of mixture on untoasted side of each round and serve. Rounds may be garnished with a sprig of parsley.

12 Pieces

Sardine Saturns

1 tin boneless, skinless sardines, drained
5 T butter, softened
  juice of ½ lemon
4 slices thin white bread
12 onion rings about 1″ in diameter
1 T chopped parsley

Cut 4 circles from each slice of bread. Toast one side. Cool. Blend butter and lemon juice and spread on untoasted side of bread circles. Trim sardines to fit circles, place one on buttered side of each toast, and arrange a small ring of onion around each sardine so that the onion ring stands upright. Chill.

12 Pieces

Cheddar Shrimp Toasts

½ cup cooked cleaned shrimp, fresh, frozen or
    canned
¼ lb. mild cheddar cheese, grated
½ small onion, minced
½ cup mayonnaise
1 small garlic clove, minced
1 t Worcestershire sauce
2 drops Tabasco sauce
    dash salt
3 slices thin white bread

Chop shrimp finely. Add cheese, onion, garlic
and blend into mayonnaise. Add remaining
ingredients except bread, and blend. Trim
bread and cut each slice into 4 squares. Toast
one side. Spread mixture on untoasted sides
and broil squares for several minutes, until
cheese melts. Serve warm.

12 Pieces

Herbed Shrimp Glace

18 large fresh shrimp
½ cup vegetable oil
¼ cup tarragon vinegar
1 clove garlic, crushed
¼ t salt
1 T chopped fresh dill
1 t capers
1 t chives, minced
3 T gelatin powder

Drop the shrimp into 1 qt. boiling water and cook for 3 minutes. Cool and peel. Mix the oil, vinegar, garlic, salt, chives and capers. Marinate the shrimp in this mixture for 3 hours; drain. Soak gelatin in just enough cold water to dissolve it for 5 minutes. Add dill and ½ cup boiling water. Cool. Spoon gelatin mixture over shrimp; chill. Repeat glazing several times. Serve on picks.

18 Pieces

Pickled Shrimp

½ cup fresh cooked shrimp, peeled
½ cup vegetable oil
½ cup white vinegar
   juice of ¼ lemon
1 stick cinnamon
½ t dill seed
½ t peppercorns
½ t ground cloves
¼ t salt
1 small onion, sliced

Place shrimp in bowl with sliced onion. Place
remaining ingredients in saucepan. Simmer
for 10 minutes. Cool. Pour mixture over shrimp
and cover tightly. Refrigerate for 24 hours.
Serve on picks.

About 20 Pieces

Shrimp Atlantis

4 oz. tiny shrimp, canned in brine
4 small cucumbers
½ cup mayonnaise
  juice of ½ lemon
1 T chopped dill

Peel cucumbers and score sides with tines of a sharp fork. Cut cucumbers into 1″ slices. With a melon scoop make a pocket half as deep as the cucumber slice. Blend mayonnaise, lemon juice and dill. Spoon about ½ teaspoon of mixture into each cup. Fill with tiny shrimp. Chill.

About 16 Pieces

Shrimp Leaves

20 endive leaves
 1 4½ oz. can tiny shrimp
¼ lb. butter (1 stick), softened
 1 t lemon juice
 1 t chopped fresh dill

Wash, pat or spin dry, and reserve endive leaves. Blend remaining ingredients. Spread about 1 teaspoonful on the broad end of each leaf. Chill and serve cold.

20 Pieces

Shrimp Sensations

 1 cup cooked chopped shrimp, fresh, frozen
   or canned
24 whole small cooked fresh shrimp, peeled
 2 14 oz. cans artichoke bottoms
 1 cup mayonnaise
¼ lemon
 1 T chopped fresh dill

Drain artichoke bottoms. Mix chopped
shrimp, mayonnaise, dill and juice of lemon
thoroughly. Spread mixture over artichoke
bottoms and cut each bottom in half. Place
one whole shrimp on top of each and refrigerate.

24 Pieces

Sturgeon Dill Squares

1 cup flaked smoked sturgeon
¼ lb. butter, softened
6 slices thin white bread
2 T chopped fresh dill
   pimiento (optional)

Mix sturgeon, butter and dill. Trim bread and cut each slice into quarters. Toast one side. Spread sturgeon butter on untoasted side of squares. Garnish with a small square of pimiento, if desired.

24 Pieces

Tuna Horseradish Rounds

1 4 oz. can white tuna packed in water
½ cup mayonnaise
1 T white horseradish
6 black olives
6 stuffed green olives
12 Melba rounds

Mix tuna thoroughly with mayonnaise and horseradish. Cut center slice from each olive and reserve. Chop remaining olive ends and add to tuna mixture. Spread tuna mixture on Melba rounds and top each with a slice of olive.

12 Pieces

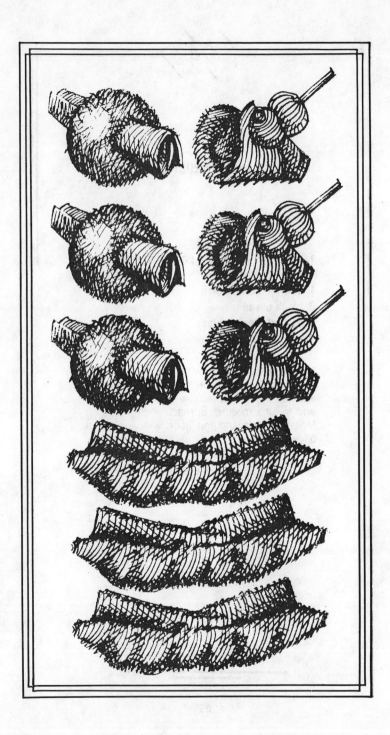

MEATS & POULTRY

Bacon Nut Canapes

¾ cup finely chopped crisp bacon
¼ cup chopped pinola nuts
Dijon mustard
4 slices thin white bread

Trim each slice of bread and cut into 4 sections diagonally, forming triangles. Saute triangles in bacon fat until crisp; drain. Spread a thin layer of mustard on each triangle and sprinkle chopped bacon and nuts on top.

16 Pieces

Bacon Wrapped Baby Corn

12 ears pickled baby corn
6 slices bacon, cut in half

Wrap corn in bacon and pan fry until bacon is crisp. Serve warm.

12 Pieces

Chicken Apple Canapes

¾ cup chopped cooked chicken
½ cup diced apple
3 slices crisp bacon, crumbled
4 T butter, softened
1 T Dijon mustard
4 slices thin rye bread

Trim crusts from bread and cut each slice into 4 squares. Combine butter and mustard and spread on each square. Combine remaining ingredients and spread on top. Bake squares in preheated oven at 350 degrees for about 5 minutes, until thoroughly heated. Serve warm.

16 Pieces

Miniature Hawaiian Skewered Chicken

1 large chicken breast, boned
1 12 oz. can pineapple chunks
1 small bottle maraschino cherries
¾ cup flavored bread crumbs
¼ cup flour, seasoned with salt and pepper
1 large egg, lightly beaten with
2 T milk
  shortening

Cut chicken breast into 1-inch squares and coat squares with flour. Dip squares into egg mixture and roll in bread crumbs. Bake chicken in a greased glass baking dish in a preheated oven at 350 degrees for about 30 min. Remove from oven. Place a wooden pick through a cherry, a pineapple chunk and a chicken square. Skewer all chicken squares and return to oven for 10 minutes, or until chicken is golden. Serve warm.

About 18 Pieces

Turkey Corn Relish Squares

⅛ lb. sliced roast turkey breast
4 oz. prepared corn relish
24 pimiento strips
6 slices thin white bread
4 T butter, softened

Trim crusts from bread and cut each slice into four squares. Toast one side. Cool. Butter untoasted sides and cut turkey to fit. Top each turkey square with a teaspoonful of corn relish and decorate with a strip of pimiento. Place turkey squares in a warm oven (about 300 degrees) for 5 min. before serving.

24 Pieces

Apricot Brandy Glazed Ham Squares

⅛ lb. thin-sliced baked ham
4 slices thin white bread
6 T butter, softened
½ cup plus 2 T apricot jam
1 T apricot brandy
  dash dry mustard

Mix butter, ½ cup apricot jam and mustard. Trim crusts from bread and cut each slice into 4 squares. Toast one side of squares and cool. Spread untoasted side of squares with jam mixture and top each square with a slice of ham trimmed to fit. Place 2 T apricot jam in a small saucepan with the apricot brandy. Heat and stir until blended. Spoon sauce over squares and cool.

16 Pieces

Curried Ham Rolls

4 thin slices baked or boiled ham
¼ cup mayonnaise
¼ t curry powder
3 stalks celery

Cut ham into 2-inch by 3-inch pieces. Remove strings from celery and cut stalks into 4-inch lengths. Blend mayonnaise and curry powder and spread on ham. Wrap ham lengthwise around middle of celery stalks and chill.

12 Pieces

Ham and Swiss Cylinders

3 oz. baked or boiled ham, sliced thin
3 oz. Swiss cheese, sliced thin
12 large cherry tomatoes
   Dijon mustard

Using a sharp knife or apple corer, cut a hole
entirely through each cherry tomato. Discard
tomato seeds and pulp and drain tomato
shells. Cut ham and cheese into 3-inch by
3-inch squares. Spread a little mustard on
each ham square, top with a square of
cheese, and roll tightly. Insert each roll
through a cherry tomato. Chill, covered, until
ready to serve.

12 Pieces

33

Ham-Filled Dill Pickles

3 medium-size dill pickles
⅛ lb. baked or boiled ham, sliced thin
  Dijon mustard

Remove and discard pickle ends. Hollow out each pickle with an apple corer and discard pulp and seeds. Coat ham slices with a little mustard. Roll ham slices and insert into hollowed-out pickles. Trim ham ends to fit. Cut pickles into one-half-inch slices and serve chilled.

About 24 Pieces

Ham Fritters

  1 cup minced cooked ham
  1 cup sifted flour
  ¾ cup milk
1½ t baking powder
  2 eggs
  2 cups vegetable oil
  ⅛ t dry mustard
  ⅛ t salt

Sift together dry ingredients. Beat eggs and add milk and dry ingredients, beating until batter is smooth. Add ham to batter. Heat vegetable oil to 365 degrees. Drop batter by spoonfuls into hot oil. Remove when golden brown and drain on paper towels. Serve warm.

About 16 Pieces

Ham Solana

8 slices baked Virgina ham, sliced thin
8 slices thin white bread
2 egg whites
¾ cup mayonnaise
2 t Dijon mustard

Place one slice of ham on each slice of bread
and trim to fit. Mix mustard and mayonnaise.
Whip egg whites until they form stiff peaks.
Gently fold in the mustard and mayonnaise
mixture. Cut each slice of bread into 4
squares. Place a spoonful of meringue on
each square and place squares in a preheated oven at 325 degrees for several minutes, until merinque is lightly browned. Serve
warm.

32 Pieces

Hazelnut Ham Squares

3 oz. baked or boiled ham, sliced thin
¼ lb. hazelnuts, roasted and salted
¼ lb. butter (1 stick), softened
5 slices thin white bread

Grind hazelnuts fine and blend with butter. Trim crusts from bread, cut each slice into quarters and toast one side. Spread untoasted sides with hazelnut butter when cool. Cut ham squares to fit bread and place over butter. Put remaining butter in a pastry tube fitted with a small rosette tip. Put a butter rosette on each ham square and chill.

20 Pieces

Mandarin Ham

1 can mandarin orange segments
2 slices baked Virginia ham
  Dijon mustard

Drain orange segments. Cut ham into 1-inch by 3-inch strips. Spread a little mustard on each strip and wrap around an orange segment. Place two wrapped segments on each pick and chill.

About 18 Pieces

Pistachio Ham Rounds

2 thin slices baked Virginia ham
⅛ cup chopped pistachio nuts
⅛ lb. butter (½ stick), softened
5 slices thin whole wheat bread

Using a cookie cutter or small glass, cut four circles from each slice of bread. Toast one side. Cool. Blend nuts and butter and spread on each round. Cut ham into half-inch by 2-inch strips and roll into rosettes. Place one rosette on each round and chill.

20 Pieces

Virginia Kumquats

12 kumquats preserved in syrup
¼ lb. baked Virginia ham
12 small parsley sprigs
    Dijon mustard

Cut a hole in the end of each kumquat with an apple corer or fruit knife. Remove pit. Cut ham into 3-inch squares. Spread a narrow stripe of mustard at one edge of each ham square. Roll squares tightly and insert the mustard-coated edge into the kumquats. Chill.

12 Pieces

Sweet and Sour Meatballs

½ lb. ground round
1 egg
¼ cup bread crumbs
1 cup canned tomatoes
¼ cup brown sugar
⅛ cup vinegar
   dash salt
1 T minced onion
½ t ground ginger

Combine ground meat, lightly beaten egg and bread crumbs. Form meatballs about 1 inch in diameter. Bake meatballs on a greased baking sheet in a preheated 350 degree oven for 8 minutes. Combine remaining ingredients in saucepan. Add meatballs and bring to a boil. Simmer for 8-10 minutes. Serve hot on picks.

12 Pieces

Roast Beef in Curried Pea Pods

¼ lb. sliced roast beef
24 snow pea pods
½ cup mayonnaise
¼ cup sour cream
¼ t curry powder
1 small clove garlic, crushed
¼ t sugar

Simmer pea pods in a little boiling water for a few minutes, until bright and crisp. Remove from saucepan and place in ice water. Trim stem and slice open one side of each pod. Cut roast beef into 3-inch squares. Mix remaining ingredients to make a sauce. Coat inside of pea pods with sauce. Roll each square of roast beef into a cylinder and insert into a pea pod. Continue until all pods are filled. Chill.

24 Pieces

42

Rolled Roast Beef

6 6-inch long strips roast beef
3 oz. cream cheese
1 T white horseradish
1 T chopped parsley

Mix cream cheese, horseradish and parsley.
Cut roast beef strips in half. Spread a thin
coating of cream cheese mixture on each beef
strip, roll and secure with a pick. Chill.

12 Pieces

43

Spicy Roast Beef Rolls

¼ lb. sliced roast beef
½ cup sour cream
1 t white horseradish, drained
2 drops Tabasco sauce

Trim roast beef into 2-inch by 3-inch pieces.
Blend remaining ingredients. Spread mixture
on roast beef and roll into cylinders. Chill.
Serve on picks.

About 12 Pieces

Pepperoni Provolone Spears

3 oz. provolone cheese
12 slices pepperoni
12 cherry tomatoes
4 slices thin white bread
4 T mayonnaise
½ t oregano

Trim crusts from bread and cut each slice into
4 squares. Toast one side and cool. Spread
untoasted sides of squares with mayonnaise
and sprinkle with oregano. Cut cheese to fit
and place on top. Add a slice of pepperoni
and a cherry tomato. Place a pick through
each. Chill.

12 Pieces

Prosciutto Melon Bars

⅛ lb. prosciutto, sliced thin
¼ persian melon or cantaloupe
¼ honeydew melon

Cut melon into bars 2 inches long and one-half inch thick. Wrap each bar in prosciutto twice, trim ends evenly and secure with a pick. Chill.

24 Pieces

Genoa Swiss Cornucopias

¼ lb sliced Genoa salami
⅛ lb. Swiss cheese
12 stuffed green olives
12 cocktail onions
    Dijon mustard

Cut rounds of Swiss cheese slightly smaller than salami slices. Spread mustard on salami slices and top with cheese. Roll each into a cornucopia shape, place an olive and an onion inside and skewer with a pick to secure the cone shape.

12 Pieces

Parsley Salami Cubes

1 small salami
4 oz. Dijon mustard
½ cup finely chopped parsley

Cut four slices salami by hand, about ¾-inch thick. Reserve the rest for another use. Cut 9 cubes from each slice. With a pick, dip each cube into mustard and then into parsley, coating all sides. Chill. Arrange on a platter and serve.

36 Pieces

48

Cocktail Wieners in Sherry Sauce

18 cocktail size wieners
1 12 oz. jar currant jam
1 8 oz. jar Dijon mustard
⅓ cup dry sherry

Boil wieners in water for 5 to 8 minutes. In a saucepan combine other ingredients and simmer 10 minutes. Add wieners. Serve in a chafing dish.

18 Pieces

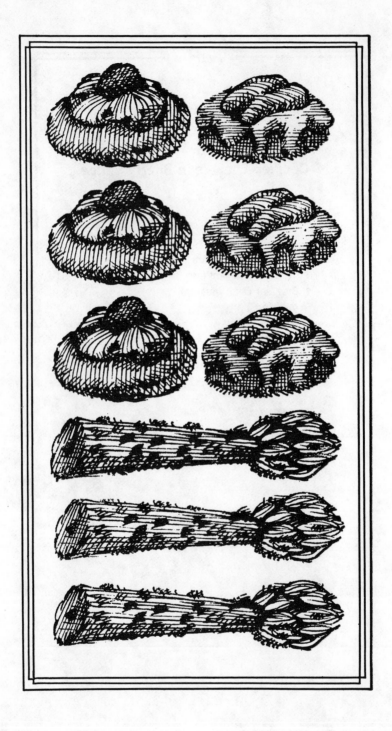

VEGETABLES

Artichoke Imperiale

1 large (14 oz.) can artichoke bottoms
12 medium to large fresh mushrooms
6 shallots
4 T butter, softened
   salt and pepper to taste

Chop mushroom caps and stems. Peel and chop shallots. Saute mushrooms and shallots in butter. Add salt and pepper. Mound mixture on artichoke bottoms using scooped side as cup. Warm thoroughly in a 300 degree oven, about 20 minutes. Remove from oven, cut each bottom in half and arrange on a plate to serve.

About 12 Pieces

Artichoke Italia

1 large (14 oz.) can artichoke bottoms
4 oz. Mozzarella cheese, grated
2 oz. tomato sauce
½ t dried oregano

Drain artichoke bottoms. Mix cheese and tomato sauce. Add oregano. Fill artichoke bottoms with cheese mixture and broil for 5 min.
or until cheese is melted. Remove from broiler.
Cut each bottom in half. Serve warm.

10 Pieces

51

Marinated Artichoke Crescents

1 large can (14 oz.) artichoke bottoms
6 T butter
½ cup vinaigrette dressing
5 slices thin white bread

Drain artichoke hearts and marinate in vinaigrette dressing overnight. Using a cookie cutter or small glass, cut 2 circles out of each slice of bread and toast one side. Cool. Spread butter on each circle and place a drained artichoke bottom on each. Cut each bottom in half, arrange on a plate and chill.

10 Pieces

52

Asparagus Sesame Spears

12 stalks asparagus
 1 egg
1½ oz. sesame seeds
 2 T butter
 2 T sesame oil

Cut asparagus into 4-inch lengths from the tip.
Reserve stems for another use. Steam tips for
5 min., until bright green and crisp. Cool.
Lightly roast raw sesame seeds in a dry skillet.
Transfer to a plate to cool. Lightly beat egg.
Dip asparagus spears into egg and roll in
sesame seeds. Refrigerate for half an hour.
Heat butter and oil in heavy skillet. Gently roll
spears in skillet until seeds are golden. Re-
move and drain on paper towel. Serve warm.

12 Pieces

Wrapped Asparagus Rolls

12 asparagus spears
12 slices thin white bread
½ cup mayonnaise
 salt and pepper to taste

Cut asparagus spears into 4-inch lengths. Place tips in boiling water and simmer for 5 min., until bright green and crisp. Reserve asparagus ends for another use. Trim crusts from bread and roll each slice with a rolling pin to flatten. Trim each slice to a 3-inch square. Spread bread squares with mayonnaise and sprinkle with salt and pepper. Roll each spear in bread, placing rolls side by side in dish. Chill.

12 Pieces

Cocktail Beets

24 whole small beets
1½ cups vinegar
¾ cup sugar
7 whole cloves
    salt and pepper to taste
1 T chopped dill

Combine vinegar, dill and spices in a glass jar.
Add beets and cover tightly. Refrigerate for 24
hours. Serve on picks.

24 Pieces

Pickled Beet Canapes

12 whole pickled beets, drained
3 oz. cream cheese
1 t chopped chives
4 slices thin pumpernickel bread

Using a cookie cutter or small glass, cut 4 circles from each slice of bread. Toast one side, cool. Mash 10 of the beets and blend with cream cheese and chives. Slice remaining beets into 6 slices each. Mound a teaspoonful of the beet/cheese mixture on each bread round, untoasted side up. Stand a slice of beet in each. Chill.

12 Pieces

Cauliflowerettes

16 medium-sized cauliflowerettes, steamed
    lightly until crisp-tender
2 eggs, beaten
½ cup matzoh meal
2 cups peanut oil
    salt and pepper to taste

Dip cauliflowerettes into beaten egg and roll in
matzoh meal crumbs. Heat oil to 325 degrees
and deep fry cauliflowerettes for about three
min., or until golden. Serve warm on picks.

16 Pieces

Cucumber Dill Canapes

1 medium-size cucumber
¼ cup sour cream
1 small clove garlic, crushed
1 T chopped fresh dill
4 slices thin pumpernickel bread

Trim each slice of bread into three rectangles about one-and-a-half by 3 inches long. Combine sour cream, garlic and dill. Cut cucumber in half lengthwise and scoop out seeds. Cut thin slices of cucumber and place on a linen towel. Spread sour cream mixture on bread strips. Arrange cucumber crescents in a fan pattern on top, and chill.

12 Pieces

Liverwurst Cucumber Cylinders

⅛ lb. liverwurst (12 thin slices)
12 thin slices cucumber
12 large cherry tomatoes
    fresh ground pepper

Using an apple corer, remove the center of each cherry tomato, leaving a ring-shaped shell. Place a slice of cucumber in the center of a slice of liverwurst and sprinkle with fresh pepper. Roll tightly and slip the roll through the tomato ring. Chill.

12 Pieces

Mock Pate Rounds

1 box Tam Tam crackers
2 carrots
1 large onion
¼ lb. margarine

Grate carrots and onion fine. Crush crackers and mix with margarine. Add carrots and onion, kneading the mixture. Roll the mixture into a cylinder and wrap tightly in tinfoil, folding ends under. Bake on a rack in a 350 degree oven for 40 min. Cool. Place in freezer overnight. Defrost and slice into ¼-inch slices. Warm in a 250 degree oven on a cookie sheet before serving.

About 30 Pieces

Broiled Yam-Filled Mushroom Caps

12 large mushroom caps about 2 inches in
    diameter
1 8 oz. can candied yams
12 pitted black olives
3 T butter, melted

Wash and drain mushroom caps. Mash yams
and fill mushroom caps level. Place an olive in
the center of each cap and brush tops with
melted butter. Broil for several min., or until
warmed, and serve.

12 Pieces

Curried Mushroom Caps

12 large mushroom caps, 1 to 2 inches in
    diameter
½ cup olive oil
¼ t curry powder

Wash and pat dry mushroom caps. Add curry
powder to oil in a glass jar with a lid. Shake to
blend thoroughly. Add mushroom caps and
marinate overnight. Serve on picks.

12 Pieces

French Fried Mushrooms

1 lb. small fresh mushrooms
⅓ cup flour
¼ cup bread crumbs
1 egg
¼ t garlic powder
¼ t fresh ground pepper
2 T chopped parsley
¼ cup light vegetable oil

Trim ends of mushroom stems and rinse mushrooms. Lightly beat egg in small bowl. Mix flour, garlic powder, pepper in another bowl. Coat mushrooms with flour, then dip into egg and last into bread crumbs. Fry 8 to 10 at a time in hot oil (325 degrees) until golden. Drain. Serve warm.

About 30 Pieces

Mushroom Almond Swirls

6 slices white bread
½ cup finely chopped fresh mushrooms
¼ cup chopped almonds
¼ lb. butter (1 stick), softened
3 t steak sauce
1 small clove garlic, minced
   dash salt

Trim crusts from bread and flatten each slice between sheets of waxed paper with a rolling pin. Combine remaining ingredients and spread on bread. Roll three cylinders, each made of two bread slices with mushroom mixture spread inside. Wrap in tin foil and refrigerate at least 2 hours, or until firm. Remove cylinders from foil and slice into half-inch rounds. Bake on lightly greased cookie sheet in preheated 400 degree oven for 8 min., or until lightly browned.

About 36 Pieces

Mushroom Royale

12 medium-sized fresh mushrooms
1 1 oz. can truffles
3 oz. pate with truffles
3 oz. cream cheese
5 T butter

Wash mushrooms, remove and chop stems
and reserve. Gently saute mushroom caps
and chopped stems in butter for 5 min. Drain
on paper towel. Mix stems, pate and cream
cheese and place one teaspoonful of pate
mixture in each mushroom cap. Slice truffle
into 12 thin slices and stand each slice in a
mound of pate. Chill.

12 Pieces

Orange-Filled Mushrooms

12 medium-sized fresh mushrooms
 1 can mandarin orange sections
 3 oz. mayonnaise
 ¼ t curry powder
12 tiny sprigs parsley

Drain orange sections. Wash and pat dry mushrooms, remove and chop stems and reserve. Blend together mayonnaise, chopped stems and curry powder. Place a teaspoonful of curry mixture in each mushroom cap. Fan out several orange segments in each cap and add a sprig of parsley. Chill.

12 Pieces

Pickled Mushrooms

2 jars small mushroom caps
½ cup tarragon vinegar
½ cup brown sugar
6 whole black peppercorns
1 small bay leaf
1 small clove garlic, crushed
 dash salt

Drain mushrooms, reserving ½ cup liquid. Place mushrooms in glass jar. In a saucepan, combine liquid, vinegar and spices and simmer 3 min. Bring to a boil and pour over mushroom caps. Cover jar tightly and refrigerate for 24 hours before serving.

About 25 Pieces

Sesame Mushrooms

15 medium-size fresh mushrooms
¼ cup bread crumbs
½ cup sesame seeds
½ cup flour
2 eggs
2 T milk
2 cups light vegetable oil

Wash and pat dry mushrooms, remove stems and roll caps in flour. Lightly beat eggs and milk. Combine bread crumbs and sesame seeds in bowl. Dip mushrooms into egg mixture and roll in sesame seed mixture. Deep fry in hot oil (325 degrees) until mushrooms are golden brown.

15 Pieces

68

Sherried Mushroom Caps

12 fresh white mushrooms
3 oz. cream cheese
1 T dry sherry
1 T chopped chives

Wash and pat dry mushrooms and remove
and chop stems. Mix chopped stems with
cream cheese, sherry and chives. Place a
mound of cream cheese mixture in each
mushroom cap. Chill.

12 Pieces

Twice Pickled Onions

2 sour pickles
12 pickled onions
4 T mayonnaise
4 slices rye bread

Cut pickles into slices about ⅜ inch thick. With a fruit knife make a small hole in the center of each slice. Insert an onion. Using a cookie cutter or small glass, cut three rounds from each slice of rye bread. Spread rounds with mayonnaise and place a stuffed pickle slice on top.

12 Pieces

Parsnips A La Creme

4 large parsnips
1 cup sour cream
½ oz. pignoli nuts
dash curry powder

Peel parsnips and cut into one-and-one-quarter inch chunks. Place in a saucepan, cover with water and bring to a boil. Simmer just until tender, refresh immediately under cold water. Roast pignoli nuts in a dry skillet until golden. Cool. Using a melon scoop, remove enough pulp from each parsnip chunk to create a pocket. Mash pulp and mix with sour cream, curry powder and sprinkle with nuts.

12 Pieces

Radish Rosettes

6 medium-sized red radishes
⅛ lb. Butter (½ stick),softened
2 T chopped parsley
3 slices thin white bread

Cut 4 rounds from each slice of bread. Toast
on one side. Cool. Blend parsley and butter
and spread on untoasted side of rounds.
Make paper-thin radish slices and arrange in
overlapping fashion to form rosettes on each
round. Lightly press into butter.

12 Pieces

Zucchini Cheddar Rounds

1 small zucchini
2 oz. sliced cheddar cheese
6 walnuts

Wash and dry zucchini and cut into quarter-inch slices. With a cookie cutter or shot glass, cut circles of cheddar cheese slightly smaller in diameter than the zucchini slices. Top each zucchini/cheddar round with a walnut half. Bake in a 250 degree oven until cheese starts to melt. Remove from oven and allow to set for several minutes before serving.

12 Pieces

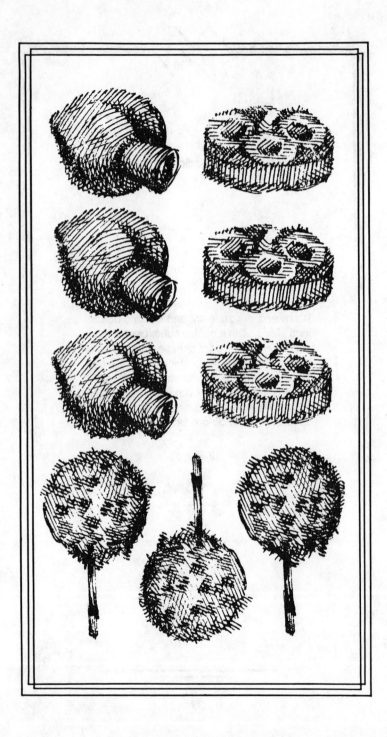

FRUIT & NUTS

Almond Cheddar-Filled Apricots

1 16 oz. can whole apricots
¼ lb. cheddar cheese, sliced thin
¼ cup sliced almonds

Drain apricots and remove pits, leaving fruit
whole. Cut cheese slices into 2-inch squares.
Sprinkle almonds on the cheese, roll cheese
into cylinders and insert into apricots.

12 Pieces

Spicy Avocado Canapes

1 medium-sized ripe avocado
1 small onion
1 small hot chili pepper
1 small clove garlic, crushed
2 T tomato paste
1 t lemon juice
  dash salt, black pepper
4 slices thin white bread

Mash avocado. Add lemon juice, salt and pepper. Chop chili pepper and onion, crush garlic and add to tomato paste. Combine avocado and tomato paste mixtures and refrigerate. Trim crusts from bread and cut bread into rectangles about 1 inch by 3 inches. Toast one side. Spread untoasted side of rectangles with avocado mixture and serve.

16 Pieces

75

Bacon-Wrapped Stuffed Dates

12 Medjool or other large dates
 6 strips bacon
12 walnut halves or
12 small pineapple chunks

Slit dates and remove pits. Stuff with your choice of a walnut half or a pineapple chunk. Cut each bacon strip in half and wrap dates, trimming off excess bacon after allowing an overlap of 1 inch. Broil or bake in a 350-degree oven for 5 min., or until bacon is crisp. Serve warm.

12 Pieces

Miniature Nut Balls

⅛ lb. blue cheese, crumbled
3 oz. cream cheese, softened
1 T minced onion
1 T mayonnaise
⅔ cup chopped walnuts
2 drops Tabasco sauce

Place walnuts in a bowl and set aside. Combine other ingredients and form into balls about 1 inch in diameter. Roll each ball in nuts and chill. Serve with picks.

18 Pieces

Miniature Spicy Nut Balls

3 oz. cheddar cheese, grated
3 oz. cream cheese, softened
2 T butter, softened
1 t Worcestershire sauce
1 t coarsely ground black pepper
¾ cup chopped walnuts

Combine all ingredients except nuts and blend thoroughly. Roll mixture into balls about 1 inch in diameter and roll balls in chopped nuts. Chill and serve with picks.

12 Pieces

78

Walnut Pate Diamonds

½ cup shelled walnuts
1 clove garlic, crushed
1 t olive oil
1 T vinegar
  dash salt
6 slices thin white bread

Puree walnuts and garlic in blender. Dampen
2 slices bread and squeeze out excess water.
Mix with pureed nut mixture to form a paste.
Add vinegar and oil in a stream to the paste,
mixing well. Add salt. Using a small
diamond-shaped cookie cutter, cut three
diamonds from each remaining bread slice
and toast diamonds on one side. Spread pate
on untoasted side of diamonds and serve.

12 Pieces

Herbed Olives

20 large pitted black olives with their liquid
1 small red chili pepper
1 garlic clove
2 sprigs fresh dill
3 T olive oil

Place all ingredients in a bowl. Cover tightly
and refrigerate for 2 days. Serve on picks.

20 Pieces

Mixed Olive and Almond Canapes

4 slices thin white bread
¼ cup chopped green olives
¼ cup chopped black olives
2 oz. sliced almonds
3 oz. cream cheese
  pimientos for garnish

Toast bread on one side and, using a diamond-shaped cookie cutter, cut four diamonds from each slice. Mix olives, almonds and cream cheese and spread on untoasted side of diamonds. Cut pimiento into small diamonds and top each canape with one.

16 Pieces

Olive Blossoms

2 T chopped green olives
2 T chopped black olives
2 T sliced green olives
2 T sliced black olives
¼ lb. butter (1 stick), softened
1 t fresh lemon juice
5 slices thin rye bread
  pimiento for garnish

Combine butter and lemon juice. Divide lemon butter into 2 bowls. Mix chopped green olives into 1 bowl, chopped black olives into the other. Using a cookie cutter or small glass, cut 4 rounds from each slice of bread. Toast one side and cool. Spread each mixture on untoasted side of 10 rounds. Place small piece of pimiento in the center of each round and encircle with sliced olives to create a "flower". Chill.

20 Pieces

Olive Cheddar Puffs

24 medium-sized stuffed green olives
 1 cup grated cheddar cheese
¼ cup butter, softened
½ cup flour, sifted
¼ t salt
¼ t paprika

Mix butter and cheese. Add flour, salt, paprika
and blend. Cover each olive with about one
teaspoonful of this mixture and place on a
lightly greased baking sheet 3 inches apart.
Refrigerate 2 hours. Bake in a preheated
400-degree oven for 10 min., or until golden.

24 Pieces

Wholewheat Almond Olive Fingers

¼ lb. unsalted butter (1 stick), softened
¼ cup ground almonds
⅛ cup sliced almonds
¼ cup sliced stuffed green olives
    dash salt
4 slices wholewheat bread

Blend butter, ground almonds and salt. Trim crusts from bread, cut slices into thirds and toast one side. Cool. Spread butter heavily on untoasted side of each bread finger. Alternately layer olive slices and almonds until ingredients are used up. Chill.

12 Pieces

Orange Hors D'Oeuvres

12 orange sections
 6 T butter, softened
 4 slices pumpernickel bread
   French dressing
12 small sprigs watercress

Marinate orange sections in French dressing
overnight. Trim crusts from bread and butter
bread slices. Using a cookie cutter or small
glass, cut 3 circles from each slice. Place an
orange section and a sprig of watercress on
each circle and chill.

12 Pieces

Polynesian Orange Sections

2 large oranges, peeled and sectioned
½ cup grated coconut
  whites of 2 eggs
1 bunch fresh parsley

Dip each orange section in egg white and roll in coconut. Arrange sections around a mound of fresh parsley. Chill.

About 18 Pieces

Spicy Pineapple Chunks

  1 medium-sized fresh pineapple
  ¾ cup vinegar
10 whole cloves
  1 5-inch stick cinnamon
1¼ cups granulated sugar
  ¾ cup water or pineapple juice

Cut pineapple into quarters, carefully leaving shell and leaves intact on each quarter. Remove fruit and trim out core. Cut fruit into ¾-inch slices. Reserve and refrigerate shells with their leaves. Place water or pineapple juice in saucepan. Add vinegar, sugar, salt, cloves and cinnamon stick. Simmer 10 minutes. Add pineapple and bring to boil. Remove from heat and cool. Refrigerate for 24 hours. To serve, skewer each fruit chunk with a pick and replace in reserved pineapple shells. Arrange shells on a platter.

About 30 Pieces

87

Fried Stuffed Prunes

18 dried prunes
⅛ lb. baked Virginia ham
1 egg, lightly beaten with
1 T milk
½ cup bread crumbs
2 cups vegetable oil

Soak prunes in water to cover for at least 1 hour. Dry, slit, and remove pit. Chop ham finely and stuff prunes. Dip prunes in egg mixture and roll in bread crumbs. Deep fry in oil (365 degrees) until golden brown. Drain and serve warm.

18 Pieces

Bacon-Wrapped Watermelon Rind

1 small jar pickled watermelon rind
4 slices bacon

Drain watermelon rind. Wrap bacon strips once around each piece of rind and trim, leaving about one-half inch of overlap. Broil until bacon is crisp. Serve warm on picks.

About 12 Pieces

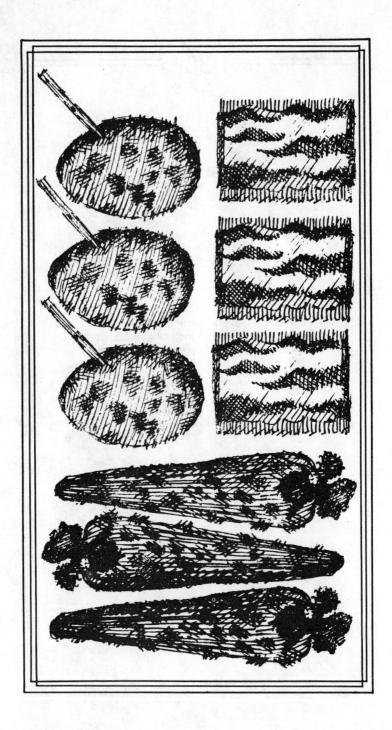

EGGS, CHEESE, ETC.

Blue Cheese Walnut Squares

¼ lb. blue cheese, crumbled
¼ lb. butter (1 stick), softened
2 t fresh lemon juice
24 walnut halves
6 slices thin white bread

Trim crusts from bread and cut each slice into 4 squares. Toast one side. Cool. Combine butter, cheese and lemon juice. Spread mixture on untoasted side of each square and press a walnut half on top of each.

24 Pieces

Carrots Carlos

½ pt. sour cream
1 cup grated carrot
2 cups grated Edam cheese
18 1-inch parsley sprigs

Blend cheese and sour cream, adding cream slowly and stopping when consistency is thick. Roll 1 tablespoonful of cheese mixture into a carrot shape. Set aside and continue until 18 cheese "carrots" are made. Place grated carrot in a flat plate. Roll each cheese "carrot" in grated carrot. Place a sprig of parsley at the blunt end of each carrot and chill.

18 Pieces

Cheese Batons

1 small package pie crust mix
½ cup grated cheese
1 T chopped fresh dill
1 T caraway seeds

Prepare pie crust mix according to box directions. Add other ingredients. Take one tablespoonful of this mixture and roll lightly into a
baton shape. Place batons on a lightly
greased baking sheet in a preheated 375-
degree oven for about 12 min., or until golden.

About 24 Pieces

Miniature Grilled Cheese and Bacon

4 slices cheddar cheese
2 T butter, softened
2 strips crisp bacon, crumbled
4 slices thin white bread

Trim crusts from bread and cut each slice into 4 squares. Butter each square. Trim cheddar cheese into squares slightly smaller than bread and lay on top. Sprinkle bacon over cheese. Broil until cheese starts to melt. Serve warm.

16 Pieces

Swiss Watercress Canapes

⅛ lb. Swiss cheese, grated
1 shallot, chopped
  dash dry mustard
½ cup chopped watercress
¼ cup mayonnaise
5 slices thin white bread

Using a cookie cutter or small glass, cut 3 rounds from each slice of bread. Toast one side. Cool. Mix remaining ingredients and spread on untoasted side of rounds. Broil until cheese melts, about 5 min. Serve warm.

15 Pieces

Chutney Baconettes

½ cup chutney
6 slices bacon
3 slices thin rye bread

Toast bread on one side. Cut each slice into 4 rectangles about 1 inch by 3 inches each. Cut bacon to fit bread rectangles and fry until ⅔ done. Remove from pan and drain on paper towel. Spread chutney on untoasted side of bread rectangles and top with a strip of bacon. Broil until bacon is crisp. Serve warm.

12 Pieces

Chutney Cheese Rounds

3 oz. chutney, chopped fine
3 oz. grated cheddar cheese
12 pickled cocktail onions
4 slices thin white bread

Using a cookie cutter or small glass, cut 3 rounds from each slice of bread. Combine chutney and cheese. Spread mixture on bread rounds and place a cocktail onion in the center of each. Place under broiler for several min., until cheese melts. Serve warm.

12 Pieces

96

Dijon Egg Delights

4 hardboiled eggs
¼ cup mayonnaise
1 t lemon juice
1 t Dijon mustard
    dash salt
12 small sprigs dill
4 slices dark pumpernickel bread

Chop eggs very fine and blend with mayonnaise, mustard, lemon juice and salt. Trim
crusts from bread and cut each slice into
thirds. Toast one side and cool. Spread egg
mixture on untoasted side of each bread rec-
tangle and place a sprig of parsley on top.

12 Pieces

Curried Quail Eggs in Herbs

24 quail eggs, hardboiled or canned
     whites of 2 large eggs
½ t curry powder
     dash salt
¼ cup chopped fresh parsley
¼ cup chopped fresh dill

Shell quail eggs or, if canned, pat dry. Combine egg whites, curry powder and salt. Combine parsley and dill in a bowl. Dip eggs in egg white mixture and then in herbs. Refrigerate for 1 hour, covered. Serve on picks.

24 Pieces

Pickled Quail Eggs

24 quail eggs, hardboiled or canned
2 T sugar
1 t salt
1 t mixed spices (peppercorns, celery seed, bay leaf, caraway seed, dill and, if desired, a small garlic clove)
2 cups cider vinegar

Shell eggs. In a saucepan mix vinegar, salt, sugar and spices. Simmer 8 minutes, strain, and pour over eggs in a glass jar. Seal tightly and let stand 2 days. Serve on picks.

24 Pieces

Cheese Herb Sticks

¼ cup grated parmesan cheese
¼ cup grated romano cheese
4 T butter
1 t dried oregano
1 t caraway seeds
¼ t salt
　pepper to taste
4 slices day-old white bread

Trim crusts from bread and cut each slice into 5 narrow strips. Heat butter in skillet and brown bread on all sides. Combine remaining ingredients and roll toast strips in this mixture. Serve warm.

20 Pieces

Cinnamon Brunch Sticks

6 slices day-old white bread
½ cup sugar
2 T ground cinnamon
4 T butter

Trim crusts from bread and cut each slice into 5 narrow strips. Combine sugar and cinnamon on a flat plate. Heat butter and brown strips on all sides. Turn warm strips lightly in sugar-cinnamon mixture and place on a plate to serve.

30 Pieces

Sesame Garlic Sticks

¼ cup sesame seeds
1 T garlic salt
¼ lb. butter (1 stick), melted
4 slices white bread

Trim crusts from bread and cut each slice into 5 narrow strips. Brush strips with melted butter. Sprinkle with sesame seeds and garlic salt. Bake in a 400-degree oven for 5 min., or until golden.

16 Pieces

INDEX